Politics for a New Generation

The Progressive Moment

Edited by

Nick Pearce
Director, ippr

and

Julia Margo
Senior Research Fellow, ippr

First published 2007 by
PALGRAVE MACMILLAN
Houndmills, Basingstoke, Hampshire RG21 6XS and
175 Fifth Avenue, New York, N.Y. 10010
Companies and representatives throughout the world

PALGRAVE MACMILLAN is the global academic imprint of the Palgrave Macmillan division of St. Martin's Press, LLC and of Palgrave Macmillan Ltd. Macmillan® is a registered trademark in the United States, United Kingdom and other countries. Palgrave is a registered trademark in the European Union and other countries.

ISBN-13: 978–0–230–52493–4   hardback
ISBN-10: 0–230–52493–1   hardback
ISBN-13: 978–0–230–52494–1   paperback
ISBN-10: 0–230–52494–X   paperback

This book is printed on paper suitable for recycling and made from fully managed and sustained forest sources. Logging, pulping and manufacturing processes are expected to conform to the environmental regulations of the country of origin.

A catalogue record for this book is available from the British Library.

A catalog record for this book is available from the Library of Congress.

10   9   8   7   6   5   4   3   2   1
16 15 14 13 12 11 10 09 08 07

Printed and bound in Great Britain by
Antony Rowe Ltd, Chippenham and Eastbourne

Institute for Public Policy Research
30–32 Southampton Street
London WC2E 7RA
Tel: 020 7470 6100
Fax: 020 7470 6111
www.ippr.org
Registered Charity No. 800065

The Institute for Public Policy Research (ippr) is the UK's leading progressive think tank and was established in 1988. Its role is to bridge the political divide between the social democratic and liberal traditions, the intellectual divide between academia and the policy-making establishment and the cultural divide between government and civil society. It is first and foremost a research institute, aiming to provide innovative and credible policy solutions. Its work, the questions its research poses, and the methods it uses are driven by the belief that the journey to a good society is one that places social justice, democratic participation, and economic and environmental sustainability at its core.

Contents

vii

List of Tables and Figures

Tables

Figures

Acknowledgements

Politics for a New Generation could not have been written without assistance from many people and organizations. ippr would particularly like to thank Joel Joffe and the Joffe Charitable Trust, KPMG, Barrow Cadbury and Peter Harper for their financial support.

We would also like to thank the external experts who have commented on drafts of the manuscript and different chapters. Thanks particularly for the time generously given by Mike Dixon, Peter Taylor-Gooby, Stuart White, Ed Miliband, Neil Sherlock, Alan Finlayson, Roberta Blackman-Woods, Liz Forgan, Nick Johnson, Alan Hunt, Greg Power, Andrew Puddephatt, Paul Williams, John Graham, Paul Maltby, Ben Jupp, Gavin Kelly, Lisa Harker, Caroline Abrahams, Jane Lewis and Duncan Fisher. Many more people have contributed to specific chapters of the book and are credited separately by the relevant authors.

We are also very grateful for the advice and guidance supplied by our colleagues at ippr. Particular thanks are due to Rob Vance, Sonia Sodha, Howard Reed, Simon Retallack, David Mepham, Kate Stanley, Ian Kearns, Guy Lodge, Glenn Athey, Victoria O'Byrne, Grae Hillary and Jim Bennett, and also to Matt Jackson, Richard Darlington and Georgina Kyriacou in our external affairs department. And we would like to thank the team at Palgrave Macmillan, particularly Amy Lankester-Owen, Gemma D'Arcy Hughes and Ian Evans, for their support and encouragement throughout the course of this project, and Ray Addicott of Chase Publishing Services.

The views expressed are those of the authors and not necessarily those of ippr or its trustees.

Notes on Contributors

Ed Balls MP was appointed Economic Secretary to the Treasury on 5 May 2006. He has been a Member of Parliament for Normanton since 2005. He was a Teaching Fellow, Department of Economics, Harvard, 1989–90, and an Economics leader writer and columnist for the *Financial Times*, 1990-94. He was Economic Adviser to the then Shadow Chancellor, Rt. Hon. Gordon Brown MP, 1994–97; Secretary Labour Party Economic Policy Commission, 1994–97; Economic Adviser to the Chancellor of the Exchequer, 1997–99; Chief Economic Adviser to HM Treasury 1999–2004; and Research Fellow, Smith Institute, 2004–05. He has co-edited the following publications: *Towards a New Regional Policy* (2000), *Reforming Britain's Economic and Financial Policy: Towards Greater Economic Stability* (2002) and *Microeconomic Reform in Britain: Delivering Opportunities for All* (2004). He is a member of the TGWU, Unison and the Co-operative Party.

Rt Hon. Hilary Benn MP is Secretary of State for International Development. He served for 20 years on Ealing Borough Council, becoming the youngest ever Chair of the Education Committee and Deputy Leader of the Council. He is a member of the House of Commons Environment, Transport and the Regions Select Committee. Between May 2002 and May 2003, he was the Home Office Minister for Prisons and Probation. He was previously the Parliamentary Under-Secretary of State at the Department for International Development, and more recently the Minister of State for International Development. In September 2003 he was appointed the Prime Minister's G8 Africa Personal Representative.

Richard Brooks is Associate Director, ippr. He leads the Public Services team at ippr, which covers health, education, criminal justice and cross-cutting issues in public service reform. He was the editor of ippr's journal *New Economy* (now *Public Policy Research*) from 2003 to 2004 and worked in the Economics team. Prior to re-joining ippr, he was Research Director at the Fabian Society, and he has also worked in the Prime Minister's Strategy Unit, the Labour Party Policy Unit, and the investment bank Warburg Dillon Read. Between 2002 and 2006, he was a Tower Hamlets Councillor, and for three of these years was the Cabinet Member for Resources at the borough.

Dawn Butler MP is Chair of the All Party Group on young people. On her election to Parliament in 2005 representing Brent South, Dawn Butler became only the third black woman to have been elected to the House of Commons, following in the footsteps of Diane Abbott in 1987 and Oona King in 1997. She worked as an officer of the GMB trade union, including time as a special adviser to the general secretary. She was also an adviser to the Mayor of London, Ken Livingstone, on employment and social issues.

Graeme Cooke is a researcher at ippr, working in ippr's Social Policy team. Before joining ippr, Graeme worked as the Senior Policy Officer at national children's charity 4Children. He has also worked on childcare and early years policy for the Local Government Association. He has a degree in Social and Political Sciences, and is a member of the government's Future of the Care Population working group.

Natascha Engel MP was elected as Labour Member of Parliament for North East Derbyshire in the general election of May 2005. Following the 2001 general election, she worked for the Smith Institute, focusing on policy areas including full employment, regional economic development and women in the economy. She co-authored *Learning to Organise*, a TUC pamphlet, with John Healey MP.

Gøsta Esping-Andersen is Professor of Sociology at the Universitat Pompeu Fabra. In September 2001 he was nominated Doctor Honoris Causa by the Roskilde University, Denmark. Prior to the Universitat Pompeu Fabra, he was Professor at Harvard University (1978–85), the Science Centre of Berlin (1985–86), the European University of Florence (1986–94) and the University of Trento (1994–2001). He has also worked extensively for international organizations (United Nations, World Bank, OECD) and for national governments (Portugal and Belgium, both in relation to the presidency of the European Union). His published books include: *Why We Need a Welfare State* (2002*), Social Foundations of Post-industrial Economies* (1999), *Why De-regulate Labour Markets?* (with Marino Regini, 2000), *Welfare States in Transition* (1996), *Changing Classes* (1994) and *The Three Worlds of Welfare Capitalism* (1990). His current research focuses on household structure, employment and income inequalities.

Stan Greenberg has advised the campaigns of Bill Clinton, Al Gore and John Kerry, as well as hundreds of other candidates and organizations in the United States and around the world. He is the founder and CEO of

Greenberg Quinlan Rosner Research, a polling firm, and co-founder of Democracy Corps, a non-profit organization which produces left-leaning political strategy.

Rt Hon. Beverley Hughes MP is Member of Parliament for Stretford and Urmston (in Greater Manchester). She has been Minister of State (Children, Young People and Families) at the Department for Education and Skills since June 2005. Before becoming an MP in 1997, she served as Leader of Trafford Metropolitan Borough Council. She has also been a probation officer, a lecturer and Head of the Department of Social Work and Social Policy at the University of Manchester.

Mike Johnson is a Research Fellow at ippr North. He joined ippr North in June 2006. Previously he worked for Durham County Council, where he coordinated the development of a five-year economic strategy for County Durham and was part of a task group that reformed the governance of the Sub-Regional Partnership. He has also worked for Tees Valley Regeneration and the Labour Party. Michael is also a Director of the Institution of Economic Development.

Dr Ian Kearns is Deputy Director of the ippr and Deputy Chair of the ippr Commission on National Security in the Twenty First Century. He has published on a wide range of issues, including democracy and empowerment, media policy, innovation in government, national security, and the use of digital technology in the public sector. He is a former adviser to David Blunkett on digital communications and privacy issues and a former director in the Global Government Industry Practice at EDS. For much of the 1990s he was also Director of the Graduate Programme in International Studies at the University of Sheffield. He is a regular media commentator on public policy issues.

Sadiq Khan MP was elected Member of Parliament for Tooting in the 2005 general election. He completed the Law Society finals at the College of Law in Guildford and trained as a Human Rights Solicitor, setting up a firm (Christian Khan) with Louise Christian. He was a Visiting Lecturer at University of North London, and a former Governor of South Thames FE College. He was Chair of Liberty (NCCL) and has been Vice Chair of the Legal Action Group (LAG).

Miranda Lewis is Associate Director of ippr. Miranda leads ippr's People and Policy team. Prior to joining ippr, she worked at Voluntary Service Overseas, where she led policy research on HIV and AIDS, carrying out research in developing countries on issues such as gender and access to medicine. Miranda has also worked at Positively Women on service user involvement and policy development. Miranda is a Board Member of the international non-governmental organization One World Action.

Julia Margo is Senior Research Fellow, ippr. She works in ippr's Directors' Research team. She is a regular commentator in the national press and other media. She is also editor of the political journal *Public Policy Research*. She spent four years at the *Sunday Times* as a commissioning editor on the News Review and prior to that she worked as a parliamentary assistant to Paddy Ashdown and Simon Hughes MP. Publications include *Population Politics* (2006), *Freedom's Orphans* (2006) and *Beyond Liberty: Is the Future of Liberalism Progressive?* (2007).

Rt Hon. David Miliband MP is Secretary of State for the Department for Environment, Food and Rural Affairs. He entered the Cabinet as Minister of Communities and Local Government in May. In May 2006 he moved to Defra where he replaced Margaret Beckett. He was previously appointed Minister for the Cabinet Office on 15 December 2004 and, prior to that, Minister of State for Schools from June 2002. He has been Labour Member of Parliament for South Shields since June 2001. He was previously Head of the Prime Minister's Policy Unit and Head of Policy in the Office of the Leader of the Opposition. From 1989 to 1994, he was a Research Fellow at ippr; and from 1992 to 1994, Secretary of the Commission on Social Justice. He has edited *Reinventing the Left* (1994) and co-edited *Paying for Inequality* (1994). He was co-founder of the Centre for European Reform.

Ed Miliband MP is Minister for the Third Sector, Cabinet Office. He was elected Labour MP for Doncaster North in May 2005. Previously he was Chair of HM Treasury's Council of Economic Advisers, advising the Chancellor of the Exchequer, Gordon Brown, on long-term policy development. Before that, as a special adviser to the Chancellor of the Exchequer after May 1997, he worked across a range of economic and social policy areas, including taxation, public spending and labour market issues. In 2003, he was a Visiting Lecturer in the Department of Government at Harvard University and a Visiting Scholar at the Center for European Studies. He holds an MSc in Economics from the London School of Economics and a BA from Oxford University.

Rick Muir is Research Fellow, ippr, working in ippr's Democracy team. He has a DPhil in Politics from the University of Oxford, where he worked as a departmental lecturer and tutor in Latin American politics. His doctoral thesis explored the contemporary political economy of the Latin American left. For four years he was an elected member of Oxford City Council, where he served on the Executive Board as Portfolio Holder for Community and Capital Projects.

Nick Pearce has been Director of ippr since 2004. He writes widely on issues ranging from social justice and community cohesion, to education policy and South American politics. His co-authored and edited books include *Freedom's Orphans* (2006), *Social Justice: Building a Fairer Britain* (2005), *Tomorrow's Citizens* (2000) and *Wasted Youth* (1998). Prior to leading ippr, Nick was a Special Adviser in the Home Office, the Department for Education and Skills and the Cabinet Office. During this time, he was involved in the creation of learndirect, Connexions and Child Trust Funds. While at the Home Office, he was a member of the UK team which negotiated the closure of the Sangatte refugee camp.

Jamie Reed MP is PPS to Tony McNulty as Minister of State, Home Office. He was elected Labour Member of Parliament for the UK constituency of Copeland in the 2005 general election. Before election as an MP he worked as a Press Officer at Sellafield, a nuclear power plant in his constituency, and had served on Copeland Borough Council.

Martin Rhodes is Professor of Comparative Political Economy at the Graduate School of International Studies (GSIS), University of Denver, Colorado. He holds a doctorate in political science from the University of Oxford and an MA from the University of Canterbury, New Zealand. Before arriving at GSIS Denver in January 2006, he worked for twelve years at the European University Institute (EUI), in Florence, Italy, first as a Research Professor in the Robert Schuman Centre for Advanced Studies, and then as Professor in the Department of Political and Social Sciences. Before arriving in Florence, he was a Senior Lecturer in the Government Department of the University of Manchester, England.

Ben Rogers is Associate Director, ippr. Ben has been Director of ippr's Democracy team since 2004. He has a doctorate from Oxford in intellectual history and has written books on philosophy and history. He has researched and published on a range of topics at ippr, and has special interests in theories of social justice, civic life, local government and criminal justice.

Alison Seabeck MP is PPS to the Rt. Hon. Geoff Hoon, Minister of State, Foreign & Commonwealth Office. Prior to her election as MP, she was for twelve years a Parliamentary Adviser to the Rt. Hon. Nick Raynsford MP, focusing on housing, planning, local government and the regions, as well as issues relating to London government and the fire service. She also served for five years as a Parliamentary Assistant to Lord Hattersley when he was Shadow Home Secretary and Deputy Leader of the Labour Party.

Sonia Sodha is a Research Fellow at ippr. Now working in the Directors' Research team, she has previously worked for ippr in its Social Policy team, primarily on asset-based welfare. Prior to joining ippr, she worked for the Home Office and the Social Market Foundation. She has an MPhil in politics and a first-class BA Hons from the University of Oxford.

Dhananjayan Sriskandarajah is Associate Director, ippr, and Head of Migration, Equalities & Citizenship. His expertise includes the economic impacts of immigration, the relationship between migration and economic development, identity and multiculturalism, and the political economy of ethnic conflict. He is or has been a consultant to the Global Commission on International Migration, the International Organization for Migration and the Global Development Network, and is an analyst for Oxford Analytica and a Trustee of Ockenden International.

Emily Thornberry MP has focused on the policy areas of housing and the environment since being elected MP for Islington South & Finsbury in 2005 and is a member of the Select Committee on Communities & Local Government. She has been a Labour activist since she was 17, and before becoming an MP she was a human rights and criminal defence lawyer for over 20 years.

Kitty Ussher MP is PPS to Margaret Hodge as Minister of State, Department of Trade and Industry. An economist by training, she previously worked as Political Adviser to Patricia Hewitt at the Department for Trade and Industry. Prior to becoming a Member of Parliament, she was the Chief Economist on the cross-party pro-European campaign group, Britain in Europe, and has also served as a local councillor where she chaired the finance and environment scrutiny committees.

Robert Vance is a Researcher in the Directors' Research team at ippr. Prior to joining ippr, Rob worked as the Commercial Director for Oxford University Student Union. He graduated from Wadham College, Oxford

University, in 2005 with an honours degree in Politics, Philosophy and Economics.

Leni Wild is a Research Fellow in the International Programme at ippr. Prior to joining ippr, she worked as a research assistant at the NATO Parliamentary Assembly, after completing a First Class Honours degree in Politics at the University of Bristol. She also worked as an intern for the late Robin Cook, the then Leader of the House of Commons.

Part 1

Preface to Politics for a New Generation

1
Introduction

Nick Pearce and Julia Margo

The 'short' twentieth century came to end in 1989, when images of the Berlin Wall collapsing under the weight of an exuberant liberation were beamed around the world to an astonished humanity. Communism had finally run its course, and as it passed into history, so too did a world structured by the great ideological divisions it had engendered. From Washington, the 'End of History' was proclaimed (Fukuyama 1992).

The twenty-first century announced its arrival in equally dramatic terms: literally out of the blue, New York's Twin Towers came crashing down, ushering in altogether darker times than those anticipated by the velvet revolutionaries of Eastern Europe or the cheerleaders of the Washington Consensus. A new ideological cleavage was observed coming over the horizon – the 'Clash of Civilizations' (Huntington 1998).

For social democrats, the passing of communism from the world stage marked less the expiration of a defensible alternative to the market economy than the funeral rites of an undemocratic, illiberal version of progressive ambitions for human potential. In truth, the accommodation between social democrats and the market had taken place much earlier, during the Keynesian modernization of post-war capitalism. But ideological soul searching on the British left started in earnest at the end of the 1970s, as the storm clouds gathered for the neo-liberal tsunami of the Reagan–Thatcher decade – one that was finally to sweep away the Keynesian consensus and dismantle the working-class power base on which social democratic politics rested (Therborn 2007).

New Labour was born of this historical defeat of socialism. In the early 1990s, it drew on a decade of modernization of the Labour Party to revalorize the progressive project, focusing its electoral energies on uniting a broad coalition behind its Third Way prospectus (even if the term itself never had widespread currency). Since 1997, it has largely stuck to this script, delivering an agenda of economic stability and growth, public service improvement, and significant constitutional reform. Despite its apparent ideological novelty and fascination with North American social policy, it has carved out a domestic policy path familiar to Northern European social democrats.

At the same time, however, the seismic shift wrought by 9/11 has transformed the British political landscape. Most obviously, the Labour government's fateful decision to join the US war in Iraq has split the progressive mainstream, and continues to reverberate, both geopoliti- cally and electorally. But new challenges that were unanticipated in the post-socialist ideological renewal of the late twentieth century have also emerged: high levels of migration, with consequences for social cohesion; the indisputable threat of catastrophe from climate change; the apparent exhaustion of the Monnet–Delors model of European Union development; and a profoundly changed foreign and security policy environment.

This volume takes these twin poles of the contemporary historical conjecture as its starting point: on the one hand, its seeks to deepen and extend the egalitarian ambitions of the progressive mainstream in the UK, against a backdrop of over a decade of centre-left political hegemony, learning from its successes as well as its failures; and, on the other, it seeks to mark out new progressive territory in the very different and uncertain conditions of a post-9/11 world. It brings together policy experts with leading progressive politicians, covering both the domestic policy terrain and Britain's role in the world. It is unashamedly normative in orientation, rooting its policy discourses in clearly stated progressive values, but rigorously empirical in how it marshals the evidence base for its arguments. And it is profoundly optimistic, for as Ed Miliband remarks in Chapter 2, hope is the hallmark of the progressive disposition. Dissatisfaction and anger are necessary attributes of those committed to even the most minimal social change; but only hope can animate emancipatory politics.

The progressive ethos

The term 'progressive' is a necessarily loose one, serving to brigade a broad spectrum of liberal, social democratic and environmentalist thinking. But insofar as it is possible to erect a conceptual architecture around a signifier of disparate political currents, contemporary progressive politics can be argued to rest on commitments to social justice and environmental sustainability, and perhaps less clearly, to a civic liberalism. Social justice is the core commitment for the progressive project – at its conceptual heart if not the sovereign virtue.

Social justice

What is social justice? Broadly speaking, a just society is one in which each has an equal opportunity to fulfil his or her potential, and in which the distribution of income and wealth is fair. A fair distribution of economic resources requires two things. First, there should be no unjust inequalities. Inequalities are just if they result from free choice and differential effort, but not brute luck or circumstance. Second, social justice requires that each member of society has access to a minimum level of resources that are needed to live a secure and dignified life. This is the principle of sufficiency. It is usually advanced as an argument for worrying only about a threshold that everyone should reach, and not about relative distributions. But it can also function in relative terms – as does Labour's child poverty target.

This concept of social justice is more demanding than some weak versions of equality of opportunity. Equal opportunities are important but not enough: first, because outcomes structure opportunities, particularly from generation to generation; and second, because, from the point of view of justice, we need to know whether outcomes are fair – that is, attributable to hard work and effort, rather than luck. It also justifies action to close social class gaps in wealth, income and well-being, and not just to lift people out of poverty. Inequality is instrumentally bad for societies, as researchers have conclusively demonstrated (Wilkinson 2006). But social justice does not demand equality of outcome, since it is liberal in its insistence that some inequalities are both just and necessary if people are to exercise meaningful choice and that in some part, we get what we deserve. It therefore has purchase on public sentiment in a liberal democracy in ways that a stronger egalitarianism of equality of outcomes does not.

We need to add a further dimension to this account of social justice to arrive at a robust definition. Social justice requires equality of citizenship – of legal, civic and political rights, including the means effectively to exercise them. A society is unjust if citizens do not have equal access to the law, or only the rich can vote. Together with the resource sufficiency principle, it helps us ground a substantive concept of basic citizenship in our theory of social justice.

This definition of social justice is therefore complex. There is no single metric or common currency of social justice – we have instead to look across different goods and bads and how they are distributed (Miller 2005). It also embraces the normative goals outlined by Ed Miliband in Chapter 2 of strong communities and individual empowerment. Community generates the solidarity upon which social justice rests, whilst empowerment ensures that the gloss of common belonging is not painted over unjust hierarchies and illiberal traditions. A society in which power is spread widely, and in which people are empowered in the different domains of their lives – from the personal to the political – is less likely to endorse tradition as fate, or inequality as inevitability.

Civic liberalism

Empowerment can ensure that communities do not suppress pluralism and difference. Empowered citizens have basic human rights and freedoms protected by law, while society respects and nurtures the autonomy of each individual to frame and pursue his or her own vision of a good life. But citizens can also recognize their mutual interdependence and participate in democratic deliberation over collective goals. This is perhaps best described as a 'civic liberalism', since it stresses the social and civic conditions of human fulfilment, and places a premium on democratic participation, but simultaneously values the diversity and freedoms of a liberal democracy (Dagger 1997; Skinner 1998; Habermas 2001; Fung 2004).

Strengthening civic belonging has emerged as a central political preoccupation in recent years, in response, on the one hand, to a lethal cocktail of home-grown terror, global geopolitical insecurity and unsettling people flows, and, on the other, to more nebulous but nonetheless real concerns about the changing nature of childhood and the moral socialization of young people. Attending to the bonds of civic belonging promises both to promote community cohesion in conditions of significant population change, and to provide answers to the challenges of raising young people in media-centric, fragmented and unequal communities. Such civic consciousness is not the preserve of progressive politics, however. It is characteristic of a long civic republican historical tradition which predates post-Enlightenment ideological divisions, and it surfaces consistently in conservative thinking, particularly its Burkean strands. It is therefore contested political territory, as much capable of articulation into a radical, participatory and progressive project as to a softer liberal conservatism.

The axis upon which the debate on these issues currently turns is the role of the state. Progressives insist that active government is a necessary precondition of strong, civic-minded communities equipped with the resources and capabilities to solve their problems. In contrast conservatives regard the state as an obstacle to civic empowerment – a blunt, ineffective instrument that crowds out social virtues. Both can find succour in strands of British political history, of course. But the evidence marshalled in this volume is that an enabling government which offers strong public services, an active welfare state and collective democratic determination of social priorities, is a sine qua non of the good society. Moreover the state does not have to be centralized; on the contrary, the most egalitarian countries in the world combine strong local government and widespread participation in decision-making with equity in socio-economic outcomes. Localism and a healthy civil society can be the partners of active government, not its enemies.

Fairness

Some civic theorists argue that a 'procedural state' cannot generate the moral resources and other-regarding virtues necessary to sustain vibrant democracies and strong communities (Sandel 1996). But civic liberalism can still attend to procedural fairness without abandoning the 'thick' social bonds necessary for community; indeed, making sure that the ground rules of a liberal democracy stick may be imperative in conditions of increased diversity.

Cross-national studies have also shown that the fairness of a society matters more for its level of social trust than its homogeneity (You 2005). Countries with high levels of procedural and distributive fairness (i.e. with democratic institutions, probity in public administration and relatively equal income distributions) have higher levels of generalized interpersonal trust ('social trust'). Diversity declines in salience as countries become more equal and more democratic. The perceived fairness or unfairness of ethnic relations in a society – related in turn to levels of discrimination, income inequality and political participation by minority groups – is more important than diversity per se.

The literature on procedural fairness gives theoretical support to evidence from recent studies such as *The New East End* (Dench et al. 2006) that hostility to migrants from indigenous populations derives from a sense of 'queue jumping' or unfairness in access to housing and welfare benefits. It also shifts the focus of race relations and community cohesion to the governance and administration of core public services: the funding and allocation of social housing, school places, GP services, and so on.

The implications for policy-makers are that greater well-being and social trust will result from policies which better reconcile procedural justice with other values, such as need, in determining access to services; and that at the same time, the legitimacy of public authorities will increase if local electorates participate more widely in the determination of policies. As Nick Pearce argues in Chapter 14, 'fair rules' or procedural fairness should form an important new focus for progressive approaches to public service reform.

Fairness is expressed not just in procedural and distributive justice but in the fulfilment of our obligations to future generations. It is a matter of social injustice that environmental degradation currently falls most heavily on the world's poor. But it will be a social injustice to future generations, not to say a potential threat to their very existence, if we allow our current resource use to deprive them of a planet in which they can live in safety and prosperity. Environmentalism therefore contains a double social justice imperative, as David Miliband makes clear in Chapter 16. Contemporary progressives must provide answers to the challenges posed by climate change and environmental sustainability, but they must also refract their policies through a social justice lens. This may involve difficult trade offs and tough choices but sustainability and social justice must be pursued in tandem if we are to avoid doing violence to both. And we honour the dead, as well as those yet to be born, if we protect and cherish our planet.

The concept of fairness also extends beyond national borders – although this is not uncontested. Most modern political philosophers may agree that people in rich countries have some obligations towards those living elsewhere, but few assert that these obligations are equal to those we owe to members of our own society (see, for example, Rawls 1999). The philosopher David Miller argues that wealthy countries are obliged – on three levels – to promote justice beyond their borders. First, there is an obligation 'to respect the basic human rights of people everywhere'. Second, wealthier individuals and societies should 'refrain from exploiting those who are vulnerable to their actions'. Third, all political communities should 'have the opportunity to determine their own future and practise justice among their members' (Miller 2000). At first glance these principles provide a strong foundation for a progressive conception of global justice, but they fall short of calling for distributive justice between nations. It is not uncommon to claim that the demand for equality should apply only when human beings participate in a common scheme of economic cooperation or share support for a particular political regime. But there are flaws in this position. In particular, it understates the degree of modern global interdependence. The ties of economic cooperation and political governance now extend well beyond national borders. Such developments suggest we should sharpen our notion of moral obligation towards people in other countries (White 2006; Mepham 2005).

Embedding progressive values

Values inform, energize and animate politics. But they have to be embedded in policies, practices and institutions in order to effect social and economic change, particularly in the long term. The most successful governments are those that put down lasting roots in the organizations, structures, habits of mind and public discourses of their societies. In the twentieth century, two progressive moments tower over the political landscape: the great Liberal-led administrations of 1906–14, and the Attlee Labour government of 1945–51. Both left substantial legacies, from the first foundations of the welfare state to the National Health Service, and both dominated political discourse for decades to come. The Thatcher governments, in their different ways, did much the same – legislating to create new economic and social forces and framing the common sense of the age.

The Labour governments of 1997 and since can tell a similar story, leaving behind significant new institutions, from the Scottish Parliament to an independent Bank of England. Public attitudes have also shifted in progressive directions, as Greenberg and Lewis demonstrate in Chapter 3, and the political centre of gravity has moved decisively to the left on core issues such as investment in public services and poverty reduction. But this progressive legacy remains fragile in parts and there is an urgent need to provide answers to new challenges facing contemporary Britain.

In particular, embedding progressive values cannot simply be about top-down institutional reform. It has to be about new forms of communication with the public and a fundamental shift in our political culture, as Ed Miliband, Thornberry, Muir and Kearns and Greenberg and Lewis argue in their respective chapters. Increasing levels of disengagement in politics represent a real challenge to progressive politics, particularly as this disengagement disproportionately affects those in lower socio-economic groups. First, new mechanisms must be found for increasing voter turnout, if necessary through some form of compulsion, as Thornberry, Muir and Kearns argue. Second, participatory democratic mechanisms must also be strengthened, particularly at neighbourhood level, if citizen involvement in the design and delivery of public services is to be meaningful. Despite problems of inertia and interest group capture, deliberative democratic procedures hold great promise, as innovative, practical experience around the world demonstrates (Fung and Wright 2004).

The onus is certainly not just on citizens. The political system has to be porous to the 'wild circuits' of opinion formation and debate in civil society (Habermas 2001) and structured spaces opened up for democratic deliberation within political processes. At heart, progressive politics is about self-government. So the battle for hearts and minds is not an optional extra: rather, it goes to the very heart of the progressive ethos.

New challenges

Equality and social mobility

New Labour's political economy is 'Anglo-Social' (Dixon and Pearce 2005), fusing a post-Thatcherite liberal economic framework and flexible labour markets with Nordic-style investments in public services. It is a model that has performed well at producing steady economic growth and relatively high levels of employment. But it continues to generate considerable income and wealth inequality and regional disparities in economic performance, while areas of concentrated socio-economic disadvantage remain stubbornly resistant to regeneration. Lacking solidaristic institutions within the labour market or strong local democratic institutions to drive growth, and sharing the global Anglo-Saxon predisposition to inflate assets, the UK relies heavily on taxation and public spending to tackle inequality and reduce poverty.

Consequently, to fulfil its egalitarian aspirations the Labour government has increased the proportion of GDP spent on public services by some 3.3 per cent since 1997 – a record amongst the G8 countries over that period. As Margo, Sodha and Vance demonstrate in Chapter 4, this has enabled it to cut child and pensioner poverty, to increase spending on education, health, and law and order significantly, and to bear down on income inequality – considerable achievements by most social democratic reckonings. Yet this strategy is now bumping up against political and fiscal limits. Absent of tax rises, public spending will increase at a rate below that of growth in the economy for the foreseeable future, curtailing the capacity of the state to redistribute resources in the pursuit of progressive ambitions. And with the political space for tax rises now constrained, increased spending on progressive goals can therefore only come from squeezing non-essential services, generating significant efficiency gains in major departments, or introducing new forms of financing, such as charges for environmentally damaging activity. None of these options is likely to be easy.

Britain's class structure has also proved remarkably intractable to public intervention over the last decade. As manufacturing employment has declined in favour of services, and technology has replaced manual labour in jobs amenable to computerized routinization, the labour market has increasingly polarized between lower- and higher-skilled work – so-called 'lovely' and 'lousy' jobs. Opportunities for labour market progression have narrowed as intermediate tiers have shrunk, limiting the structural support for social mobility among the working population. Meanwhile, school education remains heavily stratified by social class, and a socialization gap has emerged between disadvantaged adolescents and their peers, skewing the distribution of the "soft" skills that are increasingly important for career success. The school system is therefore providing little impetus for counteracting adverse trends in the jobs market (although this may be changing, as investments in early years' education, higher standards of literacy and numeracy in primary schools, and increased attainment at GCSE level feed through the system).

None of this has much to do with globalization per se, although shifts in economic activity have contributed to the decline in unskilled manual jobs. But whereas in post-war Britain a long boom in social mobility was underpinned by a burgeoning of middle-class occupations and the relative prosperity of the skilled working class, today's barbell class structure and the tightening of intergenerational transmission of life chances mitigate against social mobility. Although the demand for skilled jobs continues to grow and living standards are rising, there is little of the momentum in the contemporary British class structure towards social progress that there was for the sons and daughters of the Second World War generation. Despite the relatively healthy state of the jobs market, for millions of low-paid workers the hope of translating better employment opportunity into sustained increases in family prosperity, home-ownership or significantly brighter prospects for their children, remains elusive. Without progressive answers to how these aspirations can be met, working-class voters will turn towards right-wing populists or away from politics altogether, as Greenberg and Lewis demonstrate in Chapter 3.

Social mobility remains an important goal. An open society which rewards hard work and effort, rather than inherited advantage, will tend to be a more mobile one – whether that means up or down the ladder of opportunity. Greater social mobility is also a feature of more equal societies. The narrower the gap between rich and poor, the less distance there is to travel for the upwardly mobile. But social mobility is not the same as social justice, as our earlier discussion showed. We have to secure a social minimum for those who will never reach the top, and concern ourselves with equality of opportunity and fairness of outcomes for the whole population, not simply the talented.

Multiculturalism

These normative imperatives of social justice also bear on the debate about multiculturalism. The term 'multiculturalism' is amenable to a wide range of interpretations, both in theory and in practice. Its leading theoretical exponent, Bhikhu Parekh, argues that it is neither a political doctrine nor a philosophical world view imbued with a concept of the good life to offer its adherents. Rather it is a perspective on human life, which stresses that human beings are culturally embedded, while at the same time recognizing that cultural forms are multidimensional, interactive and dynamic (Parekh 2005).

Understood in these terms, multiculturalism is a plea for sensitivity. It asks us to recognize others' legitimate claims to cultural identity and to value differences. It seeks to cultivate our knowledge of other cultures and to nurture feelings of belonging between different communities. It insists on facilitating genuine equality of citizenship within a diverse political community. What flows from such a conception is simply a description of practices which are common to many progressive democracies: race equality strategies, public recognition of cultural diversity, and sensitivity, within the framework of public law, to religious beliefs.

Sterner critics of multiculturalism have a different target in mind, however; namely the 'ethnic enclaves' of 'mosaic multiculturalism' (Benhabib 2004). Here they are on stronger ground. Much multiculturalist thinking has been concerned with the claims to recognition of communities whose voices, experiences and cultures have been systematically marginalized and sometimes viciously oppressed over many centuries. Unsurprisingly, therefore, multiculturalism has often stressed the importance of cultural protection and the right of minority communities to receive state support for sustaining their cultural practices. Some of these practices require residential clustering of minority communities, particularly if they involve religious rites.

However, cultural claims to recognition of this kind run a number of risks in contemporary capitalist societies. As Seabeck, Rogers and Sriskandarajah argue in Chapter 10, such claims can essentialize culture and community, ignoring the diversity and contingency of cultural forms in favour of publicly recognized expressions of particular practices or norms. This is not only reductionist but it may in turn involve giving implicit (and even explicit) support to existing hierarchies of power and belief in particular communities, notably patriarchal ones. The consequence is that struggles for recognition from within minority communities – for gender equality, for example – do not receive attention or support. Similarly, cultural particularism can inhibit citizen solidarity.

There are at least two challenges here for policy-makers. First, where should we draw the line between basic liberal rights and cultural practices? Outlawing forced marriages and female circumcision is straightforward. But other cases, such as the wearing of the *jilbab* in schools, are less clear cut. Public authorities clearly have a duty to understand the depth of motivation that religious belief brings to individual lives. The evolution of what has been called a 'post-secular' society (Habermas 2002) is a means of capturing this ongoing dialogue between secular public consciousness and private belief. But this sensitivity should not prevent forceful confrontation with irrational or oppressive beliefs. Children are denied their rights when they receive wholly inadequate education in private religious schools. Muslim women have equal rights to live free and fulfilling lives, and should be supported in the assertion of those rights. Immigrant communities, as much as other citizens, can legitimately be required to cease practices that violate liberal principles.

The second challenge is to develop new forms of citizen solidarity that ensure greater integration around a common core of citizenship, while maintaining liberal respect for diverse beliefs and practices. This is not a matter of assimilation. Even if it were ethically defensible, there is no monoculture to which people could be asked to assimilate. Although liberal societies are structured by their histories, political institutions and the beliefs and practices of their citizens, they no longer have uniform dominant cultures. Instead, we should give patriotic support to our collective political citizenship, underpinned by public debate, and social interaction and association in civil society.

Civic liberalism argues for the importance of education for citizenship, the cultivation of civic virtues, and a strengthening of mechanisms for citizen involvement in democratic deliberation, in both civil society and the institutions of state. It is sceptical that the free association of rights-bearing individuals will generate the other-regarding virtues, habits and practices of mind and commonality of basic purposes that are necessary to sustain a healthy, cohesive democracy, particularly in an open market economy.

A strong version of this civic liberalism asserts that it requires commitment to a substantive vision of the good society; albeit one that prizes individual autonomy highly. A weaker version allows individuals to frame their own ends consistent with the ability of others to do likewise, but nonetheless insists that active citizenship and civic patriotism are necessary conditions for the reproduction of a liberal democracy, as well as valuable in themselves. It claims that the duties and obligations of civic belonging are compatible with liberal human rights traditions, as long as the human rights that citizens claim are basic and fundamental, not frivolous exercises in litigation or convenient covers for vested interests. Proponents of discursive democracy might add that human rights and the protection of those rights in a constitutional democracy are co-original with popular sovereignty: a citizen can only have his or her rights protected in a constitutional democracy of which he or she is a sovereign citizen member.

Global interdependence

Growing global interdependence means that our actions in Britain are increasingly impacting on the quality of life of those in other parts of the world (Mepham 2005). In Chapter 17, Benn refers to climate change, global health, global security, and governance and trade agreements as 'global public goods'. This description is particularly apt: these are all things which are fundamental to securing the prosperity of future generations, and they are all things from which not just particular nations but the whole world will derive benefits if they are achieved.

Britain can and should be a leading force in securing these public goods for the world, through our foreign, international development and environmental policies. On climate change, it is well-known that developed countries are making the biggest contribution to these global environmental problems, yet as David Miliband argues in Chapter 16, it is developing countries and their people that will suffer most adversely as a result. As Mepham and Held argue, if all the world's 6 billion people were to consume at the level of the richest, the consequences would be 'ecologically catastrophic'. It is therefore difficult to see how the world's richest people can defend a lifestyle that it would be 'impossible to extend to others and which imposes huge costs on people elsewhere'. A progressive response must involve 'a commitment to shift to more sustainable patterns of production and consumption ... and support for a more equitable distribution of global wealth' (Mepham and Held forthcoming).

The progressive moment

Shifts in three different but related spheres – public attitudes, research evidence and in politics itself – are increasingly converging to create a progressive moment. First, public attitudes appear to be changing in ways that are promising for a progressive agenda. The evidence in Part 2 of this volume indicates that despite deep insecurity over migration and the spread of diversity, and cultural conflict over faith and identity, British society has become more liberal in the last decade. For example, public attitudes are changing in relation to marriage, homosexuality and more diverse lifestyle choices. Attitudes to the environment also appear to have reached a tipping point, as public acceptance of the reality of climate change and the need for a shift to more sustainable modes of production and consumption has become widespread. And although concerns about negative public attitudes to diversity remain, new qualitative research in Chapter 3 suggests there are opportunities to lead public opinion in a more progressive direction on issues such as asylum and immigration – issues which have previously left progressives stumped.

Second, there is now a new academic evidence base which supports and adds insight to progressive values and goals. Although social justice is as much an intrinsic as an instrumental good, a range of recent research has highlighted the pernicious impact of structural inequality on societies, pointing to its various implications for crime rates and the health and happiness of a population (Gibbons et al. 2005; Kahn et al. 1998; Wilkinson 1996, 2006; Pearce and Paxton 2005; Layard 2005). Scientific research has also shown how poverty and inequality can damage the brain. For example, the neurogeneticist Professor Liz Gould has shown, using marmoset monkeys, that poverty can stunt the growth of neurons, as the brain diverts energy towards survival rather than creating new cells and connections (Lehrer 2006). Meanwhile, social and behavioural scientists have conclusively demonstrated the influence of social class on behaviour and individual life chances – a theme we develop below (see Margo et al. 2006). New research, much of it by ippr, has shown how individuals develop the capacity to exercise meaningful autonomy through childhood and adolescence – and the role of inequality and deprivation in stifling this development (Butler and Margo, Chapter 15). This evidence serves to illustrate that the progressive vision of the good society will have instrumental as well as intrinsic benefits.

Finally, the recent past has borne witness to a resurgence of politics. That might appear counter-intuitive in the context of declining voter turnout and public hostility to the political class. Yet the groundswell of social movements dedicated to tackling global poverty and climate change represents a reaffirmation of the efficacy of collective and public action. The new politics of behaviour – whether in respect of public health, social civility or sustainability – points to a renewed relationship between the private, civil and public spheres. In each case, controversial politics arise. But few now assert, with neo-liberal confidence, that the market economies of depoliticized societies can solve humanity's problems. The necessity of political action is now unanswerable.

So 2007 may well represent a progressive moment. But this moment will not automatically transform itself into a new agenda for Britain. The real question for progressive leaders across political parties and civil society is whether they can harness these forces to build a politics for a new generation. This is the challenge our contributors have taken up in this volume.

The future of the progressive project: outline of the book

Part 2: The Future of the Progressive Project

Chapter 2, 'Renewing the Domestic Agenda' (Ed Miliband)

The renewal of the progressive project begins with a reassessment of our core values. For Miliband the modern progressive project is distinguished by a commitment to the concept of social justice, enshrining a trinity of equality, community and empowerment. Instantiating these values in the fabric of British society will require confronting the core challenges to social justice set out below, and a radical new policy agenda. Lastly, the practice of politics itself must reflect the progressive ethos.

Chapter 3, 'Winning Hearts and Minds: Prospects for Progressivism'
(Stan Greenberg and Miranda Lewis)

In this chapter, Greenberg and Lewis argue that in-depth attitudinal research demonstrates genuine potential for progressive ideas to become embedded in the public consciousness. Public attitudes to redistribution, inequality, diverse lifestyles and family forms and environmental protection have all shifted to the left over the last decade. But recent gains are not irreversible. Social liberalism and environmentalism may have sunk deep roots in public consciousness, but commitment to equality and collective action for the common good remain fragile, at best.

Greenberg and Lewis examine how a progressive consensus on inequality and redistribution can be built. They argue that we need to build a new narrative about poverty that communicates what it means to live in poverty in the UK in the twenty-first century, which illustrates why the progressive ethos is so important. Rebuilding trust between citizens and government is also crucial, which will mean tackling perceptions of procedural unfairness in the system. They suggest that debates on green taxation may offer progressives a new opportunity to engage the public with debates on the tax burden and the public interest. New issues apart from these traditional ones – crime and anti-social behaviour, immigration, security and terrorism, and climate change – must also be entrenched within progressivism.

Chapter 4, 'State of the Nation: Audit of Britain' (Julia Margo, Sonia Sodha and Robert Vance)

Margo, Sodha and Vance report significant improvements in the state of the nation. The British economy has experienced steady growth since 1993, employment rates have increased and registered unemployment continues to fall. Child and pensioner poverty have been reduced and the nation is now healthier, living longer and experiencing far less crime than a decade earlier.

But levels of child poverty in Britain continue to surpass those of many of our European partners and inequalities in income, wealth and well-being remain stubbornly high. Parental social class and ethnic background still heavily determine life chances, while democratic participation has fallen and political and civic participation is polarizing according to class and wealth, with the strongest skews in the areas which hold most political influence. Moreover, the 'state of youth' has become an increasingly popular subject of debate in British academic, policy and media circles, particularly in the last year as research finds that British youth are more at risk of antisocial behaviour, self-harm, drug and alcohol abuse than those elsewhere in Europe. Thus Margo, Sodha and Vance argue that while Britain is unquestionably more progressive than it was in 1997, there is no room for complacency. Achieving progressive goals will require renewal and rejuvenation of progressive thought and policy.

Part 3: Equality

Chapter 5, 'Beyond Stability: Labour's Economic Story'
(Ed Balls, Kitty Ussher and Richard Brooks, with Robert Vance)

Improving social mobility remains a significant policy challenge for progressive ambitions over the decades to come, as examined by Balls, Ussher and Brooks. Despite improvements in employment rates; levels of worklessness among disadvantaged groups remains unacceptably high; there are still too many young people and adults in low-skill jobs without the basic qualifications they need to progress; and gaping regional inequalities mean that, too often, life chances are determined by place of birth. Tackling these deep-rooted problems will require continuing investment in schools and lifelong learning, an expansion of welfare-to-work programmes to reflect the need for better retention and progression, and increasing regional investment and connectivity.

Chapter 6, 'Mind the Wealth Gap? The Politics of Resource Inequality'
(Jamie Reed and Sonia Sodha)

Reed and Sodha argue that the gaping inequalities in wealth between the rich and the poor are showing no signs of closing, and require a more urgent focus from progressives. Inequality is indisputably harmful to societies: it damages equality of opportunity, it appears to be correlated with greater levels of social divergence, higher levels of violent crime and lower levels of mortality, and it can lead to a situation in which the voices of some groups are heard more loudly and clearly than others in the political system. Reducing wealth inequality should involve a trio of policies: an expansion of the government's asset-building agenda, increased house-building and reform of the planning system, and a renewed progressive defence of the case for wealth taxation.

Chapter 7, 'Rethinking the Welfare State' (Gøsta Esping-Andersen)

Previous chapters have focused on British policies and politics, but Esping-Andersen's chapter provides an essential international comparative perspective, setting out the challenges that all welfare states must confront: an ageing population, the revolution of women's roles in society, changes to family forms, and the rising importance of skills – both cognitive and non-cognitive – to life chances. He argues, first, that the priority for reform should be investing in children, since life chances are decided ultimately by what happens in the early years. Second, the future of the family depends on how well we support women's changing roles. Therefore some reconciliation of parenthood and careers will be essential. But the battle will only be half-won if we do not accompany standard reconciliation policies with a strategy designed to promote a 'feminization' of the male lifecycle. He also argues that we need to redefine the nexus between working life and retirement and tackle intra-generational inequity, so that those working in less-well-paid jobs do not lose out relative to those in better-paid jobs. But since the welfare of tomorrow's elderly depends crucially on the quality of their childhood and subsequent careers, our response to the ageing challenge should 'begin with babies' and focus especially on minimizing life chance inequalities. Lastly, we need to move beyond a focus on welfare and towards consolidated welfare regime accounts, and we need to be able to identify the long-term investment that certain social policies represent.

Chapter 8, 'Making Public Services Work for Social Justice' (Richard Brooks)

Brooks sets out the key challenges for the core public services, and some new progressive directions for public service reform. While education will remain a key priority because of its impact on future life chances, and the criminal justice system presents some particularly difficult problems, he argues that the health system presents perhaps the greatest and most politically important challenges for progressives. This is partly because of the apparently inexorable appetite for health spending that the UK shares with other highly developed countries, and partly because of the difficulty of reforming such a large and complex system so that it simultaneously improves outcomes, quality, trust and efficiency. Brooks argues that public service reform now requires a new set of relationships: between citizens and the state, between services and users, between government and the public service workforce, and between central and local governance. These new relationships in turn require a new set of bargains, and the chapter explores how some of these might be struck.

Chapter 9, 'Moving On Up: Progression in the Labour Market'
(Natascha Engel and Sonia Sodha with Mike Johnson)

Engel and Sodha argue that while the focus of labour market interventions on welfare to work has been the right one in the last decade, progressives need to widen the focus to labour market progression in the next one. Improving retention and progression in the labour market will be key to ensuring that work is not only the best route out of poverty, as the government has argued, but that we come closer to a point where it is a guaranteed route. Moreover, social mobility does not end with improving school-age education: inequalities in opportunities that occur later in life also need to be tackled. This chapter considers a range of policy interventions designed to improve labour market progression – from those that focus on the acquisition of 'hard' and 'soft' skills to those that promote structured career ladders within sectors and organizations.

Part 4: Community

Chapter 10, 'Living Together: Diversity and Identity in Contemporary
Britain' (Alison Seabeck, Ben Rogers and Dhananjayan Sriskandarajah)

Britain's ethnic profile has changed markedly over the last three decades, but the left has traditionally found it hard to develop a compelling narrative on immigration, multiculturalism and cohesion. Seabeck,

Rogers and Sriskandaranjah argue that in future, a progressive approach should be guided by three key principles: fair treatment, respect for ethnic identities, and fostering shared identities at both the national and the local level.

Chapter 11, 'Children, Parenting and Families: Renewing the Progressive Story' (Beverly Hughes and Graeme Cooke)

Progressives have a proud tradition of championing tolerance and social liberalism. However, in standing up to narrow-minded moralizing and prejudice towards different family forms, some on the left have been guilty of a laissez-faire attitude towards family life. Coupled with the right's fatalistic narrative of moral and social decline, this has obfuscated a primary focus on the best interests of children and young people, while failing to realize the aspirations of adults as parents and individuals in their own right.

Hughes and Cooke argue that we now need to fundamentally change Britain's working culture to improve the life chances of British children. Extending the right to request flexible working would help parents to balance work around their children, rather than their children around their work. Doubling the length of paid paternity leave to a month, and progressively increasing the rates of maternity and paternity pay, would mean that caring for young children is a realistic option for mothers and fathers in all families. Hughes and Cooke also recommend that the existing 13 weeks of parental leave be paid, so that low-income parents – especially fathers – can afford to take time off to care for their very young children.

Chapter 12, 'Crime and Punishment: A New Home Office Agenda' (Nick Pearce)

Pearce argues that crime reduction should be a core policy concern for anybody concerned with tackling social injustice. Crime falls hardest on the poorest communities, and its effects on disadvantaged victims are disproportionately large. He critically examines Labour's record on crime reduction before turning to an analysis of public attitudes to crime, arguing that the potential for a more progressive home affairs agenda exists in popular views on activities for young people, drug treatment and support for those with mental health problems. Local accountability and social justice principles should guide policy-making.

Part 5: Power

Chapter 13, 'Power Politics: Who Runs Britain?'
(Emily Thornberry, Rick Muir and Ian Kearns)

Increasing levels of popular disillusionment with politics and politicians are a key challenge to realizing the progressive goals of civic liberalism and equity. These trends have persisted despite the reforms to the political system that the government has pursued since 1997. Thornberry, Muir and Kearns argue in Chapter 13 that the strategy to increase popular engagement with democracy must therefore be two-pronged: it needs to focus not just on constitutional reform but also on the wider changes to our society that are taking place, affecting participation in civic life and the distribution of social power outside the political system. They set out an agenda for democratic renewal which reflects three progressive objectives: changing our political culture so it reflects why politics is in the public interest, redistributing political power to increase political participation and increase social justice, and extending the reach of politics into new social spheres as a way of holding power beyond the political system more effectively to account.

Chapter 14, 'Fair Rules: Procedural Fairness and the Reform of Public Services' (Nick Pearce)

Public service reform debates have neglected the importance of procedural fairness. Outcomes, and how they are distributed, matter. But so do the processes and procedures that lead to those outcomes. Social psychologists and economists have demonstrated that people care about whether the rules governing public services and service delivery are both fair and fairly applied – sometimes as much or even more than the outcomes they result in. Pearce examines the importance of these insights for public service reform debates.

Chapter 15, 'Freedom's Orphans: Raising Youth in a Changing World'
(Dawn Butler and Julia Margo)

Butler and Margo argue in Chapter 15 that the state of British youth requires an urgent reassessment of the way we raise and educate our young. According to survey evidence, young people's life chances – their educational, labour market, behavioural and social outcomes – are increasingly connected to parental background, largely because of the way that interpersonal and social skills are passed on by families or learnt through interaction with adults in the local community.

If we are to offer all young people the chance to succeed in life, youth policy now needs to focus on ensuring that all young people have access to the kinds of constructive, socializing activities that teach personal and social skills; that parents are able to spend more time with children; and children's needs are taken into account in planning decisions, so that adults and children can mix easily and safely. Legislation to protect children from the developmentally damaging effects of too much exposure to consumerism and media such as TV are also vital.

Part 6: The World

Chapter 16, 'A Greener Shade of Red' (David Miliband)

Climate change throws up one of the biggest global challenges that we face in the years to come. Miliband argues in Chapter 16 that this challenge is primarily a political one: at the global, national and regional levels. The progressive traditions of using government to shape the markets, of putting social justice at the heart of politics and of recognizing the importance of internationalism, mean that it is progressives who are best placed to respond to this challenge. Miliband argues that this response needs to focus on four areas. First, climate change requires a different political economy that accords as much importance to the welfare of future generations as to today's. Second, we need to expand our conception of citizenship to include the environmental. Third, we also need to approach the challenge through the framework of a strong European Union. Lastly, climate change needs to change the way we think about and carry out politics in the UK. Citizens need to be empowered by the political system to do their bit to tackle climate change.

Chapter 17, 'A New Agenda for International Development' (Hilary Benn)

Benn argues in Chapter 17 that increasing global interdependence, and the glaring gap between the world's richest and poorest, require British progressives to concern themselves with issues of international, as well as domestic, justice. This should place a concern for inequality at its heart, and move beyond the traditional focus on international poverty to a fuller understanding of human capabilities. Benn considers the changing aid landscape: greater diversity among donors and the increasing importance of global public goods – climate change, global governance and trade, and public health. He sets out a progressive agenda for security and development, and maintaining public support for internationalism. Ultimately, achieving global justice needs to be at the heart of a progressive international policy.

Chapter 18, 'Securing the Future' (Sadiq Khan and Leni Wild)

There is a pressing need to refresh the UK's approach to international security policy. Khan and Wild focus on four particular challenges: terrorism; the threat posed by the proliferation of weapons of mass destruction, conventional weapons and conventional arms control; the UK's involvement in major international military operations in Iraq and Afghanistan; and the 'responsibility to protect' agenda – where, when and how Britain should intervene in other countries to help prevent war crimes or violations of human rights. In each of these four areas, a progressive UK government should be advancing fresh thinking. But in almost none of these cases can the UK's security interest be pursued wholly independently. In a globalized world, it will invariably require working closely with others and building stronger global institutions to tackle the great majority of security issues that impact beyond the boundaries of the nation state. But pursuing a progressive security policy also has implications for the way in which the UK formulates its policies on security. Khan and Wild therefore consider options for strengthening multilateral institutions and reforming UK policy-making.

Chapter 19, 'The European Project Renewed' (Martin Rhodes)

The renewal of a progressive global politics would be incomplete without reference to the future of the EU. In Chapter 19 Martin Rhodes argues that the EU is facing a serious crisis of legitimacy because it has overextended itself. It therefore requires reform across four domains to slim down its menu of functions and perform them more effectively: the economy, the social dimension, foreign policy and politics. Economic reform should aim at establishing a closer link between EU monetary and fiscal policy and national reform agendas, and redefining the Lisbon programme. New means of promoting human capital growth, and research and development are essential. In the social dimension, attention should now be focused on building consensus on more concrete social policy advances, such as a European child income guarantee.

In the area of foreign and defence policy, the EU should rationalize defence spending and the European military-industrial complex, and use the money saved for other purposes. At the same time, two major 'soft' initiatives should be pursued: the creation of a European civilian expert reconstruction corps and a European humanitarian support corps.

More limited reforms are required to tackle the political and legitimacy issues facing the EU, including enhancing the European Parliament's influence over the selection of the Commission President

and Commissioners, and strengthening the links between national
Parliaments and the EU institutions.

References

Benhabib, S. (2004) *The Rights of Others: Aliens, Residents and Citizens*. Cambridge:
  Cambridge University Press.
Dagger, R. (1997) *Civic Virtues Rights, Citizenship, and Republican Liberalism*. New
  York: Oxford University Press.
Dench, G., Gavron, K. and Young, M. (2006) *The New East End: Kinship, Race and
  Conflict*. London: Young Foundation.
Dixon, M. and Pearce, N. (2005) 'Social Justice in a Changing World: The Emerging
  Anglo-Social Model', in N. Pearce and W. Paxton (eds), *Social Justice: Building a
  Fairer Britain*. London: ippr/Politico's.
Fukuyama, F. (1992) *The End of History and the Last Man*. New York: Free Press.
Fung, A. (2004) *Empowered Participation: Reinventing Urban Democracy*. Princeton:
  Princeton University Press.
Fung, A. and Wright, O. (2001) 'Deepening Democracy: Innovations in Empowered
  Participatory Governance', *Politics and Society*, 29 (1): 5–42.
Gibbons, S., Green, A., Gregg, P. and Machin, S. (2005) 'Is Britain Pulling Apart?
  Area Disparities in Employment, Education and Crime', in N. Pearce and W.
  Paxton (eds), *Social Justice: Building a Fairer Britain*. London: ippr/Politico's.
Habermas, J. (2001) 'Constitutional Democracy: A Paradoxical Union of
  Contradictory Principles?', *Political Theory*, 29: 766–81.
Habermas, J. (2002) *Faith and Knowledge in the Future of Human Nature*. London:
  Polity Press.
Huntington, S. (1998) *The Clash of Civilizations*. New York: Simon & Schuster.
Kahn, H., Tatham, L., Pamuk, E. and Heath, C. (1998) 'Are Geographic Regions
  with High Income Inequality Associated with Risk of Abdominal Weight Gain?',
  Social Science and Medicine, 47: 1–6.
Layard, R. (2005) *Happiness: Lessons from a New Science*. London: Penguin .
Lehrer, J. (2006) 'The Reinvention of the Self: A Mind-Altering Idea Reveals How Life
  Affects the Brain', *Seed Magazine*, 23 February. Available at <www.seedmagazine.
  com/news/2006/02/the_reinvention_of_the_self.php?page=all&p=y>.
Margo, J. and Dixon, M., with Pearce, N. and Reed, H. (2006) *Freedom's Orphans:
  Raising Youth in a Changing World*. London: ippr.
Mepham, D. (2005) 'Social Justice in a Shrinking World', in N. Pearce and W.
  Paxton (eds), *Social Justice: Building a Fairer Britain*. London: ippr/Politico's.
Mepham, D. and Held, D. (forthcoming) Introductory chapter in D. Mepham and
  D. Held (eds), *Progressive Foreign Policy: New Directions for the UK*. Cambridge:
  Polity Press.
Miller, D. (2000) *Citizenship and National Identity*. Cambridge: Polity Press.
Miller, D. (2005) 'What is Social Justice?', in N. Pearce and W. Paxton (eds), *Social
  Justice: Building a Fairer Britain*. London: ippr/Politico's.
Parekh, B. (2005) 'Unity and Diversity in Multicultural Societies'. Lecture delivered
  at the International Institute for Labour Studies, Geneva. Available at <www.
  ilo.org/public/english/bureau/inst/download/1parekh.pdf>.

Pearce, N. and Paxton, W. (eds) (2005) *Social Justice: Building a Fairer Britain*. London: ippr/Politico's.

Rawls, J. (1999) *The Law of Peoples*. Cambridge, Mass.: Harvard University Press.

Sandel, M. (1996) *Democracy's Discontent: America in Search of a Public Philosophy*. Cambridge, Mass.: Harvard University Press.

Skinner, Q. (1998) *Liberty before Liberalism*. Cambridge: Cambridge University Press.

Therborn, G. (2007) 'After Dialectics', *New Left Review*, 43, January–February.

White, S. (2006) *Equality*. Cambridge: Polity Press.

Wilkinson, R. (1996) *Unhealthy Societies: The Afflictions of Inequality*. London: Routledge.

Wilkinson, R. (2006) *The Impact of Inequality: How to Make Sick Societies Healthier*. London: Routledge.

You, J-S. (2005) *Corruption and Inequality as Correlates of Social Trust: Fairness Matters More than Similarity*. Working Paper No. 29, Hauser Center for Nonprofit Organizations and JFK School of Government, Harvard University.

Part 2

The Future of the Progressive Project

2
Renewing the Domestic Agenda

Ed Miliband

Introduction

By its nature, the progressive disposition tends to dissatisfaction. We have dreams for a better world, we are angry at injustice, we have a significant belief in the power of politics to change things, and we have an optimistic view of human nature. So should we be satisfied or dissatisfied with the last decade, and how should we learn the lessons and renew the progressive agenda?

The idealistic progressive sees paradox: national income significantly higher, but inequality only marginally lower; poverty down by over two million, but still one-fifth of the population; education standards higher, but working-class entry into higher education still low; public services improved, but with further to go; regeneration in cities previously neglected, but the peripheries sometimes left out; public spending higher, but the case for investment only partially won. And so we could go on across every area. Yet amidst the paradox, we can pick out the building blocks of the future. Progressive politics has shown a capacity for economic stewardship in a way it never has before in this country. Public investment has helped to regenerate our public services and create new institutions of the public realm, like Sure Start. Working people have seen gains in income and rights, from tax credits to paid holidays. The ethos of the country has shifted to the left on the environment, gay rights, development, and even taxation and spending. This is expressed not just through politics and laws, but also through, for example, the ethical consumer movement and the concept of social enterprise, firms founded for a social purpose. What matters is whether these gains are the start, or the end. This period of progressive rule was never going to be 1945–51: the 'big bang'. The model for us is surely closer to Scandinavian social democracy: sustained incremental change which knits progressive values deep into the fabric of the country. Why does this matter? Because it shifts the centre-ground of politics irreversibly onto progressive terrain.

As many have pointed out, renewal in office is one of the hardest things to achieve. But it is not impossible. There are a number of ingredients that the progressive movement needs. First of all, ethos: shining through from every action and proposal should be a sense of what progressive politics is about. I argue here for the values of equality, community and empowerment. Second, clear priorities: how does progressive politics specifically answer the challenges of building a society with the ethos we want to see? Specific policies are covered elsewhere in this book, but here I mention some of the new challenges that have arisen since 1997 and some priorities for the future. Third, political practice: can we live our values through the way we conduct politics? In particular, we need to engage with the electorate on the basis of empathy, analysis, candour and idealism.

Ethos

My starting point is the proposition that politics is about more than managerialism. Competence is necessary but not sufficient. The only protection against the passage of time in politics is a set of deep and expressed values, an ethos. This can start at a high level of abstraction, but it must be translatable into a framework for political action and for communication to normal people in everyday language.

The first building block for an ethos of progressive politics must be equality – including a belief that all should have a fair chance to achieve their potential. Part of being in progressive politics is a faith that people can achieve extraordinary things, but they need the right opportunities to do so. This belief in equality of opportunity is highly demanding, far more than most people would credit (Barry 2005). And yet, a belief in equality of opportunity is not enough. We should also worry about the outcomes in our society. Partly this is because outcomes structure opportunities, particularly from generation to generation. But even without this effect on opportunity, outcomes matter.

There is an important progressive instinct that in a rich society, nobody should fall below a certain level of income, defined in relative terms. Furthermore, there is good evidence that vastly unequal outcomes in our society have damaging effects; for example, on health as well as other aspects of well-being (Wilkinson 2005). This means, for example, the government has been right to target a relative measure in its child poverty ambition.

The view of equality must also be broad, not narrow, in its scope: as concerned with inequalities of power as income, as sensitive to issues around public services and public space as to wealth. For what we have learned from many poor communities is that inequality is a pervasive phenomenon, with multiple sources and aspects. The focus of equality must relate, then, to modern conceptions of the good life, and an understanding of the rising level not just of the social minimum, but of aspiration. It must respond to the desires of people today: for home-ownership, higher levels of consumption, education and skills and all the other things that define the good life for the person and their family.

A progressive belief in equality also has an intergenerational component. Nowhere is this more true than in relation to the environment, where climate change now threatens the very promise of progressive politics: that we can deliver a fairer world for the next generation than we enjoyed in ours (see Chapter 16).

So progressive politics in the years ahead must have equality, in all its dimensions, at its heart. We need to start from an egalitarianism which states that everyone deserves a fair chance, and that we seek fair outcomes. It is about a belief in the potential of the individual to be all they can be.

But this is only one part of the progressive ethos. There is more to the good society than the aggregation of the 'I': my health, my education, my job, my house, my pension, important as they are. The challenge also is to address the wider question not just of what each achieves for themselves, but how we relate to each other and what kind of society we are.

The central idea here is surely that the good society we believe in is underpinned by us holding a set of values in common, around solidarity and concern for others. These values are important in themselves and they also underpin our belief in equality. Their moral force animates collective action, including through the state, and private action, in our everyday lives. It gives impetus to tackling many of the great challenges of the modern age, including climate change.

These values – of what we can call community – might be claimed in some degree by all parts of the political spectrum, but there is a distinctive centre-left insight about how these values are generated. They mainly arise in the non-market sphere from opportunities to be part of common institutions and help each other. So when we think about the importance of public institutions and services, we do so not just because of the individual services they deliver, but also because of the communal values they can encourage. And these values and networks are nurtured not just in public institutions, but also in the institutions of civil society, including the voluntary sector. The renewal of the progressive project must include a commitment to finding ways of strengthening these institutions.

These two parts of our ethos, equality and community, lead us to a third: empowerment. The state is necessary for empowerment, and collective institutions can be a force for individual liberation; but equally the state alone is not sufficient to tackle the issues we face.

Empowerment is the partner of equality not just because the distribution of power is one dimension of equality: our whole notion of equality must be based on a belief about the role of the individual as author of their own life. The distinction between the progressive and conservative story is that we believe individual empowerment is the partner of the enabling state, not an alternative. And empowerment is also the partner of community, because the state – whether national or local – cannot build strong communities on its own. Its role in providing the funding and institutions is absolutely necessary but the empowered citizen – often acting as part of a group – is necessary to build a binding set of values.

Empowerment is a far more powerful notion than non-interference. It recognizes that freedom to choose is nothing without the power to choose – an empowered person must not only not be prevented from acting on their will, they must also possess the resources or capacities actually to carry it out (Sen 1999).

Earlier we cautioned against ivory towerism in the description of the progressive ethos. So what do these three parts amount to in simple terms? The proposition is this: we stand for a society where everyone has a fair chance, where we look after and care about each other and where individuals are given the power to control their lives and shape their community. But this is not yet the society we live in. Other chapters in this book are about the detailed policy to further progressive ends. In this chapter, I want to say something about how the challenges we face have changed and what the implications are for the progressive project. In this context, I will focus on some key themes and areas which are then developed in the other chapters in the book.

Equality

In our pursuit of equality, three particular challenges face us far more starkly than they did in 1997: the challenges of the environment, of globalization, and of asset-based inequality. In different ways, they make the traditional pursuit of equality more difficult but they also make the case for progressive politics clearer than ever.

The challenge of climate change means that the 1997 belief in reconciling economic efficiency and social justice must now be supplemented by environmental sustainability as an equal partner. As Miliband (Chapter 16) points out, the challenge of climate change reaches into every aspect of policy: economic, social and democratic. But more than this, it also throws into sharp relief two issues for egalitarians: our duty to future generations and the nature of our burden-sharing responsibilities with the developing world. Yet these challenges make the case for progressive politics more not less important: in particular, because, here more than anywhere, the limits of markets and the role of government becomes apparent. Achieving environmental sustainability makes a central point of progressive politics: that markets need to be embedded within the laws and norms of society, which reflect a set of social and political values.

Globalization challenges the egalitarian project in a number of ways as Balls, Ussher and Brooks point out (Chapter 5). The key insight is that while there are gains to be made from globalization for the UK, they are widely dispersed while the costs – in the loss of jobs from traditional industries for example – are more narrowly focused on individuals. This too both sharpens the challenge facing government and individuals and makes the progressive case: government playing its necessary role is essential to ensure that in these circumstances, people are not left isolated and the benefits and burdens of globalization are fairly shared.

The third challenge which more obviously confronts us now than in 1997 is that of understanding the dynamic of asset-based inequality. As Reed and Sodha (Chapter 6) demonstrate, the impact of the UK housing market over the last decade is tending to accentuate the gaps between rich and poor in access to assets. As they rightly say, the answer must be to look at the potential for giving more priority to providing greater housing, in all its forms, and looking at ways of enabling individuals to build up assets, as the government has begun to do through the Child Trust Fund and the Saving Gateway. While the specific focus on asset inequality is right, we should also recognise that asset inequality in access to housing is intimately linked to income inequality.

With this as the context then, where should the progressive egalitarian project focus in the years ahead? The starting point must be education. The impact of technology and globalization make the acquisition of skills by the population an economic and personal imperative (HM Treasury 2005). Viewing education through the lens of equality, we see that school reform and investment need to continue – Gordon Brown's commitment to increase the level of spending per state primary school pupil to current private school levels is an important ambition. But we also see that creating a more equal society cannot be done in the classroom alone. We know from the past decade that we also need a focus on what happens before children get to school, what happens out of school and their career pathways after school.

We know a lot more about the importance of the right education and care before the age of five for child development. Indeed, it has been argued that it was a failure to pay sufficient attention to the early years which explains why traditional progressive strategies around education have not had more effect on inequality (Esping-Anderson, 2005). Yet still we lag far behind the world's best in the proportion of resources we devote to the early years (Organization for Economic Cooperation and Development (OECD) 2007). Amid many competing priorities, this is one of the best long-term investments we can make in an egalitarian strategy.

Childcare and early years' services are important also for the way in which they support families. The issue of time that parents can spend out of the labour market after their children are born is also one that has been addressed, but more needs to be done. An agenda for the future must include a commitment to strengthen parental leave.

Services for teenagers outside school hours, unlike the early years, did not feature in the demands of egalitarians in the run-up to 1997. In fact, the last major investment in youth services took place after the 1960s Albemarle Report and since then it has been a neglected area. This was an important oversight. In a world where the school offers a fairly tightly regulated curriculum, it is essential to grasp the opportunity presented by good youth services and spaces to expand horizons and enable young people to make a successful transition to adulthood. Without them, class differences in soft skills will always hold some children back (Margo et al. 2006). So while proper investment in youth services is part of tackling the causes of crime, it is also essential if we are to raise aspirations and enable all young people to fulfil their potential.

After school, vocational education has been and remains Britain's Achilles' heel in education. It is striking that words written before the 1992 election, that 'At the post-16 stage, the division between academic and vocational study is the bane of our system', still resonate (Blackstone et al. 1992: 19). Britain's historic problem is that vocational qualifications have been undervalued and have failed to achieve equivalence with academic qualifications. The government is implementing important reforms to improve vocational pathways. Our aim should be to seek to build on these reforms towards greater parity of esteem.

Childcare, youth services and vocational education are united by their importance for developing the potential of everyone in our society. Like innovations such as tax credits, they lend themselves to a broad-based egalitarianism, of relevance to a large section of the population. As we move forward, we must remember that a central challenge for egalitarians is not simply to frame the right policies but to do so in a way that commands public support and this is partly done by designing programmes which have wide not narrow popular appeal.

Community

In pursuing the value of community, we must again face a number of challenges arguably greater than ten years ago. In particular, against a backdrop of geographical mobility, greater diversity and high levels of inequality, how do we build a stronger sense of community in the years ahead? We need to acknowledge the decline of some of the old institutions that used to bring together different groups in the community: young and old, people of different classes and background. As a constituency MP in an ex-mining area, I see this in the decline of the old institutions that used to be centred around the pits.

We should distinguish two different aspects of this debate: the local dimension, expressed through compassion and solidarity for those who live as one's neighbours; and the national dimension, expressed through the sense of togetherness we feel with those who inhabit our country.

Locally, new public spaces, constructed thanks to rising capital spending, have helped to build new sites where people can meet and form the bonds which create a sense of community and local pride. This is true of local libraries, play areas and the new Sure Start centres. As we look ahead, we should think about other public institutions and practices that can help bring people together. Sometimes this may be about new institutions, such as better youth services or new public spaces offering cultural or community facilities. Also, it is about how we use and build on existing institutions: schools, health centres, libraries and other public places. Public services do not simply have an impact on our pursuit of equality through the service the individual receives but also in our attempt to build community through their organization and their accountability. So in the years ahead opportunity to shape local public services from education to policing is not just right in principle but also helps build and foster social capital, as individuals work together to set priorities.

The bonds of community also come from a network of thriving community and voluntary groups. While government does not create the inspiration of the third sector, it can help or hinder it. That is why we should support more stable funding for the third sector, as well as the growing movement around community ownership and management of assets. Often there are buildings in a local community that a public authority may no longer need. Finding ways in which we can facilitate community rather than private ownership of them is an important way to protect the life and soul of the community and give residents a greater stake in the success of a local institution.

Community and public institutions do not just represent sites at which bonds of solidarity are built, but can also promote activities which connect groups that would not naturally interact. We need to consider, for example, how we can better connect younger and older people, because this is essential as a way of promoting understanding and support. And schools can play a crucial role in encouraging intergenerational volunteering, both in their openness to older volunteers and in their thinking about the role of their pupils in the community.

As well as action at local level, we need to understand that solidarity and respect come from a national consciousness. This is why the debate about Britishness (see Chapter 10) is so important, not simply because it can bind in those newly arrived in this country, but because it is a debate about what kind of country we want to be, how we want to see ourselves and how we want the world to see us. While progressives have traditionally shied away from this debate, in fact it is essential.

Empowerment

Compared to ten years ago, it is apparent today that from the private economy to public services to our democracy, people are rightly demanding more control. The decline of deference, raised expectations as well as the advent of the internet all give people a reason to believe that they can exercise a greater decision-making role in their own lives and that of their communities.

Some of the most important initiatives of the last decade – from the New Deal for Communities to Sure Start – have recognized the transformative power of government action allied to empowered individuals and communities. In public services, we have reached a stage where the kind of improvements and change we want to see require an empowered citizen and groups of citizens. In our political institutions, we need both to devolve more power to the local level and to find ways of engaging individuals in decision-making which go beyond four-yearly elections.

In public services, the importance of arguing for increased investment in key areas is essential. But, allied to resources, must be a move away from a 'letterbox' model in which we see the individual as simply having the service 'delivered' to them. Instead, we must think in terms of a more collaborative or 'co-production' model which understands the essential roles of users and communities. Take health, for instance. Around 80 per cent of visits to GPs concern chronic conditions (Cottam and Leadbeater 2004). The steps taken to ensure greater access to primary care are obviously important, but if we are really to tackle the problems people face then we need to ensure the patient can have the right sort of conversation with their GP which meets their needs. That is why new ways of empowering the patient have been pioneered (Cottam and Leadbeater 2004). This empowerment of the user is not simply right in principle but is also part of an essential insight about the contribution that the individual or groups of individuals can make to the success of the service. In chronic disease, often it is the ability to self-manage their condition which will have an important effect on an individual's quality of life. That is why the Expert Patient Programme started by the Department of Health (DoH) helps people with chronic health conditions to train others to manage their situations better (DoH 2006). By bringing patients together, it creates powerful peer networks. The same insights about personalization around the user can be applied across public services, including through a greater focus on the engagement of the user.

Just as we need to recognise the importance of personalisation to the user, so too there is an irreducibly collective element to public services. Take policing. The Chicago Alternative Policing system (CAPS), through its monthly beat meetings, not only provides accountability to the community but is also an important part of successful policing, as the community makes an important contribution to the service. Or take schooling. Every day Britain's hundreds of thousands of school governors play a heroic role in many of our schools – and at their best, they are freed from administrative tasks to mediate with parents, represent their views and shape the character of the school. In the coming years, we need to focus on how to strengthen the role that school governors can play as a source of accountability and voice.

How does this case for empowerment impact upon the debate about the strength of and interest in local democracy? In the years ahead, we need to see both a strengthening in the institutions of representative democracy and a greater willingness to engage in more experimental forms of participatory democracy.

People's disengagement from the political process must, in part, be explained by a belief that their involvement will not make a difference. At a local level, for example, part of the agenda for the future must be about the strengthening of the institutions of local democracy to improve the accountability of local services. The government has announced welcome moves to return greater powers over local bus services to councils. There is also a case for strengthening local accountability in other areas such as setting local policing priorities. Yet at the same time as understanding the importance of strengthening local and national democratic institutions, we need to recognize that, for a range of reasons, this can be supplemented with more participatory engagement (Fung 2006). This is not about consulting more but consulting better including through the use of citizens' juries and other deliberative methods.

Political practice

Having spelt out the ethos that should guide us in the years ahead, and given a sense of the key themes and priorities, I come now to the crucial question of political practice. In my view, our political practice needs to be guided by four different characteristics: empathy, analysis, candour and idealism (cf. Nuder 2002).

The attraction of the progressive project before 1997 was its sense of empathy: a notion that we, better than the alternative, understood the struggles and aspirations of families. The process of government involves difficult decisions which make retaining that sense of empathy an important challenge. In the years ahead, it is particularly important we stay connected to key parts of the progressive constituency: for example, families concerned about their children getting on the housing ladder; the white working class feeling under pressure from globalization, and public service professionals under pressure to deliver and subject to necessary but rapid reform. The job of government is not to satisfy every group in each demand, but it is essential for progressive politics to convey a sense that we understand the perspective needs of these groups.

After empathy comes analysis. We need a story about Britain and about people's lives which points to the role of progressive politics. For the low-paid worker subject to housing, employment and security pressures, the message of the far right provides a story about their lives, albeit a grotesque and inaccurate one. Any problem is down to the impact of immigration. The progressive project needs an alternative story. For the worker subject to these pressures, more than a message about globalization being good, it needs to be a story about the need for a government which is on the side of people and can help them manage their way through the changes they face in their lives.

After analysis comes candour about the challenges and dilemmas facing government and our society. Respect for politics will rise if politicians are more able to level with people about the difficult choices that our country faces. This is hard in many respects, partly because people will try and find ways round these dilemmas. But the only way of dealing with them is to reason with citizens. This demands a style of politics that is more open and more consultative.

Finally, comes idealism. Make Poverty History, the environmental movement and many other causes show people's willingness to engage in politics if they feel it changes things. The danger is of a politics that becomes centred on managerialism and turns people off – not just natural supporters and members of parties, but the wider public. The momentum behind debt and development also shows how we can build alliances which go beyond government and party to embrace a wider cause and community. We need to do the same on big domestic issues like child poverty, where we need to also tap into people's willingness to be part of a big movement for change.

The progressive project in particular relies on convincing people that politics has the capacity to change things. This is partly about the terms of political trade and the way we talk about politics, but it is also about the scale of our ambitions and our willingness to take on difficult issues.

Conclusion

Should we be more or less optimistic about the progressive project after ten years of centre-left government? Those of us who have been involved in government are more aware of the difficulties and dilemmas that we face. But the progressive project should take heart: a centre-left government has helped changed the ethos of the country in a more progressive direction. What matters most to the course of political history is not simply the institutional legacy – institutions built by government – but the ideological legacy – the terrain in which politics is played out. And the most encouraging thing of all for progressives is that politics is now being played out in a very different terrain to that of ten years ago. The success of progressive politics has been to win not just votes, but also arguments.

Today an explicit agenda around tax cuts, shrinking the state, blaming the poor, and anti-environmentalism seems as out of the mainstream as nationalization, penal tax rates and withdrawal from the EU did in

1997. This is because winning key political battles has helped changed the mood of the country. The prize then of continued progressive rule is to continue to shift the terms of debate. This is why the notion of the 'progressive consensus' is so powerful. It is an argument about political change. By winning big arguments for what we believe in, whether it is combating child poverty or tackling climate change, not only can we change the country, but we can also open up further space for progressive politics. To do that we need a strong, clear ethos of equality, community and empowerment. We need this ethos to translate into clear priorities. And it has to be put into practice with empathy, analysis, candour and idealism. If we do that, we can continue to make this a more progressive and more prosperous country in the years to come.

References

Barry, B. (2005) *Why Social Justice Matters*. Cambridge: Polity Press.
Blackstone, T., Cornford, J., Hewitt, P. and Miliband, D. (1992) *Next Left: An Agenda for the 1990s*. London: ippr.
Brown, G. (1996) John Smith Memorial Lecture, 19 April.
Brown, G. (1997) Anthony Crosland Memorial Lecture, 13 February.
Cottam, H. and Leadbeater, C. (2004) *RED Paper 01 Health: Co-creating Services*. London: Design Council.
DoH (2006) *The Expert Patient Programme*. London: DoH.
Esping-Andersen, G. (2005) 'Putting the Horse in Front of the Cart: Towards a Social Model for Mid-Century Europe'. The Hague, WRR Lecture, 8 December.
Fung, A. (2006) 'Democratising the Policy Process', in M. Moran, M. Rein and R. Goodin (eds), *The Oxford Handbook of Public Policy*. New York: Oxford University Press.
HM Treasury (2005) *Globalisation and the UK: Strength and Opportunity to Meet the Economic Challenge*. London: TSO.
HM Treasury (2006) *Report of the Shared Equity Taskforce*. London: TSO.
Margo, J. and Dixon, M. with Pearce, N. and Reed, H. (2006) *Freedom's Orphans: Raising Youth in a Changing World*. London: ippr.
Miliband, E. (2005) 'Does Inequality Matter?', in A. Giddens and P. Diamond (eds), *The New Egalitarianism*. Cambridge: Polity Press.
Nuder, P. (2002) 'A Manifesto for Reformers', *Progressive Politics*, 1 (1), September.
OECD (2007) *PF10: Public Spending on Childcare and Early Education*. Paris: OECD.
Putnam, R. (2000) *Bowling Alone: The Collapse and Revival of American Community*. New York: Simon & Schuster.
Sen, A. (1999) *Development as Freedom*. Oxford: Oxford University Press.
Titmuss, R. (1968) *Commitment to Welfare*. London: George Allen & Unwin Limited.
Wilkinson, R. (2005) *The Impact of Inequality: How to Make Sick Societies Healthier*. London: Routledge.

3
Winning Hearts and Minds: Prospects for Progressivism
Stanley B. Greenberg and Miranda Lewis

Having established the ethos that should guide the renewal of progressive thought in the previous chapter, this chapter provides part one of the analysis of the changing condition of Britain, laying out the attitudinal and political background for what follows. Here we draw on new qualitative research not only to ascertain the state of the modern political battleground in which progressives must fight to occupy territory, but also to set out the areas where there is scope to shift the terms of discussion, to lead public opinion and to entrench progressive values in political and public debate over the next decade and beyond.

The chapter starts by examining the electoral realities and widespread public disengagement from formal politics. It then sets out the areas where the gap has grown between progressive and public priorities. Finally it addresses the policy issues upon which progressives need to take a stronger lead and consider new initiatives if a newly invigorated progressive project is to be achieved. Although this chapter focuses on the challenges this project must confront, it indicates considerable cause for optimism. As the introductory chapter noted, the current constellation of social and political forces suggests that this could be a vital moment for progressive ambitions.

Enduring political change comes when voters are convinced that a particular party is uniquely relevant to addressing the key problems and challenges facing the country. This happened in 1979 when Thatcher's Conservatives rode the wave of post-materialist value change and again in 1997 when the New Labour project emerged from the particular socio-political landscape of the time. But after a decade of Labour governance, we have again reached a period when new and growing problems demand a different kind of politics. As the next chapter indicates and as we detail here, the British public have been deeply discontented with their political parties, the government's priorities and the direction of the country. But they have also been prepared to embrace the challenges of living in a technologically advanced global society and have increasingly engaged in the new issues this context throws up: responding to climate change, the consumer culture, changes to families, and demographic change more generally, such as increased migration and asylum. Therefore, for progressive values to become entrenched in the coming years, we must update our policies and ideas and inhabit new political territory on the centre-left. This is a vital and daunting goal. Failure to achieve this means a likely retreat of the progressive project.

As this chapter will demonstrate, there are significant new challenges facing the UK which progressives must tackle if they are to forge a strong political legacy. These go far beyond a narrow focus upon public service reform, and include how to fund the state and security in retirement, and how to address rising immigration and cultural and racial diversity, climate change and new energy demands, a new world of extremism and terrorism, and, above all, the new forms of inequality and brakes to rising living standards. These are major challenges, particularly for progressives who have tended to struggle in articulating a publicly convincing account of security issues. At the same time, they represent an opportunity to seize some ground and demonstrate that progressive answers to these larger issues will work. And there is every indication that this is possible. But in essence, this analysis poses a challenge to Labour and its claims to be a leading progressive force. If it takes up this challenge it has the opportunity in the coming decade to emerge, as in 1997, as a modernizing, indispensable party, but only – as we argue here – if it builds an agenda that makes progressive ideas newly relevant.

The electoral realities

If we broadly take votes for the parties on the centre-left to represent votes for progressive politics, the simple electoral mathematics should lead progressives to take a fresh look at the challenges facing the country. In the 2005 general election, Labour won only 35.2 per cent of the vote, down 5.5 points from 2001 and 8 points from 1997, even as the

Conservatives remained stuck at just under a third of the vote (Electoral Commission 2005). The Liberal Democrats picked up their vote share by 3.7 points to 22 per cent in 2005, but with the Conservatives now showing signs of life, both Labour and the Liberal Democrats have fallen below their 2005 levels – Labour to around 33 per cent and the Liberal Democrats to below 20 per cent in the polls at the end of 2006 – together, a bare majority in the country (Polling Report 2007). (As of February 2007, the average of the most recent polls on voting intention from the four most regular polling groups (YouGov, MORI, Populus and ICM) were: Conservatives 37.25 per cent, Labour 32.75 per cent, Liberal Democrats 19.75 per cent, giving Labour and the Liberal Democrats combined a total of 52.5 per cent.) These numbers do not preclude waging a pitched battle on the current terrain, as each percentage point regained in a future election can bring up to ten additional seats.[1] But the erosion of support for the centre-left parties has also revealed a series of gaps on the economic, social and political landscape that allow for a bolder call for action.

Over the period 1997–2007 an estimated 5 million voters have been lost to the national electoral process. Many of these would be natural Labour supporters – 'working class' voters such as trade union members, council tenants and the unemployed (Heath et al. 2001). Turnout in the 1997 general election dropped to 71 per cent, the lowest since 1945, but the disengagement did not end there: the election of 2001 produced a drop-off of a wholly different kind – down over 10 points to 59 per cent, the lowest turnout since 1918. The 2005 election turnout of 61 per cent affirmed the lost electorate one more time and the reality of political disengagement. So what accounts for this large-scale electoral flight?

The abrupt disengagement during this period is part of a longer-term problem of party decline that has fewer and fewer people taking up membership and fewer and fewer 'strongly' identifying with any party (Power Inquiry 2006). Britain has evolved from an industrial to a post-

---

1. This estimate is based on a computer simulation that takes the increased vote from all the other parties according to their share of the vote; a second, more cautious simulation assumes that the Conservatives cannot be further eroded, so all additional Labour gains come from other parties. On 5 May 2005, if the Labour share was 1 point higher, the party would have held ten additional seats and achieved an 87-seat majority; a 2 point improvement (to just 37 per cent of the vote) would have enabled Labour to hold 18 more seats, with a 103-seat majority. Running the model with the most cautious assumptions that lock in the Conservative vote, a 2 point gain in the Labour share would have allowed Labour to hold 13 more seats and a 93-seat majority.

industrial society, with a parallel change in the parties and the character of the party conflict. The parties are now less ideological and class-defined (Labour is no longer seen as the party for the working class), without clarity on where the new battle lines lie or what their new convictions might be; indeed, even without clarity on the core problem that needs to be addressed. These developments account for the flight of the less educated and those in manual occupations out of the electorate in disproportionate numbers, particularly in the most recent period; the same has happened for younger age cohorts, who seem to lack moorings in the current political order (Keaney and Rogers 2006).

The sense of unease about the new political order is evident in focus group research. In particular, there is a sense that differences between the main parties have evaporated (Green and Holbolt 2006). People also feel that the government is behaving like any other government of the past and is therefore indistinct. As one respondent put it:

> Politics in Britain is like those cheap chocolate boxes: 'Six different flavours, one single taste.' Where is the choice? What's the point?
> (Public submission to the Power Inquiry (2006))

That it is the working class and young people who have been quickest to disengage and reject formal politics is particularly worrying. The middle classes are most likely to vote and most likely to be involved in informal politics (Working Party on Active Citizenship 2004). Some of those most disenchanted with politics are turning to far right extremist parties as the only parties that appear to be listening to their concerns. This is particularly the case in seats not targeted by the mainstream parties (John et al. 2006).

So disengagement ought to engage progressive sensibilities, given the centrality of civic values to progressivism, and the social class differences in participation. This is discussed in greater detail in Chapter 13. But we shall also see that disengagement is a leading indicator for so many other problems.

The 2006 independent inquiry into Britain's democracy was right to conclude that Britain is facing a 'democratic malaise' that may take us well beyond disappointing voter turnout. The inquiry reports its own realization about 'just how wide and deep is the contempt for formal political institutions' (Power Inquiry 2006: 28–9). It is important to be clear that, as Chapter 13 points out, this alienation is specifically from formal politics. People continue to engage locally in voluntary sector organizations and local public services and schools, and they are more likely to take part in demonstrations and marches (Norms 2002). From the mid 1970s to the mid 1990s, the number of people signing a petition doubled from 32 per cent to 60 per cent; attendance at demonstrations rose from 7 per cent to 19 per cent, and those taking part in a consumer boycott rose from 5 per cent to 15 per cent. The Power Inquiry found that 37 per cent of those who do not vote in general elections are members of, or active in, a charity, a community group or a public body (Power Inquiry 2006). So what is going on?

It is pretty well documented that people feel disconnected from their representatives, as if ordinary people have been forgotten. They suspect that politicians are 'in it for themselves'. Quotes for research undertaken by the Institute of Public Policy Research (ippr) in 2005 show that people have little connection with, or respect for, those who politically represent them:

> After the election and its promises, nothing's changed. I voted, but have actually forgotten his name, as I haven't seen nor heard of him since.

> They are disconnected from the real world.

> He does not refer to me for my opinion on any question. Mainly he follows the party line.

> He is a publicity machine – not a politician.

> They treat us as if we were invisible, and do what they want, not what the people they represent want. (Coleman 2005)

Currently, 80 per cent of voters do not feel involved in the political decisions that affect them, and 76 per cent believe that their vote makes little or no difference to the decisions made in Westminster (ICM 2007).

In relation to the current Labour government, this sense manifests itself in widespread disillusionment about broken promises. While the government's achievements (particularly the strong economy) are recognized, this sits alongside deep frustration with its perceived inability to champion the interests of ordinary people. Despite significant gains in poverty reduction (Sutherland et al. 2006) the public is not convinced that improvements are always visible in their own lives, and do not necessarily feel that government plans to change public services will bring sufficient change.

But trust in politicians and the government is a long-term problem. While the above suggests that current disenchantment is related to whether the promises of 1997 have been fulfilled, the reality is that levels of trust in politicians have remained remarkably stable over the last 20 years or so – in 1983, 18 per cent of people trusted politicians to tell the truth, with an identical number doing so in 2003. At the same time, trust in specific aspects of political processes and institutions has declined significantly. In particular, people are much less trusting of official statistics and information, fearing 'spin'. As one focus group respondent put it, 'Everything – there's spin on it. Even when you don't think it has got spin, it's got spin on it' (Duffy et al. 2005).

It also appears that the broad experience of the public with public institutions and politics leaves them doubtful of the government's integrity and confidence, regardless of the actual services delivered or their experiences of them. This is important: people tend to assume that where their own experience of local services is good, this is the result of a happy accident or their own ability to work the system, rather than of government policy or competence. There is a general assumption that services elsewhere in the UK are much worse (Cabinet Office 2004).

With the main party battles not yet centred on the issues that now engage the public, and with the emergence of new economic and political elites, large portions of the electorate feel alienated from the political centre. Without a new kind of politics, they lack an instinctive confidence in the government or the parties of the centre-left. Reinvigorating British democracy requires a very different kind of politics, and one in which the majority of people feel that what happens in our political institutions is relevant to them and their lives. This chapter now turns to examine how these key electoral issues could be impacted by a progressive agenda that picks up emerging currents in public opinion.

Building a progressive consensus on inequality and redistribution

In important areas, progressive values are now entrenched more successfully into the public debate than ever before. The British public is in some respects more socially liberal than ever before, particularly in their attitudes towards race and sexuality (Taylor-Gooby 2007). The terms of debate on public services have also shifted: they now centre upon delivery rather than upon questions over the role of the state (Rothon and Heath 2003), and support for spending on universal public services, such as education and health, is high (Taylor-Gooby 2007). The Labour government has made an important contribution to this. In particular, it has restored the funding and legitimacy of the public services. But, as we show below, there remains a gap between public attitudes and progressive values on issues of inequality and redistribution. Closing this gap – and winning hearts and minds over to progressive values – remains a challenge: but it is not an insurmountable one.

As the following chapter will show, the period of Labour governance has brought a remarkably strong economy that, against the trends in North America and Europe, has produced sustained macro-growth and low unemployment; a rise in real incomes of well over 2 per cent a year for all but the bottom decile; a fall in poverty rates, particularly among children and pensioners; a steady rise in life expectancy and public health; and a fall in overall income inequality, particularly after government taxation, credits and benefits (Dixon and Paxton 2005; Dixon and Margo 2006). Yet despite these gains, the majority of Britons do not think of themselves as better off: last year only around a third of those in the lowest social class and half of those in the highest social class thought they were better off than in 1997 (ICM 2006a). Similarly low proportions thought that poverty had actually fallen under Labour.

This is understandable. Britain today also faces a reality of stubborn and entrenched inequalities despite the improvements outlined in the next chapter, and on some measures this inequality has worsened under Labour governance. The income gains for the middle have been accompanied by an explosion of income for the top 1 per cent, which has doubled its share of total income since 1997 (Sikka 2006). Wealth inequality is nearly twice as high as income inequality (using a Gini coefficient) and has remained at these high levels over the past decade or so. This is reflected in a growing inequality among regions in the country, with London, the East and the South East of England growing more prosperous relative to the national average, with other regions falling back. Moreover, an already not very mobile society has become less mobile. Parental background, including education and ethnicity, appears to be making more of a difference to one's life chances (although this process is not uniform across different social and ethnic groups). Labour's goal of moving 50 per cent of school leavers into higher education has been taken up disproportionately by those of higher socio-economic status: attendance has risen from 35 per cent to 50 per cent for those from wealthier backgrounds, but for those from more deprived backgrounds, the number in higher education rose from 11 per cent to just 19 per cent, well short of the national goal. During the 1990s, children whose parental incomes were in the highest 20 per cent were around five times more likely to acquire a degree by the age of 23 than children whose parental incomes were in the lowest 20 per cent (Blanden and Machin 2004).

Britons themselves tend to greatly underestimate the extent of inequality in the UK: when asked in 1999, the average person thought that chairs of large corporations earned 14 times more than the average shop assistant; the real figure was 55 times more (Taylor-Gooby 2005b). The public have a correspondingly poor understanding of the current tax system and tend to overestimate how progressive it is: almost two-thirds of respondents in a British Social Attitudes (BSA) survey thought that high-income earners pay a greater share of their income in taxes than lower earners, despite the fact that the reverse is actually true, as discussed in the next chapter. Moreover, despite low public tolerance of inequality, people are wary of overt and explicit redistribution. Just under half of respondents in the BSA survey agreed that it is the government's responsibility to reduce income differences, and only a third believed that the government should redistribute income from the better-off to the less affluent. The preference was for implicit redistribution through government provision and subsidies rather than explicit redistribution through taxation (Sefton 2005). But despite their underestimations of inequality and the impact of the tax system, analysis of BSA data shows that four out of five people agreed that 'the gap between those with low and high incomes is too wide', underscoring the centrality of fairness for the progressive project (Taylor-Gooby 2005a). Legitimately focused on maximizing other values, the Labour government has seemed to promote fairness and greater equality through stealth rather than design. Yet the old and new economy entrenches inequalities and rewards elitism, both of which undermine progressive designs for the future.

That four out of five people think inequality is too high in Britain is a beacon, as progressives are much better positioned to make the conclusion central to their new agenda and narrative. A vast terrain may open up with a fresh and unapologetic discussion of fairness. We are proposing new kinds of thinking that may allow as yet untested innovations in policy.

First, the continued desire for greater fairness and rising living standards, combined with misperceptions about the extent and character of inequality, suggest the need for a new narrative, a framework of understanding that allows people to interpret the new and changing economic realities, including the growing role of markets, choice and global competition. If progressive politicians are the voice for this narrative, they are in a position to play an educative role and put the spotlight on areas misaligned with progressive values. Progressives have to build a narrative about poverty, beginning with what it means to live in poverty in the UK. Rather than talking about poverty in technical terms only – children living in households with an income of less than 60 per cent of the median – we also need to talk about the number of children going without necessities such as a warm coat in winter. There is evidence to suggest that using striking and practical examples is a much more powerful way of illustrating the realities of poverty in the UK (Fabian Commission on Life Chances and Child Poverty 2006). People are also struck by discussion of the strides made by the government in reducing child poverty, and heartened by knowing that policy can make a difference (ibid.).

Second, progressives will want to introduce new policies, or revisit old ones, with the explicit goal of ensuring greater fairness and opportunity. It goes beyond the remit of this chapter to set out in detail what these policies may be, although subsequent chapters flag up key areas where greater fairness and opportunity can be realized. Many of these ideas emerge out of real gaps in progressive policy, as discussed earlier, and may take on a new import in the context of a new narrative.

Third, building a narrative rests on building trust between government and citizens. As outlined above, we are witnessing increasing scepticism in political institutions and processes. Some of this distrust may lie in the perceptions of procedural unfairness in housing allocation and prices, and in access to vital services such as long-term care, that people expressed in recent ippr focus groups on fairness (Lewis and Margo forthcoming; see also Chapter 14 for a fuller discussion). To win people to the progressive project and to make a case that distributional fairness also matters, progressives will have to push the government to place these concerns about fairness on the centre-stage in a way that it has not yet done.

Fourth, new debates on environmentalism and green taxes offer new opportunities to build consensus around contributions to achieving public goals. As we describe below, public concern about the environment and climate change is growing rapidly. This does not, of course, mean that the public are willing unconditionally to accept higher levels of environmental taxation: as with any form of taxation, people are concerned about this becoming simply another revenue-raising instrument, although ippr research suggests that support is much greater when revenues are hypothecated to transport infrastructure improvements (Bird and Morris 2006). The public also tend to be reluctant to bear the costs of any environmental regulation, usually underestimating their own impact and preferring upstream regulation on business (Retallack et al. 2007). But these new issues offer progressives the opportunity for renewed debate on the tax burden and the public interest. After a decade of Labour government, the lowest and highest earners each pay about a third of their income in taxes (income and value added tax (VAT)). There are good progressive reasons to think about the necessary costs in ways that bring better results.

Entrenching new issues within progressivism

There are some key areas in which the Labour government, despite a great deal of effort, has thus far failed to build a progressive consensus or public confidence. These tend to be the areas in which the left has traditionally struggled with the public, particularly on crime and immigration. Labour has responded with tough policies and speeches, but has failed to convince voters that its policies work or that they are part of a distinctive approach that is best for Britain. The needs of the economy are creating new issues regarding migration that leave the public unsettled and the elites sounding elliptical at best.

This has been reflected in a vast change in the concerns of voters – away from the economic issues of the 1980s and the public service concerns of the 1990s to the cultural and security-focused issues of the 2000s. At the end of 2006, the most important issues for voters were race relations and immigration (23 per cent); defence and international terrorism (18 per cent); and crime, law and order, and violence (13 per cent) – all of which form the priorities for a good majority of Britain – ahead of the NHS (9 per cent) and schools (5 per cent) (Ipsos MORI 2006). While thus far the traditional issues of health and education have continued to drive voting behaviour, one cannot assume that Britain will be immune to the dynamics that impacted voting in the Netherlands, France and Austria (Green and Holbolt 2006). Progressives must continue to show that safety and security are central to their agenda and that these issues can be tackled using progressive approaches. A failure to address these issues effectively would risk losing the public debate and undermining progressive values.

Crime and anti-social behaviour

The British public fears rising crime and is anxious about anti-social behaviour. This is despite evidence cited in Chapter 12 that recorded crime is dropping, as are levels of anti-social behaviour. A wealth of research suggests that while some crimes and disorders – for example, domestic violence, which is often carried out behind closed doors – may pass almost unnoticed by the general public, other incidents are widely perceived to pose a much greater threat to the civic order. People particularly see local, highly visible disorders, such as graffiti and groups of young people loitering in a particular place, as threatening to local safety (Dixon et al. 2006). While the incidence of many kinds of crime has been declining over a period of time, incivilities, violence and anti-social behaviour in public have only begun to decline relatively recently (Walker et al. 2006). Levels of perceived anti-social behaviour rose substantially between 1996 and 2002/03 (Margo et al. 2006), and in 2005, Britons were more than three times as likely to complain about groups of young people loitering than about noisy neighbours – up from 1.75 times more likely in 1992 (Walker et al. 2006). Moreover, nearly 80 per cent of Britons thought that 'young people today have too much freedom and not enough discipline' (Page and Wallace 2004).

The Labour government has brought in a raft of measures to tackle crime and anti-social behaviour, including on the spot fines, Anti-Social Behaviour Orders (ASBOs) and 'acceptable behaviour contracts'. While there is evidence that these measures are reducing the incidence of these behaviours, public perceptions of the reality and the government's larger purpose lag behind. The more progressive policies that will have an impact upon crime and anti-social behaviour – for example, Sure Start and child poverty reduction targets – are long term and the link between policy and problem is not necessarily clear to the public. It will need highlighting if the British public are to believe there is a uniquely progressive approach to these problems.

While the public are justifiably worried about anti-social behaviour, progressives should respond in ways that do not make it harder to address the problem effectively. Many policy responses to concerns about anti-social behaviour centre upon the use of public spaces by young people. This feeds into a wider public narrative about 'yob Britain', binge drinking, lack of respect and out-of-control youth. The story told is one of dangerous city centres inhabited by feral young people. There is a real danger that this narrative will further fuel public anxiety and fear about young people.

To some extent this is simply the product of an ongoing intergenerational conflict about how young people are perceived and how public spaces are used. But it is important for progressives to recognize that there are now some qualitative differences in behaviour, giving rise to a clear need to tackle the issue. In particular, it is critical to address those behaviours as many have a disproportionate effect upon the most deprived communities. There is potential to move towards a more progressive debate in which a new politics of public spaces is developed. ippr's deliberative research has found that bringing older and younger people together to discuss the use of space can offer a rich means with which to begin to rebuild intergenerational trust (Hatch 2003).

Alongside this, some punitive measures are important so as to send strong social signals about the acceptability of particular behaviours. That progressives send such signals is important to the overarching narrative. At the same time, a more convincing account of how parents can be supported to take control of the issue needs to be developed. This involves recognizing the many differences in the ability and desire of parents to tackle their children's behaviour. Some, particularly those leading chaotic lives as a result of drug or alcohol misuse, require significant support to be able to parent well. Others are doing well, but may need reassurance about their abilities to nurture their children in the twenty-first-century environment.

Addressing the role of parents effectively involves empowering them to take control. However there are key questions to be raised here about the growing influence of advertising and the media on the definition and cultural norms of childhood and youth culture. In effect, media and advertising have taken power away from parents in determining the leisure activities and the communication and behavioural norms influencing young people (Margo et al. 2006).

Government policy has also served in some instances to disempower parents. Re-categorizing behaviour which would normally be dealt with by parents, particularly behaviour in the home, as 'anti-social' – thus requiring police action, or ASBOs and other punitive responses – means that the responsibility for disciplining children is removed from both parents and the local community. Rather than empowering local groups of parents to assert behavioural norms, as has traditionally been the case in well-functioning communities with high levels of collective efficacy, in some instances they are encouraged to rely on the police and other local community figures, who in turn are encouraged to use more punitive methods. Tackling anti-social behaviour effectively requires a new public discussion about the role of parents and the wider community in dealing with behaviour.

Immigration

Immigration has been one of the most contested issues of the last decade. It was bitterly fought over in the 2005 election, and continues to dominate the public's concerns. While Tory leader David Cameron has gone silent on immigration and while the government has sought to 'transform' the Home Office after a range of breakdowns, there has been a much bigger process and set of issues at work. It is critical that progressives get to grips with these changes, as they are part of their approach to a modern and successful Britain. Labour's account has been viewed with suspicion by the public, and has not succeeded in convincing them either that the issue is being dealt with or that a progressive approach could succeed.

The public fears competition for resources, particularly over public services and employment. This is especially the case for many working-class people, who perceive their wages as vulnerable to competition and who are not able to opt into private health or education if local services are unsatisfactory. A less tangible fear is that British culture (or more specifically English culture) is being undermined by the presence of immigrants (Lewis 2005, 2006). This is partially driven by attitudes towards Muslims who are widely deemed to be reluctant to integrate or to adopt British culture, in contrast to polls demonstrating that the vast majority of Muslims want greater integration. In ippr focus groups, many people have expressed concern over terrorism and the presence of Muslims in Britain (Lewis 2005, 2006).

The drivers of these concerns are complex. The reality is that Britain's population has changed dramatically in the last 30 years. The British public see a Britain that is increasingly multicultural and pluralistic, and unevenly integrated. The public believe that the political class has lost control of our borders and somehow seems indifferent to the change in the nature of Britain. Increased pressure on housing and education in particular are felt acutely. People in ippr's focus groups expressed vivid concerns that their lives were being negatively affected while richer people were benefiting from migration. The public are aware that since 1997 the Labour government has overseen an uninterrupted period of accelerating net in-migration – the only such period in the last four decades (Office for National Statistics (ONS) 2006; Connolly and White 2006).

Although concerns about immigration mirror the changing face of Britain, in many cases concerns about the impacts are greatly exaggerated and based on myth. ippr's focus groups found that a very significant number of people believed that anyone from an ethnic minority background was routinely given priority access to all public services. A 2007 ippr survey found that 20 per cent of the British public believe there to be more than 1 million asylum seekers in the UK. Concerns were highest in areas where there were the fewest immigrants, and lowest in areas with the greatest concentration (Lewis and Newman forthcoming).

The challenge for progressives is to untangle legitimate concerns from racism and the xenophobic way in which fears are often expressed.

Progressive arguments consistently fail to win ground with the public, partly because deeply held views on fairness are rarely addressed. Progressives will lose ground to reactionary forces unless they are uniquely committed to fairness and a new national identity.

More difficult is the notion of Britain as a multicultural nation. It is unlikely that progressives will be able to make the case for multiculturalism unless the government is understood to be serious about gaining control over immigration. One of the key challenges is to get the public to accept that measures are being taken. ippr's focus groups found that the public were unwilling to accept that any measures on asylum have been taken to date. Those measures which people do have faith in – such as the detention of asylum seekers – have done little to diminish hostility, and may in fact increase it (for example, some people believe that asylum seekers are detained because they have committed a crime). On this issue more than perhaps any other, the role of the media is critical.

To be trusted, progressives need to understand that this is not just about creating effective instruments of control; this is about threatened values. People believe that unity, security and a fundamental fairness are being lost.

The evidence suggests that people are increasingly accepting of many kinds of diversity. The public no longer believe that being white – or even being born in Britain – is a prerequisite for being British. There is increasing acceptance that belief in British institutions underpins British identity. The demand for full integration and the preservation of an underlying national unity and identity are the preconditions for accepting and perhaps heralding Britain's new diversity. This is the time to create the framework that can move people to a different place – one that allows people to value what globalization will surely bring. This may also be a moral imperative, as the alternative is surely a divisive, racist politics.

Security and terrorism

The issue of global terrorism is so centrally identified with Tony Blair and the choices he made after 9/11, and with the Iraq war, that progressives may think that the issue would recede with his retirement, but they would almost certainly be wrong. A centre-left government will not be trusted to lead unless keeping the country safe in a dangerous world is second nature for the progressive project. Progressives need to address this lack of trust. Before 9/11, just 2 per cent of Britons cited international terrorism, defence and foreign policy as the top issue, but this figure jumped to 60 per cent after the attack on the Twin Towers and again after the 2005

London bombings, dropping to roughly 40 per cent in 2007. However, it remains one of the top two issues for voters (MORI 2007).

Public opposition to the Iraq war and to a foreign policy so closely identified with President Bush has made it difficult to win public confidence more generally on security issues. Immediately following the London bombings, almost two-thirds of the public believed the British presence in Iraq was a contributing factor in the bombings. At the end of 2006, more than two-thirds of the public believed that American foreign policy under President Bush has made the world a more dangerous place (ICM 2006a, 2006b). But it is likely that Tony Blair's analysis and the reality of extremism and a 'reactionary Islam' will outlast not only Blair's tenure as Prime Minister but also Bush's presidency (Blair 2006). The public certainly see dangers abroad and, with the reality of the London and Madrid bombings, an extremist threat at home.

Going forward in the post-Iraq period, it will be imperative for the left to reform its image and ideas in the eyes of the public and be seen to be committed to security and fighting terrorism while rejecting the neo-conservative framework that has characterized the present debate. There is also a deeper need for progressives to press the government to adopt a more progressive agenda on security and foreign policy, as detailed in Chapter 18. Disconnected from the neo-conservative world view, progressives may yet be the indispensable champions of moderation, tolerance, human rights, modernization and gender equality – the ideas that allow societies to develop while containing conflict and violence.

Climate change

The Stern Report recently set out in dramatic terms the consequences of failing to act on climate change. ippr's own modelling work takes an even bleaker view, and demonstrates that we need to make very significant cuts to avoid the most dangerous levels of climate change (Baer and Mastrandrea 2006). Achieving this requires unprecedented partnership between citizens, governments and the private sector. Personal behaviour change is vital if the necessary cuts are to be made: individuals are directly responsible for nearly 44 per cent of the UK's CO_2 emissions, and are indirectly responsible for much more (Retallack et al. 2007).

The government has signalled its commitment to addressing climate change, and the Climate Change and Sustainable Energy Act became law in June 2006. Among other measures, this demands an annual report on greenhouse gas emissions. However, attempts to address climate change are hampered by the political challenge of implementing the most effective solutions. Focusing on taxation rather than incentives and bringing in more enforcement measures would undoubtedly be more effective at reducing emissions, but this has to be weighed up against people's reluctance to bear the personal costs associated with reducing emissions. In order to create the space to do this, communications and information need to be improved so that people understand the effect their actions have on the environment. Effective public engagement is a critical part of this.

The public believe that climate change is real and happening, and 71 per cent think that their children's or grandchildren's lives will be a little or a lot worse as a result (YouGov 2006). In polls, people have demonstrated an increased willingness to tolerate some sacrifice – but actual behaviour change lags far behind (Retallack et al. forthcoming). David Cameron is keen to present himself as environmentally friendly, although few concrete policies are evident as yet. Nonetheless, for the first time in two decades the environment is taking the political centre-stage. The furore caused by Tony Blair's announcement that he had no intention of reducing his personal air travel shows just how far this debate has come.

The progressive political challenge is to move beyond the current rhetoric and constraints of public opinion to address climate change in new and bolder ways that only progressives will be trusted to take up.

Conclusion

While New Labour has shown diverse sets of voters that it can manage the economy in a new period of globalization and restore the funding and legitimacy of public services, it has not yet created a forward-moving political project that engages voters and unifies the country around progressive values. Overcoming these gaps will require a focus not on past promises, but on a changing Britain and the new issues that require a new politics. The challenge for progressives is to recognize and address the problems that the political order has not tackled or put centre-stage.

The coming years offer an opportunity for progressive values to become more deeply entrenched in the public and political debates. However, making this happen requires a new shift in the political debate in which old challenges are addressed head-on and new challenges are made politically salient for voters. It is critical that progressives in government and beyond lead public opinion to a more progressive space on issues such as fairness and diversity, using the opportunities afforded by the public debate.

References

Baer, P. and Mastrandrea, M. (2006) *High Stakes: Designing Emissions Pathways to Reduce the Risk of Dangerous Climate Change*. London: ippr.

Bird, J. and Morris, J. (2006) *Steering through Change: Winning the Debate on Road Pricing*. London: ippr.

Blair, T. (2006) 'We Will Win against Global Terrorism'. Speech at the Los Angeles World Affairs Council, 1 August.

Blanden, J. and Machin, S. (2004) 'Educational Inequality and the Expansion of UK Higher Education', *Scottish Journal of Political Economy*, Special Issue on the Economics of Education, 51 (2): 230–49.

Cabinet Office (2004) Unpublished paper.

Coleman, S. (2005) *Direct Representation: Towards a Conversational Democracy*. London: ippr.

Connolly, H. and White, A. (2006) 'The Different Experiences of the United Kingdom's Ethnic and Religious Populations', *Social Trends 36*. London: TSO. Available at <www.statistics.gov.uk/articles/social_trends/ST36_Overview.pdf>.

Duffy, B., Hall, S. and Williams, M. (2005) *Who Do You Believe? Trust in Government Information*. London: Ipsos MORI.

Dixon, M. and Margo, J. (2006) *Population Politics*. London: ippr.

Dixon, M. and Paxton, W. (2005) 'State of the Nation: An Audit of Social Injustice in the UK', in W. Paxton and N. Pearce (eds), (2005) *Social Justice: Building a Fairer Britain*. London: ippr/Politico's.

Dixon, M., Reed, H., Rogers, B. and Stone, L. (2006) *Crimeshare: The Unequal Impact of Crime*. London: ippr.

Electoral Commission (2005) *Election 2005: Turnout*. London: Electoral Commission. Available at <www.electoralcommission.org.uk/files/dms/Election2005turnoutFINAL_18826-13874__E__N__S__W__.pdf>.

Fabian Commission on Life Chances and Child Poverty (2006) *Narrowing the Gap*. London: Fabian Society.

Green, J. and Holbolt, S. (2006) 'Owning the Issue Agenda: Party Strategies in the 2001 and 2005 British Election Campaigns'. Paper prepared for presentation at the Midwest Political Science Association Annual Meeting.

Hatch, B. (2003) *Whose Town Is It Anyway? A Report of a Citizen's Forum with Under 25s and Over 65s in Bournemouth*. London: ippr.

Heath, A., Jowell, R. and Curtice, J. (2001) *The Rise of New Labour: Party Policies and Voter Choices*. Oxford: Oxford University Press.

ICM (2006a) July *Guardian* poll. Available at <www.icmresearch.co.uk/reviews/2006/Guardian%20-%20July/guardian-july-2006.asp>.

ICM (2006b) World Leaders poll. Available at <www.icmresearch.co.uk/reviews/2006/Guardian%20-%20world%20leaders/guardian-world-leaders-2006.asp>.

ICM (2007) *Political Report. Survey for the Power Enquiry between 17–18 January 2007*. Available at <www.icmresearch.co.uk/reviews/2007/Power%20Enquiry/power-inquiry-jan.asp>.

Ipsos MORI (2006) *Survey of 1966 Adults*, 7–12 December. Available at <www.ipsos-mori.com/polls/2006/mpm061212.shtml>.

58   *Politics for a New Generation*

John, P., Margetts, H., Rowland, D. and Weir, S. (2006) *The BNP: The Roots of its Appeal* (Democratic Audit). York: Joseph Rowntree Charitable Trust.

Keaney, E. and Rogers, B. (2006) *A Citizen's Duty: Voter Inequality and the Case for Compulsory Turnout*. London: ippr.

Lewis, M. (2005) *Asylum: Understanding Public Attitudes*. London: ippr.

Lewis, M. (2006) *Warm Welcome: Understanding Attitudes to Asylum in Scotland*. London: ippr.

Lewis, M. and Margo, J. (forthcoming) *Procedural Fairness*. London: ippr.

Lewis, M. and Newman, N. (forthcoming) *Communicating Asylum*. London: ippr.

Margo, J. and Dixon, M., with Pearce, N. and Reed, H. (2006) *Freedom's Orphans: Raising Youth in a Changing World*. London: ippr.

MORI (2007) *Long-Term Trends*. Available at <www.ipsos-mori.com/polls/trends/issues.shtml>.

Norms, P. (2002) *Democratic Phoenix: Reinventing Political Activism*. Cambridge: Cambridge University Press.

ONS (2006) *Foreign Labour in the UK: Current Patterns and Trends*. Available at <www.statistics.gov.uk/pdfdir/lmt1006.pdf>.

Page, B. and Wallace, E. (2004) *Families, Children and Young People – Key Issues*. London: MORI.

Polling Report (2007) *Current Voting Intention*. Available at <www.ukpollingreport.co.uk/blog/voting-intention/>.

Power Inquiry (2006) *Power to the People. Report of the Power Enquiry*. York: Joseph Rowntree Reform Trust. Available at <www.makeitanissue.org.uk/>.

Retallack, S., Lockwood, M. and Lawrence, T. (2007) *Stimulating Climate Friendly Behaviour*. London: ippr.

Rothon, C. and Heath, A. (2003) 'Trends in Racial Prejudice', in A. Park, J. Curtice, K. Thompson, L. Jarvis and C. Bromley (eds), *British Social Attitudes: The 20th Report*. London: Sage.

Sefton, T. (2005) 'Give and Take: Public Attitudes to Redistribution', in A. Park, J. Curtice, K. Thomson, C. Bromley, M. Phillips and M. Johnson (eds), *British Social Attitudes: The 22nd Report – Two Terms of New Labour: The Public's Reaction*. London: Sage.

Sikka, P. (2006) 'Ethical Gaps in Accountancy Bodies Claims and Practices', *International Accountant*, December. Basildon: Association of International Accountants.

Sutherland, H., Sefton, T. and Piachaud, D. (2006) *Poverty in Britain: The Impact of Government Policy since 1997*. York: Joseph Rowntree Foundation.

Taylor-Gooby, P. (2005a) 'The Work-Centred Welfare State', in A. Park, J. Curtice, K. Thomson, C. Bromley and M. Phillips (eds), *British Social Attitudes: The 21st Report*. London: Sage.

Taylor-Gooby, P. (2005b) *Attitudes to Social Justice*. London: ippr.

Taylor-Gooby, P. (2007) 'In Tune with the People? Analysing Attitudes', in J. Margo (ed.), *Beyond Liberty: Is the Future of Liberalism Progressive?* London: ippr.

Walker, A., Kershaw, C. and Nicholas, S. (2006) *Crime in England and Wales 2005/6*. London: HMSO. Available at <www.homeoffice.gov.uk/rds/pdfs06/hosb1206.pdf>.

Working Party on Active Citizenship (2004) *Lonely Citizens*. London: ippr.

YouGov (2006) Poll for the *Daily Telegraph* 30 October–1 November 2006. Available at <www.yougov.com/archives/pdf/TEL060101021_1.pdf>.

4
State of the Nation: Audit of Britain

Julia Margo, Sonia Sodha and Robert Vance

In this chapter we draw together an audit of the key trends in Britain in recent years. In so doing, we set out to assess how progressive Britain is after a decade of Labour government. As the introduction to this volume argued, progressivism is about much more than reducing distributional inequity – although of course, this remains a core goal that sits at the heart of progressivism. We therefore examine how Britain is faring using a wide range of indicators that span the key tenets of the progressive ethos as set out by Ed Miliband in Chapter 2: equality, community and empowerment. Detailed analysis of these trends, and what they mean for the next decade of progressive thought and practice, is left to the proceeding chapters.

In the pages that follow, we consider some of the key areas affecting equity in the UK – poverty, inequality, social mobility, family, the achievement of young people, the quality of public services and the changing nature of the labour market. Many of these have long been progressive concerns. We then move on to look at community: trends in people's feelings about their community, identity, crime and the local environment and public space. Political power and democratic participation then form the focus. We finish by considering the place of Britain in the world: our role in tackling climate change, international development, and promoting international peace and security.

Equality

There is no question that as a nation we are steadily growing richer. In 2005, the average Briton was more than twice as rich in real terms as in 1971 and 21 per cent richer than in 1997, measured using the mean average of gross domestic product (GDP) per head at 2003 prices (Office for National Statistics (ONS) 2006a).

This is good news. But for progressives, the key question is to what extent everyone is able to share in these gains, and to what extent some groups are left out.

Poverty

The standard definition of poverty used by government and analysts is a relational measure: as average standards of living increase, the poverty line too is raised. This is in recognition that poverty is not an absolute state – but is much more complex and contextual. The extent to which someone can participate fully in society is determined not only by their own resources, but also by how these compare to the resources of the wider community. There is now consensus on this right across the political spectrum – from progressives to conservatives (see, for example, Clark and Franklin 2006).

In the UK, the poverty line is commonly defined at a level of income that is 60 per cent of median income. This standard can be assessed either before or after housing costs. In 2004/05 the contemporary after housing cost (AHC) threshold was £183 a week for a couple with no children (Department for Work and Pensions (DWP) 2005). We have chosen to focus here on AHC measures, as these arguably provide a better indication of living standards. We also provide a measure of poverty for children on a before housing cost (BHC) basis as this is the government's target measure. (For a more detailed discussion see Dixon and Paxton 2005; DWP 2005.)

Overall poverty rates have fallen considerably over the last few years, as shown in Figure 4.1 – by 17 per cent since 1998/89 (DWP 2006). The decline in poverty among some specific groups – such as children and pensioners – has also been marked. The child poverty rate has fallen by 23 per cent when measured before housing costs and 17 per cent after housing costs since 1998/89, which represents 700,000 fewer children living in relative low income households (ibid.). This unquestionably reflects the Labour government's focus on reducing poverty.

However, these successes have several caveats. First, severe and persistent poverty have been resistant to change. Although child poverty rates have fallen, the proportion of children in severe poverty remained static between 1997 and 2002 at 3 per cent (Magadi and Middleton 2005). A child is defined as living in severe child poverty if they have to go without one or more necessities, their parents have to go without two or more

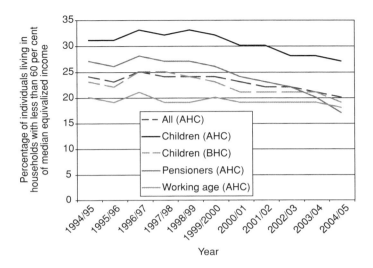

Figure 4.1 Trends in poverty, 1994/95–2004/05

Note: We have chosen to focus on trends AHC, except for children where a BHC measure is also included. Other trends measured before housing costs are available in DWP (2006).

Source: DWP (2006).

necessities and the household has an income of below 40 per cent of median income (Adelman et al. 2003). Looking at the population as a whole, persistent poverty, defined as the percentage of the population who live in poverty for three out of four years in a four-year window, only fell 3 percentage points from 15 per cent to 12 per cent from 1992–95 to 2000–03 (DWP 2005), and while this modest fall in persistent poverty gives cause for optimism, the resilience of severe and persistent poverty indicates the scale of the task.

Second, within these overall trends, poverty continues to have an ethnic, disability-related and geographical dimension. Pakistani and Bangladeshi households were 2.75 times more likely to be in poverty than the average household, Indian households 1.75 times more likely, and black or black British households 1.5 times more likely (DWP 2005). Similarly, for disabled households this figure was 1.4, and for households in the North East, 1.3 (ibid.).

Third, working-age adults have also experienced less marked falls in poverty than either children or pensioners. This has been as a direct result of the Labour government explicitly focusing resources on reducing poverty rates among these groups, particularly children, which is certainly justified; particularly given the fact that rates of working-age poverty after housing costs have consistently been lower than child and pensioner poverty since 1997.

Fourth, child poverty in Britain still remains high by historic standards: in 1968 just 10 per cent of children lived in poverty (Dixon and Paxton 2005). The steep increases in poverty in the 1980s are proving hard to reverse. The government looks likely to miss its target of halving child poverty by 2010, and meeting the 2020 target of ending child poverty will be even more difficult: to reduce child poverty to below 5 per cent would require doubling key tax credits and benefits in real terms between 2010 and 2020 at a cost of £28 billion (Hirsch 2006).

Fifth, levels of in-work poverty are still high – particularly for families with children. This reflects poor incentives for two-earner couples to increase hours for the second earner (Harker 2006: 49).

International comparisons also give cause for concern. It is true that Britain has improved its relative position from the bottom of the EU15, where it sat in the late 1990s, so that it has become close to the European average – and has made the biggest improvement of any EU country. But in 2007, Britain ranked lowest out of the 21 industrialized nations in the Organization for Economic Cooperation and Development (OECD) with a child poverty rate that was more than six times higher than that in Denmark, nearly four times higher than Sweden and more than double that of France (United Nations Children's Fund (UNICEF) 2007). So it is clear that although poverty rates have significantly improved since 1997, there is still a long way to go before we achieve the vision of eliminating child poverty by 2020.

Material inequality

These falling poverty rates have only recently begun to be reflected in falling inequality, suggesting that the richest continued to get richer in relation to the rest of the income distribution for much of this period. During the mid and late 1980s, post-tax and benefit income inequality, as measured by the Gini coefficient,[1] rose steadily (Figure 4.2). Commentators were beginning to think that rising inequality was an inevitable result of the changing world (Dixon and Pearce 2005; Dixon and Margo 2006). But more recent trends belie this assessment. Since

1. The Gini coefficient is a standard and internationally comparable measure of inequality. A value of 0 represents complete equality, in which each person earns the same income, and a value of 100 represents complete inequality, in which one person receives all of a country's income. For more details see Jones (2006).

2000, post-tax and benefit income inequality has tentatively begun to decline, although it remains historically and internationally high (Dixon and Paxton 2005).

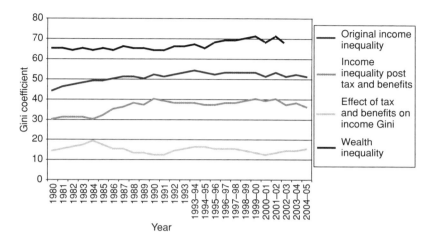

Figure 4.2   Income and wealth inequality, 1980–2004/05

Sources: Jones (2006); HM Revenue & Customs (HMRC) (2006).

However, wealth inequality remains much higher than income inequality (HMRC 2006). In many ways this is unsurprising – it reflects the magnification of income inequality over time, particularly the high inequality of the 1980s, historically high levels of house price growth, and the unequal impact of inheritance. But this makes it no less concerning, as Reed and Sodha argue in Chapter 6. First, the amount of wealth someone has is a more accurate representation of the resources they have access to than of income, and so wealth inequality must be examined alongside income inequality. Second, recent research suggests that wealth may have positive benefits that go above and beyond its function as a store of financial assets: it is thought that assets have positive psychological benefits because they bring security, and thus the capability for longer-term planning and taking more productive risks (Bynner and Paxton 2001).

One of the key drivers of post-tax and benefit income inequality is inequality in labour market pay. For much of the period since the 1980s, real earnings growth has been highest for the richest, as shown in Table 4.1. It is only since the mid 1990s that pay growth has been fastest for those towards the bottom of the income distribution (see also Jones 2006). It should be noted, however, that the richest 1 per cent have seen faster income growth during the period 1997–2005 than any other group (Dixon and Paxton 2005).

Table 4.1   Real pay growth across time

Year	10th percentile	50th percentile	90th percentile
1968–77	39.00	26.84	19.64
1977–87	17.41	29.11	49.80
1987–97	13.38	16.50	18.54
1997–2004	18.42	15.13	14.23

Source: Family Expenditure Survey (FES).

As we would expect, the tax and benefit system plays a significant role in reducing income inequality. But the burden is carried entirely by benefits and tax credits: the British taxation system is regressive overall. The poorest households pay a higher proportion of their income in tax than any other group, largely through indirect taxation such as value added tax (VAT) (see Figure 4.3) – a fact of which most Britons remain unaware.

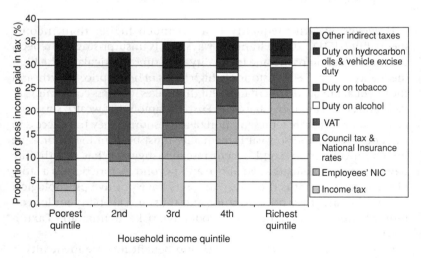

Figure 4.3   Tax paid in 2004/05, as a percentage of gross income, by income quintile

Source: Jones (2006).

As Figure 4.2 shows, the welfare state became much less redistributive from 1984 until the early 1990s, when economic recession and rising unemployment increased dependence on benefits (Dixon and Pearce 2005). But recent reforms appear to have reversed the trend: since 2000/01, the welfare state has begun to work much harder at reducing income inequality through transfers and benefits.

Other factors have also been important in reducing inequality, particularly more favourable conditions in the macro-economic climate (Adam et al. 2006).

Social mobility

As Ed Miliband argues in Chapter 2, another dimension on which a progressive society needs to be judged on equality is social mobility. But social mobility – a measure of the degree that individual life chances are independent of family background – has declined in recent decades, at least up to the millennium. (Unfortunately, no comparable data will be available to assess the extent of social mobility for later cohorts until at least 2025 because of reduced funding availability for cohort studies in the 1980s and early 1990s.) The latest research shows that young people born in 1970 were less likely to be upwardly mobile in their early thirties than those born twelve years before (Blanden 2006), as shown in Figure 4.4. If family background made no difference to life chances, then the income quartile that people fall into in their early thirties would be made up equally of people born into the first, second, third and fourth quartiles. But as Figure 4.4 shows, starting off disadvantaged has a profound influence on later life chances, and this effect increased for those born in 1970 compared to those born in 1958: 38 per cent of those born to parents in the poorest income quartile in 1970 remained in that quartile in their early thirties, compared to just 30 per cent of those born in 1958; and only 15 per cent of those born to parents in the poorest income quartile in 1970 had climbed to the top quartile by their early thirties, compared to 19 per cent of those born in 1958.

This is perhaps the most damning evidence that social mobility in Britain has not improved dramatically over the last 30 or so years. Internationally, Britain does not compare well: the social mobility experienced by the British 1970 cohort was 18 per cent lower than their contemporaries in Canada, Denmark, Norway and Sweden; 17 per cent lower than in Finland; and 14 per cent lower than in West Germany. In fact, this figure was only worse in the US – but even there, there was nothing like as severe a decline in social mobility from previous cohorts (Blanden et al. 2005).

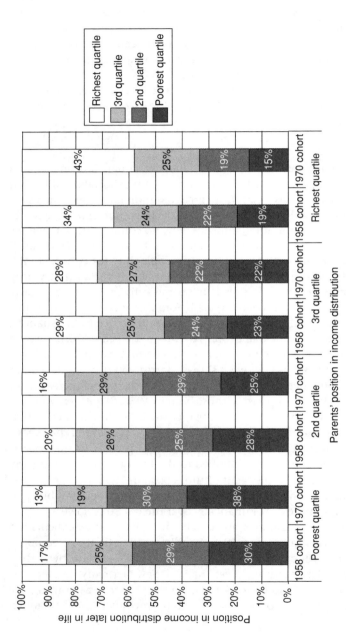

Figure 4.4 Social mobility for young people born in 1958 and 1970

Note: Position in later life determined by earnings in early thirties.

Source: Blanden et al. (2004).

Family

Family life has changed immensely over the past few decades. As marriage rates have fallen from their 1972 peak, divorce rates have risen, fertility rates have fallen and both unmarried cohabitation and solo living have become more common (Babb et al. 2006). For the most part, these are trends that are expected to continue into the future (Dixon and Margo 2006).

Perhaps the most important trend affecting families is that children are much less likely to grow up with both natural parents. In the early 1970s, 92 per cent of children lived in a two-parent family and just 7 per cent lived in a lone-parent family, but by early 2005, this picture had changed. Although two-parent families are still the norm, lone parenting has become much more common, rising to affect 24 per cent of children in early 2005, nine out of ten of whom live with their mother (Babb et al. 2006). This trend is more marked for some minority ethnic groups: around half of children of black Caribbean background born in 2000 were living with one parent in 2006, compared to 13 per cent of children from a white British background and 5 per cent from Indian or Bangladeshi backgrounds. At the same time, as a result of more complex family formation and partnership patterns, stepfamilies are far more common and large families much less so (ibid.).

In combination, these trends have meant that the impact of traditional familial 'socializing' influences in which natural parents and siblings traditionally share responsibility for imparting the norms and conventions of society to the younger generation, have become more differentiated. Research shows that several factors relating to 'parenting' are important in young people's social development. Parental warmth and interest is by far the most important factor in predicting whether young people develop as emotionally secure and well-behaved individuals (Margo et al. 2006), but recent research has shown that family structure is important too: children born in 1970 who lived with a lone parent were, by the age of 30, 5 per cent more likely than their counterparts in two-parent families to be single, separated or divorced; 2 per cent more likely to be in social housing; 4 per cent less likely to achieve level three qualifications (A levels or equivalent); and 4 per cent more likely to have a low income (Feinstein et al. 2005).

For the majority of children growing up with siblings and both natural parents, their familial experience is relatively similar to that of previous generations. But for the increasing numbers of children who have more complex living arrangements, or no siblings, their contact with these socializing influences can be more limited: for example, nearly four in ten children born in 2000 who lived with just their mother had no contact at all with their father in 2003 (Calderwood 2004). This will have implications for their personal and social skills. Moreover, these differences are exacerbated by trends in caring and employment. The implications of these social trends are discussed in Chapters 11 and 15.

Young people

There is a wealth of research that shows that later life chances are related to experiences earlier in life. Unemployment in youth imposes a wage scar as large as 12–15 per cent on individuals at the age of 42 (Gregg and Tominy 2004). Yet participation rates in education or training for those aged 16 have flat-lined over the past decade, following an improvement from 1985 to 1993 (Figure 4.5). The proportion of 16–19-year-olds not in education, employment or training (NEET) has also remained broadly constant at around 12 per cent since 1997: this rate has not fallen in line with national unemployment rates (Department for Education and Skills (DfES) 2006) – and is higher than in Sweden, Germany, the US, Canada and Spain (OECD 2005). For those in work, earnings prospects have declined, following the collapse of youth labour markets in the early 1980s (Bynner et al. 2002). Moreover, the likelihood of unemployment among young people is related to social class: 6 per cent of 19-year-olds growing up in professional/managerial households fall into the NEET category, compared to nearly 20 per cent in unskilled households (Figure 4.6).

Participation in full-time post-compulsory education is similarly related to social class: young people whose parents are 'higher professionals' are nearly 50 per cent more likely to be in post-compulsory full-time education than the children of those in 'routine' occupations (Babb et al. 2004).

Participation in higher education has also trailed off. Between 1970 and 2003/04 the numbers participating in higher education grew from 416,000 and 205,000 to 1,054,000 and 1,392,000 men and women respectively (Babb et al. 2006), with the middle classes taking up the bulk of new places (Galindo-Rueda et al. 2004). But over the past few years the higher education initial participation rate (HEIPR) has flat-lined: it was 41 per cent in 1999/2000 and was just 1 percentage point higher five years later in 2004/05 (DfES 2006). Looking at social class, the differences are even more pronounced than for post-compulsory full-time education. Figure 4.6 clearly demonstrates that the likelihood of participation in higher education is strongly related to social class; Figure 4.7 depicts the vast gap in skills between people from parents

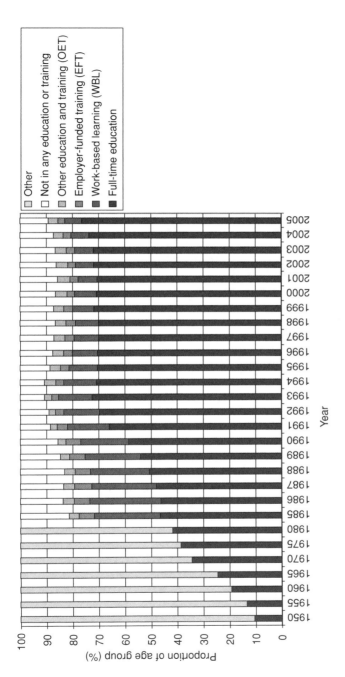

Figure 4.5 Participation in education and training, 16-year-olds, 1950–2005

Note: Trends for 16–18-year-old participation are very similar post-1985; data pre-1995 is unavailable for this group. Time series includes a change in the source of further and higher education data in 1994. Figures pre-1985 are available for full-time education only.

Sources: DfES (2005a, 2006).

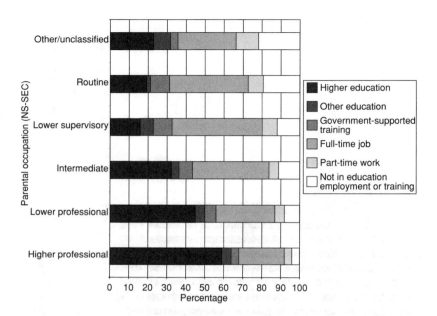

Figure 4.6   Education, training and employment status of 19-year-olds, 2005

Note: 'Other/unclassified' includes a high proportion of respondents who had neither parent in a job. 'NS-SEC' = National Statistics Socio-Economic Classification.

Source: DfES (2005b).

of different occupational classes. Yet as the DfES argues in *The Future of Higher Education* White Paper:

> Graduates and those who have 'sub-degree' qualifications earn, on average, around 50 per cent more than non-graduates. Graduates are half as likely to be unemployed, and as a group they have enjoyed double the number of job promotions over the last five years, compared to non-graduates. (DfES 2003)

The most comprehensive international comparison of pupil achievement that includes the UK is the 2000 OECD PISA study, which compares the achievements of students aged 15 in reading and mathematics. This shows clearly that although young people in the UK perform well on average, with a mean score in reading literacy that sits well above most other countries in the OECD – including Sweden, France, Norway, Germany and the US – there is much greater inequality of outcome than

in most other countries (OECD 2001). This has profound implications
for outcomes later in life.

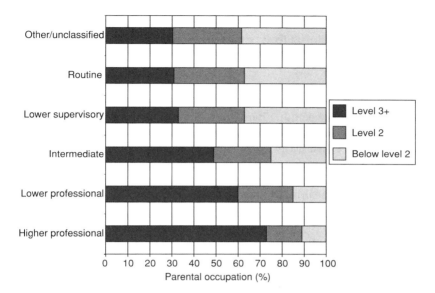

Figure 4.7   Highest qualification level achieved by 19-year-olds, 2005, by
parental occupation

Note: 'Other/unclassified' includes a high proportion of respondents who had neither parent
in a job).

Source: DfES (2006).

On a broader range of indicators, social class remains a strong divider.
British children are generally healthier than ever before: more than nine
out of ten say they are in 'good' or 'very good' health in each year. But
the last decade has seen a rapid rise in childhood weight problems, with
children from more disadvantaged households nearly 25 per cent more
likely to be obese (Department of Health (DoH) 2006a). Meanwhile,
issues such as teenage pregnancy remain intractable. In 2003 the UK
had the highest rate of live births to teenagers in the EU25, with rates
more than four times higher than those in Cyprus, Slovenia, Sweden and
Denmark (Babb et al. 2006). Despite a concerted policy effort focused
on halving teenage pregnancy rates between 1999 and 2010, progress
remains frustratingly slow: there were 41.4 conceptions per 1,000 women

under the age of 18 in 2005 – just 2.9 per 1,000 lower than in 1991 (DoH 2006b). The picture for teenage sexual health is even worse.

It seems clear that a particular group of young people, those from disadvantaged backgrounds, are consistently and increasingly underperforming, explaining at least in part the growing public sense that young people are 'in crisis'. This is considered further by Dawn Butler and Julia Margo in Chapter 15.

Public services

Although public spending hardly rose during the three years after 1997, as the newly elected Labour government kept to the budgeted plans of the previous Conservative government, total spending grew at nearly 5 per cent a year in real terms between 2000/01 and 2005/06 – about twice as fast as the economy. In most areas, outcomes have been improved, particularly in health. To take just two examples, 67,000 people were waiting more than a year for inpatient treatment in 1998, compared to fewer than 1,000 in 2005; and median waiting time for outpatient treatment fell from around 15 weeks to 8.5 weeks over the same period. Public opinion has also improved significantly since 1997: British Social Attitudes (BSA) data reveal that the proportion of Britons who say they are 'very' or 'quite' satisfied with the NHS declined from 56 per cent in 1983 to 34 per cent in 1997, but had then risen to 44 per cent by 2004 (Appleby and Alvarez-Rosete 2005). But questions still remain as to whether increased spending has led to sufficient improvements, particularly given future slowdowns in public sector spending (HM Treasury 2005).

However, there are two key challenges facing public services: rising public expectations and improving equity. Public expectations are becoming ever more demanding (Rankin forthcoming). As people get richer they tend to spend more of their income on healthcare and education and consequently are more demanding of public services (Hills 2004). And as the private sector has focused on offering increasingly tailored, professional and personal services, people have expected more from the NHS and state schools. The upshot is that public expectations are often simply unrealistic: for example, our research shows that in mid 2006, 31 per cent of Britons thought that the NHS should provide *all* drugs and treatments, no matter how much they cost (Rankin forthcoming).

The second challenge is to ensure that public services are as equitable as possible. Although spending on public services is broadly progressive, outcomes are far from equitable, and the provision of services is often skewed by middle-class pressures away from distributional equity. For example, in many types of preventative healthcare services, such as health checks for cardiovascular disease and MMR (combined measles/mumps/rubella) vaccinations, the deprived are less likely to access care, as well as being less likely to have inpatient treatment, and research suggests that children from low-income households may use fewer health services in relation to their needs than other children (Dixon et al. 2003; Sefton 2004). These inequities in access feed through into outcomes.

On many outcome measures, although the general trend is one of improvements, public services have fared poorly with respect to equity, particularly in healthcare. Between 1997–99 and 2005–06, the gap between infant mortality rates between the lowest and highest social classes rose from 13 per cent to 19 per cent (DoH 2006c).

Labour market

The macro-economic stability achieved over the last decade has been good news for the labour market. Unemployment is at a historic low, employment at a historic high, and both inflation and interest rates remain stable (HM Treasury 2006; Lindsay 2003, 2006). Yet it would be wrong to focus solely on these encouraging trends. As we pull closer to the government's ambitious target of reaching an 80 per cent employment rate by 2020, increasing employment further will become more difficult.

The overall rate masks different experiences among disadvantaged groups. Of the 3.6 million disabled people of working age, less than one-third had a job in 2006, compared with three-quarters of non-disabled adults (Bertoud 2006); and in 2003, more than 1 million disabled people said they wanted to work but were unable to find employment (Regan and Stanley 2003).

Although minority ethnic employment rates have risen 1.9 percentage points since 2003, some groups remain much more likely to be unemployed: 15 per cent of black Caribbean and 12.7 per cent of Bangladeshi men were unemployed in 2004, as were 19.9 per cent of Pakistani and 12.6 per cent of black African women (Babb et al. 2006). Older men are also much more likely to be inactive than their younger counterparts, particularly in areas that have experienced rapid deindustrialization (Dixon and Paxton 2005; Lindsay 2006). As Balls, Ussher and Brooks show in Chapter 5, regional diversity is also a problem.

A further, though long-standing, problem is that British labour productivity is poor by international standards. Despite recent efforts, the UK continues to lag behind many OECD countries in terms of productivity. On an output per worker basis, US productivity is 27 per cent higher than the UK, and French productivity 11 per cent higher – although German productivity is similar to that in the UK (Department for Trade and Industry (DTI) 2006). It is important to note that there may well be a tradeoff, particularly in the short-term, between increasing per capita productivity and getting lower-skilled workers back into the labour market.

Gender inequities, although they are slowly closing, continue to persist in the labour market. Female employment rates have steadily risen from the post-war period, from 45.9 per cent in 1955 to 70.1 per cent in early 2006 (Walsh and Wrigley 2001; ONS 2006b). But despite this growing equality in participation, there are still considerable differences between the kinds of work done by men and women.

In the UK, women remain much more likely to work part time and in the service sector than their male counterparts: in 2004, 67 per cent of employees in the non-marketed (public) services and 46 per cent of those in business and other services were women, compared to just 9 per cent in construction and 30 per cent in manufacturing (Wilson et al. 2006). Partly as a result, women are systematically paid less than their male counterparts. As Figure 4.8 shows, although there has been a renewed drop since 2002, the gender pay gap remains stubbornly high. This gap is much wider for women working part time: the average full-time female

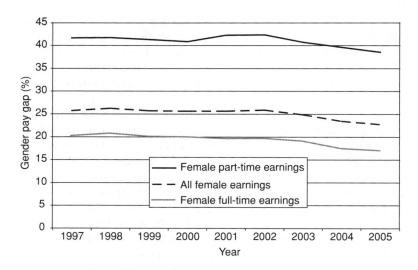

Figure 4.8   Gender pay gap, 1997–2005

Sources: ASHE data, 1998–2006; Grimshaw (2007).

worker earned 83.2 per cent of average male full-time hourly earnings in 2005 – but the average part-time female worker only 61.5 per cent (Grimshaw 2007). The figures we have used are based on the Annual Survey of Hours and Earnings (ASHE), in which average gross hourly pay for men includes overtime.

The shift towards greater female employment has, perhaps surprisingly, exacerbated inequality between households by creating a growing disparity between affluent two-earner households and others (Goodman and Oldfield 2004; Dixon and Margo 2006). It has also had important implications for the structure of the economy by stimulating demand for services over manufactured goods: many of the jobs that women were doing unpaid in the home and community have moved out of the domestic sector into the commercial sector.

The nature of work has been characterized by two significant shifts: towards a service-based economy with a shrinking manufacturing sector (Wilson et al. 2006), and relatedly, increasing polarization of the labour market into low-skilled and high-skilled jobs (Goos and Manning 2004). The implications of these trends for skills policy and labour market progression are discussed in Chapters 5 and 9.

Community

Our analysis of British Crime Survey (BCS) data shows that community spirit and feelings of neighbourhood solidarity appear to be improving since their mid 1990s nadir. As Figure 4.9 shows, Britons are more likely to say that 'people in this neighbourhood tend to help each other' than at any point since 1988.

Other evidence supports this picture. Despite an often-cited decline in trust (Layard 2005), public attitudes data show that popular conceptions of a more isolationist, individualist society are ill-founded (Margo et al. 2006). Britons' trust in the professions, ordinary people and even politicians has remained broadly stable since at least the early 1980s (MORI 2005a), while the proportion of people who think that 'many people in this neighbourhood can be trusted' rose from 40 per cent to 48 per cent between 2001 and 2005. Similarly, the proportion who felt they 'very strongly' belonged to their neighbourhood rose from 28 per cent to 32 per cent between 2003 and 2005 (Kitchen et al. 2006). So it seems that Britons are increasingly feeling positive about their communities.

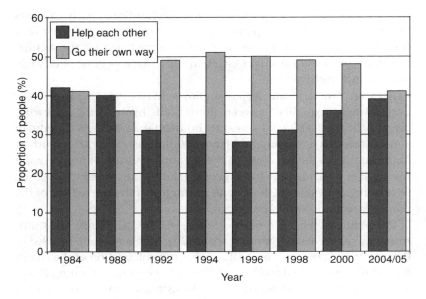

Figure 4.9   Trends in community spirit, 1984–2004/05: 'People in this neighbourhood tend to ...'

Source: ippr analysis of BCS data.

Identity

British identity is changing. Recent evidence suggests that younger generations are much less likely to equate Britishness with ethnicity, instead focusing on the importance of civic factors such as citizenship, respect for laws and institutions and the sharing of customs and traditions, while the proportion who have an exclusively civic conception of national identity has doubled between groups born before and after 1964 (Tilley et al. 2006). However, fewer people now than in the late 1990s say that 'British' is the best way of describing themselves, and this is only partly due to an increase in feelings of 'Englishness' (Muir 2007).

Britain's ethnic composition is also continuing to evolve over time. Between 1991 and 2001, the non-white minority ethnic population of the UK rose from 3 million to 4.6 million (8.1 per cent of the British population). More established groups, such as the black Caribbean population, grew at a much slower rate than more recent immigrant populations, such as the Bangladeshi and black African populations (Babb et al. 2006). Although migration is an important factor in explaining this growth, much has also been due to higher fertility rates among minority ethnic groups: nearly 20 per cent of births in England and Wales in 2004 were to mothers born outside the UK; and in January 2006, 18.7 per cent of primary school pupils and 16 per cent of secondary school pupils were from minority ethnic backgrounds (ONS 2005b). The minority ethnic population is expected to grow significantly over the coming decades, but to remain concentrated in particular areas (Kyambi 2005).

Although Britain remains predominantly Christian, with 49 per cent of people saying in 2001 that they were Church of England and 11 per cent saying they were Catholic, Britain is steadily becoming both more secular and more religiously diverse, in step with growing ethnic diversity (Crockett 2004). For example, the proportion of people saying that they were Muslim doubled from 1 per cent to 2 per cent between 1997 and 2001, and it is likely that rates have risen further since then. But the implications are by no means a simple weakening of British identity: in 2005, 86 per cent of British Muslims said they felt 'very' or 'fairly' strongly that they belonged to Britain (MORI 2005b).

In general, attitudes toward multiculturalism in Britain are encouraging: 62 per cent of Britons polled in 2005 believed that 'multiculturalism makes Britain a better place to live', while only 32 per cent agreed that it 'threatens the British way of life' (John et al. 2006). Additionally, despite recurrent terrorism scares, Britons are more likely than the citizens of other European countries to associate positive attributes with the Muslim communities in their midst (Pew Global Attitudes Project 2006).

However, such statistics belie the complexity of British attitudes toward multiculturalism. More than 30 per cent have recently expressed concern about immigration, compared to just 5 per cent in 1997 (MORI 2006), and 24 per cent of Londoners questioned in an ICM poll said that they might vote for the British National Party – although only 5 per cent said that they closely identified with it (Joseph Rowntree Reform Trust 2004).

The attitudes of British Muslims towards Westerners are the least positive in Europe (Pew Global Attitudes Project 2006). At the same time, many Britons feel their country is becoming more racist. When asked in 2003 whether racism had increased in the last five years, 45 per cent of respondents answered yes, compared to 34 per cent in 1997 (MORI 2006). There is a significant challenge for the future in ensuring that all groups feel effectively integrated into society. This challenge is addressed in Chapter 10.

Crime

Improvements in community solidarity have been accompanied by falling crime rates, although people's perceptions of crime have not followed suit. For around four decades, recorded crime rates had spiralled upwards. Police recorded crime figures in 1995 were nearly ten times those of 1951 (Margo et al. 2006). Although changes to policing and recording practices explain some of this rise, there is wide consensus that crime rates escalated dramatically over this period. But they began to fall in the mid 1990s and have continued to do so, as shown in Figure 4.10.

According to the British Crime Survey – the most accurate measure of actual crime rates – crime in Britain had fallen by 44 per cent in 2004/05 from its peak in the early 1990s, and the risk of being a victim was 23 per cent, lower than at any time since 1981, although the fall has not been uniform, with some measures such as rates of gun crime and violent crime remaining static or even rising (Walker et al. 2006). There are also signs that the government's focus on cutting inequality in victimization is paying dividends: research shows that such inequality increased during the 1980s (Trickett 1995) but has fallen since then. The very poorest were 7 per cent less likely than the richest households to be victims of violent crime last year, compared to 29 per cent more likely in 1997 (Dixon et al. 2006). However, they still remain more likely to be victims of burglary. Inequalities in the impacts of crime mean that tackling it is as much a social justice as a law and order issue, as Nick Pearce argues in Chapter 12.

The reality sits at odds with public perceptions, which now appear more than ten years out of date: in 2006, 63 per cent of people thought national crime had risen (ONS 2006c). Media coverage, although an easy scapegoat, is undoubtedly partly responsible. In 2006, tabloid readers were around twice as likely as broadsheet readers to think the national crime rate had increased 'a lot' in the previous two years. This is partly because reports often fail to discriminate adequately between two measures of crime. As Figure 4.10 shows, there has been a growing discrepancy between police recorded crime figures, which show rising crime levels, and the BCS, which shows falling crime rates. The latter is widely regarded as more accurate by academics and policy-makers alike as police-recorded figures often simply reflect improved police recording practice, but the media often presents the latter as being the more accurate representation. For example, violent crime remained stable between 2004/05 and 2005/06 according to the BCS, but most newspapers

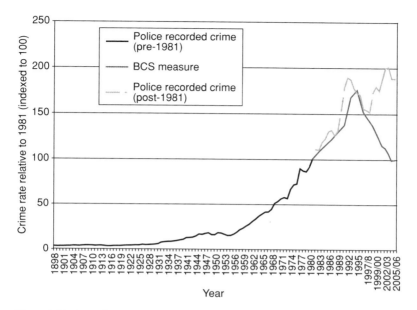

Figure 4.10 Trends in crime, 1905–2005/06

Note: The BCS is a more accurate measure of trends in crime. Changes to recording practices in the late 1990s resulted in an increase in police recorded crime figures that does not reflect victimization rates. Rates are indexed to 100 in 1981 for ease of comparison but are not adjusted for population growth.

Sources: Home Office (2005a, 2005b).

reported the 2 per cent increases in 2006 in *recorded* violent crime as significant. The *Observer*'s coverage was typical:

> John Reid's efforts to turn around the embattled Home Office will be dealt a major blow this week by figures revealing a surge in muggings and other robberies over the last year, suggesting police forces are struggling to control street crime. (*Observer*, 16 July 2006)

Given such reporting, it is hardly surprising that most people are reluctant to believe crime is falling.

Similar levels of concern exist over anti-social behaviour. There was a 44 per cent rise in the proportion of people perceiving 'very' or 'fairly big' problems with vandalism and graffiti in their local area between 1996 and 2002/03 and a 42 per cent rise in the complaints about 'teenagers hanging around', while the overall level of crime fell by 36 per cent. And there are worrying signs that perceptions of rates of anti-social behaviour are increasing once more: in 2006 there were increases in all measures (Margo et al. 2006).

Local environment

The quality of the local environment has an important effect on people's satisfaction with their neighbourhoods: people understandably want to live in areas where the public space is pleasant and welcoming, buildings and street furniture are in good repair, and traffic problems are minimized. As Figure 4.11 shows, these concerns are often underrated by policy-makers and the media: in neighbourhoods with poor-quality environments, concern over litter in the streets is more widespread than fear of burglary.

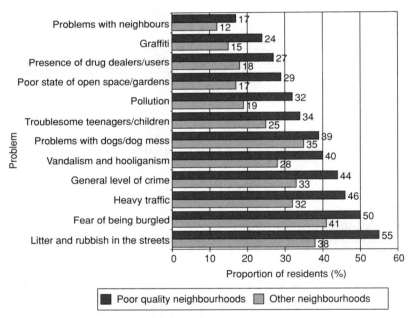

Figure 4.11 Residents' views of problems in the local area, by quality of environment, 2003

Note: 'Poor' neighbourhoods refer to local areas where the English House Condition Survey surveyor visually assessed whether any one or more of the following problems apply: (1) over 10 per cent of dwellings in the local area visually assessed to be seriously defective; (2) the presence of serious problems related to any of the following: vacant sites or derelict buildings; vacant or boarded up buildings; litter, rubbish or dumping; vandalism; graffiti or scruffy buildings, gardens or landscaping; neglected buildings; (3) very poor visual quality of the local area.

Source: Babb et al. (2006).

And despite the current national obsession with anti-social behaviour, concern over the poor state of open space and gardens ranks only very slightly below concern over troublesome teenagers in ordinary Britons' assessment of problems in their local area (Babb et al. 2006).

Although it is unsurprising that those living in poor-quality environments are more likely to cite a range of concerns, looking at the differences between neighbourhood types is revealing. While residents in poor-quality areas are 1.2 times more likely to be worried about burglary, they are 1.7 times more likely to comment on pollution and the poor state of open spaces and gardens – a bigger gap than in any other domain, suggesting that differences in the quality of public spaces are important in distinguishing the best and worst areas. In combination with research suggesting that the quality of public spaces and urban design are crucial to reducing anti-social behaviour and fostering collective efficacy (Dixon et al. 2006), this indicates how important public space should be to urban renewal strategies.

It is not only the quality of people's environment that we should be concerned with, but also the distinctive effect that the space people live in has upon both their experiences and life chances independent of other factors. This is evident both in the statistics depicting gross regional inequality (explored in more depth by Balls, Ussher and Brooks in Chapter 5) and in the empirical evidence of the importance of 'neighbourhood' or area effects on individual outcomes (Midgley 2006; Gibbons et al. 2006; Margo et al. 2006).

Power: democratic participation

Formal participation in local and general elections has long been in decline. Despite the closeness of the 2005 election, turnout was up just 2 per cent on 2001 at 61 per cent (Electoral Commission 2006). But more worryingly, the gap in turnout between social classes had grown: 71 per cent of those in the top social class voted, compared to just 54 per cent of those in the bottom, compared to 68 per cent and 53 per cent four years previously (MORI 2005b). More positively, turnout in the 2006 local elections was 6 percentage points higher than in 2000, at 36 per cent (Rallings and Thrasher 2006).

Declining interest in more traditional forms of participation may reflect that people are increasingly likely to participate in new ways – for example, joining single-issue campaigns rather than using formal mechanisms such as voting or contacting their MP (Dixon and Paxton 2005). The anti-war marches in 2003 were the largest public demonstra-

tions in British history and the 2005 Make Poverty History campaign
resulted in more than 500,000 people contacting the Prime Minister and
8 million wearing the associated white wristband (Make Poverty History
2005). Twice as many people in 2001 as in 1974 had been involved in
a demonstration, and nearly four times as many had signed a petition
(Power Inquiry 2006). Union and political party membership has fallen
but English Heritage and similar charities have experienced considerable
increases in membership and support (ibid.). People are also increasingly
expressing their political preferences by contacting the media rather than
politicians, and boycotting products (Dixon and Paxton 2005). But these
newer forms of political participation are also characterized by social
class. As Reed and Sodha outline in Chapter 6, better-off households are
more likely to perform 'individual political actions' such as boycotting

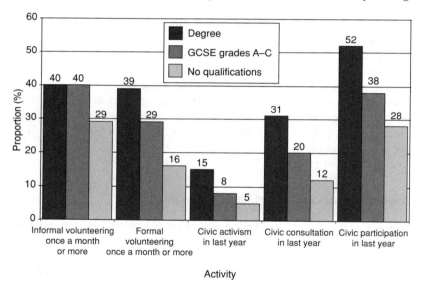

Figure 4.12   Civic participation by educational attainment, 2005

Note: 'Civic activism' consists of undertaking specific responsibilities in the community (being
a councillor, a school governor, a magistrate or a special constable) and involvement in groups
which have a decision-making role in local services. 'Civic consultation' consists of taking part
in consultation about local services or problems in the local area by completing a questionnaire,
attending a public meeting, or being involved in a group set up to discuss local services or
problems in the local area. 'Civic participation' consists of contacting a local councillor, an
official working for the local council, an MP, a government official, an elected member of or
an official working for the Greater London Assembly (for people living in London); attending
a public meeting or rally; taking part in a public demonstration; or signing a petition.

Source: Kitchen et al. (2006).

products or raising money for a pressure group, and 'contact actions' such as writing to their MP.

These trends are reflected in the way people engage in civic society. As voting declines, volunteering appears to be on the rise. In 2005, more than 20 million people undertook some form of formal or informal volunteering at least once a month – 2 million more than in 2001 – and more than three-quarters had given to charity in the four weeks before they were interviewed (Kitchen et al. 2006). However, social class differences are apparent here too, as shown in Figure 4.12. Across almost all forms of civic engagement, education strongly predicts participation. Similar patterns can be seen in terms of area deprivation and ethnicity (ibid.).

Worryingly, the strongest skews appear to be in the two areas that hold most political influence: civic activism and civic consultation. The concern is that if these trends continue, political power will be increasingly related to income and the ability to pay for change, further shifting the balance away from the poor and disadvantaged (Dixon and Pearce 2005). It illustrates why reducing inequality is important not just in lifting barriers to opportunity, but also in preserving the principles of democracy, as Reed and Sodha argue in Chapter 6.

This shift in forms of engagement has many underlying causes. But one important factor may be a growing dissatisfaction with the current political system. In 1973, 49 per cent of people said the present system of governing the UK could be improved 'quite a lot' or 'a great deal', compared to 54 per cent in 1998 and 62 per cent in 2005 (Electoral Commission/Hansard Society 2006).

Britain in the world

Climate and sustainability

Climate change is arguably the most important long-term challenge facing Britain. Yet despite a commitment to reduce CO_2 emissions by 20 per cent from 1990 levels, the UK's emissions rose by 2.2 per cent in 2003 and 0.5 per cent in 2004 (Department for Environment, Food and Rural Affairs (Defra) 2006). If this trend persists, the government's target will be missed by a substantial margin.

The two sectors in which the government has been least effective in controlling emissions are domestic energy use and transport, which account for around 40 per cent of total emissions. Between 1990 and 2004, fossil fuel emissions increased by 12.5 per cent in the domestic sector, and in the transport sector by 10 per cent. These are areas in which personal responsibility and individual behaviour are paramount. The figures are not encouraging: in 2004, Britons travelled 7 per cent further in cars and vans than in 1997 (Babb et al. 2006).

Yet in other areas, there are signs that Britons are behaving more sustainably, although there is still a long way to go. For example, the amount of waste per person that is recycled or composted has increased steadily each year for a decade, and at 17 per cent was three times higher in 2003/04 than in 1995/96 (Defra 2006) (the more sophisticated measuring systems in use from 2006 have made it more difficult to compare data).

These trends have both international and domestic social justice implications. Internationally, climate change will have the most profound effect on the world's poorest people (Department for International Development (DfID) 2006; Foley 2005). Domestically, it is the poorest communities which are often most affected by environmental problems, such as poor air quality or lack of green spaces, and the resulting health implications, such as respiratory diseases and obesity (Duxbury 2004). In 2002, those living in the most deprived wards were exposed to 41 per cent higher concentrations of poisonous nitrous dioxide gas than those in average wards. In a number of studies the quantity of emissions were consistently related to the level of deprivation (Walker et al. 2005).

In England there is a strong relationship between risk of flooding and deprivation, with eight times more people in the most deprived decile living in a tidal floodplain than in the least deprived decile (Foley 2005).

Regional pressures within the UK also add to the problem. Over the past decade, growth in London and the South East has been faster than in other regions, with both internal and international migrants being attracted there (ONS 2006d). Changing living patterns and the increasing trend in solo living have contributed to the average household shrinking from 2.9 people in 1971 to 2.1 in 2005 (Babb et al. 2006). This has created even greater demand for housing in London and the South East region, and elsewhere, putting increased pressure on dwelling stock and land use. Although the government has committed to increasing housing supply in England to 200,000 homes a year by 2016, there are concerns that even this increase will fall short of demand, with serious implications for future affordability, particularly for low-income groups (Bennett et al. 2006). Significant challenges also remain in ensuring that new communities are mixed, inclusive, sustainable and attractive (Commission on Sustainable Development in the South East 2005; Bennett et al. 2006).

International development

Growing cultural diversity has altered Britain's links with the rest of the world: it means that an increasing proportion of Britons have family ties in other countries, particularly developing nations. Heightened public concern and support for global poverty has helped to make international development a key feature of Labour's agenda, illustrated by the doubling of international aid between 1997 and 2005, the commitment to spend 0.7 per cent of GDP on development by 2013, and the cancellation of debt owed by the poorest, most indebted countries in the world (DfID 2006). The 2005 G8 Gleneagles summit led the way on greater commitments to poverty and disease reduction and increased trade opportunity, particularly in Africa (Oxfam International 2005). The evidence suggests that these efforts are working: DfID estimates that British aid helps take 2 million people permanently out of poverty each year (DfID 2006). And the British government has led the world in debt cancellation by cancelling £2.8 billion of Nigerian debt, the largest ever one-off international debt cancellation.

Yet there is still a way to go. The 0.36 per cent of gross national income (GNI) spent on international aid each year is only just over half the amount Blair had committed Britain to by 2013 (DfID 2006). Moreover, diminishing headline world poverty levels mask the unequal spread of international development. Although, according to the World Bank, 390 million fewer people lived in poverty in 1981 than in 2001, the period saw 400 million Chinese escape poverty; while in Eastern Europe and Central Asia, Latin America and the Caribbean, India and Africa, numbers living in poverty were increasing (Chen and Ravallion 2004).

International conflict

Britain's increasing international influence is both a cause and consequence of the growing visibility of the British military in conflicts worldwide. At a financial cost of £4.17 billion (Ministry of Defence (MoD) 2006), a human cost of somewhere in the region of 40,000 lives (BBC News 2007) and a perceived ethical cost (for example, as photos of abuses at Abu Ghraib prison were published worldwide), it is widely believed that the Iraq war has diminished the public's faith in Blair's foreign policy initiatives. By March 2005, 63 per cent of Britons disapproved of the government's handling of the war (MORI 2005). In addition, 72 per cent of Britons believe that government policies in Iraq and Afghanistan have made Britain more of a target for terrorists. Further animosity is directed toward the US, with 63 per cent of Britons believing that Blair has made Britain 'too close' to it (ICM 2006).

Future international actions will need to respond to a rapidly changing world (DfID 2006). In 1950 there were twice as many people living in the developing than in the developed world, and by 2050 this proportion is expected to have risen to six times as many (Population Reference Bureau 2005). The pace of economic growth is picking up: by 2015, India and China between them will make up 26 per cent of the world economy, compared to just 6 per cent in 1985 (Leitch Review 2005). Looking ahead, Britain's place in the world will be decreasingly determined by its economic influence, creating new challenges for both development and foreign policy. And other global trends, particularly the increased risk of terrorist attacks, will require new international and domestic responses.

Security

National security has become an increasingly important issue in recent years. Both at home and abroad, new pressures have combined to create new security risks. Globalization, a potential return to multipolarity; extensive international poverty; climate change and sustainability; revolutions in digital communications and scientific advances; the UK's foreign policy, and integration challenges at home, all heighten security risks. Yet the UK is yet to develop a new national security strategy to respond to the new challenges we face. These issues are considered by Khan and Wild in Chapter 18.

Conclusion

Britain is unquestionably more progressive than it was in 1997. On key indicators of distributional equity, it is, on the whole, doing better: overall poverty rates, and child and pensioner poverty, are falling. Income inequality also seems to have taken a downward turn. Crime levels have fallen and higher levels of investment in our public services have paid off. With respect to global justice, Britain has punched above its weight in international development, particularly with respect to aid to Africa.

But there is no room for complacency. We are still a long way off the progressive ideal outlined in the Introduction and by Ed Miliband in Chapter 2. There are a number of key challenges facing Britain in the years to come – some new, and some old. As we make progress on some of the government's ambitious and laudable targets, such as ending child poverty and achieving 80 per cent employment, meeting those targets becomes harder as doing so means drawing in ever-harder to reach groups. While income inequality is showing tentative signs of a fall, wealth inequality remains high, and, as Reed and Sodha argue in Chapter 6, will continue to do so unless progressives rethink policy in this area. The changing labour market – the growing importance of soft skills, and the polarization of the economy into increasing numbers of low- and high-skill jobs – means that our education and skills and work support policies need reforming in light of these trends. Issues of security will become more important both on the international scene and abroad, and as a result there are key questions for progressives about identity and integration at home, and foreign and security policy abroad.

So the medicine cannot be more of the same. Achieving progressive goals will require renewal and rejuvenation of progressive thought and policy. This is a process the authors of the proceeding chapters are seeking to begin.

References

Adam, S., Brewer, M. and Shephard, S. (2006) *The Poverty Trade-Off: Work Incentives and Income Redistribution in Britain*. Bristol: Policy Press.

Adelman, L., Middleton, S. and Ashworth, K. (2003) *Britain's Poorest Children: Severe and Persistent Poverty and Social Exclusion*. London: Save the Children. Available at <www.savethechildren.org.uk/scuk/jsp/resources/details.jsp?id=1431&group =resources&section=publication&subsection=details&pagelang=en>.

Appleby, J. and Alvarez-Rosete, A. (2005) 'Public Responses to NHS Reform', in A. Park, J. Curtice, K. Thomson, C. Bromley, M. Phillips and M. Johnson (eds), *British Social Attitudes: The 21st Report*. London: Sage.

Babb, P., Butcher, H., Church, J. and Zealey, L. (2006) *Social Trends 36*. London: TSO. Available at <www.statistics.gov.uk/downloads/theme_social/Social_Trends36/ Social_Trends_36.pdf>.

Babb, P., Martin, J. and Haezewindt, P. (2004) *Focus on Social Inequalities*. London: TSO.

BBC News (2007) Iraq violence in figures. Available at <news.bbc.co.uk/1/shared/ spl/hi/guides/456900/456995/html/nn2page1.stm>.

Bennett, J., Hetherington, D., Nathan, M. and Urwin, C. (2006) *Would You Live Here? Making the Growth Areas Communities of Choice*. London: ippr.

Bertoud, R. (2006) *The Employment Rates of Disabled People*. Department for Work and Pensions Research Report No. 298. London: TSO. Available at <www.dwp. gov.uk/asd/asd5/rports2005-2006/rrep298.pdf#search=%22disabled%20empl oyment%20rates%22>.

Blanden, J. (2006) 'Persistent Child Poverty and "Bucking the Trend"'. Unpublished memo. London: CEP.

Blanden, J., Goodman, A., Gregg, P. and Machin, S. (2004) 'Changes in Inter-generational Mobility', in M. Corak (ed.), *Generational Income Mobility*. Cambridge: Cambridge University Press.

Blanden, J., Gregg, P. and Machin, S. (2005) *Intergenerational Mobility in Europe and North America. A Report Sponsored by the Sutton Trust*. London: Centre for Economic Performance, LSE.

Bynner, J., Elias, P., McKnight, A., Pan, H. and Pierre, G. (2002) *Young People's Changing Routes to Independence*. London: Joseph Rowntree Foundation. Available at <www.jrf.org.uk/bookshop/eBooks/184263108X.pdf>.

Bynner, J. and Paxton, W. (2001) *The Asset Effect*. London: ippr.

Calderwood, L. (2004) 'At First the Infant: Children of the New Century', in I. Stewart and R. Vaitilingam (eds), *Seven Ages of Man and Woman*. Swindon: Economic and Social Research Council.

Chen, S. and Ravallion, R. (2004) 'How Have the World's Poorest Fared Since the Early 1980s?', *World Bank Research Observer*, 19 (2).

Clarke, G. and Franklin, P. (2006) 'First Principles: Poverty is Relative and Social Exclusion Matters', in Social Justice Policy Group, *Draft Interim Report: Volume 1 – Economic Dependence and Worklessness*. Available at <http://povertydebate. typepad.com/home/files/volume_1_worklessness.pdf>.

Commission on Sustainable Development in the South East (2005) *Final Report*. London: ippr.

Defra (2006) 'Experimental Statistics on Carbon Dioxide Emissions at Local Authority and Regional Level: 2004', *Defra Statistics Summary*. London: TSO. Available at <www.defra.gov.uk/environment/statistics/globatmos/regionalrpt/ localghgdefrasum20061127.pdf>.

DfES (2003) 'Participation Rates in Higher Education: By Social Class'. *Social Trends 34*. London: TSO. Available at <www.statistics.gov.uk/StatBase/ssdataset. asp?vlnk=7308&More=Y>.

DfES (2005a) Unpublished figures on 16-year-olds' participation in education and training, 1950–2005.

DfES (2005b) *Youth Cohort Study: The Activities and Experiences of 19 Year Olds: England and Wales 2005*. SFR 49/2005. London: TSO.

DfES (2006) *Participation in Education, Training and Employment by 16–18 Year Olds in England: 2004 and 2005*. SFR21/2006. London: TSO.

DfID (2006) *Eliminating World Poverty: Making Governance Work for the Poor*. White Paper. London: TSO.

Dixon, A., Le Grand, J., Henderson, J., Murray, R. and Poteliakhoff, E. (2003) *Is the NHS Equitable? A Review of the Evidence*. LSE Health and Social Care Discussion Paper No. 11. London: LSE.

Dixon, M. (2006) *Rethinking Financial Capability: Lessons from Economic Psychology and Behavioural Finance*. London: ippr.

Dixon, M. and Margo, J. (2006) *Population Politics*. London: ippr. Available at <www. ippr.org.uk/publicationsandreports/publication.asp?id=341>.

Dixon, M. and Paxton, W. (2005) 'The State of the Nation: An Audit of Social Injustice in the UK', in N. Pearce and W. Paxton (eds), *Social Justice: Building a Fairer Britain*. London: ippr/Politico's.

Dixon, M. and Pearce, N. (2005) 'Social Justice in a Changing World: The Emerging Anglo-Social Model', in N. Pearce and W. Paxton (ed.), *Social Justice: Building a Fairer Britain*. London: ippr/Politico's.

Dixon, M., Rogers, B., Reed, H. and Stone, L. (2006) *CrimeShare: The Unequal Impact of Crime*. London: ippr.

DoH (2006a) *Health Survey for England 2004. Updating of Trend Tables to Include Childhood Obesity Data*. London: TSO. Available at </www.ic.nhs.uk/pubs/ hsechildobesityupdate>.

DoH (2006b) *Health Statistics Quarterly 30, Summer 2006*. London: TSO.

DoH (2006c) *Department of Health. Departmental Report 2006*. London: TSO.

DTI (2006) *UK Productivity and Competitiveness Indicators 2006*. DTI Economics Paper No. 17. Available at <www.dti.gov.uk/files/file28173.pdf>. Accessed 26 January 2007.

Duxbury, T. (2004) 'Sustainable Communities: Regeneration and a Just Society', in J. Foley (ed.), *Sustainability and Social Justice*. London: ippr.

DWP (2005) *Households Below Average Income (HBAI) 1994/95–2004/05*. London: TSO. Available at <www.dwp.gov.uk/asd/hbai/hbai2005/contents.asp>.

DWP (2006) *Making a Difference: Tackling Poverty – A Progress Report*. London: TSO. Available at <www.dwp.gov.uk/publications/dwp/2006/poverty/tackling-poverty.pdf>.

Electoral Commission/Hansard Society (2006) *An Audit of Political Engagement 3*. Research Report, March. London: Electoral Commission/Hansard Society. Available at <www.electoralcommission.org.uk/templates/search/document.cfm/14653>.

Feinstein, L., Bynner, J. and Duckworth, K. (2005) *Leisure Contexts in Adolescence and Their Effects on Adult Outcomes*. London: Centre for Research on the Wider Benefits of Learning.

Foley, J. (ed.) *Sustainability and Social Justice*. London: ippr.

Galindo-Rueda, F., Marcenaro-Gutierrez, O. and Vignoles, A. (2004) *The Widening Socio-economic Gap in UK Higher Education*. London: CEE.

Gibbons, S., Green, A., Gregg, P. and Machin, S. (2006) 'Is Britain Pulling Apart? Area Disparities in Employment, Education and Crime', in N. Pearce and W. Paxton (eds), *Social Justice: Building a Fairer Britain*. London: ippr/Politico's.

Goodman, A. and Oldfield, Z. (2004) *Permanent Differences? Income and Expenditure Inequality in 1990s and 2000s*. London: Institute for Fiscal Studies.

Goos, M. and Manning, A. (2004) *Lovely and Lousy Jobs: The Rising Polarisation of Work in Britain*. CEP Discussion Paper 0604. London: Centre for Economic Performance.

Gregg, P. and Tominey, E. (2004) *The Wage Scar from Youth Unemployment*. Bristol: Centre for Market and Public Organisation, Department of Economics, University of Bristol.

Grimshaw, D. (2007) 'Gender Pay Gap in the UK: The Key Issues'. Presentation to HM Treasury Workshop, January.

Harker, L. (2006) *Delivering on Child Poverty: What Would it Take?* Report for the DWP. London: TSO.

Hills, J. (2004) *Inequality and the State*. Oxford: Oxford University Press.

Hirsch, D. (2006) *What Will it Take to End Child Poverty: Firing on All Cylinders*. London: Joseph Rowntree Foundation. Available at <www.jrf.org.uk/bookshop/eBooks/9781859355008.pdf>.

HMRC (2006) *Distribution Among the Adult Population of Marketable Wealth* (Series C, Table 13.5). London: TSO.

HM Treasury (2005) *Long-term Public Finance Report: An Analysis of Fiscal Sustainability*. London: TSO.

HM Treasury (2006) *Pre-Budget Report*. London: TSO. Available at <www.hm-treasury.gov.uk/pre_budget_report/prebud_pbr06/prebud_pbr06_index.cfm>.

Home Office (2005a) *Summary of Recorded Crime Data from 1898 to 2004/05*. London: TSO.

Home Office (2005b) *British Crime Survey*, various years. London: NATCEN.

ICM (2006) *Guardian* August 2006 poll. London: ICM. Available at <www.icmresearch.co.uk/reviews/2006/Guardian%20-%20August/guardian-august-2006.asp>.

Ipsos MORI (2005a) *Trust in the Professions*. London: Ipsos MORI.

Ipsos MORI (2005b) *MORI Final Aggregate Analysis*. London: Ipsos MORI.

Ipsos MORI (2006) *Concerns about Race Relations and Immigration, 1997–2006*. Available at <www.ipsos-mori.com/ethnic/index.shtml>.

John, P., Margetts, H., Rowland, D. and Weir, S. (2006) *The BNP: The Roots of its Appeal* (Democratic Audit). York: Joseph Rowntree Charitable Trust.

Jones, C. (2006) *Briefing on* Power to the People*: The Final Report of the Power Inquiry into the State of British Democracy*. London: Power Inquiry.

Joseph Rowntree Reform Trust (2004) *State of the Nation Poll 2004: Summary of Main Findings*. Available at <www.jrrt.org.uk/FINDINGS.pdf>.

Kitchen, S., Michaelson, J., Wood, N. and John, P. (2006) *2005 Citizenship Survey. Active Communities Topic Report*. London: DCLG.

Kyambi, S. (2005) *Beyond Black and White: Mapping New Immigrant Communities*. London: ippr.

Layard, R. (2005) *Happiness: Lessons from a New Science*. London: Penguin.

Leitch Review (2005) *Skills in the UK: The Long-Term Challenge*. Interim Report of the Leitch Review. London: TSO.

Lindsay, C. (2003) 'A Century of Labour Market Change: 1900 to 2000', *Labour Market Trends*, March: 133–44.

Lindsay, C. (2006) *Labour Market Analysis and Summary: May 2006 Assessment* London: TSO.

Magadi, M. and Middleton, S. (2005) *Britain's Poorest Children Revisited: Evidence from the BHPS (1994–2002)*. Loughborough: Centre for Research in Social Policy. Available at <www.savethechildren.org.uk/scuk_cache/scuk/cache/cmsattach/3796_BPC2_Research_Report.pdf>.

Make Poverty History (2005) *White Band*. London: Make Poverty History.

Margo, J. and Dixon, M., with Pearce, N. and Reed, H. (2006) *Freedom's Orphans: Raising Youth in a Changing World*. London: ippr.

Midgley, J. (2006) *A New Rural Agenda*. Newcastle: ippr North.

MoD (2006) *Operating in Iraq: Key Facts and Figures*. Defence Factsheet. Available at: <www.mod.uk/DefenceInternet/FactSheets/OperationsFactsheets/OperationsInIraqKeyFactsFigures.htm>.

MORI (2005) 'Iraq war', 21 March. Available at <www.mori.com/polls/2005/help-the-aged2.shtml>.

Muir, R. (2007) *The New Identity Politics 2007*. London: ippr.

Observer (2006) 'Fresh blow to Reid as violent crime rises', 16 July.

OECD (2001) *Knowledge and Skills for Life: First Results from PISA 2000*. Paris: OECD.

OECD (2005) *Labour Productivity Growth – Data: Gross Domestic Product, Average Hours Worked per Person, Total Employment, Total Hours Worked, Total Hours, GDP per Hour*. Paris: OECD.

ONS (2005a) *First Release: 2005 Annual Survey of Hours and Earnings*. London: TSO.

ONS (2005b) *Birth Statistics 2004*. Series FM1 No. 33. London: ONS.

ONS (2006a) *Gross Domestic Product (Average) per Head, CVM Market Prices (IHXW): SA Not Seasonally Adjusted Constant 2003 Prices. Updated on 21/7/2006*. London: ONS. Available at <www.statistics.gov.uk/statbase/TSDdownload2.asp>.

ONS (2006b) 'Labour Market Analysis and Summary', *Labour Market Trends*, 114 (7): 213–40.

ONS (2006c) *Crime in England and Wales 2005/6: A Summary of the Main Statistics*. London: ONS.

ONS (2006d) *NUTS1 Regional Gross Value Added (1989–2004) (data tables)*. London: ONS.

Oxfam International (2005) *Gleneagles: What Really Happened at the G8 Summit*. Oxford: Oxfam. Available at <http://publications.oxfam.org.uk/oxfam/display.asp?K=_2005080816034356&sort=sort_date%2Fd&sf_01=CAT_CLASS&ds=Trade&st_01=280%2C090%C050%2C230&m=36&dc=270>.

Pew Global Attitudes Project (2006) *The Great Divide: How Westerners and Muslims View Each Other*. Washington DC: Pew Research Center. Available at <http://pewglobal.org/reports/pdf/253.pdf>.

Population Reference Bureau (2005) *Population Bulletin: Global Demographic Divide*. Washington DC: Population Reference Bureau.

Power Inquiry (2006) *Power to the People. Report of the Power Inquiry*. York: Joseph Rowntree Reform Trust. Available at <www.makeitanissue.org.uk/>.

Rallings, C. and Thrasher, M. (2006) *Local Elections 2006: Report to the Electoral Commission*. Plymouth: LGC Elections Centre, University of Plymouth.

Rankin, J. (forthcoming) *Great Expectations: A Sustainable Health System Beyond 2008*. London: ippr.

Regan, S. and Stanley, K. (2003) *The Missing Million*. London: ippr.

Sefton, T. (2004) *A Fair Share of Welfare: Public Spending on Children in England*. London: CASE/LSE. Available at <http://sticerd.lse.ac.uk/dps/case/CR/CASEreport25.pdf>.

Tilley, J., Exley, S. and Heath, A. (2006) 'Dimensions of British Identity', in A. Park, J. Curtice, K. Thomson, C. Bromley and M. Phillips (eds), *British Social Attitudes: The 21st Report*. London: Sage.

Trickett, A., Osborn, D. and Ellingworth, D. (1995) 'Property Crime Victimisation: The Roles of Individual and Area Influences', *International Review of Victimology*, 3: 27395.

UNICEF (2007) *An Overview of Child Well-Being in Rich Countries*. Florence: UNICEF. Available at <http://news.bbc.co.uk/nol/shared/bsp/hi/pdfs/13_02_07_nn_unicef.pdf>.

Walker, A., Kershaw, C. and Nicholas, S. (2006) *Crime in England and Wales 2005/06*. HOBS 12/06. London: TSO.

Walker, G., Mitchell, G., Fairburn, J. and Smith, G. (2005) *Industrial Pollution and Social Deprivation: Evidence and Complexity in Evaluating and Responding to Environmental Inequality'*, Local Environment, 10 (4), August. Available at <http://taylorandfrancis.metapress.com/(1r145smn0o22afz2yis4bwyv)/app/home/contribution.asp?referrer=parent&backto=issue,3,8;journal,9,36;linkingpublicationresults,1:104534,1>.

Walsh, M. and Wrigley, C. (2001) 'Womanpower: The Transformation of the Labour Force in the UK and the USA Since 1945', *Recent Findings of Research in Economic and Social History*, 30: 1–4.

Wilson, R., Homenidou, K. and Dickerson, A. (2006) *Working Futures 2004–2014 National Report*. Warwick: Institute for Employment Research, University of Warwick. Available at <www.ssda.org.uk/ssda/pdf/Working%20Future%2020042014%20National%20R%20060215.pdf>.

Part 3
Equality

5
Beyond Stability:
Labour's Economic Story

Ed Balls, Kitty Ussher and Richard Brooks, with Robert Vance

Introduction

Over the past decade, Britain has changed. Most progressives believe it has changed for the better. We should be proud of some of the achievements of the Labour government – on stability and rising employment, the minimum wage, the investment and improvements in health and education and the fight against poverty (see Chapter 4). It is this track record of progress on stability, jobs, poverty and public services that has enabled the government to confound the defeatism of the free market right and, step-by-step, to win the globalization argument. We are showing every day that a centre-left government – in a competitive and open world – can deliver economic stability and advance the cause of both prosperity and social justice.

But our task is getting more difficult. We have many more arguments to win, challenges and fears to overcome and opportunities we cannot afford to miss. In the next decade Britain and the world will see even faster economic change and integration – bringing with it both opportunities and challenges to our individual and collective security; and new challenges, most importantly climate change, which threaten our ability to deliver rising prosperity and tackle poverty at home and abroad.

The right are – as ever – pessimistic. They claim it cannot be done – that governments are powerless and need to 'get out of the way', that cooperation in Europe and internationally is not in our best interests and that rising inequality is inevitable. As progressives, our task in the decade to come is to prove, once again, that centre-left governments can deliver economic growth as well as fairness – and to show, at the same time, we can respond to an ever-changing security situation, resist protectionism and protect our environment for our children and their children too.

If we get it wrong, we face decades ahead of division, protectionism, stagnation and conflict. If we get it right, we can win public trust that progressive politics has the answers not just here in Britain but round the world – and no country is better placed than Britain to prosper and lead in the twenty-first century.

This is our challenge for the next decade. In this chapter we will argue that the progressive response to these economic challenges is the only one that will allow us to achieve sustainable growth and employment, social justice and fairness. This response involves maintaining an economy that is internationally competitive and highly productive; making markets work for people and ensuring equitable access to work; endowing people with the skills necessary to progress with a particular emphasis on those in less-well-paid jobs; and giving local and regional economic leaders more of the tools they need to grow their local economies.

Britain's political economy in a global context

The challenge of globalization

We start with our changing world. On the one hand, we are faced with the rapid integration of markets across an ever-shrinking globe, with cross-border competition from large and rapidly industrializing countries threatening our domestic economic stability and security. On the other hand, advances in technology are quickly changing the way we work, the jobs we do and the structure of our economy. These economic challenges in turn sit alongside other pressures from demographic and social change, international uncertainty and conflict, and the imperative of environmental sustainability. The result is that we are now in a new era of global economic change and industrial restructuring – as dramatic as the industrial revolution of the 18th century.

Politicians have all debated and discussed at length the challenge of globalization and technological change, and seen in our own country and in our travels abroad how these globalizing trends manifest:

- the way in which, in a world of global brands and companies, a decision by a company's headquarters in one part of the world can impact directly on local communities in another
- the widening wage gap in the developed world between skilled and unskilled workers

- the pace at which events in one country impact round the world, be it a stock market crash in the US, an outbreak of bird flu, or the publication of a tendentious cartoon
- the insecurity, alienation or nationalism that change has sometimes brought in its wake.

Globalization is not just an economic process or theory, it is a human challenge – a reality for businesses and working people who often have to make daily decisions about how to stay competitive, keep their jobs or update their skills. And while the public sees the benefits in terms of new investments from abroad and cheaper goods in the shops, people also fear the effect it can have on their own lives and their security.

Yet despite these pressures, things are radically different today to how they were 10 or 20 years ago. Today unemployment is low and employment across the UK is at record levels. In the 1980s and 1990s when coal mines closed, National Union of Mineworkers (NUM) members moved from well-paid employment to redundancy and unemployment. In 2002, when the Pontefract Prince of Wales pit finally closed for geological reasons, all of the 400 miners had a new job to go to.

As the example of MG-Rover showed, when large employers announce plans to shed jobs, our economic development agencies and the local Employment Service's Rapid Response Taskforce step in to help skilled workers to find new jobs and unskilled workers to retrain. We do not, in any way, underestimate the shock and suffering for any man or woman who, after 20 years of service, is told they are losing their job and must retrain – or the stress and insecurity that the risk of losing a job can cause. But while we know that we cannot stand in the way of these global forces of change and restructuring, we are not passive in the face of change because a modern industrial and employment policy can intervene to help companies and trade union members cope with change, win new investment and sustain good and skilled jobs.

So this is our starting point. With more jobs in our economy than ever before, record levels of foreign direct investment and lower prices for many consumer goods, Britain is benefiting from these global economic forces. Britain's financial services industry has become the global market leader. In areas like clean coal and other environmental technologies, British industry is already in the lead and can win new investment and jobs from around the world. At the same time, our policy of allowing skilled and needed migrants to come to our country has once again, as in centuries past, brought new ideas, tackled skill shortages and boosted our economy.

Embracing change, being innovative and open to new ideas, encouraging ownership and talents from around the world, investing in skills and new technologies – these are the keys to success in the modern economy.

The risks of globalization

Yet at the same time, global economic integration is dislocating. There are losers as well as winners, and while the gains are widely dispersed, the short-term costs are concentrated, making them more visible and more keenly felt. And with manufacturing jobs in decline across the developed world, there are worrying signs of reaction, protectionism and economic nationalism rising up in many countries and continents.

In the US, protectionist sentiment has been on the rise – in ports, steel, and threats of retaliatory trade sanctions against China. In Latin America, the talk is of a new economic nationalism; while closer to home, in parts of Europe, protectionist sentiment has manifested itself, often under the banner of 'economic patriotism'. Just look at recent and widely publicized cases of government interference in cross-border mergers. At the same time, the world trade talks have now stalled, with many siren voices hailing their demise and seeking instead to start negotiating bilateral arrangements which would risk locking out the poorest countries from the benefits of trade and fuelling a new mercantilism. And these protectionist pressures are growing just as we face new challenges which demand international cooperation, not isolationism.

As Sir Nick Stern's landmark report made clear, climate change is a real threat to our prosperity, the poorest countries are most at risk, and the only feasible solutions require multilateral action and global leadership (Stern 2006). The Stern Report makes a compelling and overwhelming case. And it could prove to be the turning point we need in the climate change debate. But whether his warnings will be heeded around the world remains to be seen. And how we respond is critical. For while some on the right deny that climate change is a real threat, others – on left and right – argue that protecting the environment means economic growth cannot continue or that open trade should be curtailed. That is a recipe for economic stagnation at home, while keeping poor countries poor – and must be resisted by modern progressive politics. This is discussed in greater detail by David Miliband in Chapter 16.

But what is true on the environment is also true in other critical areas. It is only by global cooperation – America, Europe and Asia, developed and developing countries, Christian and Arab nations, working together – that we can deliver global security, tackle nuclear proliferation, root out Islamic extremism and promote a fair and lasting peace in the Middle East.

So the threat to global prosperity and security from these protectionist and nationalist trends must not be underestimated. Nor should we be fooled into thinking that Britain is immune. We have a fine and long-standing open tradition and commitment to tolerance. Yet, at the same time, in many parts of Britain in recent local elections, the British National Party (BNP) had their best ever results.

The BNP's campaigns start from concerns which many hold in our communities – about insecurity, and identity and too often very local issues of poor housing or inadequate transport. And they then build on top of that a pernicious narrative in which external threats and racial difference are at fault – a message which ends in a prescription based on nationalism, xenophobia and racism.

Confounding the global pessimists

Our argument in this chapter is that we must act now to counter these anti-globalization pressures before they take root. But that means first confronting the pessimists – from both left and right – who say it cannot be done.

For some on the left, a commitment to social justice and environmentalism quickly turns to oppositionism. At its most extreme you have a demonstrator outside a recent G8 Summit with a placard reading 'World wide movement against globalization'. They claim that national governments are impotent in the face of global capital markets, that free trade inevitably means lower standards, rising inequality and environmental damage. And then they claim that the only solution is protectionism and a retreat from global markets. We are clear that this is not the right model within which to pursue progressive policies for our future.

And while there are some in the labour movement who lean towards protectionism in trade, or would seek to rule out outsourcing as a matter of principle, in the main, the British labour and trade union movement – with the British people – has stood apart from its brother and sister trade unions in other parts of the world, including America, in its opposition to protectionism.

At the same time, the right is clear and consistent in its response: that globalization places great, indeed decisive, limits on the ability of government – any government – to pursue an active economic policy, deliver social justice at home or abroad, or cooperate internationally. And this is a view which you consistently see from right-wing parties and governments round the world – a right-wing response to global change designed to nip progressive politics in the bud.

There are four myths which characterize this right-wing pessimism:

- Myth 1 is that national governments are impotent because national governments are just too small, Keynesian intervention has proved ineffective and full employment is just not consistent with stability. And so the only thing government can do is try to deliver low inflation and cut the size of the state. Whatever the share of gross domestic product (GDP) on public spending, globalization means it must go down.
- Myth 2 is that only free markets work, that the only way to sustain jobs is to deregulate and let markets rip, cut taxes and hope that by keeping costs down we can compete.
- Myth 3 says that internationalism is over, that the world is just too complex and national self-interest now rules, making cooperation in Europe or globally on security policy or climate change futile. Indeed, even national governments can't credibly deliver – which is why the response to the desire for local involvement is to replace the state with charity and local voluntary organizations.
- Myth 4 says that rising inequality is inevitable, because government cannot support the burden of an active welfare state without stifling the economy and destroying jobs.

We reject each of these myths. After a decade of Labour government, we are not pessimistic about globalization or the ability of national governments, if they choose to pursue, win and sustain public support for progressive policies in government. As a 2002 Trades Union Congress (TUC) report on globalization concluded: 'The task is neither to halt globalisation in its tracks nor to simply accept that an unregulated capitalism is inevitable' (TUC 2002).

On the economy, we on the centre-left know that when the pace of change is so rapid in the modern world, people need a government on their side to open up new opportunities and deliver security and strong communities. The fact is that globalization can be managed well or badly, fairly or unfairly. And government, working with business and trade unions, can make genuine political choices about the kind of society in which we want to live.

The inheritance: stability and growth

Over the past eight years the global economy has suffered the sharpest world downturn since the early 1970s – with recessions in America, Japan,

France and Germany. Britain has bucked the trend and has demonstrated outstandingly good overall economic performance over the past ten years. The last decade has been one of almost unprecedented macro-economic stability and personal prosperity. The economy is in much better shape than it has been since before the early 1970s, when inflation rose dramatically, and the mid 1980s and early 1990s which saw boom and bust macro-economic cycles, as shown in Figure 5.1 (Lindsay 2003; Bank of England 2006; ONS 2006a). As the Chancellor noted in his 2006 Budget speech, the current government is the first 'in British history to be entering the tenth consecutive year of uninterrupted economic growth' (Brown 2006).

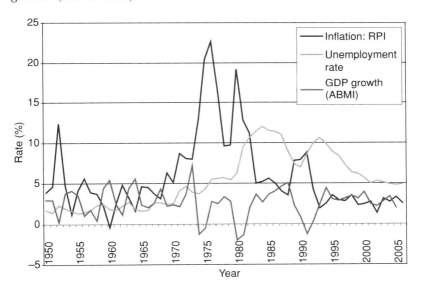

Figure 5.1   Long-run macro-economic indicators, 1950–2006

Sources: Lindsay (2003), ONS (2006a), Bank of England (2006).

Here in Britain we have shown we can put in place a new economic policy to establish and entrench stability, backed with a new employment policy to generate new employment opportunities and equip young people and the long-term unemployed with the skills they need to be flexible and adapt to new technologies. We have shown that you can have a national minimum wage and rising employment, and far from being driven to lower standards, we have proved that in today's global economy we can have a full employment economy and legislate for enhanced rights at work (Burkitt 2001).

When some argue that the rise of China and Asia and the globalization of manufacturing means that we must sacrifice our goals of full employment and good, decent paying jobs; that globalization means accepting rising wage inequality (Glennerster 1999; Rhodes 2000; Scharpf 2000) or fewer rights at work or a privatized NHS, our response must once again be to confound the sceptics.

We know that in an open and more rapidly changing global trading economy, flexibility – the ability to respond quickly – is not an option. It is a necessary precondition of success and of delivering greater prosperity, fairness and security. We know, too, that it is the responsibility of government to equip companies and people to master change – through investment in skills and training, through the best transitional help for people moving between jobs, and by combining the national minimum wage with tax credits within a progressive tax system. And in this era of global change and insecurity it is right that we have a system of managed migration. We need to control our borders so we know who is coming in and coming out, but at the same time we need to make the case for the benefits of economic migration within a managed system. In this way, workers from across the world who have a contribution to make to our economy can come here and do so – adding value to our economy without reducing the employment opportunities of British workers.

And on the environment, too, over the last 30 years, with the right kinds of intervention and standards, we have shown we can have economic growth and at the same time make our air less polluted and our rivers and beaches cleaner and safer. Our challenge now is to go much further in showing, through global cooperation, that we can have growth and open trade while reducing carbon emissions. As the Stern Report concludes: 'the world does not need to choose between averting climate change and promoting growth and development' (Stern 2006). If we put in place the right global incentives to cut carbon and emissions, we can be both pro-growth and pro-green. As Stern makes clear, the only feasible solutions to a problem of such magnitude as this are through multilateral action and international cooperation. Action in one country alone will not do the trick. This is why we were right to put the environment on the G8 and EU Presidency agendas in 2006. This is why we need the EU emissions trading scheme to become the hub of a global carbon market. If Britain continues to take a lead in Europe and in international negotiations, as we have done on both Kyoto and European emissions trading, we can meet our environmental obligations at the same time as having a growing economy. But we must not be complacent either about the challenge of maintaining the currently benign economic environment, or about the specific challenges that lie beneath this impressive overall picture.

With high oil prices, and ever more rapid global capital movements, the world economy is far from a benign environment. And in Britain today, there are still real challenges:

- too many young people are still leaving school at 16 without a course or an apprenticeship to go on to
- thousands of men and women are still locked out of employment because of incapacity or a lack of affordable childcare
- millions of working people are without the skills they need to get higher-paying jobs
- there is still not enough affordable housing.

And while our levels of employment are high, productivity – which must also be high for our overall prosperity to be top of the international league – still lags behind the United States. There are five areas which the Treasury and Department of Trade and Industry (DTI) are focusing on as drivers of productivity within the UK:

- strengthening **competition** to encourage firms to innovate, reduce costs and provide better-quality goods and services to the consumer
- promoting **enterprise** to maximize the contribution of businesses to employment, productivity, prosperity and social cohesion
- supporting **science and innovation** to harness the potential of new ideas, technologies and working practices
- improving the **skills** base to maximize the contribution of human capital to growth
- encouraging **investment** to improve the UK's stock of physical capital in every sector and industry.

There is a growing body of evidence on progress in these areas which the Treasury drew on recently in their report on productivity:

- The 2005 Global Competition Review rated the UK's competition authorities as second only to those in the US.
- The Organization for Economic Cooperation and Development (OECD) has rated the UK as having the lowest barriers to entrepreneurship of any major economy.

- With only 1 per cent of the world population, the UK is responsible for 5 per cent of world science, publishes over 12 per cent of all cited papers and almost 12 per cent of papers with the highest impact.
- The percentage of those who are economically active with skills lower than level two (that is, GCSEs) declined to 27 per cent in 2005, from 37 per cent in 1996.
- Whole economy investment in 2005 was 37 per cent higher than in 1997 (HM Treasury 2006a).

It is in these areas, alongside the goal of continuing to raise productivity in the public sector, that we must focus our attention if we are to achieve our full potential as a nation and deliver rising prosperity alongside high employment.

The challenges

The pressures of demographic and social change

Before we turn to raising the productivity of those in work, there is still more to be done to get more people into the labour market in the first place. Changes to the way we live have created some groups who are particularly in need of support to get into work and stay in work.

The average size of households in the UK fell from 2.64 in 1982 to 2.46 in 1992, and is projected to fall further to 2.19 by 2016 (Office of the Deputy Prime Minister (ODPM) 2004). This is partly due to an increase in single-person households and single-parent households. Such households are less able to pool the risks of unemployment and the resources required to keep a family out of poverty. These people are more likely to require care services as they age.

As in all developed countries, the UK's population is ageing. In 2000, 15.6 per cent of the population was over 65 compared with 13.2 per cent in 1971. By 2050, this will have risen to 24.4 per cent and the proportion over the age of 80 will have more than doubled, from 4 per cent in 2000 to 9.1 per cent in 2050 (ibid.). This has profound implications for the labour market, particularly in terms of gender and the need to facilitate longer working lives, with a more gradual shift into less intensive activity as people get older, rather than the 'cliff edge' of retirement. At the same time we will need to create a framework for balancing work and caring responsibilities at both ends of the lifecycle, facilitating the provision of informal care for both children and older people (Hughes and Cooke examine this in more detail in Chapter 11).

Despite a prolonged recent period of economic growth, levels of worklessness are still unacceptably high among a number of disadvantaged groups. We cannot be satisfied with current rates of employment for disabled people, ethnic minorities (especially women) and men over the age of 50. Their situation is especially difficult in areas that have experienced rapid deindustrialization since the early 1980s (Regan and Stanley 2003; Dixon and Paxton 2005; Babb et al. 2006; Bertoud 2006; Lindsay 2006, Johnson et al. 2007). The proportion of people who consider themselves disabled has increased substantially over recent decades. Moreover, a significant rise in the number of people reporting mental health problems is particularly worrying, as they have the lowest employment rate out of all impairment groups (ONS 2004; Stanley and Regan 2003). Well over 1 million disabled people who are not employed nonetheless say that they want to work (Department for Work and Pensions (DWP) 2005). In Burnley, which was a pathfinder pilot area for the new reforms to incapacity benefit, people who had found voluntary and part-time paid work under this highly targeted scheme said that they had been given their lives back (ibid.). Ensuring that everyone who is able has access to work, decent pay and the opportunity for progression is fundamental not only to social justice but to the functioning of our economy.

Towards a highly skilled economy

The best way to get a good job is to start by getting a job. But that is not enough. We need to understand the structural changes taking place in our economy and what our policy response should be.

In 1982, a third of UK employment was in manufacturing, construction and utilities, and two-thirds was in the service sector. Two decades later, in 2002, manufacturing employment had shrunk by 35 per cent and service employment had grown by 20 per cent (Wilson et al. 2006). As national income increases we tend to spend a higher share of our income on services rather than manufactured goods (Hills 2004), and the manufactured goods we do buy tend to make greater use of technology. This shift towards a service economy, plus rapid productivity increases in manufacturing industry, will continue to change the structure of UK employment. As Table 5.1 shows, the distinction between manufacturing and services is likely to diminish in importance, being replaced by high- and low-skill jobs. The sectors of the economy that rely on highly trained people, with correspondingly higher salaries, are set to expand. Conversely, the proportion of people employed in low-skilled operations, whether in offices or on shopfloors, is set to decline or remain stagnant (Leitch Review 2005).

Table 5.1   Changes in the occupational structure of employment, 1984–2020

	% of total employment				Average gross hourly earnings (2003), UK = 100
	1984	1994	2004	2020 est.	
1. Managers and senior officials	12	14	15	17	160
2. Professional	8	10	12	14	149
3. Associate professional & technical	10	12	14	15	114
'Higher occupations' combined	30	36	41	46	
4. Admin/clerical/secretarial	15	15	13	11	75
5. Skilled trades	16	14	11	10	81
'Intermediate occupations' combined	31	29	24	21	
6. Personal services	4	6	8	9	60
7. Sales/customer services	6	7	8	9	62
8. Plant & machine operatives	12	10	8	7	69
9. Elementary occupations	16	14	11	8	60
'Lower occupations' combined	38	37	35	33	

Notes: Percentages have been rounded.

Sources: Leitch Review (2005, Table 3.1), with additional data from ippr.

What this analysis shows is that there is nothing inherent about manufacturing that means it is doomed to decline. But it is the case that prospects are not good for low productivity operations, employing people on low salaries, regardless of the sector they are in. An individual company in the manufacturing sector that decides to employ more highly-trained people and invest in smarter technology may, unless it is simultaneously expanding, end up employing fewer people. But it could just as well gain new markets and employ more. And there is no reason why our economy cannot support many more of such companies, leading to a corresponding increase in the number of people employed in so-called 'advanced' manufacturing.

The point that is relevant to this analysis is that there appears to be a steady increase in the share of employment in the 'higher' managerial, professional and technical occupations, most of which demand qualifications at degree level and above. At the other end of the skills spectrum, there has been a decline in the overall share of lower-skilled occupations. The sharp decline in manual jobs has been partly offset by rising employment in the personal services and sales occupations, particularly retailing and care. However, it is the share of 'intermediate' occupations, with qualifications typically at levels two or three (that is, GCSE/A level or equivalent), which has shown the fastest decline.

These shifts have profound consequences for people with lower skill levels, and they also demand a change in the kind of skills required for successful employment and progression (Margo et al. 2006). The economy has become more service sector-dominated, and interpersonal, communication and 'people' skills are now more important than in the past, as low-skilled service jobs require more communication skills than their manufacturing equivalents. As we move towards a service-based economy, individuals will increasingly require both 'hard' cognitive skills and 'soft' interpersonal communication skills if they are to get a job and progress in the labour market (see Chapters 9 and 15 for a fuller discussion).

A recent survey of nearly 75,000 companies revealed that when thinking about the skills requirements of their staff, employers are most concerned about gaps in 'soft' skill areas; in particular, 'team working and customer handling skills' (Learning and Skills Council (LSC) 2006: 12): in 2006, nearly 40 per cent of British employers reported shortages in customer handling skills and around 35 per cent reported shortages in oral communication and team working skills. Importantly, employers' perceptions of 'soft' skill shortages were more pronounced for elementary occupations than for higher-level occupations. At the same time, as Butler and Margo illustrate in Chapter 15, there is a strong socio-economic influence on the acquisition of such skills, with those from lower socio-economic groups being less likely than their more affluent peers to develop good interpersonal and communication skills. The suggestion therefore is that many disadvantaged workers may be effectively trapped by their lack of soft skills and that these may lie behind limited prospects for progression (Margo et al. 2006) (again, this is discussed more fully in Chapter 9).

As mentioned above, the shift to a service economy may partly explain these changes (Blanden et al. 2006; Margo et al. 2006). But the impact of technological change should not be overlooked. Recent research shows that the rise of information and communications technology (ICT) in firms has increased the return to general (softer) skills and reduced the relative importance of job-specific technical skills (Kirby and Riley 2006), partly because ICT has 'polarized' the labour market – widening the gap between 'lovely' and 'lousy' jobs as computers and technology replace labour in the middle of the labour market (Autor et al. 2003; Goos and Manning 2004; Dixon and Pearce 2005).

This illustrates the increasing importance of 'lifelong learning' both to individuals and to Britain's economic prospects. Lifelong learning and progression within the labour market are now the key issues facing our economy which will make the difference between whether we are able to compete internationally or not. We do not want to compete on wages, but we can compete on brainpower, skills and the raw potential of our people. This is an area over which there is a perhaps surprising degree of consensus, with both employers and trade unions saying that skills are the key challenge facing the British economy, and welcoming the Leitch Review which was published in December 2006 (TUC 2006; Confederation of British Industry (CBI) 2005, 2007).

Unfortunately, many of these problems in terms of skills and progression in labour markets are not just a question of individual education, attainment and training. The concentration of economic opportunities in some areas of the country and the paucity of access to work for people in areas of low labour-demand also result in serious regional inequalities.

Regional inequalities and transport

There are three reasons why progressives should care about regional inequalities. First, it is an injustice that the accident of birth should strongly determine your life chances. Second, utilizing the full capacity of an educated, skilled and hard-working population would lead to significant economic growth, the benefits of which would be shared across the UK. Third, the unbalanced growth that Britain experienced during the nineteenth and twentieth centuries is unsustainable, as congestion and pollution in economically successful areas seriously jeopardize the quality of life of millions of people.

Progressives believe in equality of opportunity, and this principle is clearly breached by gross regional inequality. While social justice does not require the complete equalization of incomes across the whole country, it does demand that individuals have equitable access to employment and that people are not grossly disadvantaged by where they are born.

This government therefore rightly has an objective that nobody should be disadvantaged by where they live. Nonetheless, geographical inequalities have been very stubborn. In spite of a range of area-based interventions, outcomes across key factors such as employment, crime, health, education and housing continue to be substantially worse for people living in relatively deprived areas and regions (Berube 2005).

As Figures 5.2 and 5.3 show, life expectancy has improved dramatically in the past ten years – advancing from an average of 73.84 to 76.61 years. However, not only does life expectancy vary dramatically across different geographies, but it has also preserved many of its distributional characteristics over the past ten years. Male life expectancy increased in Wakefield from 73.0 to 75.8 years between 1994 and 2004, and in Burnley from 72.1 to 74.5 years. These are tremendously significant gains, but they still leave people born there below the national average and far behind the most advantaged communities.

While overall economic growth has been strong, regional inequalities have been stubborn. Figure 5.8 compares output (gross value added (GVA)) per capita for each region, with all the data rebased each year so that the UK average is 100. First, it is clear that the differences between regions and within regions are substantial, and that they have not narrowed significantly since 1989. On the other hand, there has been some relative improvement in the position of the worst-performing regions since 2002.

Employment rates have also improved markedly over the past ten years, from a Great Britain average of 72.1 per cent in 1996 to 74.3 per cent in 2006 (74.1 per cent for the UK in 2006) (ONS 1996, 2006a), but again there are significant and persistent geographical variations. In particular there are acute geographical 'blackspots' with very low employment rates (see Figures 5.4 and 5.5). Some of these are inner-city areas with well-documented problems, such as Tower Hamlets (54.1 per cent), Inner Manchester (61.5 per cent), and Central Glasgow (64.7 per cent). However, some are relatively distant from areas of strong economic activity, such as Fenland in Cambridgeshire (68.2 per cent), Merthyr Tydfil (61.4 per cent) and West Somerset (59.3 per cent) (ONS 2006a).

Skill levels in the working population have risen significantly. In 1995, just 14 per cent of the working-age population in Normanton had a degree-level qualification. In 2006 the figure was 25 per cent. For Burnley the figures are similarly stark: 11.8 per cent in 1995 up to 20.4 per cent in 2006. However, Figures 5.6 and 5.7 show once again persistent geographical inequalities in the distribution of high-level skills.

There are substantial costs arising from the concentration of deprivation, including negative impacts on employment, crime, education and other outcomes for residents through neighbourhood effects (Gibbons et al. 2005). There is also a worrying circularity to these problems: they deny opportunities to people who are already deprived.

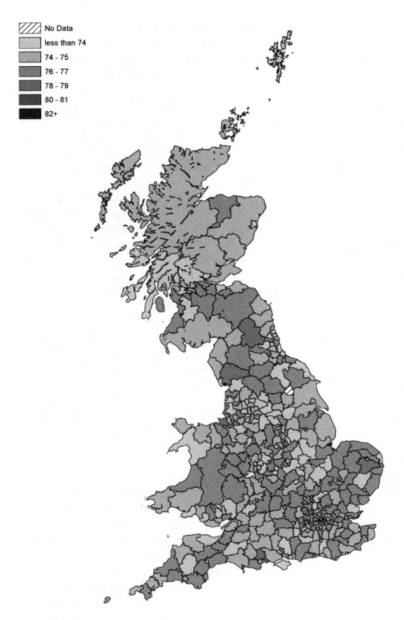

Figure 5.2   Male life expectancy at birth, 1996 (years)

Source: ONS (2006b).

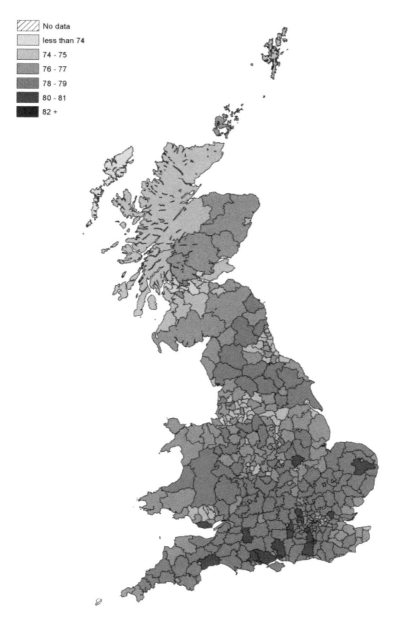

Figure 5.3 Male life expectancy at birth, 2006 (years)

Source: ONS (2006b).

Figure 5.4   Employment rate, 1996 (%)

Source: ONS (1996).

Figure 5.5   Employment rate, 2006 (%)

Source: ONS (2006c).

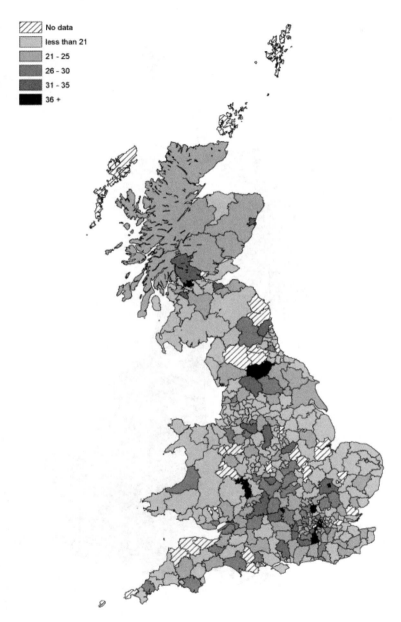

Figure 5.6   Proportion of working population with NVQ4+, 1996 (%)

Source: ONS (1996).

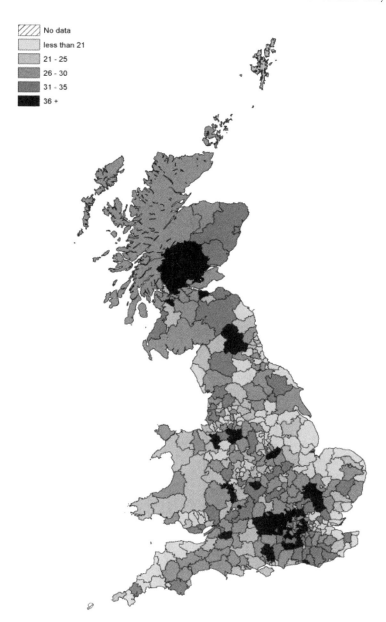

Figure 5.7   Proportion of working population with NVQ4+, 2006 (%)

Source: ONS (2006c).

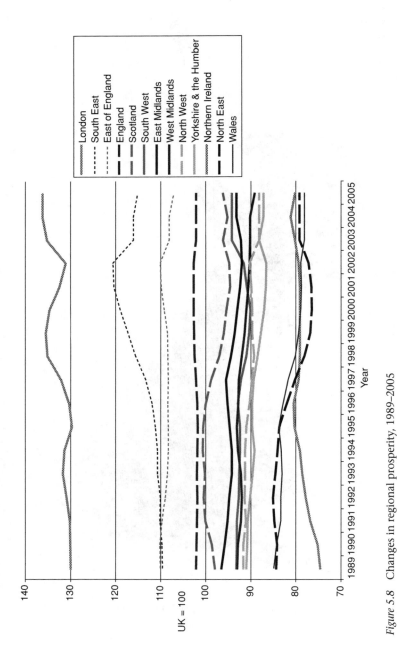

Figure 5.8 Changes in regional prosperity, 1989–2005

Note: Compares output (gross value added (GVA)) per capita for each region, with data rebased each year so that the UK average is 100.

Source: ONS (2006d).

Meanwhile, substantial costs also arise from congestion in areas of intense economic activity, and these are also disproportionately borne by disadvantaged people. This is usually thought of as a problem for London and the South East of England, but it also happens elsewhere. Roads into and around major regional economic centres such as Manchester, Leeds and Sheffield (like the M56, the M62, the M66 and stretches of the M1 and the M6) are almost as congested as the M25 and arterial routes out of London. Income inequalities across the population also tend to widen property and other price differentials, and this is likely to make residential segregation more extreme (Cheshire et al. 2003).

Poor health, low skill levels and a weak economy form a self-reinforcing vicious circle. In addition, there are powerful forces that reinforce local economic success. Highly skilled employees are likely to be high earners, supporting the economy where they live. At the same time, firms often benefit from being located close to each other, so areas that are already doing well are the ones most likely to attract new economic activity. Firms seek skilled employees and a good local business environment, just as skilled employees seek appropriate job opportunities and a good local living environment.

While there is an effectively national graduate labour market, low-paid jobs do not function in the same way (Green and Owen 2006). Regional mobility is only marginally higher among the unemployed than the employed, but it is much higher (two or three times) among the better educated than the least qualified. This means that the distribution of skills is intimately related to the extent to which different areas of the country have progressed towards a high productivity, high employment, knowledge-based economy. Highly skilled people congregate to high-value employment, but lower-skilled people do not migrate to employment opportunities to the same degree.

It is clear that those without qualifications are at a disadvantage in the labour market, and while the possession of qualifications helps to protect people from unemployment, they are not by themselves a sufficient shield. Compare Brixton in London and Burnley in Lancashire. In both places there are many families who are not well off. The difference between the two places is that if you are ambitious and work hard to gain good qualifications in Brixton, then there are many good jobs nearby in the London economy. In Burnley, however, you can have the best qualifications in the world but it won't alter the fact that local wage levels are low (and falling); that there is no direct train to booming Manchester, despite it being a mere 30 miles away; and it is practically impossible to commute reliably by bus in the rush hour to any city at all. In Burnley you are forced to choose between your career and your community; in Brixton, you are not.

Meeting the challenges

A strong foundation

The foundation for meeting all of these challenges must be a strong and stable macro-economy. We cannot make progress in an environment of economic instability and uncertainty for businesses, families and the public sector. Although we have established a robust framework for maintaining stability, we must not allow ourselves to become complacent about the gains we have won over the last ten years – including the politically valuable reputation for good economic stewardship that has been the Achilles' heel of previous Labour governments.

The UK's monetary policy framework combines the appropriate flexibility to meet the needs of our particular economic circumstances, with the clarity and transparency necessary to achieve a high level of credibility and therefore effectiveness. Meanwhile, the fiscal policy framework supports monetary policy in the short term (by not causing unexpected monetary pressures), ensures sound public finances in the medium term (by borrowing only to invest over the economic cycle), and achieves a fair distribution of tax burdens across generations in the long term (by keeping overall borrowing below a prudent level) (HM Treasury 2006b).

The important thing for progressives to recognize is that these apparently technical rules have profound social and political consequences. They constrain government action in the short term while liberating it to make decisions for the long term. Over the past ten years we have been able to address some of the worst failures of unemployment and high national debt repayment, and have thus been able to reinvest considerably in public services and other priorities. As we enter a period where these early gains are no longer available and the public finances are more constrained, it would be a cardinal error to sacrifice the stability that we have achieved through rash tax cuts or through unaffordable spending promises.

Investment in education and skills

The most successful economies of the twenty-first century will be those that most effectively invest in the skills and capacities of their people. The UK has nothing to fear from economic globalization and technological change if it is able to combine a world-class business environment with a workforce that has world-class abilities. The progressive approach to achieving high skill levels is distinctively different from an outdated emphasis on selection and excellence for the few. It is based on a vision of universal opportunity that wastes no one's talent, and is motivated by concerns for individual and community empowerment as well as prosperity. It is also informed by our fast-developing understanding of the way in which a partnership between individuals, public services and employers can help everyone develop to their maximum potential.

The early foundation of educational success must be high-quality, affordable and flexible childcare available to all, and with more help focused on those who need it most. Over the last ten years childcare has been developed as the new frontier of the modern welfare state, largely because we now understand what a huge difference a secure start in life can make for children who would otherwise suffer persistent disadvantage that is much more difficult – and more expensive – to address later in their lives.

Children's Centres and the childcare element of the working tax credit represent a huge investment in our collective future, as do our improvements to the rights of parents to enjoy working arrangements that allow them to balance employment with family life. Over the coming decade we should go further, extending the financial support available for parents, improving the flexibility of employment for carers of both genders who look after adults as well as looking after children, and increasing the availability and quality of childcare near home and work (HM Treasury et al. 2004).

In education we have seen significant improvements in standards and a sharp fall in the number of failing schools. However, there is still further to go so that every child leaves primary school with the best possible grasp of the basics, and then goes on in their secondary education to acquire the skills necessary to thrive in the modern economy. Our vision here must be for every child to reach their full potential, with personalized teaching and learning in every classroom, especially to support those who fall behind (Gilbert 2007). This requires a long-term commitment to increase funding for maintained schools so that they can match the resources available in the private sector.

Two major challenges for the UK as a whole are to increase the number of young people staying on in education or training until at least the age of 18, and to raise the level of skills in the adult population. Our progressive approach to these issues must be to ensure that young people have the best possible opportunities to continue their learning in a way that is engaging and relevant to them, and that adults have access to high-quality, flexible and appropriate education and training provision that enables them to progress in the labour market. The 14–19 Diplomas will be the cornerstone of this strategy, with the first four (in ICT, engineering, health and social care, and creative and media) being available from 2008, and another twelve being introduced by 2015. Over the coming decade we will need to continue working to break down the outdated divide between vocational and academic education for young people.

Adult skills in the UK are rising as better-educated young people leave improved schools, colleges and universities to join the workforce. But our ambitions here must be very high. Practically everyone should be skilled to the level required to achieve five good GCSEs, and the majority rather than the minority should be achieving graduate-level skills. The system to achieve this should be twin-track and flexible: it should be easy for learners to get the qualifications and information they need for their wages to rise, but at the same time it should be easy for employers to get the bespoke local training they need to raise their company's performance.

We believe there is a growing recognition that in skills policy the old voluntary and ad hoc approaches have not worked – as the recent Leitch Review confirmed. The Leitch Review challenges us to move to a post-voluntary approach to skills training with a new relationship between the government, employers and individuals in which everyone plays their part and accepts their responsibilities – government to provide the resources and opportunities, employers to ensure all their employees have opportunities to train, trade unions and individuals to take up the opportunities on offer.

Just as unemployment benefit set the direction for post-war employment policy, with a new framework of rights and responsibilities our central reform in 1997, so rights and responsibilities in skills policy will define the employment policy of the twenty-first century.

The New Deal has done a lot to get people into work. Now that long-term unemployment has been virtually eliminated, we need a discussion, in the context of framing our next manifesto, on a New Deal for those in work. Specifically, we should target those on low wages to give them proper, individualized, advice on the options available to them to open up greater opportunities for advancement in the labour market, as Engel and Sodha argue in Chapter 9. Working through trade unions where appropriate, and directly through government agencies elsewhere, nobody should be denied access to higher-paid work by not knowing what options would be available if greater training was undertaken, in their current sector or elsewhere.

We have conceded the principle: we are now adopting the New Deal approach to offer highly targeted advice to those on incapacity benefit. The next step is to explore the potential for offering individual, personalized career-enhancing support to all those on low wages. It is a nonsense that careers advice should end at sixth form college. People need to know in later life what the effect of a change of tack or investment in training would give them in terms of increased quality of life for them and their families. Since higher-paid jobs are only available to higher-productivity people, the economy would also benefit hugely from such an approach.

The creation of new ideas, technologies and processes tend to have 'spillover' effects that create wider benefits for the overall economy, as well as the benefits that accrue to the person or firm who create the innovation. These spillovers can increase productivity of all firms as new processes and ideas are emulated and new technologies, such as mobile communications, can have similarly significant effects creating new products and markets (HM Treasury 2006a). Globalization puts an even higher premium on innovation and the economy will increasingly need to be built on successfully generating and exploiting innovations and new technologies (Hay 2004; Dixon and Pearce 2005). Encouraging innovation and investment in science and technology is therefore crucial, and government has a clear role in ensuring both the transfer of ideas from scientists to entrepreneurs and the spread of process innovation and best practice is between companies. Business Link and the Small Business Service are good examples of how government can have a large impact in this area.

Meeting the regional challenge

We must also aspire to achieving economic justice across the whole of the UK, so that no one is disadvantaged by where they are born and everyone enjoys decent prospects of rewarding employment and prosperity for themselves and their family, regardless of where they live. As well as a foundation of overall economic stability and the right national economic policies and institutions, and a world-class system of childcare, education and training, this also requires a distinctive approach to economic development at the regional and sub-regional level.

This is an issue where globalization and technological change do present a real challenge, because both of these forces tend to increase the agglomeration of economic activity through increasing specialization and increasing returns to high-level skills. As progressives we need to recognize this challenge and meet it, aiming not just for growth in every region but to narrow the gap in economic performance between regions and to ensure that no neighbourhood is left behind (HMT 2004).

This has implications at the national level, the regional level and also at the very local level where pockets of deprivation can coexist beside economic success. The role of Regional Development Agencies (RDAs) in a modern economic policy is not to replace market activity, but to help the market work better by addressing failures such as where there are coordination problems or externalities preventing investment. RDAs have played a valuable role in supporting major regeneration projects across the UK, including pump-priming public investments on a scale which local authorities could not have undertaken on their own – for example, the Markets project in Barnsley town centre, in which Yorkshire Forward invested £34 million. In addition, we should not think of 'regional policy' being restricted only to regions with relatively poor economic performance. Because local market failures can coexist next to areas of economic success, regional development agencies will have a role to play even in affluent regions.

Local leadership is one of the conditions of effective economic regeneration. One of the great successes of the past ten years has been the transformation of great cities such as Manchester, Leeds and Birmingham. The challenge now is to capitalize on their success, recognizing the importance of cities to their surrounding regions and supporting their continued development, but to balance this with an approach which ensures that nowhere is left out. The unique strength of RDAs is that they have this whole-region focus. However, we do not need to choose between cities and regions as the focus of our efforts, and the right approach will vary from place to place (Balls et al. 2006).

Conclusion

It is a competitive world out there, and it requires a policy response. British progressives know that we are better placed to succeed if the unique talents of all our people are better utilized. We have made huge progress in many areas, evidenced by our strong inward investment flows and good record on job creation. But we must do more to help people to get the training and support they need to find the good jobs they want. And once they have that training, they have to be able to physically get to where those jobs are located. In a twenty-first century progressive Britain, nobody should have to choose between their career and their community.

In the face of global pressures, we need both economic prosperity and security with strong and fair communities. There are still too many people in our country who feel that the quality of the public services they use are not good enough. And too easily they blame migrants for jumping the queue for social housing or claiming benefits they somehow do not deserve. However unfounded these accusations, we know that despite all the progress made over the last decade, great social challenges remain.

Our task is to show that progressive politics can meet the challenges of globalization, invest in skills, tackle climate change and build a fairer society. Progressives can succeed not just because of the competence of our ideas but because of our values – our commitment to social justice, and to the ethos set out by Ed Miliband in Chapter 2.

References

Autor, D., Levy, F. and Murnane, R. (2003) 'The Skill Content of Recent Technological Change: An Empirical Exploration', *Quarterly Journal of Economics*, 118: 1279–333.

Babb, P., Butcher, H., Church, J. and Zealey, L. (2006) *Social Trends 36*. London: TSO. Available at <www.statistics.gov.uk/downloads/theme_social/Social_Trends36/Social_Trends_36.pdf>.

Balls, E., Healey, J. and Leslie, C. (2006) *Evolution and Devolution in England: How Regions Strengthen our Towns and Cities*. London: NLGN.

Bank of England (2006) *Statistical Interactive Database – Official Bank Rate History*. London: Bank of England.

Berube, A. (2005) *Mixed Communities in England: A U.S. Perspective on Evidence and Policy Prospects*. York: Joseph Rowntree Foundation.

Bertoud, R. (2006) *The Employment Rates of Disabled People*. Department for Work and Pensions Research Report No. 298. London: TSO. Available at <www.dwp.gov.uk/asd/asd5/rports2005-2006/rrep298.pdf#search=%22disabled%20employment%20rates%22>.

Blanden, J., Gregg, P. and Macmillan, L. (2006) *Explaining Intergenerational Income Persistence: Non-cognitive Skills, Ability and Education*. Working Paper No. 06/146. Bristol: Centre for Market and Public Organisation <www.bris.ac.uk/Depts/CMPO/workingpapers/wp146.pdf>.

Brown, G. (2006) Chancellor of the Exchequer's Budget Statement, 22 March. London: TSO. Available at <www.hm-treasury.gov.uk/budget/budget_06/bud_bud06_speech.cfm>.

Burkitt, N. (ed.) (2001) *A Life's Work: Achieving Full and Fulfilling Employment*. London: ippr.

CBI (2005) *CBI Response to Leitch Review on Skills*. Available at <www.cbi.org.uk/ndbs/positiondoc.nsf/1f08ec61711f29768025672a0055f7a8/531C3A10BA2B1F348025711B00509B1E/$file/leitchresponse0605.pdf>.

CBI (2007) *Promoting Economic Prosperity: Considering the Implications of Eddington, Barker and Leitch*. Available at <www.cbi.org.uk/

ndbs/positiondoc.nsf/1f08ec61711f29768025672a0055f7a8/
9C546E47EAE22CFB8025726F005AC17E/$file/lyonsresp190107.pdf>.

Cheshire, P., Monastiriotis, V. and Sheppard, S. (2003) 'Income Inequality and Residential Segregation: Labour Market Sorting and the Demand for Positional Goods', in R. Martin and P. Morrison (eds), *Geographies of Labour Market Inequality*. London: Routledge.

Dixon, M. and Paxton, W. (2005) 'The State of the Nation: An Audit of Social Injustice', in N. Pearce and W. Paxton (eds), *Social Justice: Building a Fairer Britain*. London: ippr/Politico's.

Dixon, M. and Pearce, N. (2005) 'Social Justice in a Changing World: The Emerging Anglo-Social Model', in N. Pearce and W. Paxton (eds), *Social Justice: Building a Fairer Britain*. London: ippr/Politico's.

DWP (2005) *Department for Work and Pensions Five Year Strategy – Opportunity and Security Throughout Life*. London: TSO.

Gibbons, S., Green, A., Gregg, P. and Machin, S. (2005) 'Is Britain Pulling Apart? Area Disparities in Employment, Education and Crime', in N. Pearce and W. Paxton (eds), *Social Justice: Building a Fairer Britain*. London: ippr/Politico's.

Gilbert, C. (2007) *2020 Vision: Report of the Teaching and Learning in 2020 Review Group*. London: HMSO.

Glennerster, H. (1999) 'Which Welfare States are Most Likely to Survive?', *International Journal of Social Welfare*, 9. Oxford: Blackwell.

Goos, M. and Manning, A. (2004) *Lovely and Lousy Jobs: The Rising Polarisation of Work in Britain*. London: Centre for Economic Performance.

Green, A. and Owen, D. (2006) *The Geography of Poor Skills and Access to Work*. York: Joseph Rowntree Foundation.

Hay, C. (2004) 'Common Trajectories, Variable Paces, Divergent Outcomes? Models of European Capitalism Under Conditions of Complex Economic Interdependence', *Review of International Political Economy*, 11 (2).

Hills, J. (2004) *Inequality and the State*. Oxford: Oxford University Press.

HM Treasury (2004) *Spending Review 2004: Stability, Security and Opportunity for All: Investing in Britain's Long-Term Future*. London: HMSO. Available at <www.hm-treasury.gov.uk/spending_review/spend_sr04_spendsr04_index.cfm>.

HM Treasury (2006a) *Productivity in the UK 6: Progress and New Evidence*. London: HMSO.

HM Treasury (2006b) *Pre-Budget Report: Investing in Britain's Potential: Our Long-Term Future*. London: HMSO.

HM Treasury, DfES, DWP and DTI (2004) *Choice for Parents, the Best Start for Children: A Ten Year Strategy for Childcare*. London: TSO.

Johnson, M., Schmuecker, K. and Reed, H. (2007) *The Sand Timer: Skills and Employment in the North West*. Newcastle-upon-Tyne: ippr North.

Leitch Review (2005) *Skills in the UK: The Long-Term Challenge*. Interim Report of the Leitch Review. London: HMSO.

Lindsay, C. (2003) 'A Century of Labour Market Change: 1900 to 2000', *Labour Market Trends*: 133–44.

Lindsay, C. (2006) *Labour Market Analysis and Summary: May 2006 Assessment*. London: HMSO.

Kirby, S. and Riley, R. (2006) *The Returns to General versus Job-Specific Skills: The Role of Information and Communication Technology*. NIESR Discussion Paper 274. London: NIESR.

LSC (2006) *National Employers Skills Survey 2005: Key Findings.* London: LSC. Available at <http://readingroom.lsc.gov.uk/Lsc/2006/research/commissioned/nat-nationalemployersskillssurvey2005keyfindings-re-june2006.pdf>.

Margo, J. and Dixon, M. with Pearce, N. and Reed, H. (2006) *Freedom's Orphans: Raising Youth in a Changing World.* London: ippr.

ODPM (2004) *Household Estimates and Projections: Great Britain, 1961–2021.* London: TSO.

ONS (1996) *Labour Force Survey.* Available at <www.nomisweb.co.uk/>.

ONS (2004) *Labour Force Survey.* London: TSO.

ONS (2006a) 'Labour Market Analysis and Summary', Labour Market Trends, 114 (7): 213–40.

ONS (2006b) *Life Expectancy at Birth by Health and Local Authorities in the United Kingdom, 1991–1993 to 2003–2005.* Available at <www.statistics.gov.uk/statbase/Product.asp?vlnk=8841>.

ONS (2006c) *Annual Survey of Population.* Available at <www.nomisweb.co.uk/>.

ONS (2006d) *Regional Trends 39.* London: TSO. Available at <www.statistics.gov.uk/StatBase/Product.asp?vlnk=14356>.

Rhodes, M. (2000) 'Restructuring the British Welfare State: Between Domestic Constraints and Global imperatives', in F. Scharpf and V. Schmidt (eds), *Welfare and Work in the Open Economy.* Oxford: Oxford University Press.

Scharpf, F. (2000) 'Globalisation and the Political Economy of Capitalist Democracies', in D. Held and A. McGrew (eds), *The Global Transformations Reader.* Cambridge: Polity Press.

Stanley, K. and Regan, S. (2003) *The Missing Million.* London: ippr.

Stern, N. (2006) *Stern Review: The Economics of Climate Change.* London: TSO. Available at <www.hm-treasury.gov.uk/independent_reviews/stern_review_economics_climate_change/stern_review_report.cfm>.

TUC (2002) *Globalisation: Myths and Realities.* London: TUC.

TUC (2006) TUC Briefing on the Leitch Review of Skills – Final Report. Available at <www.tuc.org.uk/skills/tuc-12778-f0.pdf>.

Wilson, R., Homenidou, K. and Dickerson, A. (2006) *Working Futures 2004–2014 National Report.* Coventry: Institute for Economic Research. Available at <www.ssda.org.uk/PDF/Working%20Future%2020042014%20National%20R%20060215.pdf>.

6
Mind the Wealth Gap?
The Politics of Resource Inequality

Jamie Reed and Sonia Sodha

Debates around inequality have historically represented an intractable left–right dividing line in British politics. Crudely, the last century has been characterized by a political left arguing passionately for egalitarianism against a political right who, to all intents and purposes, acquiesced to inequality. But at the time of writing, many progressives feel that New Labour has not paid sufficient attention to the egalitarian vision in the past decade (see, for example, Compass 2006; Toynbee 2006). At the same time, we are now hearing noises from the political right which, taken at face value, suggest the potential for a left–right consensus on the importance of distributional equality. Despite the lack of substantive policy development, David Cameron has asserted the party as 'the champion of progressive politics in Britain' (2006), and the party's Social Justice Policy Group has affirmed its commitment to relative rather than absolute definitions of poverty (Clark and Franklin 2006). The Liberal Democrats too are apparently committed to lifting more people out of relative poverty (Campbell 2006).

But we should not be too sanguine about this apparent consensus on inequality. The case against inequality has, if anything, been underplayed in progressive debates over the last ten years. It is therefore increasingly urgent that progressives restate the rationale for addressing inequality, and articulate where it sits in the progressive vision. Only in this way can we hope to illustrate the difference between true progressivism – which focuses on the policy solutions needed to tackle inequality – and those merely paying lip service to the notion in the normative debate that has surfaced in recent months. We argue that despite this emergence of a shallow consensus, it continues to be progressives who have the courage to sell the case for tackling inequality to a sceptical public, and to champion the policies that are needed to do so.

We begin this chapter by outlining the progressive view of egalitarianism and the role of reducing inequality of material resources in this vision. We argue that reducing resource inequality matters: first, because gaping material inequalities hinder any meaningful notion of equality of opportunity; and second, because the progressive vision of a good society is not one that is only structured along an equality of opportunity principle. As Pearce and Margo argue in the Introduction, it is also one in which those who are not fortunate enough to be endowed with highly valued talents are treated with respect and have access to a basic minimum. Moreover, there is a growing evidence base that inequality has wider ill-effects for society.

Partly because the data is more complete, debates on resource inequality have tended to focus on income. But there is a good case for rebalancing this focus to look at wealth also – because someone's wealth is a much better indication of their resources and opportunities. We thus go on to outline trends and drivers of wealth inequality. It is clear that although our nation's wealth is steadily increasing, it is not the case that everyone is able to share in these gains. Wealth inequality remains stubbornly high and there are no signs of it falling. We therefore set out a progressive framework for policy responses to wealth inequality.

Promoting meaningful equality means reducing inequality of resources

All three main parties are signed up to the uncontroversial goal of promoting equality of opportunity. In many ways this is unsurprising – who in the twenty-first century would defend a society aligned along principles of birthright and class? To get at why reducing resource inequality is important, we need to unpick exactly what promoting equality of opportunity means to progressives, and why this sets them apart from other political traditions.

Two clear beliefs distinguish progressives from conservatives. First, progressives have a more demanding view of what it means for two people to have the same opportunities. For example, while a conservative might think it is enough for government to ensure that all children have access to a free education until age 18, progressives believe, in light of evidence which shows that structural inequalities create barriers to opportunities, that equality of opportunity cannot be achieved without some reduction in resource inequality. Resources themselves shape opportunities in the meaningful sense. Gaping inequalities hinder social mobility, which has deteriorated over the last ten years (see Chapter 4). Resource inequality today is one determinant of opportunity inequality tomorrow.

This stands in stark contrast to the argument that the goals of reducing inequality and of extending opportunity are unrelated. Some might also argue that reducing inequality need only mean raising the position of those at the bottom, by equipping them with a decent minimum (see, for example, Laws 2007). But this positively requires redistribution, because this minimum has to be sourced. This book contains many proposals to open up opportunities for all, all of which require resources. Lifting up those at the bottom necessitates some measure of redistribution; improving equality of opportunity requires reducing inequality of resources. It is disingenuous to claim otherwise.

Second, our vision of a good society is not one solely based on equality of opportunity – indeed, such a society was satirized by the progressive who coined the term 'meritocracy' (Young 1958). It is not enough that people endowed with the talents valued by society should be able to rise to the top, unhindered by where and when they were born. For progressives, the demands of social justice are stronger. While they recognize that some inequalities are the just result of individual choice (see the Introduction), they also believe that society should treat all its citizens with equal respect and dignity regardless of their talents, which again means providing a decent minimum.

Wealth matters

It is worth elaborating why this chapter is mainly about wealth inequality, when it is income inequality that has been the traditional focus of policy-makers. Both are important economic indicators of resource inequality. Perhaps part of the reason that income inequality has attracted more attention is that we have more accurate, extensive data on income than we do on wealth – which we define as someone's total stock of assets, including their financial assets, property and pension wealth. But we believe that wealth offers a better snapshot of the resources that people have access to at a single point in time than income. Some people may choose not to work and therefore have a low income but own a large amount of assets – which is of less concern than someone who earns very little and owns nothing. Focusing on wealth inequality alongside income inequality also highlights the cumulative effects of income inequality. Over time, income inequality translates into ever-increasing wealth inequality.

We also need to consider wealth inequality in light of emerging evidence that owning an asset brings positive psychological benefits. In the cold light of neoclassical economics, assets are simply considered to be a store of future consumption or investment potential. But research has suggested that by allowing for upfront costs, assets can act as a springboard, working not just to alleviate immediate poverty but also to open up opportunities through a number of different effects (Paxton 2001).

First, owning an asset can provide security – a financial cushion for when things go wrong. For those without assets, especially those on lower incomes, the risk of unexpected events, such as the breakdown of a car, or one-off 'lumpy' costs, such as a child starting school, can create uncertainty and insecurity, which bring stress and other psychological costs (Lister 2006). Second, by improving security, assets enable individuals to take productive risks – for example, starting their own business, or undertaking training. In an analysis of the National Child Development Study, Blanchflower and Oswald (1998) have shown that people aged 23 who had in the past received at least £5,000 of inheritance by 1981 (in 1981 prices) were approximately twice as likely to be self-employed in that year as someone who had received no inheritance, controlling for factors such as certain personality traits, regional employment levels, and father's occupation when the respondent was 14.

Owning an asset can make it easier for individuals to plan ahead by reducing shorter-term budgeting problems, which enables individuals to lift their eyes from week-to-week budgeting to the long term. Assets are also thought to influence an individual's self-efficacy – the extent to which they believe they can change their future situation by their own actions. Sherraden (1991) has argued that asset-holding can change the way people think, and several political philosophers have explored the idea that assets increase people's freedom from interferences and dependency on others (Ackerman and Alstott 1999; Dowding et al. 2003).

If these effects do indeed operate as has been proposed, we would expect to find that assets have an independent effect on positive outcomes. There is emerging evidence to suggest that this is the case. Bynner (2001) finds that among respondents in the National Child Development Study, owning a financial asset of between £300 and £600 (in 2001 prices) at age 23 is positively associated with a greater chance of employment and improved mental health outcomes at age 33, controlling for a range of other factors. This simple association requires further investigation to determine in which direction the causality runs; this relationship is the subject of ongoing ippr work with the Centre for the Analysis of Social Exclusion at the London School of Economics (LSE).

The ill-effects of inequality

The arguments for tackling resource inequality go beyond a normative commitment to social justice. There is a growing body of evidence that suggests not only that increasing inequality is fundamentally unjust but also that more unequal societies also tend to experience greater levels of social divergence. It seems that increasing economic divergence pulls at our societal fabric, increasing social tensions (Halpern 2004). Because it is more easily measured in an international context, most of this evidence inevitably pertains to income rather than wealth inequality – but it is also relevant to debates on the latter.

Cross-national empirical research suggests that levels of trust and civic cooperation are higher in countries with relatively low levels of income inequality (Knack and Keefer 1997), and this result has also been found to hold in the US (Kawachi and Kennedy 1997). Causality may run in both directions, but it should come as no great surprise that societies that are more polarized in terms of income and wealth seem to be less able to sustain social trust and cooperation. Opinions and attitudes towards others seem also to be shaped by the structure of society: one study of 17 countries has found that countries with greater inequality between the 50th and 90th income percentiles have significantly lower levels of public spending (Schwabish et al. 2003). The ill-effects of inequality can also be felt in a geographic and spatial sense within the UK. In the same way in which material inequality can lead to less social mobility for individuals, it can also disable the economic growth of more discrete, remote geographical areas.

Levels of violent crime have also been shown to be associated with income inequality in the US (Wilkinson et al. 1998). Wilkinson et al. have argued that wide income disparities generate invidious social comparisons, which themselves create feelings of exclusion, alienation, low social status and lack of self-esteem among low-income groups. They have suggested that violent crime is in part a desire to seek respect from others, pointing to psychiatric work with violent offenders as an example.

It has long been established that individual income is positively related to health, as measured by mortality (see, for example, Townsend and Davidson 1982). But recent research has shown that health and the distribution of income within society are also correlated (Wilkinson 2006).

Numerous studies have shown a link between income distribution and mortality between different states in the US (for example, Kennedy et al. 1996; Kaplan et al. 1996) and between the states in the US and provinces in Canada (Ross et al. 2000). Moreover, more recent international research has highlighted the same trend: Ross et al. (2005) examined data for 528 cities in the US, the UK, Sweden, Canada and Australia and showed that mortality rates tended to be higher in more unequal cities. It has been suggested that the negative impact of inequality on health may be mediated by a range of factors: underinvestment in social goods such as public education and healthcare, disruption of social cohesion, and the harmful psychosocial effects of invidious social comparisons (Kawachi and Kennedy 1999).

But is inequality healthy for the economy? Economic liberals have traditionally claimed that reducing inequality through redistribution will inevitably curb economic growth (Laws 2007). Yet there is little evidence that this is in fact the case. There is a large economic literature on the empirical links between inequality and economic growth. Most of these cross-country studies have found that lower levels of income inequality are positively associated with growth, controlling for a range of other factors (see, for example, Alesina and Rodrick 1994; Persson and Tabellini 1994; Knack and Keefer 1997). These studies have not gone uncontested (Forbes 2000), but they at least suggest that the assumption that reducing inequality is bad for growth cannot go unchallenged. For example, Nordic democracies have higher levels of taxation and redistribution than liberal economies such as the US and the UK, but their economic health does not seem to have suffered adverse impacts – for instance, Sweden was enjoying growth rates of 5.6 per cent in the second quarter of 2006.

Power, rules and resources: when fair's not fair

Economic inequalities tend to translate into inequality in political participation and representation. The corrupting influence of wealth on democracy is an age-old concern, troubling the very earliest Western democratic theorists from Solon, the early architect of the Athenian constitution in 600 BC, onwards. In the words of Louis Brandeis, US Supreme Court Justice, 'we can have a democratic society or great concentrated wealth in the hands of the few. But we cannot have both.'

As highlighted in Chapter 3, the least affluent are least likely to vote in democratic elections: controlling for other factors, income was a strong predictor of voting in the 2001 and 2005 general elections (Keaney and

Rogers 2006). The decline in turnout since the mid 1960s has been most marked for those in the lowest income quartile. And almost four times the number of young people living in households with an annual income of less than £15,000 think 'it's not really worth voting' than those in households with an income of more than £50,000 (ibid.). Moreover, the more affluent are more likely to be politically active in other ways. People in households with annual incomes greater than £70,000 performed nearly twice as many 'individual political actions', such as boycotting products or raising money for a pressure group, and one and a half times as many 'contact actions', such as writing to their MP, than those in households with annual incomes of less than £10,000 (Patty et al. 2003, 2004).

Some studies have found that politicians are also more responsive to more affluent citizens (see, for example, Bartels 2005; Gilens 2005; Jusko 2005). The evidence is, however, sparser, and relates to the US and Canada rather than the UK, where data limitations make a reliable examination of the link between income inequality and representation almost impossible (Soroka and Wlezian 2006). Bartels (2005) has found that the voting record of US senators suggests they are significantly more responsive to the views of higher-income constituents, controlling for differences in turnout, political knowledge and constituent contact. Gilens (2005) has reported similar relationships between income and political decisions in the US over a 20-year period: he found that when preferences of the 90th income percentile diverge with those of the 10th and 50th, government policy appears to reflect that of the 90th percentile to a much greater extent. Soroka and Wlezian (2006) looked at changes in political preferences over time in the US and Canada with more mixed results, but they did find that in some policy domains (for example, welfare spending) there was a high-income bias. Of course, these correlations do not explain why outcomes appear to be more responsive to the more affluent, and the effects also may not be so marked in the UK – without better data, it is difficult to tell. But it is deeply worrying that material wealth seems to be related not just to political participation, but also to political influence. This corrosive trend poses a unique challenge for progressives – how can democratic movements effect change for the disadvantaged and the dispossessed when these very same groups are the least likely to engage with the political process?

In fact, this evidence on political representation is symptomatic of a wider problem. No matter how procedurally fair the rules of the game may be, it is not necessarily fair in a wider sense if the playing field is hugely uneven. It might seem that the epitome of democratic legitimacy, the 'one man, one vote' principle, could never be anything *but* fair, but to make this assumption is to take an overly simplistic view of what constitutes fairness. Resources allow people to play the rules to their advantage, and so we need to take them into account. We only have to look to our school system as an example. School quality is strongly related to property prices, with a difference of 10 percentage points in a school's league table at age eleven adding at least 3 per cent to the price of a house located next to it (Gibbons and Machin 2005). So although the system is procedurally comprehensive, more affluent parents can afford to purchase houses in areas with good schools – and thus effectively buy their child a better state education.

Some might argue, however, that this is a case for reforming our procedures – the rules that structure our societies – rather than for tackling inequality. But when we look at examples of reform, we find that where there is a will and, more importantly, the resources, to play the system, there is a way. Perhaps one of the best examples of this is reform of political financing in the US – a recent ban on unlimited large donations to political parties to use on 'issue ads' which do not expressly advocate the election or defeat of a candidate has simply resulted in a diversion of funds to campaign groups set up for the purpose of running these advertisements outside of the formal party system in the 2004 and 2006 election cycles.

Wealth inequality: trends and drivers

As Chapter 4 illustrates, although there are some tentative signs of a downward trend in income inequality, we can by no means take this trend for granted. Moreover, wealth inequality remains stubbornly high – approximately twice as high as post-tax income inequality as measured by the Gini coefficient (HM Revenue & Customs (HMRC) 2006). The richest 1 per cent of the population owned a staggering 21 per cent of the nation's wealth in 2003, the latest year for which we have figures, while at the same time, the bottom 50 per cent of the wealth distribution owned just 7 per cent, and almost a quarter of the population owned assets worth less than £5,000 (HMRC 2006).

It is difficult to build up a more complete picture of who owns what in the UK because there is no single large-scale survey that asks people of all ages about what they own with respect to financial assets, their home, their pensions, and debts. Even if such a survey did exist, involvement in it would be likely to suffer from a firmly established cultural suspicion about precisely how this data would be used – itself an illustration of the challenges facing progressives in tackling the issue of wealth inequality.

The best available information is on financial wealth – the British Household Panel Survey (BHPS) asks questions about people's stocks of financial assets every five years. In 2000, 50 per cent of families owned less than £600 in net financial assets, but mean net financial wealth was £12,636 (Banks et al. 2002). Some of this inequality will be explained by a cohort effect – younger people will have had less time to save and accumulate assets than those who are older. Because accumulating wealth is a dynamic process, we would also expect inequality to become progressively greater within older age cohorts. This is borne out by the evidence: in the 2000 BHPS, inequality increased within age groups until the age of 75 (ibid.).

If data on wealth holdings is limited, data on what drives wealth inequality is even more so. Income inequality and differential saving rates are obviously important drivers of wealth inequality: very crudely, the more someone earns, the greater their ability to save, given a certain fixed amount of outgoings. While the sharp rise in income inequality that was allowed to occur in the late 1980s has slowed, and since 1997 has begun to reverse, there is no room for complacency. The richest 1 per cent have seen higher rates of income growth over the last decade than any other group (see Chapter 4).

Fast-increasing house prices are also a significant driver (Maxwell and Sodha 2006). Nominal house prices have increased by over 500 per cent since 1983 – a house bought for £100,000 then would now be worth on average £530,000. But this average masks a spatial dimension: over the period 1983–2003, the increase in property values in the tenth most expensive areas of the UK was almost twice that of the least expensive tenth (Thomas and Dorling 2004). This is reflected in average house prices, which are almost £300,000 in London, compared to just under £150,000 in the North East (Department for Communities and Local Government (DCLG) 2006).

The effect of increasing house prices is magnified by the leverage effect of mortgages (Maxwell and Sodha 2006). Because most people tend to buy their houses using mortgages, the debt to equity ratio in homes also tends to be high. This means that both gains and losses that result from changes in house prices are very high relative to the net amount invested in a home. As an example, consider someone who puts down a £10,000 deposit on a £100,000 house and takes out an interest-only £90,000 mortgage to cover the rest. If house price inflation is 10 per cent, their house will be worth £110,000 by the end of the year. In that time they will have paid £4,500 in interest charges on their 5 per cent interest mortgage, but the net equity they have invested in their home is now

£20,000. So they will have made a net profit in one year of £5,500 – a return of 55 per cent. Of course, if house price inflation falls below their mortgage rate, the flipside is that losses are magnified too – but this has not historically been the case in the most affluent areas of the UK. So investing in housing using mortgage debt has historically led to huge gains for home-owners, increasing their relative wealth compared to non-owners. Perhaps unsurprisingly then, one US study of home-ownership found that in 1999, people who owned their own home in 1984 were 2.2 times wealthier than people who rented in 1984, controlling for a wide range of income and demographic variables (Di et al. 2003).

So home-ownership is an excellent way to accumulate wealth when house price inflation is greater than mortgage rates. But it is becoming progressively harder to get onto the housing ladder: house price inflation delivers gains to those who can make the jump but takes those gains further and further out of reach of those who cannot. The number of unassisted first-time buyers has fallen steadily from 140,000 in 1996 to just under 20,000 in 2005, and in the same period, the number of assisted first-time buyers has almost doubled (Tatch 2006) – it is increasingly harder to buy without financial help from parents or others. Because house price inflation simply redistributes wealth from non-owners to owners, policy needs to tackle the fundamental causes of the supply–demand imbalance.

Inheritance also contributes to high levels of wealth inequality. People from higher social classes are more likely to inherit: one Joseph Rowntree Foundation/MORI survey found that 70 per cent of senior professionals (social class A) had inherited during their lifetimes, compared to just three in ten in social class E (Rowlingson and McKay 2005). There were also significant differences in the amount inherited: in social classes A and B, one in ten had received an inheritance worth at least £50,000 in 2006 prices, compared to just 1–2 per cent in social classes D and E (ibid.).

These trends combined increasingly mean that getting richer means being rich in the first place. Children with wealthy parents who bought their homes in the right place and at the right time will always find it easy to get on the housing ladder with financial support and inheritance from their parents. They will continue to get rich faster, but the rest will only be able to watch from the sidelines. If this process is allowed to continue unconstrained, there is a danger that the dividing line between the 'haves' and 'have-nots' will become ever starker. This must be of deep concern to progressives in the next decade.

The policy challenge

Any comprehensive strategy aimed at reducing wealth inequality needs to tackle its core drivers – income inequality and the housing market in particular. Reducing income inequality is a theme running throughout this book. But there will be limits to the extent to which the income gap can be reduced. Wealth-based strategies are thus another important way of reducing inequality, directly targeting wealth inequality itself. There are two kinds of strategies. One is asset-building, which looks to build wealth for those who own nothing or very little. The second is wealth taxation, a potentially alternative form of progressive taxation that can be used to supplement progressive income taxes to fund redistributive policies such as education, policies to promote labour market progression, asset-building policies and tax credits and benefits.

Asset-based welfare

It is important to stress that asset-building policies have a long, established tradition in the UK. But they have historically been based on the principle of tax relief – tax relief on interest on saving products such as Individual Savings Accounts (ISAs) and Personal Equity Plans (PEPs); tax relief on pensions saving; tax relief on mortgage payments from 1920 to 1998; and exemptions from capital gains tax for a home-owner's main residence. Yet tax relief is intrinsically regressive, offering the greatest incentives to the highest earners. This is perverse in light of the link between income and asset inequality, which demonstrates that it is those on low incomes who most need support in building up assets.

It is only recently, however, that asset-building policies have begun to take on a progressive sheen, with the government even suggesting they could become a fourth pillar of the welfare state (HM Treasury 2001). Asset-based welfare has represented a new policy-making frontier since 1997. Since an ippr paper first recommended an asset-based complement to other social policies in the UK (Kelly and Lissauer 2000), the government has introduced a number of reforms to spread asset ownership. The boldest of these was the Child Trust Fund – as a result of this policy, every child born since 2002 will have access to a modest asset when they turn 18. The government is also piloting the Saving Gateway, a matched-saving scheme targeted at those on low incomes. Additionally, it introduced ISAs in 1997, which meant that for the first time, savers did not have to sacrifice one or the other of liquidity or the relatively low risk of cash to benefit from tax relief on short-term savings.

These policies are hugely important in enabling an increasing number of people to share in the benefits of asset ownership, but they only represent a starting point. Now the immediate priority for asset policy in the UK must be to roll out the Saving Gateway as a national scheme, so that for the first time, people from across the whole income distribution are supported in saving, not just the more affluent (Sodha and Lister 2006). This is particularly the case in light of the very positive evidence from the pilots (ibid.; Kempson et al. 2005).

In the long term, the challenge lies in being more ambitious. The Child Trust Fund and Saving Gateway have very much been introduced as part of the 'social investment' paradigm of the state that has been so influential in centre-left thinking in recent years (Pearce et al. 2006). This philosophy of the state sees its primary role as building people's capacities and opening up opportunities so they can be more self-supporting. Under this view, supporting people to build up assets is useful because it allows them to be more productive and self-sufficient. Thus the emphasis in these policies has been on building up propensities to save over time, rather than focusing on some of the other benefits assets can bring – for example, in allowing people to interact more flexibly with the labour market, which can improve quality-of life-measures other than income. But as the Introduction to this book has argued, progressives need to move beyond a measure of well-being that is based solely on income. This could be incorporated into asset-based policy; for example, in encouraging employers to establish 'time-use' accounts, which allow employees to bank leave or defer salary so they can take sabbatical leave during their working lives (Boyes and McCormick 2006).

Support for home-ownership has also become more progressive since 1997 with the abolition of mortgage interest tax relief and the introduction of shared-equity schemes targeted at those on low incomes. These schemes have real benefits: in the long term, they are a cheaper form of state housing support than housing benefit. But they do not tackle the fundamental problem in the housing market: the UK has a relatively unresponsive housing market (Swank et al. 2002, quoted in Barker 2003) and supply is not keeping pace with demand. These demand-based subsidies can actually further buoy-up the housing market – so while they may help those who benefit to start building up a substantial asset, they take home-ownership even further out of reach for those who do not, by contributing to higher prices. Instead, the fundamental mismatch between supply and demand needs to be tackled directly. Our current planning system is overly cumbersome and places too many limitations on new development. Extensive restrictions on development are regressive: they benefit current owners at the expense of those yet to own. The government needs to commit to increased levels of house building in order to meet demand (Commission on Sustainable Development in the South East 2005). But the focus of longer-term reform should be the planning system. This may be politically difficult because the current system enjoys public support – but this is based on a public misperception that half of the UK is urbanized, while the actual figure is around 10 per cent (Evans and Hartwich 2007). Progressives need to dispel these myths and make the case that objections to further development can be not only regressive and unfair but also prejudicial to the interests of disadvantaged social groups and geographic areas within the UK. As house prices continue to rise at a rate which the incomes of most people have no prospect of matching, there is a compelling case for housing supply to be far more responsive to housing demand. Such a bold move would deliver progressive policy aims far more quickly than wealth taxation policies ever could.

Wealth taxation

Wealth taxation has been an issue that politicians from across the political spectrum have been reluctant to touch in the last ten years. While conservatives have widely criticized inheritance tax, progressives have failed to respond by making a case, choosing to fight battles elsewhere. Britain's current system of wealth taxation is widely perceived as unfair – and in many ways it is, which makes the system difficult to defend. But problems in the system are an argument for reform not abolition. Reform and building support must go hand in hand.

Crucially, progressives do not view wealth taxation as something that should be pursued simply as a burden on the rich. Taxation can and often has been used as an indiscriminate, blunt instrument in pursuing the progressive cause. In discussing how wealth taxes can be raised most fairly – and indeed, in whether they are inherently fair – we must not lose sight of the redistributive goal of any form of progressive taxation: to raise revenue that can be spent on further reducing inequality. So the question is not whether we should impose wealth taxes on the affluent in order to reduce inequality through a 'levelling down' effect, in a 'if not everyone can have it, nobody can' kind of sentiment. Rather, the question is that, given inequality is too high and there is a greater need for redistribution, is taxing wealth a *fair* way to reduce inequality through redistribution?

The current system

Wealth in the UK is mainly taxed under the auspices of two taxes: inheritance tax, and capital gains tax. Inheritance tax (IHT) is a tax on estates, levied when the owner dies. The first £285,000 of an estate can be passed on tax-free (rising to £350,000 in 2010 (HM Treasury 2007)); wealth above this threshold is subject to a 40 per cent tax. There are a number of important exemptions, including transfers to spouses or charity and small gifts, and reliefs for agricultural property and family and private businesses. People can also make gifts tax-free so long as they live for seven years after they are made ('potentially exempt transfers'). It is a tax currently paid by only 6 per cent of estates each year (Brown 2006).

Capital gains tax (CGT) is a tax on gains to people's wealth over a period of time. It is a transactions tax: people pay the tax when they sell assets that have appreciated in value. The appreciation is taxed at the same rate as an individual's maximum income tax band, although everyone has a separate CGT tax-free allowance (£8,800 in 2006/07). Again, there are some important exemptions. The most significant is the complete exemption of people's principal private residences – which means that any increases in the value of their homes go untaxed in their lifetimes. This is a huge tax bonus – estimated at £15 billion in 2006/07 (HM Treasury 2007, Table A3.1). Second, the amount of the gain that is taxable on other assets decreases over time to just 60 per cent after ten years for non-business assets, and just 25 per cent after two years for business assets (shares in a company in which an individual does not have a material interest) – again, this tax bonus is significant at £6 billion in 2006/07 (ibid.).

Critics are right that significant problems exist within the current system. First, IHT is notoriously easy for the very wealthy to avoid. This is because they can afford to pay for expensive tax-avoidance advice. Although many IHT loopholes, most notably those on trusts, have been closed, the biggest and most easily exploited loophole remains wide open: because IHT is designed as a tax on the estates of the deceased rather than the gifts of the living, people can always avoid paying it by gifting their wealth to others so long as they live for seven years after they have done so. It is easiest for the wealthiest to take advantage of this provision because it is usually they who can afford to give away their wealth, whereas for the moderately affluent, it tends to be locked up in their homes. One report has suggested that inheritance tax receipts are only 16 per cent of what they would be were it not for avoidance and exemptions (Wadsworth 2006).

How should progressives respond?

The main reason that politicians have shied away from an informed, rational debate about wealth taxation is because of understandably negative public attitudes. It is true that inheritance tax seems to be unpopular. But looking at the figures more closely suggests that the idea of taxing inheritance is not as unpopular as media coverage of inheritance tax would lead us to expect.

A Fabian Tax Commission survey found that only a very slight majority of the public, 51 per cent, are completely opposed to a tax on inheritance (Fabian Commission on Tax and Citizenship 2000), demonstrating significant resistance, but certainly not unanimous opposition. Interestingly, attitudes were least hostile among older groups and the most affluent social classes. Yet misperceptions about inheritance tax are widespread. In one Joseph Rowntree Foundation/MORI poll, only 6 per cent of respondents were able to correctly identify the number of estates that pay IHT each year – the most common assumption among those who gave an answer was that somewhere between 25 per cent and 49 per cent of estates pay inheritance tax, far higher than the actual figure of 6 per cent (Rowlingson and McKay 2005).

Moreover, widespread polls provide only a superficial snapshot of people's beliefs about inheritance tax, and do not always reveal the depth of those beliefs, and whether they hold common misperceptions. Deliberative polling or workshops can enable policy-makers to get a sense of how fixed public views are and of the overall potential for change (Lewis and White 2006). ippr has conducted deliberative workshops on IHT with a broadly representative sample of 32 people. At the start of the workshops, there were similar levels of hostility to IHT as those revealed by the Fabian Commission survey. However, once people were presented with balanced arguments in favour of and against inheritance tax, and an informed debate ensued, there was a modest shift in support for IHT (ibid.). While half of participants were opposed outright both before and after the workshops, there was a clear increase in support among those who were ambiguous or unsure about the idea. Hypothecation seemed to increase support further: a clear majority said after the workshops that they would be more willing to support IHT if it were put aside to spend on a particular area of public services.

There is also some evidence of changing attitudes, with there being a stronger level of support for inheritance among older age groups. In the Joseph Rowntree Foundation/MORI survey, only 15 per cent of potential bequeathers said it was 'very important' to leave an inheritance, with most saying it was 'fairly important' (50 per cent) or 'not very important' (28 per cent). When asked to select between two statements, most potential bequeathers said they wanted to 'enjoy life and not worry about bequests' (67 per cent), with only 28 per cent saying they 'would be careful with money to leave bequests'. Breaking down attitudes by age, it transpires that the older age groups (70 plus) were more likely than younger groups to agree with the statement 'older people should be careful with their money so they can leave an inheritance'. It may be that the current middle-aged generation takes these attitudes into retirement with them, or that their attitudes become more like today's older generation as they become older. Further research is needed, but this data certainly suggest that public attitudes are not as intractable as might be assumed.

New research has also probed public attitudes into other forms of wealth taxation (Prabhakar forthcoming). In broadly representative focus groups, this research found that people were more positively disposed to a tax on land value than inheritance tax: some recognized that an increase in land value caused by social investment near their home should be taxed. Others, though, maintained that any increases in value of their land were rightfully theirs. There were also some concerns expressed about the affordability of such a tax for those who live in expensive homes but without large incomes (ibid.).

All this suggests that it would indeed be possible for progressives to build a consensus in favour of the social benefits which could be realized through wealth taxation, but this possibility is contingent on three factors. First, progressives need to start from a position of realism. There will always be some people for whom making bequests is important, and it would be futile, and indeed wrong, for politicians to try to argue against this. In a time of unprecedented economic growth, low unemployment, low inflation and economic stability, this is an attitude which is shared by many of those sections of society who have benefited from ten years of Labour government. The goal of progressivism is not to eliminate all advantage that may be passed down through a family in an attempt to level down, but instead to extend this advantage to all as far as possible. A tax on wealth should therefore be understood as a way of funding the expansion of opportunities for those who are not lucky enough to receive an inheritance. One way of doing so would be to link revenues from a tax on wealth to expenditure on policies that explicitly expand opportunities. Public support should be easier to build if citizens can see that this link exists. Second, progressives need to defend the purpose of wealth taxation from first principles using the facts – so people are aware of the arguments in favour of as well as against wealth taxation, and the reality of how it operates. But in order to make this case, wealth taxation needs to be clearly linked to the principles that lie behind it. Third, making the case for wealth taxation will also be easier if the tax is clearly understood by the public as being unquestionably fairer, and this gives further impetus for reform.

Conclusions

Moving forward into the next ten years, resource inequality will become an increasingly important dividing line between the left and right in British politics. After a decade of Labour government, progressives have the opportunity to recast their agenda for the twenty-first century, based on a firm commitment to tackle resource inequality.

However, it is clear that reform is a long way off. Progressives need to start thinking about how they can realize the social benefits of wealth redistribution through policies which are clearly understood and acknowledged as fair to all. Those conservatives serious about expanding opportunities and reducing inequalities should also contribute towards the production of policy solutions which could achieve these desired outcomes. The current system requires meticulous analysis now so that a better, fairer system can be established.

Regrettably, recent proposals from the Conservatives' Tax Reform Commission move in entirely the opposite direction to that of a policy platform designed to reduce inequality. Their proposals to abolish CGT and IHT accompanied by the introduction of a short-term capital gains tax represent a significant step backwards for progressive ambitions. Not only would these proposals entrench social, individual and regional inequalities, but they also expose a widening gulf between British progressives and the Conservative Party on the issue of inequality. As we have argued in this chapter, there are a diverse set of reasons why progressives should care about inequality that range from the normative to the empirical. The focus needs to be expanded to wealth inequality as well as income inequality – because someone's wealth in many ways gives a better understanding of the resources they have to draw upon.

Wealth taxation is a little-used method of redistribution: inheritance tax and capital gains tax between them only raise a small fraction of the huge gains to personal wealth we see year on year – over £400 billion in the last year in the property market alone. But this is an argument for reform, not abolition. Research shows that public opposition to wealth taxation is not as intractable as we might think. But it will be exceptionally difficult to win support for reform so long as the taxes are perceived to be unfair and progressives fail to make the case not only for the fairness of wealth taxation and the social, individual and macro-economic benefits which it could bring, but also of the socially ruinous consequences of policies which actively work against the reduction of asset and wealth inequality. It is in the best interests of the nation that inequality is reduced; this requires a meaningful political consensus underpinned by broad public support. Defence and reform must go hand in hand.

Acknowledgements

The authors are grateful to the Public and Commercial Services Union for its generous funding which made the writing of this chapter possible, and would also like to thank Charles Cochrane, Alan Finlayson, Julia Margo, Nick Pearce, Howard Reed and Stuart White for their helpful comments on earlier drafts of the chapter.

References

Ackermann, B. and Alstott, A. (1999) *The Stakeholder Society*. New Haven: Yale University Press.

Alesina, A. and Rodrick, D. (1994) 'Distributive Politics and Economic Growth', *Quarterly Journal of Economics*, 109 (2): 465–90.

Banks, J., Smith, Z. and Wakefield, M. (2002) *The Distribution of Financial Wealth in the UK: Evidence from 2000 BHPS Data*. London: Institute for Fiscal Studies.

Barker, K. (2003) *Barker Review of Housing Supply: Securing our Future Housing Needs Interim Report*. London: HM Treasury and ODPM.

Bartels, L. (2005) 'Economic Inequality and Political Representation'. Unpublished manuscript, Princeton University.

Blanchflower, D. and Oswald, A. (1998) 'What Makes an Entrepreneur?', *Journal of Labour Economics*, 16: 26–30.

Boyes, L. and McCormick, J. (2006) 'Having the Time of Our Lives: Reworking Time', in W. Paxton and S. White (with D. Maxwell) (eds), *The Citizen's Stake*. Bristol: Policy Press.

Brown, G. (2006) *Budget Statement*. Available at <www.hm-treasury.gov.uk/budget/budget_06/bud_bud06_speech.cfm>.

Bynner, J. (2001) 'Effect of Assets on Life Chances', in J. Bynner and W. Paxton, *The Asset-Effect*. London: ippr.

Cameron, D. (2006), 'We are the party of class mobility', *Guardian*, 3 December 2006.

Campbell, M. (2006) 'Poverty and Opportunity: The Liberal way'. Speech to the ippr, 19 December. London: ippr.

Clark, G. and Franklin, P. (2006) *The State of the National Report: Economic Dependency*. London: Conservative Party.

Commission on Sustainable Development in the South East (2005) *Commission on Sustainable Development in the South East Final Report*, London: ippr.

Compass (2006) *The Good Society: Compass Programme for Renewal*. London: Compass.

DCLG (2006) *House Price Index October 2006*. Available at <www.communities. gov.uk/index.asp?id=1002882&PressNoticeID=2311>.

Di, Z.X., Yang, Y. and Liu, X. (2003) *The Importance of Housing to the Accumulation of Household Net Wealth*. Joint Center for Housing Studies Working Paper W03-5. Cambridge, Mass.: Harvard University Press.

Dowding, K., De Wispelaere, J. and White, S. (2003) *The Ethics of Stakeholding*. Basingstoke: Palgrave Macmillan.

Evans, A. and Hartwich, O. (2007) *The Best Laid Plans: How Planning Prevents Economic Growth*. London: Policy Exchange.

Fabian Society on Taxation and Citizenship (2000), *Paying for Progress: A New Politics of Tax for Public Spending*. London: Fabian Society.

Forbes, K. (2000) 'A Reassessment of the Relationship between Inequality and Growth', *American Economic Review*, 90 (4), September: 869–87.

Gibbons, S. and Machin, S. (2005) 'Paying for Primary Schools: Supply Constraints, Popularity or Congestion'. Paper presented at the Royal Economic Society's Annual Conference, University of Nottingham, 22 March.

Gilens, M. (2005) 'Inequality and Democratic Responsiveness', *Public Opinion Quarterly*, 69 (5): 778–96.

Halpern, D. (2004) *Social Capital*. Cambridge: Polity Press.

HMRC (2006) 'Table 13.5: Distribution Among the Adult Population of Marketable Wealth (Series C)'. Available at <www.hmrc.gov.uk/stats/personal_wealth/ table13_5.pdf>.

HM Treasury (2001), *Savings and Assets for All*. London: HM Treasury.

HM Treasury (2007), *Budget 2007: Building Britain's Long-Term Future: Prosperity and Fairness for Families*. London: HM Treasury.

Jusko, K. (2005) 'The Political Representation of the Poor: A Research Note Using CSES Data'. Paper presented at the Plenary Meetings of the Comparative Study of Electoral Systems, Washington DC, 30–31 August.

Kawachi, I. and Kennedy, B. (1997) 'The Relationship of Income Inequality to Mortality – Does the Choice of Indicator Matter'?, *Social Science and Medicine*, 45 (1): 121–7.

Kaplan, G., Pamuk, E., Lynch, J., Cohen, R. and Balfour, J. (1996) 'Inequality in Income and Mortality in the United States: Analysis of Mortality and Potential Pathways', *British Medical Journal*, 312: 999–1003.

Keaney, E. and Rogers, B. (2006) *A Citizen's Duty: Voter Inequality and the Case for Compulsory Turnout*. London: ippr.

Kelly, G. and Lissauer, R. (2000) *Ownership for All*. London: ippr.

Kempson, E., McKay, S. and Collard, S. (2005) *Incentives to Save: Encouraging Saving Among Low-Income Households*. Bristol: Personal Finance Research Centre, University of Bristol.

Kennedy, B., Kawachi, I. and Prothrow-Stith, D. (1996) 'Income Distribution and Mortality: Cross Sectional Ecological Study of the Robin Hood Index in the United States', *British Medical Journal*, 312 (1): 4–7.

Knack, K. and Keefer, P. (1997) 'Does Inequality Harm Growth Only in Democracies? A Replication and Extension', *American Journal of Political Science*, 41 (1): 323–32.

Laws, D. (2007) 'Size Isn't Everything: Debating the State', in J. Margo (ed.), *Beyond Liberty: Is the Future of Liberalism Progressive?* London: ippr.

Lewis, M. and White, S. (2006) 'Inheritance Tax: What Do the People Think?', in W. Paxton and S. White (with D. Maxwell) (eds), *The Citizen's Stake*. Bristol: Policy Press.

Lister, R. (2006) 'Poverty, Material Insecurity and Income Vulnerability', in S. Sodha and R. Lister, *The Saving Gateway: From Principles to Practice*. London: ippr.

Maxwell, D. and Sodha, S. (2006) *Housing Wealth*. London: ippr.

Patty, C., Seyd, P. and Whitely, P. (2003) 'Civic Attitudes and Engagement in Modern Britain', *Parliamentary Affairs*, 56: 616–33.

Patty, C., Seyd, P. and Whitely, P. (2004) *Citizenship in Britain: Values, Participation and Democracy*. Cambridge: Cambridge University Press.

Paxton, W. (2001) 'The Asset-Effect: An Overview', in J. Bynner and W. Paxton, *The Asset-Effect*. London: ippr.

Pearce, N., Paxton, W. and White, S. (2006) 'Conclusion', in W. Paxton and S. White (with D. Maxwell) (eds), *The Citizen's Stake*. Bristol: Policy Press.

Persson, T. and Tabellini, G. (1994) 'Is Inequality Harmful for Growth?', *American Economic Review*, 84 (3): 600–21.

Prabhakar, R. (forthcoming) 'Taxing Wealth: Public Attitudes Towards Policies for Overcoming Wealth Inequality'. Paper for presentation at the 2007 Political Studies Association Annual Conference.

Ross, N., Dorling, D., Dunn, J., Hendricksson, G., Glover, J. and Lynch, J. (2005) 'Metropolitan Income Inequality and Working Age Mortality: A Five Country Analysis Using Comparable Data', *Journal of Urban Health*, 82 (1): 101–10.

Ross, N., Wolfson, M., Dunn, J., Berthelot, J., Kaplan, G. and Lynch, J. (2000) 'Relation Between Income Inequality and Mortality in Canada and in the United States: Cross Sectional Assessment Using Census Data and Vital Statistics', *British Medical Journal*, 320: 898–902.

Rowlingson, K. and McKay, S. (2005) *Attitudes to Inheritance in Britain*. York: Joseph Rowntree Foundation.

Schwabish, J., Smeeding, T. and Osberg, L. (2003) 'Income Distribution and Social Expenditures: A Crossnational Perspective'. Available at <www.popcenter.umd.edu/conferences/rsf/papers/Smeeding.pdf>.

Sodha, S. and Lister, R. (2006) *The Saving Gateway: From Principles to Practice*. London: ippr.

Soroka, S. and Wlezian, C. (2006) 'Heterogeneity and Homogeneity in Opinion-Policy Dynamics'. Paper presented at the Annual Meeting of the Elections, Public Opinion and Parties Specialist Group of the Political Studies Association, Nottingham, September.

Swank, J., Kanes, J., and Tieman, A. (2002) 'The Housing Ladder, Taxation, and Borrowing Constraints', *De Nederlandsche Bank Staff Reports*, 1–26.

Tatch, J. (2006) 'Will the Real First Time Buyers Please Stand Up?' *Housing Finance*, Q3: 1–16.

Thomas, B. and Dorling, D. (2004) *Know Your Place: Housing Wealth and Inequality in Great Britain 1980–2003 and Beyond*. London: Shelter.

Toynbee, P. (2006) 'The welfare state needs to be policed at the top as well', *Guardian*, 19 December.

Wadsworth, M. (2006) *Tax, Benefits, Pensions: Keep it Simple Part 2.* Available at <www.bowgroup.org/harriercollectionitems/Tax+Simplification.doc>.

Wilkinson, R. (2006) *The Impact of Inequality: How to Make Sick Societies Healthier.* London: Routledge.

Wilkinson, R., Kawachi, I. and Kennedy, B. (1998) 'Mortality, the Social Environment, Crime and Violence', *Sociology of Illness and Health*, 20 (5): 578–99.

Young, M. (1958) *The Rise of Meritocracy.* London: Thames & Hudson.

7
Rethinking the Welfare State

Gøsta Esping-Andersen

Introduction: how to analyse welfare futures

Previous chapters have focused on British policies and politics. But if our concern is with welfare state reform it is useful to adopt an international, comparative perspective. The experience of other countries, be it in terms of failure or success, provides us with benchmarks against which we are better informed and through which we gain perspective. This chapter sets the debates that play out in other parts of the book in this broader context, considering the role of the welfare state in responding to changes to our families, labour markets, political economy and demography.

Any rigorous discussion of welfare reform must consider four questions:

1. How are social needs and risks evolving; what are the challenges that lie ahead?
2. Which instruments are best suited to address our priorities?
3. Can such instruments deliver efficiency and equity simultaneously?
4. What, if any, egalitarian aspirations should we saddle welfare policy with?

A sound diagnosis of the challenges that lie ahead requires a suitable analytical method. First, we need to move beyond the standard, overly myopic, focus on the welfare state to a welfare regime approach. This approach focuses on the interplay of family, markets and government in the production (and consumption) of the total welfare pie and the reciprocal effects these three elements exert on each other. For example, if markets fail, this will necessitate recourse to either the family or to government. If the family is unable to provide support, the government becomes more important, and so on. Care for the frail elderly is susceptible to double failure since commercial services are expensive while families' caring ability is eroding. Also, any given welfare mix will inevitably produce consequences that influence equity and efficiency: for example, if childcare is unaffordable, prospective parents may have fewer children or the mother may decide to curtail employment. The former generates a societal child gap; the latter lowers employment levels and, hence, tax revenue and it reduces income among the families that most need it.

Second, we need to move beyond the practice of defining policy around discrete groups, be they the 'elderly', the 'working class' or the 'excluded'. This leads to very ineffective policy and it easily nurtures counter-productive equity conflicts. Adopting a 'life course perspective' permits us, in contrast, to identify the interconnectedness of citizens' risks and needs. An effective response to welfare needs requires us to identify when and how in the human life course we might best invest resources so as to minimize the need for later, costlier and often ineffectual remedial policies.

The evolving structure of risks and needs

Ongoing societal transformation is spearheaded by a set of endogenously driven structural trends. Many of these trends have been assessed in previous chapters, particularly Chapter 5, so they will be mentioned only in passing here.

Population ageing is undoubtedly the best-documented trend, affecting Britain and other European countries. There is widespread fear that this will make us financially insolvent and unleash a major generational clash. Ageing is driven by low fertility, but also by rising longevity, and the latter is occurring at an especially rapid pace, as Chapter 5 illustrated. Increasing longevity generates greater demand for caring, but most families are priced out of the elderly care market, and the stock of available family carers is disappearing. Hence, we must urgently devise a workable formula to meet future caring needs.

The second trend comes from the 'revolution' of women's roles, outlined in Chapters 9 and 11. Across Europe, as well as in Britain, we are beginning to see the spread of the Nordic model of full-time, lifelong employment as the norm for all women. This has major repercussions for labour and product markets. It also implies that families' ability to internalize caring responsibilities will diminish. The traditional welfare model that is based around the family must therefore be reconsidered. The challenge for Britain and the whole of Europe is to reconcile women's new preferences with our continued desire to form families. Failure to do so will produce either of two evils: a 'childless' society or a 'sub-employment' economy.

The third trend stems from the new family demographics (that are very much a by-product of women's changing roles). These include rising marital homogamy (marriage between partners of the same social group), postponed family formation, fertility levels that are far lower than citizens desire, increased marital instability and the proliferation of 'atypical' families – many of which are economically vulnerable.

The fourth trend stems from the emerging knowledge economy and, in particular, from the centrality of skills for citizens' life chances. The distribution of skills among today's youth will determine the quality of tomorrow's working-age population and, further ahead, the well-being of the retirement population. This gives added weight to concerns about school dropout rates and skill levels discussed in Chapters 3, 9 and 11.

Table 7.1 utilizes data from the Programme for International Student Assessment (PISA), a triennial worldwide test of 15-year-old school-children's scholastic performance, developed by the Organization for Economic Cooperation and Development (OECD); the Luxembourg Income Study (LIS), which monitors household income in 30 countries; and the OECD's social indicators database. It shows three 'warning signals': (1) the incidence of 'cognitive dysfunctionality' among youth;

Table 7.1 Early warning signals

	% below PISA minimum[a]	Literacy inequalities[b]	Lone mothers[c]	Trend in lone mothers[d]	Jobless households[c]	Trend in jobless households[d]
Denmark	15	88	14	+2	9	+2
Germany	21	109	13	+4	16	+3
Netherlands	10	85	8	0	11	−2
Spain	19	95	7	+2	13	−1
Sweden	12	96	18	+4	6	+1
UK	13	100	22	+6	13	0
US	18	101	20	−1	5	−2

Note: Trends are based on 1996–2006.
[a] Percentage of 15-year-olds who score below 400 (level 1 and below) on the PISA 2003 reading test. Falling below the 400 score implies a dysfunctional skill level.
[b] Standard deviation on PISA reading test. Note that UK data refer to PISA 2000.
[c] Per cent.
[d] Percentage points.

Sources: Jobless household data are from the OECD's social indicator database. Lone mother data are from the LIS.

(2) the degree of cognitive inequality; (3) the share of lone mother families; and (4) jobless households (the latter including, of course, also jobless single parents). It is particularly apparent that the UK has higher rates of lone parenthood than elsewhere in Europe and high rates of literacy inequalities.

Reform priorities

The contemporary debate across Europe is almost exclusively concerned with retirement reform. Yet the nature of structural transformation tells us that our first priority must be to invest far more in children. It is no secret that school success and subsequent life chances are powerfully dictated in early childhood. The ability of schools to equalize children's opportunities and to rectify a bad start is, at best, limited. The mainsprings of child outcomes lie in the family of origin. To ensure a good life, today's youth will require not only more education but also the pursuit of continuous lifelong learning. This presupposes strong cognitive skills to begin with. Considering the looming demographic imbalances that are on the horizon, we can ill-afford large skill deficits within the population. Large-scale immigration adds to the urgency of homogenizing children's learning abilities.

The second upshot is that we need to redesign family policy. Unless we 'de-familialize' welfare responsibilities we will never succeed in reconciling motherhood with employment. Low fertility is not a signal that citizens do not want children but rather that the constraints of family formation are mounting. The family remains the key institution of society and the challenge is to forge policies that support it.

Third, we need to minimize the child penalty of motherhood. This implies a reconciliation of motherhood and careers, but we are mistaken if we believe that the standard menu of 'family-friendly' policy will suffice. Some of the major obstacles are hidden in the labour market, especially with regard to job security.

Fourth, we need to redefine the nexus between working life and retirement. The most difficult challenge that ageing presents is not so much how to finance it as how to ensure equity. It is easy to envisage a retirement regime that is sustainable while equitable in intergenerational terms: raising the retirement age is one way of doing this. In the UK, there is now consensus in the policy-making community around this (see, for example, Pensions Commission 2005) – although winning public support for such a reform will be a challenge (Robinson et al. 2005). It is more difficult, and also more urgent, to design one that also delivers *intragenerational* equity – so that those working in less well-paid jobs do not lose out relative to those in better-paid jobs. The current system is, almost everywhere, inherently inequitable because life expectancy is powerfully associated with social class. I believe that the solution must be some form of basic pension guarantee and a more progressive system of financing ageing and dependency. But since this debate is so well-rehearsed in a British context, I do not dwell on it here.

The fifth, and final, upshot is that current social accounting systems fail to provide us with a clear picture of the long-term benefits of welfare reform. We need to move towards consolidated welfare regime accounts so that we can identify the long-term investment that certain social policies represent.

Supporting the revolution of women's roles

One does not need to be a feminist to realize that women are very much the vanguards of ongoing change – and that the conventional male breadwinner society is unworkable. There is good and bad news connected to women's embrace of lifelong employment. It will stimulate jobs because families will externalize servicing needs, from eating and cleaning to child and elderly care. The job multiplier that is created is potentially huge, particularly within personal and social services. It also gives women greater autonomy over their life course decisions and provides an effective bulwark against income loss due to divorce, and deprivation in old age. But it also implies greater marital instability, declining fertility and more vulnerable households, among which lone-parent families loom large.

Women's altered life course preferences are also very good news for welfare state finances. A back-of-the-envelope calculation may be illustrative of the magnitudes. If women on average earn 75 per cent of male wages and their employment rate jumps from 50 per cent to 75 per cent (from Spanish to Danish levels), their additional contribution to national income will be about 15 per cent and, at a mean taxation rate of 30 per cent, this would add 10–12 per cent to government tax revenues. As Hakim (1996) insists, women's preference sets are quite heterogeneous. A disappearing minority continues to cling to the traditional housewife ideal and another minority (certainly less than one-fifth) puts careers before family. The vast majority, in other words, embrace a dual-role preference of combining a life commitment to work with marriage and motherhood. It is to this majority that we must address policy. If the dual preferences cannot be reconciled satisfactorily we face negative-sum tradeoffs both in terms of individual welfare and the collective good. Failure to reconcile motherhood and careers will, for citizens, provoke a tradeoff between having children, on the one hand, and pursuing employment, autonomy and increasing household income, on the other. At the societal level this translates into one of two suboptimal equilibria: a childless 'low fertility equilibrium' or a 'low income, low employment equilibrium'.

We must first come to grips with the low-fertility syndrome. Since survey data repeatedly show that most adults desire at least two children, low fertility cannot simply be ascribed to 'post-materialist' tastes. The child gap is modest in some countries (the US total fertility rate is 2.1, and the Danish, Norwegian, British and French rates hover around 1.8), and substantial in most EU countries (the Dutch fertility rate is about 1.5–1.6) and, at a fertility rate of 1.2, it is huge in Southern and Eastern Europe. In some regions the fertility rate is as low as 0.8. For citizens, low fertility represents a welfare deficit – the inability to form families as desired. For society, even small differences in the fertility rate will, in the long haul, have massive consequences. Holding all else constant, a fertility rate of 1.3 will produce a population that is only 25 per cent its present size at the end of the twenty-first century. In contrast, a fertility rate of 1.9 will produce only a 15 per cent population decline. (Projections are made on the basis of a demographic forecast provided by Eurostat and agreed assumptions on key economic parameters (labour force participation rates, unemployment, productivity growth and real interest rates).) Together with ageing, population decline will lower our living standards. One typical simulation concludes that, for the EU15, ageing lowers per capita gross domestic product (GDP) by 0.4 per cent annually (McMorrow and Roeger 2003). OECD estimates are a bit higher.

There are, similarly, major costs to both citizens and society if women's pursuit of lifelong employment is frustrated. Here we must consider the rising importance of women's earnings for family welfare. Men's earnings have eroded, especially among the young and less skilled, and the conventional male breadwinner is less and less able to guarantee sufficient income. Hence, mothers' earnings are increasingly the key to child welfare. Child poverty rates decline by a factor of three or four when mothers work. Additionally, women who are compelled to interrupt their careers to care for either small children or dependent elderly family members will accumulate fewer pension credits and thus risk poverty in old age. Most importantly, rising female education, now surpassing that of males, implies that the opportunity cost of career interruptions becomes very large in terms of foregone earnings.

We need to recognize that the cost of children is rising and that, concomitantly, parenting brings important benefits that are felt by society as a whole. US research estimates that the social benefit of an average child runs to £50,000 (Preston 2004). Most importantly, the social value of children is bound to rise simply because there are so few of them. For equity reasons, therefore, redistribution in favour of children is called for. At present, even the most generous family benefit schemes, such as the Danish, cover only a fraction of added consumption spending – although they are very effective in minimizing poverty. In any case, the major – and rising – cost of children lies in the financial penalty women face due to lost earnings associated with having children and not in the added consumption outlays. This is why the most important family support is policy that reconciles motherhood and careers.

The standard 'family-friendly' package includes a neutral, individual taxation regime, maternity-cum-parental leave with job security, and subsidized childcare. Joint taxation penalizes wives' marginal earnings and is discriminatory. If paid maternity leave is too short (or too long) it discourages employment re-entry of less-educated women and fertility among highly educated women. And, as I discuss below, if mothers are compelled to return to work too soon this can harm children's development. Access to affordable quality childcare is a sine qua non for any workable future equilibrium.

It is important to understand that childcare costs are the equivalent of a regressive tax on mothers' labour supply. The typical price of full-time, full-year quality commercial care in European countries approaches £6,700, which means that many parents are effectively priced out of the market. Worse, the price structure has a strong social bias since low-income mothers are especially likely to curtail employment – and yet it is especially these mothers' earnings that are vital for family welfare. Subsidizing our way to universal coverage does not come cheap. Sweden provides what is probably the most generous system, subsidizing 85 per cent of the total cost of childcare; the Danish subsidy is somewhat less generous at 66 per cent, but is still able to support universal coverage, in part because low-income parents have access to free childcare. The total cost to the Danish exchequer comes to a little less than 2 per cent of GDP.

In Denmark, the typical mother will take leave benefits during the first year of the child's life, return to work for a brief period on a part-time basis, and then resume on a full-time basis. Research shows that the lifetime income loss is quite marginal, and this means that over the course of their lifetimes, mothers end up in practice repaying (with interest) the initial subsidy via their enhanced lifetime earnings and tax payments. In contrast, motherhood incurs major opportunity costs in most EU countries (Sigle-Rushton and Waldfogel 2004; Rake 2000). Estimates suggest that the median lifetime income penalty for a woman is around 40 per cent in Germany and the Netherlands.

Subsidizing universal childcare is not only necessary for equity – it is also doubly efficient because it enhances family income and government revenues. And quality childcare can be a very effective tool in the pursuit of equal opportunities and lower school dropout rates. If we were to rely on the market, as in the US, families' uneven purchasing power translates into uneven childcare quality, which in turn manifests itself in unequal child outcomes.

Within the EU there is now broad consensus in favour of the standard subsidy model. But we will fool ourselves if we conclude that this will suffice. The incompatibilities of motherhood lie also in the labour market and in the resilience of traditional familialism. Testifying to women's new life priorities, research shows that precarious jobs and unemployment have become major impediments for women to having children (Dolado et al. 2002; Adsera 2006). Similarly, we know that job guarantees and flexible working schedules are key to reconciliation of parenthood with labour market participation.

Feminizing the male lifecycle

Women's fertility choices depend less and less on their partner's breadwinner potential and more and more on their own career prospects. This does not mean that childbearing has become purely individualized – only that the relevance of fathers is being redefined. There is strong evidence that low fertility is a manifestation of the incongruence between women's new life course preferences, on one hand, and lingering traditional gender roles, on the other (McDonald 2000). Women have adopted a more 'masculine' life course while men have not really proceeded to 'feminize' theirs. True, men's contribution in the domestic sphere is increasing, but as Chapter 11 shows, the gender gap remains large. Men may also experience more career interruptions, but this is largely due to unwanted unemployment.

Gendered life course asymmetries are obviously linked to incentive structures and constraints. The gender pay gap remains substantial, and the typical spousal age gap also implies that the male's opportunity cost of dedicating time to home production will be relatively greater. And to the extent that women select themselves into family-friendly jobs while men are more likely to work in the hard economy, the career penalties of 'feminizing' the male life course will be substantial. Gendered life course asymmetries therefore present a major obstacle to women's quest for autonomy. How might we encourage men to interrupt careers and share the domestic burden? One answer would be to design parental leave so that fathers are encouraged to take it, as Hughes and Cooke argue in Chapter 11. This would require not only full income compensation but also that a couple's lifetime earnings are not harmed as a result of men taking time out. The gender wage gap is a barrier to this.

The dilemma is aggravated because men's contribution to domestic work is socially skewed towards the highly educated. This undoubtedly has something to do with growing marital homogamy, especially at the top of the social pyramid. Highly educated women have substantial bargaining power in the partnership. We face, in other words, not simply a gender issue but a broader question of social inequalities. Marital homogamy contributes to widening household income and work inequalities.

The problem is that highly educated dual-earner couples have the means to embrace greater gender equality in domestic and work life; they are also far better positioned to reconcile careers and parenthood. At the other end of the social spectrum, low-educated women are more likely to interrupt or end employment when children or, later, caring obligations to elderly family members arrive; and both partners in such households are concomitantly more likely to face unemployment and precarious working lives. Work-poor households are concentrated at the bottom end of society. The upshot is a growing gap in couples' potential labour supply and hence earning power. When we add to this the proliferation of lone-parent families we see the potential for an increasingly polarized household welfare scenario.

We can remedy this the old-fashioned way, by more redistribution in favour of low-income households. But a more effective policy would be to equalize the earnings potential of households by removing the barriers to labour supply that those at the bottom face. A major barrier lies in the cost of accessing child and adult care and this can be resolved via a sliding subsidy scale.

A more formidable barrier lies in the nature of low-skilled jobs in our new economy. Uneven productivity growth in services – as discussed in Chapter 9 – means that low-end service jobs will offer low wages or disappear. Given that families increasingly need two incomes, and that marital homogamy is increasing, low individual wages will probably go hand in hand with low family income. In the medium term, we cannot ignore the fact that a substantial share of tomorrow's workforce is already handicapped by their lack of skills. While lifelong learning policies can go some way to addressing skills deficiencies, it will be difficult to avoid some form of income support unless we are willing to accept rising household welfare inequalities.

Investing in children

Industrialized societies are swimming upstream in terms of securing a good life for children. The knowledge economy requires more and more competences, families are increasingly fragile, and economic inequalities are widening. This means that parents' ability to invest in their children's futures is also becoming more unequal.

So children face an increasingly hostile environment within which they must maximize their life chances. The knowledge economy is raising the human capital requirements needed to ensure good jobs. Of course, not all jobs require strong skills and we will inevitably see substantial growth in low-end service jobs catering to families' needs. Unless in the public sector, the latter are likely to be low paid and precarious simply because they tend to be low value added and labour intensive. There are good arguments in favour of such low-end service jobs. They provide a large pool of easy-entry jobs for youth and immigrants with few skills or experience. But from a life chances perspective this labour market may prove problematic if it cultivates a new 'post-industrial proletariat', condemned to lifelong low-wage employment. Strong human capital is the main prerequisite for mobility.

The question is, what skills? Formal educational credentials are, as always, a sine qua non, especially for early career moves. As mentioned, we might consider completed upper secondary equivalent education as a bottom-line requirement. But other human capital dimensions are gaining in saliency. As Chapter 5 outlines, many employers look for social skills, initiative and emotional intelligence. But virtually by definition it is cognitive skills that reign supreme. First, cognitive abilities and the motivation to learn are the preconditions for successful schooling. Second, knowledge-intensive production assumes that people have the skills to understand, interpret and apply information. Third, lifelong learning is becoming the norm, but it depends on a good educational base and on strong cognitive abilities. The economic returns to cognitive skills are rising strongly (Farkas 2003).

The evidence that key competences such as cognitive skills, discipline and learning motivation are developed very early in life must guide policy-making on this front (Karoly 1998). This helps explain why a half-century of educational expansion has done very little to diminish the impact of social origins on opportunities: the first years of childhood are decisive and this is usually when children are most 'privatized'. Inequalities in parental stimulus are transmitted to the school experience and schools are typically poorly equipped to rectify differentials in learning abilities. How should we then invest in our children's life chances?

There are two sides to this coin: one has to do with raising the level of skills overall, and the other has to do with ensuring more equality of opportunity. At this point it is important to note that equalization need not lower the common denominator. To illustrate, some of the best PISA performers (like Finland and Sweden) also boast very modest differentials in terms of cognitive abilities or school completion. For efficiency reasons we cannot permit ourselves to squander our human capital potential.

Ignoring genetic transmission, child outcomes are primarily the result of parental income and 'cultural' status. Even if education is free of charge, parental income matters greatly for health and schooling. In most countries, quality preschool enrolment depends on household income. Well-off parents can give their children an edge by investing in private schools or in extra-curricular activities. At the other end, poverty and economic insecurity can have very adverse consequences. There is ample evidence that parental unemployment, lone motherhood and low income are harmful for an array of outcomes, such as sociability, studying, health and delinquency. US research shows that poor children will have two years' less schooling than the better-off (Kamerman et al. 2003). Similar but less dramatic findings also exist for Europe. The Nederlandse Gezinsraad shows that up to 15 per cent of children from long-term low-income families manifest poor developmental outcomes (Nederlandse Gezinsraad 2001). Worse, the effects persist through children's lives. As adults, the same children are very likely to become poor parents. Children of lone mothers end up with incomes that are just 66 per cent of those of two-parented children in the Netherlands and the UK; in the US the penalty is even greater (Kamerman et al. 2003). Here we are, once again, swimming upstream because child poverty, lone parenthood and, in some countries, workless households are on the rise. Despite a booming economy, Dutch child poverty has doubled in the past two decades, reaching 10 per cent in 2006 (UNICEF 2006).

We must take note that the income effect is not linear. The really harmful effects begin to spiral when economic conditions are very poor, in particular when children are small. Fortunately, it is both simple and cheap to combat the poverty problem. First, it will diminish simply when more mothers work. Second, generous family benefits are very effective in limiting poverty. Indeed, I believe, the added cost to the exchequer of abolishing child poverty altogether would be surprisingly modest. Adopting 50 per cent of median income as the poverty line, the complete elimination of child poverty would in a typical EU country amount to 0.2–0.3 per cent of GDP. In the Nordic countries where virtually all mothers work, the price tag is less than 0.05 per cent.

On balance, however, the income effect is probably less salient than the 'culture effect'. Analyses of the PISA data show that children's cognitive performance (at age 15) is less connected to income than to families' 'cultural' resources. There are three types of culture effects that operate. One is related to Bourdieu's idea of class reproduction in terms of transmitting the proper 'middle-class' cultural baggage to their children. A second has to do with parents' education, which can be decisive for making the best school choices on behalf of their offspring. Low-educated parents suffer from information failure and lack the means to navigate their children through the education system. And a third refers to the family's learning environment, parental stimulation and nurturing. Analyses of the PISA data show that the number of books in the home is one of the single most powerful predictors of children's learning abilities. I use the Dutch PISA data to illustrate the point: the reading ability of children from families with ten or more books is 9 per cent higher than those with fewer books in the home (estimated from regression analysis of the Dutch PISA files). This is examined in more detail in Butler and Margo in Chapter 15.

Inequalities on all three dimensions are huge, with immigrant and lone-parent families especially disadvantaged. The inequalities are particularly large in countries – like Italy or Spain – where a substantial share of the parental generation had only minimal education. Young women's educational attainment is rising rapidly and, hence, part of the problem will gradually diminish. But large-scale immigration constitutes a worrisome counter-tendency. Even in Sweden, where efforts to rectify the immigrant disadvantage have been extraordinary, we find that the probability of school failure among immigrant children is five times higher than for natives. In the Netherlands, immigrant children score more than 10 per cent lower on PISA's problem-solving tests (which are less likely to be immigrant-biased than literacy tests).

The spread of lone parenthood represents a second problematic trend. Coleman (1988) reports that school dropout rates are 30 per cent higher among children living with a solo parent. But the negative effect largely disappears when we control for income and employment (Biblarz and Raftery 1999). Hence, encouraging more employment among lone parents should constitute an effective counter-measure. Research reviewed in Chapter 11, however, warns us that outcomes for lone-parent children are especially threatened unless they benefit from high-quality childcare (Bernal and Keane 2005).

At first glance it would appear impossible to remedy cultural deficits through policy. How can we compel parents to read to their children or to take an active interest in their homework? The good news is that compulsion is unnecessary because early childcare programmes that help reconcile motherhood and careers can be a very effective tool for equalizing children's cognitive stimulus and school preparedness. There are three major findings from evaluation research. One is that external care during the child's first year can be harmful. But, second, from year one onwards, childcare participation has very positive effects on child outcomes, particularly for underprivileged children (Karoly 1998; Waldvogel 2002; Kamerman et al. 2003). The third is that 'neighbourhood' and school effects matter far less than family effects (Brooks-Gunn et al. 1997; Farkas 2003). In other words, the thrust of policy must be directed more at the family than at the education system. The key is to ensure optimal parent–child interaction during the first year, and to secure a strong pedagogical quality of child rearing thereafter.

Indirectly, evidence from the Nordic countries confirms the vast potential of high quality, universal early childcare. Denmark, Norway and Sweden demonstrate a substantial (and unique) decline in the effect of parents' education, 'cultural capital' and socio-economic status on children's educational attainment. Most strikingly, this decline coincides almost perfectly with the universality of childcare for the under-3s – namely for children born in the 1970s onwards. The equalizing effect is especially notable for children from disadvantaged homes, in which parents tend to have very low levels of educational achievement. In Denmark, the chance of completing upper secondary education has doubled for the youngest cohorts, and in Norway it has tripled (Esping-Andersen 2004).

There are two potential problems with the childcare strategy. One is that mothers' employment may cause children to suffer from inadequate parental interaction. The evidence suggests that such harmful effects disappear if children remain with the mother during their first year (Ruhm 2004; Waldfogel 2002; Gregg et al. 2005), if mothers have quality jobs and if childcare quality is high. These are three difficult 'ifs'. The first can be solved by providing adequate parental leave entitlements, as set out in Chapter 11. In the Netherlands, only the first 16 weeks of leave are fully compensated, while the remaining 24 weeks provide a very low benefit. This means that career-minded women rush back to work very soon (60 per cent of Dutch mothers return to work within six months of giving birth), but also that a substantial number (in excess of 25 per cent) disappear from the workforce (Gustafsson and Kenjoh 2004). Extending parental leave to one year is not merely a concession to women – or a means to get fathers involved – but also an investment in superior child outcomes. And investing in quality childcare will largely pay for itself. The remaining dilemma we face is how to ensure that mothers are employed in quality jobs – a question that falls beyond the scope of this chapter.

Tomorrow's society will inevitably be far more ethnically and culturally heterogeneous, and we face a major challenge in terms of how to ensure that immigrant children do not fall behind in the knowledge economy. There is a substantial native-immigrant gap not only in reading literacy but also in mathematical and problem solving abilities. The 10 per cent performance gap I found for the Netherlands jumps to 15 per cent in Germany. It is undoubtedly feasible to narrow the gap – in France, Denmark and Sweden it is less than 5 per cent.

This is one case where 'neighbourhood' effects matter greatly. Here we encounter a very complex interaction process: an oppositional enclave culture is especially likely to evolve if the minority group is physically concentrated and sees itself as systematically distanced from the economic opportunity structure. In this environment minority groups will adopt performance criteria and behavioural norms that are in opposition to the mainstream, emphasizing 'street-smartness' rather than study, and this can produce self-reinforcing spirals of marginalization, oppositional culture, and underachievement (for an overview, see Portes and Rumbaut 2001).

Enrolment in quality childcare would no doubt help, but is surely an inadequate answer since disadvantages are compounded by residential segregation and economic exclusion. We can diminish segregation by more residential dispersion – a policy that has met with substantial success in Chicago – or by limiting minority concentration in the school system, perhaps using positive bussing. One thing is clear: immigration is here to stay and if we do not take urgent steps to combat excessive segregation and scholastic underperformance now, we will find ourselves with a major social divide tomorrow.

A new welfare mix?

A paradox of our times is that family well-being presupposes 'de-familialization'. This obviously does not imply coercive intrusion in family life.

The essence is to give families realistic options. Nor does it automatically threaten the quality of family life, more likely to the contrary. What, then, are the relative merits of markets or the state in terms of substituting for familialism and meeting the challenges ahead? The debate on privatization frequently pits opponents, who insist that all private is bad, against supporters, who maintain that all public is bad. The truth lies in the details, not in ideology. The menu of privatization is ample, ranging from a purely commercial regime to quasi-market principles in public provision. In between exist non-profit, regulated or subsidized private providers, voucher schemes, and so forth.

The first point to stress is that, macro-economically speaking, total welfare costs will probably not change much however we combine markets and state. Denmark and the US occupy the polar ends in terms of public spending but end up virtually identical when we examine total net social outlays (for details, see below). If the market is truly competitive we may expect a quality dividend and, in some cases, it is demonstrably possible to achieve cost savings via private provision. For example, home help services staffed by public functionaries are inevitably more expensive than if provided by contracted personnel. But in most private provision of welfare the per unit service cost will normally exceed the public sector equivalent. This is partially due to the profit margin but mainly to higher transaction costs (such as marketing or billing administration). If commercial welfare providers are pricier, this does not automatically imply that government provision is the only alternative. Religious welfare organizations play a massive role in some countries' welfare delivery. In Denmark a third of childcare centres are established and run by parental associations, and in Sweden one in ten schools are independent. The real issues we should address are the distributional and behavioural second-order effects of any given mix.

Unless subsidized (say by tax concessions or by vouchers), commercial social services are typically priced out of the market for most households below the median income. The same goes for private health insurance and retirement plans. A tragic example is health insurance in the US: in excess of 40 million Americans have no coverage whatsoever. The important point here is that we must always measure any efficiency gains against equity. As a rule of thumb, the equity price we pay will almost invariably overshadow any efficiency gain.

In terms of second-order behavioural effects, there are three that especially merit attention. One refers to incentive effects – primarily the incentives to save and to work. Although unambiguous empirical findings are hard to come by, it is a plausible argument that a primarily publicly financed welfare model implies a level of taxation that will distort work incentives and reduce household savings. Vice versa, we should expect more savings and labour supply if citizens need to personally finance their welfare. Until we have credible estimates of the relative savings and labour supply effects of either alternative for each and every welfare item we will be in no position to make an educated choice one way or another.

A second has to do with information deficits and asymmetries. Competition may be very positive for quality but many areas of policy involve substantial expertise that citizens are unlikely to possess. Very few are able to choose between competing heart transplant offers, and even selecting between alternative schools may pose major difficulties. Asymmetries arise because customers become captive to the sellers' expertise. Citizens' ability to inform themselves is also highly unevenly distributed. The low educated can be severely disadvantaged in a competitive market. The high risk may be additionally disadvantaged if competitive markets lead to client creaming and exclusion.

The third refers to social externalities. If a large segment of the population is priced out of welfare services this may have non-trivial societal repercussions. For example, if low-income parents are unable to afford quality childcare, they may respond by placing children in substandard care (parked in front of a TV, for example) or by withdrawing the mother from employment. The former is undeniably harmful to children. The latter reduces aggregate employment (and tax revenues) and raises child poverty (that necessitates public income transfers). Alternatively, if childcare is inaccessible the birthrate may suffer.

My argument is that we must factor all these second-order and distributional effects into our accounting practices. And we must compel the advocates and enemies of either preference to furnish us such a complete kind of social accounting.

The strongest case in favour of privatization is that it enhances freedom of choice and competition; either may raise quality. The weakness of this position is, however, that the implementation of 'quasi-market' principles in public (or publicly regulated) services may yield the same benefits. Julian Le Grand makes a very persuasive argument that greater choice is fully compatible with egalitarian goals, too, if competing providers are adequately regulated and consumers are adequately informed (Le Grand 2003). Empirical research is replete with good and bad practice from which we can learn a lot. If providers are permitted to cream the best risks or to set fees as they like, the likely result is welfare segregation. The question boils down to a consistent and effective regulatory framework.

Financing the future

The welfare equilibrium that I am promoting will certainly not come cheap. The main items in my design will require an additional spending burden that, realistically speaking, may run to 10–12 per cent of GDP. (This is assuming that pension spending will increase by 5 per cent of GDP, that full coverage of dependency is attained (another 3–4 per cent of GDP), and that we reach universal (quality) childcare (another 2 per cent of GDP). Rising healthcare needs will require at least another 1 per cent of GDP. In addition, we should include added costs of extending parental leaves and providing a guarantee against child and pensioner poverty that, combined, might run to yet another 1 per cent of GDP.)

The real problem we face is that current accounting practices are simply not up to the task of furnishing the kinds of numbers we really need. We need to revamp our social accounting systems so that we can think more clearly about substance. I have already emphasized the need for accounting that explicitly factors in second-order effects. There are two additional changes that need to be considered.

Investment accounts

As I suggested earlier, expenditure on childcare will, in a dynamic perspective, pay for itself. It would accordingly be helpful to distinguish long-term investments from current consumption, and then be able to estimate the real returns. This is no mean challenge, considering that existing social accounts (which basically date back to the mid-twentieth century) consider public social spending as purely consumption expenditure. There are good reasons why we might promote a separation of current and capital accounts in our welfare state, just as we do in private companies.

The post-war welfare state was exceedingly income-transfer (and especially pension) biased, so the need to distinguish social investment from consumption was minor. It becomes a more urgent question when spending must be redirected in favour of proactive policies: servicing families, building lifelong learning opportunities, or active labour market programmes. It is not easy to separate social investment from consumption. It is only modest progress to distinguish 'passive' from 'active' policies. It would appear obvious to classify income support as a passive 'consumption' that yields few economic returns. Yet things get complicated when we consider that transfers to families may enhance child outcomes. Or take programmes in support of working mothers: once again, simply the fact that they work means sharply reduced child poverty, an implicit job-multiplier and additional tax revenue to governments. Care for the elderly is likewise Janus-headed: taking care of the frail may not constitute an investment in our future productive potential, and yet failure to do so implies that many women must reduce their labour supply.

Besides education and training, there are a number of social policies that are easy to identify as investments in individual productivity and collective wealth creation. Most generically, all spending towards child welfare has a potential payoff. Cash benefits to families with children create financial security and prevent child poverty, crucial for child outcomes. Early preschool programmes and universal, quality childcare have a powerful equalizing effect on children's learning abilities.

It is more complicated to pinpoint precisely the investment component of many income maintenance programmes for working-age households – such as unemployment benefits. The reasoning is more circumscribed, but it has for long been recognized that strong welfare guarantees stimulate greater risk-taking during the working life. Also, workers will arguably be less resistant to change if their welfare is assured in the event of redundancies. Generally speaking, flexible and dynamic labour markets need to be offset with greater social security provision.

This is not intended to be an exhaustive overview of how to set up a system of social investment accounts, but rather simply to pinpoint the need to revise existing practice.

Welfare regime accounts

Our social accounts are too myopically limited to public expenditures. The reawakened international interest in the Nordic model is a case in point: while admired, it is broadly rejected for its huge spending and taxation requirements. In 2001, gross public social expenditures were 34 per cent of GDP in Denmark and 35 per cent in Sweden (based on OECD estimates). To most accountants this compares unfavourably with the UK's 25 per cent.

The first problem is that these numbers are meaningless because they fail to consider that much spending is taxed back immediately – particularly in big-spending welfare states like the Nordic countries. They also ignore hidden tax expenditures in the form of tax deductions and subsidies for social purposes. Tax subsidies loom large in 'residual' type welfare models. The second problem is that meagre public provision will stimulate market alternatives – in particular if mandated or given tax subsidies. Private (net) social spending is predictably marginal in Scandinavia (only 0.8 per cent of GDP in Denmark) but substantial in the UK (4 per cent). The Netherlands has experienced very rapid growth in private welfare in tandem with major cutbacks in public programmes. Studies that focus on pension spending come to similar conclusions: there is basic convergence in total GDP use for pensions however we mix markets and government. Table 7.2 provides an overview.

Table 7.2   Apparent and real social expenditure as a percentage of GDP

	Denmark	Sweden	Germany	Netherlands	US
Gross *public* social spending	34	35	31	24	16
Net *public* social spending	26	28	28	20	17
Net *private* social spending	1	3	3	5	11
Total net social spending	27	31	31	25	28

Source: Adema and Ladaique (2005: Table 6).

One lesson is that some forbiddingly heavy spenders, like Denmark, in reality are quite lean. So the important issue is not so much the overall burden but rather from whose pocket the money is drawn, and the welfare outcomes for any given level of expenditure. In Denmark and Sweden almost all the money is taken out of the taxpayers' pocket; in the Netherlands and the US, a lot is taken out of the consumers' pocket. At the end of the day the average Dane, Dutch and American ends up paying pretty much the same. But clearly the non-average Dane, Dutch and American will not *receive* the same.

Not all citizens are average and this is where total welfare regime accounting becomes relevant. If a large chunk of the money must come from the consumers' pocket, access to welfare will hinge on our spending power. To cite a British example, in the late 1990s the Blair government embarked on a massive expansion of childcare, establishing within a few years 600,000 new places. The policy was based on commercial centres and, since the public subsidy was modest, families had difficulty accessing the service. As a result, almost half were subsequently closed due to 'lack of demand'.

The added spending burden of 10–12 per cent of GDP must be considered as a realistic scenario. The very simple point that needs to be driven home is that if we do want to realize such welfare goals, this added financial burden is inevitable however we combine private and public provision. And if the added spending is not forthcoming we should expect major welfare lacunae.

The added financial burden will inevitably vary across the EU. The Scandinavian countries are far better positioned to meet future spending requirements than most other EU nations. In short, we need a consolidated system of accounts that allows us to identify real (and not misleading) public spending, and examine the joint expenditure trends in markets and government alike. It is total GDP use that matters. The value of such an approach is that it puts us in a far better position to assess the distributional aspects of our social model. The relevant question is not whether we can afford more welfare spending, because this will happen anyway. The really relevant question has to do with who are the winners and losers, and what may be the second-order consequences when we opt for a particular public–private mix. If we could also develop a credible system of measuring the implicit costs of non-monetarized family servicing, we would be able to approach a genuine system of welfare regime accounts.

Conclusion

This chapter has focused on what I believe to be the three (plus one) greatest challenges to our welfare model. First, since life chances are so overdetermined by what happens in childhood, the flagship of our strategy must be a comprehensive child investment strategy that combines a strong accent on early childhood development with a deliberate and explicit commitment to equality of opportunities. Second, since the future of our families depends on how well we resolve the dilemmas associated with women's new life course preferences, it is impossible to imagine a positive equilibrium without an effective reconciliation of parenthood and careers. But the battle will only be half-won if we do not accompany standard reconciliation policies with a strategy designed to promote a 'feminization' of the male lifecycle. Women – at least in Scandinavia and the US – are reaching the limits of 'masculinization' of their lifecycle and it is increasingly this which provokes new disequilibria. And, third, since the welfare of tomorrow's elderly depends crucially on the quality of their childhood and subsequent careers, our response to the ageing challenge should 'begin with babies' and focus especially on minimizing life chance inequalities. The 'plus one' challenge lies in the development of a superior system of social accounting and may arguably be our first priority.

The quality of jobs can be a major stumbling block for both our child investment and parenthood–career reconciliation strategy. We can promote more equality of opportunities in early childhood, but what if opportunities are not there when young people reach adulthood? Likewise, even the most brilliant reconciliation policy may fail if women's job conditions contradict motherhood. And, likewise again, we will have to expect widespread old age poverty in the future if a substantial proportion of tomorrow's workers find themselves trapped in a life of bad jobs. Suffice to say that we should most realistically assume the following scenarios: first, that labour markets will become more flexible, in particular in terms of wage setting and job protection; second, that post-industrial job growth is highly biased in favour of 'good' jobs (that require skills); third, that flexibilization plus the continuous rise in female employment plus ageing will nurture the growth of a sizable amount of low-end (low-skill) servicing jobs; and fourth, that income inequalities are likely to increase.

These trends, in other words, give mixed signals. Greater flexibility and widespread low-wage employment suggest a scenario of overall insecurity for possibly sizeable population groups. It is unrealistic, therefore, to believe that the importance of traditional 'passive' income maintenance will disappear. Indeed, I would consider it a sine qua non that we build a genuine unconditional anti-poverty guarantee for families with children and the elderly alike.

Postscript: what about equality?

My treatment has emphasized equity in the sense of fairness, not equality. Should we also pursue an egalitarian agenda? If so, which? Academics and policy-makers routinely equate the welfare state with egalitarianism while, paradoxically, this is less so in the general public – for whom the welfare state represents security. In the very good old days the egalitarian promise was often framed in terms of the class divide. In the post-war era it became a more diffuse and plural idea, embracing meritocracy and equal opportunities but also a redistributive here-and-now equality of condition. Do we need a new egalitarian commitment for the twenty-first century?

We must first recognize that ongoing structural change promotes substantial inequality, be it from widening earnings differentials, marital homogamy, immigration, or the evolving household structure. There are also counter-tendencies buried within these same trends. The gender pay gap is narrowing and female employment is becoming more universal. Household income inequalities can be held at bay when less-educated women embrace the lifetime employment model. Such counter-movements are important but are, in any case, unlikely to turn the basic tide of inequality around.

There are reasons why we should not be especially alarmed by rising here-and-now inequality. Low wages or bad jobs are not per se problematic if they are transitory experiences. Our poverty headcounts are misleading if many of the poor are simply youth and students. The real question has to do with mobility, that is, with life chances. When we measure inequality in terms of lifetime incomes we find that there is far less inequality than we were led to believe. To illustrate, the Danish Gini coefficient is reduced to half when calculated on the basis of lifetime incomes but, at the same time, we discover that 92 per cent of Danes have been poor at one or another moment in their lives!

But there are also reasons for alarm. There is substantial evidence that mobility is negatively correlated with the overall level of income inequality. The notion that inequality nurtures more mobility is simply wrong. Most comparative data show that there is substantially less mobility in the US than in many if not most European countries. Worse, the opportunity structure is adversely affected by prevailing levels of inequality. If there are strong inequalities in the parental generation this implies more unequal abilities to invest in the life chances of children.

All this considered, there are at least two fundamental principles that must underpin any future egalitarian policy: first, it should emphasize life chances rather than here-and-now redistribution; second, it should centre on those mechanisms that lie at the heart of social inheritance and unequal opportunities. We are well-placed to identify where our egalitarian efforts should focus. We must prioritize child investments and family welfare not because children are sweet and innocent but because the key triggers of life chances lie in childhood conditions. No policy will solve all problems, but guaranteeing a strong start to all children is one that will surely pay off. It is for this reason that we should consider an income guarantee and also access to quality childcare for all families with children. Very committed life chance egalitarians might go further and advocate affirmative action for disadvantaged children and mobility guarantees to adults who find themselves entrapped in a persistently poor welfare position.

In the end we should expect that an unchecked rise in income inequality will worsen the opportunity structure, and this implies that it does, indeed, need to be checked. Government redistribution via taxes and spending is demonstrably a very effective instrument, especially if, as I advocate, we sharpen the progressiveness of old-age financing and favour universalistic principles of entitlement.

To wrap it all up, Table 7.3 presents an idea of the distance we need to travel in order to come anywhere close to the kind of improvement I advocate. To define the target towards which we can move, I first set as our benchmark as zero child and pensioner poverty, and for other indicators I use the best performance that can be currently identified within the EU15.

Table 7.3 The distance to travel to reach main objectives: select EU countries, 2006 data

	Sweden	Germany	Netherlands	UK	Spain
	(A minus sign identifies shortfall in reaching objective)				
Poverty targets:					
Zero % child poverty	−4	−9	−10	−15	−16
Zero % pensioner poverty	−7	−10	−2	−21	−23
Invest in children:					
Minimize school dropout[a]	0	−4	−7	−9	−23
Maximize average cognitive level[b]	−45	−65	−33	−71	−96
Maximize cognitive homogeneity[c]	−13	−15	−12	−20	−1
Reconciliation					
Two children on average[d]	−0.3	−0.5	−0.4	−0.2	−0.8
Employment of mothers with small children[e]	0	−23	−8	−19	−32
Equality of opportunity					
Impact of ascriptive factors on child outcomes[f]	−6	−15	−10	−8	−7

Notes: [a] Sweden and Denmark, with a dropout rate of 8 per cent among 18–24-year-olds is the reference. Dropout is defined as no education beyond lower secondary level.
[b] Cognitive score levels refer to PISA's maths tests, and Flemish-speaking Belgium is the reference with the highest EU mean score of 562.
[c] Cognitive homogeneity is derived from the standard deviation (SD). Iceland with the lowest SD of 73 is the reference.
[d] Target here is defined as a total fertility rate (TFR) = 2.0.
[e] Denmark (and Sweden) is the reference with a 73 per cent employment rate.
[f] Regression estimated combined effects of parents' socio-economic status and cultural capital (number of books in the home) on PISA 2000 reading scores. I include a control for immigrant status since the relative size of the immigrant population differs substantially across nations. Finland is again the reference because it exhibits the OECD's lowest family effects. The numbers reflect how much a country must reduce the percentage variance explained by the family effects to reach the Finnish minimum (R-squared = .075).

Note

This chapter is an edited and revised version of a paper originally prepared for the Dutch Social Insurance Bank, December 2005.

References

Adema, W. and Ledaique, M. (2005) *Net Social Expenditure, 2005 Edition*. OECD Social, Employment and Migration Working Paper No. 29. Paris: OECD.

Adsera, A. (2006) 'An Economic Analysis of the Gap Between Desired and Actual Fertility: The Case of Spain, *Review of Economics of the Household*, 4 (1): 75.

Bernal, R. and Keane, M. (2005) 'Maternal Time, Child Care and Child Cognitive Development. The Case of Single Mothers'. Unpublished paper, Department of Economics, Northwestern University, 15 September.

Biblarz, T. and Raftery, A. (1999) 'Family Structure, Educational Attainment and Socioeconomic Success', *American Journal of Sociology*, 105 (2): 321–65.

Brooks-Gunn, J., Duncan, G. and Aber, L. (1997) *Neighborhood Poverty. Context and Consequences for Children. Volume 1*. New York: Russell Sage.

Coleman, J. (1988) 'Social Capital in the Creation of Human Capital', *American Journal of Sociology*, 94: 95–121.

Dolado, J. J., Garcia-Serrano, C., Jimeno, J. F. (2002) 'Drawing Lessons from the Boom of Temporary Jobs in Spain', *Economic Journal*, 112 (480). Oxford: Blackwell.

Esping-Andersen, G. (2004) 'Untying the Gordian Knot of Social Inheritance', *Research in Social Mobility and Stratification*, 21.

Farkas, G. (2003) 'Cognitive Skills and Noncognitive Traits and Behaviours in Stratification Process', *Annual Review of Sociology*, 29: 541–62.

Gregg, P., Washbrook, E., Propper, C. and Burgess, S. (2005) 'The Effects of Mothers' Return to Work Decision on Child Development in the UK', *Economic Journal*, 115: 48–80.

Gustafsson, S. and Kenjoh, E. (2004) 'New Evidence on Work Among New Mothers'. *Transfer. European Review of Labour and Research*, 10: 34–47.

Hakim, K. (1996) *Key Issues in Women's Work*. London: Athlone.

Kamerman, S., Neuman, M., Waldvogel, J. and Brooks-Gunn, J. (2003) *Social Policies, Family Types and Child Outcomes in Selected OECD Countries*. OECD Social, Employment and Migration Working Paper No. 6. Paris: OECD.

Karoly, L. (1998) *Investing in our Children*. Santa Monica: Rand Corporation.

Le Grand, J. (2003) *Choice: What Role Can it Play in Helping Local Public Services Evolve?* (e-pamphlet). New Local Government Network. Available at <www.nlgn.org.uk/pdfs/upload/Choice%20and%20local%20services.pdf>.

McDonald, P. (2000) 'The Tool-box of Public Policies to Impact on Fertility'. Paper presented at the European Observatory on Family, Seville, 15–16 September.

McMorrow, K. and Roeger, W. (2003) *Economic and Financial Market Consequences of Ageing Populations*. European Economy Economic Papers No. 182. Brussels: European Commission.

Nederlandse Gezinsraad (2001) *Gezin: Beeld en werkelijkheid* (Family: Image and reality). Den Haag: Nederlandse Gezinsraad.

Pensions Commission (2005) *A New Settlement for the Twenty-First Century: Second Report*. London: TSO. Available at <www.pensionscommission.org.uk/publications/2005/annrep/main-report.pdf>.

PISA (2000) Online data available at <http://pisaweb.acer.edu.au/oecd/oecd_pisa_data.html>.

PISA (2003) Online data available at <http://pisaweb.acer.edu.au/oecd/oecd_pisa_data.html>.

Portes, A. and Rumbaut, R. (2001) 'Conclusion: The Forging of a New America', in R. Rumbaut and A. Portes (eds), *Ethnicities: Children of Immigrants in America*. Berkeley: University of California Press.

Preston, P. (2004) 'The Value of Children', in D. Moynihan, T. Smeeding and L. Rainwater (eds), *The Future of the Family*. New York: Russell Sage.

Rake, K. (2000) *Women's Incomes over the Lifetime*. London: Cabinet Office.

Robinson, P., Gosling, T., and Lewis, M. (2005) *Working Later: Raising the Effective Age of Retirement*. London: ippr.

Ruhm, C. (2004) 'Parental Employment and Child Cognitive Development', *Journal of Human Resources*, 34: 155–92.

Sigle-Rushton, W. and Waldfogel, J. (2004) *Family Gaps in Income: A Cross National Comparison*. Maxwell School of Citizenship and Public Affairs Working Paper No. 382. Syracuse, NJ: Center for Policy Research.

Waldfogel, J. (2002) 'Child Care, Women's Employment and Child Outcomes', *Journal of Population Economics*, 15: 527–48.

UNICEF (2006) *Child Poverty in Rich Countries 2005*. Florence: UNICEF Innocenti Research Centre.

8
Making Public Services Work for Social Justice

Richard Brooks

Public services are at a crossroads, and at this crossroads there are three possible new roads to travel. The road straight ahead combines stable and relatively high levels of public funding in the core services, high ambitions set and regulated by central government, and user choice and provider markets to create incentives for performance improvement. Another road involves a more explicit recognition of the limits of the state, puts more weight on individual responsibility, private funding and voluntary provision, but shares with the status quo a focus on market-based mechanisms to improve service performance. The third road, the one that progressives should want to travel, has a different character. It recognizes the need for a new set of relationships, between citizens and the state, between services and their users, between government and the public service workforce, and between central and local governance.

Why do the public services matter?

What should count as 'public services' was one of the key political battlegrounds in the UK during the twentieth century, and is likely to remain so for the foreseeable future. Economists and social scientists have attempted to impose a degree of order and rigour on where and how markets fail, and thus where and how government should intervene; for example, via the concepts of public goods (Samuelson 1954), merit goods (Musgrave 1959), externalities (Buchanan and Stubblebine 1962) and information asymmetries (Arrow and Lind 1970). The public itself works with a softer and more intuitive understanding: for them a public service is a vitally important publicly funded service, on which they or people close to them rely, and with which they have regular and face-to-face contact for extensive periods of their lives. This makes schools, the NHS and the police the 'paradigmatic' public services, the ones by which the others are defined, compared and understood. Similarly, there is a non-technical, political condition of a service being public: voters must be prepared to politically support its continued public funding.

Health, education and public safety are not services in themselves, they are the outcomes that the national health service, schools and colleges, the police and a multitude of other public and private organizations seek to achieve. Outcomes such as increased life expectancy, improved skill levels or lower crime rates are rarely determined entirely by the services themselves; rather, they result from the interaction of individuals within a complex social and economic context, where public services are just one of the major influences. Nonetheless, it is the importance of these outcomes that is the fundamental motivation of our concern for public services.

In addition to making the best contribution to outcomes, we also want public services to perform at a high level of quality, often regardless of the impact of this on the final result. Thus in addition to our hospitals making us healthy, we also expect to be treated with care and respect by the staff – we want services that 'look us in the eye'. Public services also need to generate trust and legitimacy (Kelly and Muers 2002). If a local community does not support its police force, then community safety is likely to suffer, and if people do not believe the advice of health professionals then their health is likely to be worse as a result.

Progressives tend to attach a particular importance to social justice, seeing this, as the political philosopher John Rawls put it, as 'the first virtue' of social institutions. Much of the value that they attach to public services derives from their belief that these have an important contribution to make to promoting social justice. The political theorist David Miller argued that social justice demands that social 'goods and bads' should be distributed in accordance with four principles: equal citizenship, the social minimum, equality of opportunity and a fair distribution (Miller 2005).

It is the central role of public services in achieving social justice that makes them so important to progressives. To start with, public services both make equal citizenship possible, by maintaining its basic institutions such as elections, government and courts, and facilitate the degree of its actual enjoyment. Literacy and numeracy equip us to enjoy the liberties that come with being a citizen, and citizen education helps ensure that we can be politically engaged. The NHS in part attempts to ensure that all people, irrespective of class or background, enjoy the health necessary to exercise their citizenship rights. The police and other criminal justice services play an even more direct role in safeguarding our liberties, protecting us not only from our fellow citizens but also from the state itself. We look to the criminal justice system to uphold the rule of law, and to prevent political corruption and bureaucratic abuse.

Public services have an important role to play in ensuring that no citizen falls below minimum standards of existence and capability. Our schools system, for instance, is meant to guarantee that all children leave with a minimal set of skills and knowledge, and our police are meant to ensure social order for all citizens. Social care is a classic 'safety net' service, acting not so much to promote equality of opportunity as to prevent any member of society falling below a minimum standard. However, we can take a more expansive view of the social minimum and consider what capabilities everyone needs to be able to pursue their goals in life, including reasonable mental and physical health, a good level of education, and so on (Sen 1999).

When we take this more expansive view of the human capabilities that public services support, achieving the social minimum becomes more and more closely related to promoting equality of opportunity. Of all the public services it is early years' care, schools and adult education that perhaps contribute most to this goal. However, all the major services have an important role to play. Without health, the most basic opportunities are denied, and both the experience and the fear of crime are debilitating as well as hurtful (Home Office 2006a). We are increasingly aware of the links between health in the early years of childhood and achievement later in life (Bamfield and Brooks 2006).

The principle of fair distribution dictates that those inequalities permitted by the three earlier principles, like income, should reflect relevant factors like choice and desert. It insists that we should, as far as is possible, only permit inequalities that are earned rather than arise from luck and inheritance. However, this principle leads us straight into difficult issues to which we will return later: to what extent should we hold people responsible for the consequences of their choices? Should people who fall ill due to smoking, poor diet or recklessness be entitled to exactly the same medical treatment as those who fall ill due to factors completely beyond their control? The principles of equal citizenship and social minimum forbid us from letting people fall into indigence, but the principle of fair distribution might lead us to be less generous to certain 'irresponsible' groups than we would otherwise be.

This is an instance of the more general point that these four principles of justice can give rise to conflicting imperatives. As Miller puts it, 'there are likely to be hard choices to make, since each of the principles makes demands on our resources. Money spent on community policing to protect equal rights to security is money that cannot be spent on increasing the state pension (part of the social minimum) or on pre-school education (necessary for equal opportunity). Faced with these choices, no one principle takes automatic priority' (Miller 2005: 19).

Social justice also relates closely to other core progressive values including sustainability and democratic engagement. As we have discussed, public services engender a society in which citizenship rights are upheld and their exercise promoted. However, in addition we expect public services themselves to be democratically accountable. Because the principles of justice sometimes conflict both within themselves and with other principles (like sustainability), the only way of ensuring decisions are fair and legitimate is to make them democratically.

The objectives of public services should thus not be considered solely in terms of distributive justice, but also in terms of procedural justice: how decisions are made, as well as what is decided. This aspect of social justice and some of the implications for public services are developed at more length by Nick Pearce in Chapter 14.

Finally, we should also consider public satisfaction. In one sense, the need to sustain adequate satisfaction with public services is obvious. Given that the core public services are so important to the wider political agenda and strongly affect voting intentions, excessive dissatisfaction is politically perilous for any governing party (Ipsos MORI 2007a). However, in other ways satisfaction is a highly controversial objective.

To start with, satisfaction could plausibly be achieved by holding public expectations down, so that even poor services were perceived relatively well. More fundamentally, however, we should not prioritize satisfaction as our overarching objective for the public services for the same reason that we reject utility or happiness as our overarching more general political objective. As Nick Pearce explains in Chapter 14, 'Utilitarian ambitions of this kind suffer numerous conceptual problems, well-attested in the academic literature. In addition, there may be tradeoffs between procedural utility, distributive justice and other principles of social justice.' Satisfaction should thus take its place among our objectives for public services, but should not be elevated to *the* objective which all others serve.

Health, education and the criminal justice system – the inheritance and the challenges

This section provides a very brief overview of a few key trends in the core public services, and outlines some of the future challenges. Spending on the public services has grown very significantly over the last decade, not just in real terms, but as a share of national income too. Public spending on the core services of health, education and public order increased from 12.2 per cent of gross domestic product (GDP) in 1997/98 to 15.5 per cent of GDP in 2005/06. As Table 8.1 shows, the big winner has been the health service. While education spending is at around twice the level of spending on public order and safety, both these areas have seen similar proportionate increases in resources.

Table 8.1   Public spending as a percentage of GDP, 1997/98–2005/06

	1997–98	*2005–06*
Public order and safety	2.1	2.5
Health	5.4	7.3
Education and training	4.7	5.7
	12.2	15.5

Source: Public Expenditure Statistical Analyses (PESA), Home Office (2006d).

This, of course, raises the following questions: what has been the result of this huge increase in resources, and has the money been well spent? Unfortunately, neither question is at all straightforward to answer. This is principally because of the twin difficulties of measuring public service outputs (and thus measuring efficiency) and establishing causal relationships in the very complex environment in which public services operate. We can start, however, by looking at some of the key outcomes in each area.

In health, one of the big advances of the past decade has been the reduction in waiting lists and average waiting times. Table 8.2 tells the story clearly: at the end of March 2000 there were a quarter of a million people waiting longer than 26 weeks for their inpatient appointment. Six years later, almost no one was in this position. Overall, the number of people waiting had fallen by a quarter, and average waiting times had fallen significantly.

These figures reflect huge increases in hospital activity. In 1999/2000, the NHS in England carried out 12.2 million finished consultant episodes (periods of inpatient care), but this increased to 14.4 million care episodes in 2005/06 (Department of Health (DoH) 2006b). However, putting these figures alongside the waiting list numbers brings to light a puzzle: how is it that the NHS is delivering over 2 million more periods of care each year, but waiting lists have only fallen by 250,000? The answer is that the new resources have been accompanied by a huge surge in demand. In 1999/2000, the NHS in England admitted 8.6 million patients, whereas in 2005/06 the corresponding figure was 10.3 million (ibid.).

Table 8.2 Inpatient waiting lists, England, 2000 and 2006

	Total	0–13 weeks	13–26 weeks	26 weeks plus
31 March 2000	1,037,066	524,314	244,477	268,275
31 March 2006	784,548	589,906	193,727	915

Source: Department of Health (DoH) (2006a).

This surge in demand does not reflect a worsening of the health status of the population over this period. Across England as a whole, life expectancy at birth rose by over a year for women and by nearly two years for men between 1996–98 and 2002–04. Infant mortality rates also fell significantly, from an average of 5.7 per 1,000 live births in 1996–98 to 4.8 per 1,000 in 2003–05 (Office for National Statistics (ONS) 2006a). Mortality rates for major killers such as heart disease and cancer have also fallen.

Despite these increases in health system activity and improvements in overall population health, inequalities have remained extremely stubborn. The significant differences in life expectancy between more affluent and more deprived areas, and in infant mortality between parents from professional and routine occupations, did not fall at all over this period. However, mortality rates from heart disease are falling and converging across different regions of the UK (British Heart Foundation 2007).

The most effective response to both improving the health of the population and addressing health inequalities is likely to lie outside the acute health sector that has traditionally taken the lion's share of health resources. In addition, the balance of health need is likely to shift to long-term conditions, in part as a result of demographic change and in part because of medical advances that transform acute into chronic problems. Both of these considerations point to the need to progressively shift resources into illness prevention, health promotion and primary care on the one hand, and to break down the boundary between health and social care on the other. However, this will require a different kind of public discussion around priorities for health spending, and we return to this issue when we discuss the relationship between citizens and the state.

Resources have not increased quite so dramatically in the education system as they have done in the NHS, and this is reflected in the somewhat less dramatic change in activity rates in the education sector. Average class sizes at secondary school did not change significantly between 1997 and 2005. However, class sizes have diminished in primary schools, and in particular large infant classes of more than 30 pupils have almost been eradicated. In 2000, nearly 10 per cent of infant classes that were taught by one teacher contained 31 or more pupils, whereas in 2006 the corresponding figure was 1.6 per cent.

School results have improved significantly at both primary and secondary level, although it has proved impossible for the government to reach its target of 85 per cent of all pupils reaching level four in all the core subjects at the end of primary school. Nonetheless, the pattern is of considerable improvement since 1997, albeit with most of the gains concentrated in the early years between 1997 and 2002, and quite limited gains more recently (see Table 8.3). The gap in attainment in English between boys and girls is striking, and has major implications for their subsequent performance at secondary school, where it is difficult for pupils to progress successfully without a solid foundation in literacy. This suggests the need for a major focus on those pupils falling behind early in primary school, with extra resources focused on helping them catch up (Brooks and Tough 2006).

Table 8.3 Percentage of pupils achieving level four+ in English and Maths at the end of primary school, 1997, 2002 and 2006

	English		*Mathematics*	
	Boys	*Girls*	*Boys*	*Girls*
1997	57	70	63	61
2002	70	79	73	73
2006	74	85	76	75

Source: Department for Education and Skills (DfES) (2006a).

There has also been significant progress at secondary school, where GCSE results have improved steadily and not flatlined in the same way they have at primary school. One major concern, however, must be that this levelling out will eventually happen as the primary school pupils move up through the schools system. Another serious problem is the number of pupils, roughly one in ten, who leave secondary school without even five GCSEs at G grade, and thus face very poor labour market opportunities and other poor life chances (see Table 8.4). Our education system is not currently making significant progress in reducing the size of this group.

Table 8.4 Percentage of children achieving GCSEs at the end of secondary school, 1997, 2002 and 2006

| | 5 or more A*–C (or equiv.) | | 5 or more A*–G (or equiv.) | |
	Boys	Girls	Boys	Girls
1997	41	50	84	89
2002	46	57	87	91
2006	53	63	87	92

Source: DfES (2006a).

Educational inequalities have been almost as stubborn as those in the health sector, with significant and persistent gaps in attainment at all levels by class, income and ethnicity. While the proportion of young people entering higher education has risen significantly, there has been relatively little progress made in respect of the one in four young people who are not in any form of education or training by the age of 18 (Delorenzi and Robinson 2005). The further education sector, both for young people and adults, must form a more important focus for progressives over the coming decade than it has been over the past one, with more resources supporting structured courses for young people and new flexible entitlements focused on adult learners (Delorenzi 2007).

There is perhaps more controversy about the measure of success in the field of public order and safety than in relation to any other public service. To start with, there are two major sources of information about the prevalence of crime: the British Crime Survey (BCS) and recorded crime. Because the BCS is a household survey it is not an appropriate indicator for certain types of crime, including crime that is not committed against households or individuals (for example, theft from a business, or possession of drugs), or certain types of very serious crime such as murder and serious sexual offences. However, many crimes are not reported to the police, so for this reason, and also because it has been collected on a consistent basis for longer, the BCS is a more accurate measure of the level and trend of most crime. The BCS indicates that overall crime has fallen substantially over the past ten years. In particular, the levels of burglary and vehicle theft have roughly halved over this period, while violent crime as measured by the BCS has also fallen by some 40 per cent (see Table 8.5).

Table 8.5   Incidence of major categories of crime in England and Wales, 1997, 2001/02 and 2005/06 (in thousands)

	Vandalism	Burglary	Vehicle theft	Violence
1997	2,866	1,621	3,511	2,455
2001/02	2,603	969	2,494	1,724
2005/06	2,731	733	1,731	1,490

Source: BCS, Home Office (2006e).

Anti-social behaviour is an unusual category, including some activities that are clearly criminal (drug dealing) and some that may seem threatening but are perfectly legal (teenagers hanging around on the streets). In some ways it can be seen as a composite of crime and the fear of crime. Whereas crime as measured by the BCS has fallen significantly over the past ten years, the proportion of people reporting a high level of anti-social behaviour in their area has remained relatively stable, at just over one in six (17 per cent in 2005/06) (Home Office 2006b).

While the fear of crime has declined since 1998, nonetheless at the time of the 2005/06 survey a quarter of men and a third of women believed that the national crime rate had increased 'a lot' in the past two years. Part of the key to understanding this puzzle is to note that many fewer, just 13 per cent of men and 17 per cent of women, thought that the same was true of their local area. The perception that violent crime is increasing may perhaps be explained by the fact that its composition is changing: the incidence of violence by strangers has slightly increased over the past ten years, and thus makes up a much higher proportion of total violent crime. The number of recorded murders, on the other hand, did not increase over the period from 1997/98 to 2005/06 (Home Office 2007).

One area of criminal justice that looks particularly unsuccessful is the prison system. The prison population roughly doubled from 40,000 in 1992 to 80,000 in 2006. On current projections it will continue to increase to at least 90,000 by mid 2013 (Home Office 2006c). Meanwhile, the reoffending rate is staggeringly high: two-thirds of young men aged 18–24 who are released from prison are convicted of an offence they committed within two years of their release. Given that, very roughly, one crime in four is detected and sanctioned (that is, the offender is identified and dealt with via a judicial sanction), half of these are then charged or summonsed, and half of these are then sentenced, the true picture in relation to reoffending is likely to be grim indeed.

One final, critical matter is the public's attitude to services in these areas. By the end of 2006, voters were just barely optimistic about the prospects for improvement in education, on balance pessimistic about law and order, and were especially negative about the NHS, where survey respondents expected the service to get worse rather than better by a ratio of two to one (Page and Nicholls 2006). After such huge increases in resources and some significant measured successes, this is an extraordinary situation for the government to find itself in. It is also a politically perilous situation to be in, with these core public services regularly accounting for three of the six most important issues facing Britain, according to the public (Ipsos MORI 2007b).

It is difficult to summarize even the broad outlines of such a complex picture. However, in general we can say that for each of these core public services, there have been significant improvements in some of the headline outcome measures over the past decade to accompany the large increases in resources. In relation to each we can also identify major issues that demand either a new focus (such as reoffending or further education) or a new approach to an old problem (such as school standards or health inequalities). In part the rise to prominence of these concerns is a mark of success: public expectations will always move on as old problems are addressed.

A new relationship between citizens and the state

Without the right relationship between citizens and the state, public services cannot function effectively. The progressive response to this critical relationship should involve public honesty and realism about the limitations of public services, meaningful engagement of citizens with difficult decisions around the use of limited resources, a new approach to personal behaviour which recognizes the importance of responsibility but also empowers behaviour change, and a focus on procedural fairness.

It is politically inconceivable that the recent rate of growth of funding could be sustained even in the short- to medium-term future, let alone over the coming decades. Yet it is clear that there are fundamental upward pressures on expenditure in a number of areas. This is most obviously true for the NHS, where rising public expectations are being met by rapidly developing and often expensive medical practices and technologies (Rankin 2007). Social care presents another area that will experience major cost pressures over the coming decades, as the UK population ages and more older people require assistance due to long-term health conditions

(Brooks et al. 2002). The expansion of high-quality childcare would also create significant new public costs (Pearce and Paxton 2005).

One way of seeing the relationship between citizens and the state is as a set of claims that we make on each other. When we pay our taxes we are supporting fellow citizens in their use of public services, and when we make claims on services we are making claims on each other. Few public services are public in the economic sense of the term in which my use does not diminish your possible use. My occupancy of a hospital bed is exclusive, and your child's place at a popular school is one less for other parents. It is this aspect of public services as a collective endeavour that injects such heat into debates about the entitlements for groups such as economic immigrants and asylum seekers.

We can use the example of the health system to think about the public services more widely. In the short term, a sustainable health system must meet the requirements of affordability. In the medium term, costs are strongly affected by factors such as technological and demographic change and rising public expectations. In the longer term, the extent and sustainability of the service is determined by public political support. So a sustainable system is one where:

- the public are willing to maintain the system through their financial contributions
- there is an acceptance of the limits of the provision of healthcare, according to a reasoned and robust analysis of the costs and benefits of additional spending
- health is promoted across the health system and the health service takes a proportionate share of financial resources and political capital
- there is a fair distribution of resources across the population
- there is a clear understanding of the roles and responsibilities of government and individuals in securing health.

This does not describe the health system that we have at the moment. While public support for the NHS remains high, at the moment only a minority (one in four) of the public recognizes the need to provide drugs and treatments on the basis of value for money and effectiveness (Rankin 2007). The idea of rationing health services on any basis is highly emotive and strongly resisted by the public. Yet rationing happens every day, at every level of the health service, when managers make decisions about the level at which various services are offered, and when clinicians make decisions about the appropriateness of individual treatments. This disjuncture between public attitudes and the limitations of the service can only lead to political conflicts, perverse decisions and corrosive disappointment.

Since 1997, governments have placed huge public emphasis on increasing health service resources, and trumpeted the consequent (very significant) increases in staff numbers and activity. Yet even at the new, much higher level of resources, not all needs and expectations can be met simultaneously. Technological advance tends to drive down the cost of a given activity (such as a particular kind of hip replacement), but also creates new possibilities (a better but more expensive hip prosthesis), that then generate their own new demand.

Given limited resources at any one time, we need to decide which possibilities to prioritize. This is a fundamentally political process involving incommensurable interests. The creation of the National Institute for Health and Clinical Excellence (NICE) was an important step towards making rational and systematic decisions about the pattern of health spending in the NHS. However, the organization's guidance about the cost-effectiveness of new drugs and treatments does not remove the need for political decisions over what activities are in fact funded – it merely provides some of the necessary evidence to inform such decisions.

One problem is that after years of being told by politicians that record levels of resources are being invested in the NHS, the public is resistant to the idea that they will have to face hard choices after all. This means both that it is almost impossible to have rational public debate about priorities, and also that public expectations are likely to be consistently disappointed when reality bites. This is likely to result in ad hoc decisions over the actual pattern of provision, and in the longer term may undermine support for the publicly funded service more generally.

In retrospect, it was a serious political error for governments since 1997 not to tell a more complex story. A progressive government should balance high ambitions for the public services, with the promotion of a mature public discourse about their necessary limits. Examples such as the Pension Commission (Turner et al. 2005) have shown that it is possible to develop public understanding about the need for difficult choices without incurring unacceptable political costs, and that this can open the door to policy change. Some of these hard decisions will always need to be made at the national level, but others can be taken more locally. One of the responses to the need to make hard choices must be to devolve some of the responsibility for these decisions. The alternative is to impose uniform standards that may not meet local preferences, and thus to nationalize blame for disappointment.

Private behaviour has a profound impact on the outcomes that the public services are seeking to achieve, both for the individual and often for the wider community. Health is perhaps the most compelling example of these two issues. On the one hand, individual behaviour – for example, smoking, diet and exercise – is often far more important for individual health outcomes than any action by the NHS. On the other hand, treating diseases that arise because of smoking, poor diet and lack of exercise uses resources that cannot then be deployed elsewhere. Different patterns of private behaviour imply radically different demands on the health service, with major implications for long-term costs (Wanless 2002). Yet it is important to recognize that this issue of private responsibility goes far beyond the field of health. Another particularly controversial area is that of parenting, where our growing understanding of how parental behaviour affects child development rubs up against our instinct that the family is a private sphere.

One response to these issues would be to simply clarify the limits of what the public services will offer and insist on personal responsibility beyond that point. This would not have much appeal if it implied personal costs for large numbers of people, but could be dangerously popular if it was used to withdraw support from groups which do not currently elicit much public sympathy, such as addictive drug users or families stuck in a cycle of low income, poor attainment and anti-social behaviour. Insisting on personal responsibility could also be used as a long-term way to shrink the state, by fixing the boundary of what can be expected from public services.

Instead, our response to these issues should balance clarity about what our public services will offer, realism about what they can achieve, and more explicit expectations about personal responsibility. We should not be afraid to be open about using the state to change behaviour. There is a strong philosophical case for doing so grounded in a positive conception of liberty: we often require assistance to be free (for example, via education, the rule of law, and the removal of undue influences), rather than the simple absence of constraint. 'Rights and responsibilities' was an important theme for the Labour Party in the mid 1990s, and the idea of strong reciprocity between citizens remains powerful. We now need to supplement these ideas with a progressive approach to behaviour change.

The two key principles that should guide a progressive approach to behaviour change are equity and empowerment (Lewis 2007). Equity implies that attempts to change behaviour do not disproportionately load costs onto disadvantaged groups. This is a real danger, because the same people are likely to end up being targeted by programmes to address (for example) binge drinking, unhealthy eating, smoking and anti-social behaviour: these behaviours are all correlated with social class. (In addition to being a matter of equity, this kind of overload is likely to reduce the effectiveness of interventions.) Empowerment implies that behavioural interventions should help develop the capacities of the target group, and in particular should help develop their sense of self-efficacy – the belief that one is both capable of effective action and responsible for one's own outcomes. One of the critical frontiers of public policy over the coming years will be developing our understanding of how to change individual behaviour in ways that are both effective and seen to be legitimate.

New relationships between the government and the public service workforce

A very significant proportion of the new resources flowing into public services over the past decade has been spent on expanding the workforce and improving its terms and conditions. Indeed, the two are likely to go hand in hand, because good terms are likely to attract more applicants. The increases in numbers of some of the core categories of public servants are striking, as shown in Table 8.6.

Table 8.6 Numbers of public servants in core categories, 1997 and 2005/06

	1997	*2005/06*	*Increase (%)*
All regular teachers	399,000	436,000[a]	9
Total police	127,000	141,000[a]	11
Doctors and GPs	83,000	112,000[b]	45
Nurses	256,000	322,000[b]	26

[a] 2006.
[b] 2005.
Sources: DfES (2006b), DoH (2005), Bullock and Gunning (2007).

Over the period 1997–2006, average earnings including bonuses rose by almost exactly the same amount in both public and private sectors as a whole (46 per cent in nominal terms according to National Statistics' average earnings index). The Annual Survey of Hours and Earnings (ASHE) indicates that by 2006, *average* pay levels in the private sector were 13 per cent higher than in the public sector, while *median* earnings were 5 per cent higher in the public sector. This reflects the different pattern of pay in the two sectors, with fewer very low-paying jobs in the public sector and more very highly paid jobs in the private sector. In 2006, median public and private sector pay increased at exactly the same rate, up 3 per cent since 2005. At the same time many private sector workers saw their pension schemes scaled back, while defined benefit pensions and a retirement age of 60 have remained protected for most public servants (Department of Trade and Industry (DTI) 2005).

Yet despite these increased numbers and improved pay, there is a sense that Labour is losing the support of the public service workforce, and that this in turn is damaging the wider public's perception of the services. If this were true, it would represent a remarkable failure given the party's political focus on the public services and the huge investment of resources in the sector. It is important to be clear about objectives here. Public services must always serve public interests, not the interests of any particular group, and certainly not the interests of their own staff. But at the same time, no enterprise is likely to succeed in the face of serious dissatisfaction and particularly opposition from its own staff. This is especially important for public services because the attitude of staff is likely to affect both service quality and public trust.

Are public servants dissatisfied or alienated? Data on sickness absence, grievances, disciplinary sanctions and industrial action are inconclusive. In particular, although sickness absence rates are higher in the public than the private sector, this difference is principally accounted for by compositional differences in age and gender. Resignation rates are perhaps more useful, and indicate a particular problem in the health sector (see Table 8.7).

Table 8.7 Public servant resignations, 2004

	Resignations per 100 employees
Public administration	5.7
Education	7.2
Health and social work	12.4
All workplaces	13.7

Source: Work Employment Relations Survey (WERS), DTI (2004).

Industrial action is much more common in the public sector, being threatened or taken in 16 per cent of public sector workplaces in 2003 compared to 3 per cent in the private sector, but this reflects much higher levels of unionization in the public sector as a whole. There is also survey data that illuminate public servants' perceptions of their organizations and particularly their management. Employee views of management are around 10 percentage points worse in the public sector compared with the private sector, on assessments of trust in senior management, confidence in senior management, and belief that senior management has a clear vision for their organization (Ipsos MORI 2005). Public servants are also relatively pessimistic about how their organization is perceived in terms of its customer and quality focus, value for money and efficiency.

Table 8.8   Public servants' perceptions of their organization, 2005

'Which of these words, if any, do you think your customers, clients or people who use your organization's services or products would use to describe your organization?'

	Public sector (%)	Private sector (%)
Customer focused	33	42
Efficient	27	38
Good value for money	20	33
Quality driven	17	27

Source: Ipsos Mori (2005).

One complaint that is often heard is that central control has inappropriately constrained professional discretion, such as by forcing teachers to focus on Key Stage results, or requiring medical professionals to prioritize patient waiting times. In part this may reflect individual instances of poor performance management leading to services 'hitting the target and missing the point'. For example, the school assessment system may facilitate shallow and narrow teaching ('teaching to the test') because of the nature of the examinations. In this kind of circumstance the response may well be a technical one; for instance, while maintaining a strong focus on literacy and numeracy at primary school, the assessment system could be changed in a way that would make it impossible to teach to the test, by using ongoing teacher assessment and moderating the results with a sample test of the students (Brooks and Tough 2006).

However, a more profound problem occurs when the workforce does not believe in the legitimacy of the objectives that they are being asked to achieve. Once again, the health service provides wider lessons for the rest of the public services. The pace of change in the health service has been ferocious since 1997. This is challenging enough in itself, but more importantly the direction of reform has been inconsistent, with Labour halting the previous Conservative government's market-based reforms in its first term, leaning heavily on target-driven regulation as it poured in resources in its second term, and now racing towards a radically ambitious quasi-market in elective care in its third term. As a result, the reforms lack legitimacy among the workforce that is required to carry them out.

Current dissatisfaction in the health service workforce thus seems to be related in part to the way that change has been implemented, in part the pace and scale of reform, and in part the objectives and the lack of strong public legitimacy for both the objectives and the mechanisms of reform. A healthy relationship between the government and the public service workforce would therefore be one where:

- government is realistic about the pace and scale of change it expects the workforce to implement
- government is consistent in the direction of its policy decisions
- central and local government make strong efforts to legitimize their objectives for each service
- the workforce plays an active role in constantly improving service performance
- the workforce becomes more accountable to service users and local citizens.

Conclusion

The core public services will continue to become increasingly important over the coming decades. Health and protective services will become more valuable in the context of rising incomes and wealth, and education will become more important in the context of a labour market that places an ever higher premium on advanced skills. Public services will continue to be critical for the achievement of social justice through enabling citizenship, guaranteeing minimum standards of human existence, and enabling equality of opportunity. The pressure for improvements will not slacken, even if resources become more constrained.

At the same time we can now see more clearly the dangers of over-reliance on centrally driven performance management and quasi-markets as the mechanisms to achieve such improvements. The first generates exactly the same coordination problems that bedevilled state monopoly public service providers, and the second runs up against the problems that were identified 50 years ago by the original theorists of market failure. The future thus lies in a more balanced system of more engaged citizens, more sophisticated performance monitoring, provider markets where appropriate, more local governance and priority setting, and more accountable public service professionals. The next stage of public service reform will be about facilitating these new relationships, and information about citizens and services will be the key.

References

Arrow, K. and Lind, R. C. (1970) 'Uncertainty and the Evaluation of Public Investment Decisions', *American Economic Review*, 60 (3): 374. Nashville, Tenn.: American Economic Association.

Bamfield, L. and Brooks, R. (2006) *Narrowing the Gap: The Final Report of the Fabian Commission on Life Chances*. London: Fabian Society.

British Heart Foundation (2007) Heartstats. Available at <www.heartstats.org/homepage.asp>.

Brooks, R., Regan, S. and Robinson, P. (2002) *A New Contract for Retirement*. London: ippr.

Brooks, R. and Tough, S. (2006) *Assessment and Testing: Making Space for Teaching and Learning*. London: ippr.

Buchanan, J. M. and Stubblebine, W. C. (1962) 'Externality', *Economica*, 29 (116): 371–84. Oxford: Blackwell.

Bullock, S. and Gunning, N. (2007) *Police Service Strength England and Wales*, SB04/07. Available at <www.homeoffice.gov.uk/rds/pdfs07/hosb0407.pdf>.

Delorenzi, S. (2007) *Learning for Life: A New Framework for Adult Skills*. London: ippr.

Delorenzi, S. and Robinson, P. (2005) *Choosing to Learn: Improving Participation After Compulsory Education*. London: ippr.

DfES (2006a) School and College Achievement and Attainment Tables. Available at <www.dfes.gov.uk/performancetables/>.

DfES (2006b) *School Workforce in England (Including Pupil:Teacher Ratios and Pupil: Adult Ratios), January 2006 (Revised)*. Available at <www.dfes.gov.uk/rsgateway/DB/SFR/s000681/index.shtml>.

DoH (2005) *All NHS Doctors: Hospital and Community Health Service (HCHS) Medical and Dental Staff and General Medical Practitioners*. Available at <www.ic.nhs.uk/pubs/nhsstaff/mdbulletintab/file>.

DoH (2006a) Hospital Waiting Times/List Statistics. Available at <www.performance.doh.gov.uk/waitingtimes/>.

DoH (2006b) Hospital Episode Statistics. Available at <www.hesonline.nhs.uk/Ease/servlet/ContentServer?siteID=1937&categoryID=192>.

DTI (2004) *Work Employment Relations Survey*. Available at <www.dti.gov.uk/employment/research-evaluation/wers-2004/>.

DTI (2005) 'Agreement Reached on Public Sector Pensions'. Press release, 18 October. London: DTI. Available at <www.gnn.gov.uk/environment/fullDetail.asp?ReleaseID=173937&NewsAreaID=2&NavigatedFromDepartment=False>.

Home Office (2006a) *The Economic and Social Costs of Crimes Against Individuals and Households*. Home Office Research Study No. 296. London: Home Office.

Home Office (2006b) *Crime in England and Wales 2005/06*. London: Home Office.

Home Office (2006c) *Prison Population Projections 2006–2013, England and Wales*. London: Home Office.

190   *Politics for a New Generation*

Home Office (2006d) Public Expenditure Statistical Analyses. Available at <www.
hm-treasury.gov.uk/economic_data_and_tools/finance_spending_statistics/
pes_publications/pespub_pesa06.cfm>.
Home Office (2006e) *British Crime Survey*. Available at <www.homeoffice.gov.uk/
rds/bcs1.html>.
Home Office (2007) *Recorded Crime Statistics 1898–2005/06*. London: Home
Office.
Ipsos MORI (2005) *Growing Disaffection with Public Service Workers*. Survey on
behalf of the Work Foundation. Available at <www.ipsos-mori.com/polls/2005/
theworkfoundation3.shtml>.
Ipsos MORI (2007a) *Political Monitor*, February. London: Ipsos MORI. Available at
<www.ipsos-mori.com/polls/2007/mpm070129.shtml>.
Ipsos MORI (2007b) *Political Monitor: Recent Trends*. Available at <www.ipsos-mori.
com/polls/trends/issues12.shtml>.
Kelly, G. and Muers, S. (2002) *Creating Public Value: An Analytical Framework for
Public Service Reform*. London: Cabinet Office.
Lewis, M. (2007) *A New Social Contract: Personal Responsibility and Public Policy*.
London: ippr.
Miller, D. (2005) 'What is Social Justice?', in N. Pearce and W. Paxton (eds), *Social
Justice: Building a Fairer Britain*. London: ippr/Politico's.
Musgrave, R. A. (1959) *The Theory of Public Finance*. New York: McGraw-Hill.
ONS (2006) *Mortality Statistics: Childhood, Infant and Perinatal* (Series DH3). Available
at <www.statistics.gov.uk/STATBASE/Product.asp?vlnk=6305>.
Page, B. and Nicholls, J. (2006) *What State Are We In?* London: Ipsos MORI. Available
at <www.ipsos-mori.com/publications/bp/what-state-are-we-in.shtml>.
Pearce, N. and Paxton, W. (2005) *Social Justice: Building a Fairer Britain*. London:
ippr/Politico's.
Rankin, J. (2007) *Great Expectations*. London: ippr.
Samuelson, P. (1954) 'The Pure Theory of Public Expenditure', *Review of Economics
and Statistics*, 36 (4): 387–9. Cambridge, Mass.: MIT Press.
Sen, A. (1999) *Development as Freedom*. Oxford: Oxford University Press.
Turner, A., Hills, J. and Drake, J. (2005) *A New Pension Settlement for the Twenty-First
Century*. London: TSO.
Wanless, D. (2002) *Securing our Future Health: Taking a Long Term View*. London:
TSO.

9
Moving On Up: Progression in the Labour Market

Natascha Engel and Sonia Sodha, with Mike Johnson

Whether you work to live or live to work, jobs are about more than just earning money. They can bring satisfaction, stimulation, self-esteem, a sense of worth, purpose and the opportunity to develop and progress. But – although it would be wrong to assume that low-skill work can never provide some or all of these things – there is no question that they can be more difficult to achieve in routine, low-skill jobs, many of which offer poor opportunities (Dickens 2000, cited in Hoggart et al. 2006). Yet the nature of our economy means that there are vast numbers of such jobs in the UK.

Take the example of a lone parent, living in poverty and with a child in secondary school, moving off Income Support into work under the voluntary New Deal for Lone Parents. This lone parent may have few formal qualifications and have been out of the labour market for a number of years. Their choice of first job is likely to be limited. The chances are that they will move into one of millions of jobs in the low-paid service industries, paying a wage not much more than the minimum wage of £5.35 an hour.

This lone parent has done all that can be asked of them. They have looked for and taken up a job that pays a low wage, which, alongside tax credits and benefits, is enough to take them out of poverty. They are no longer wholly dependent on the state. But a very fair question that this individual might ask is: 'What lies in store for me from here?' What support and help is there for this lone parent – who may have been out of the labour market for many years – to remain in work, and to progress

191

into more highly-skilled, highly-paid work? More broadly, what does progressive politics have to offer them?

In debates about work, poverty and social justice in the last ten years, much of the focus has been on the impact of the move off welfare and into work on poverty rates, and how to facilitate this move. This focus has been the right starting point. But we suggest here that in the next decade we need to expand our thinking beyond simply moving people back into work, to a greater extent than has been the case in the past. We need to look at what happens to people once they are in work.

Labour market retention and progression need to form an integral part of the progressive project. This is because achieving social justice is not simply about ensuring all individuals achieve a decent minimum standard of living. Nor is it just about helping the able and talented to climb the social ladder without a thought for those left behind. What social justice requires is a simultaneous commitment to both. Retention and progression – an individual's trajectory in the labour market – are vital to everyone.

In this chapter we examine the extent of retention and progression, particularly in the low-skill labour market, and consider why they pose significant challenges for social justice and our economy. We then move on to consider why rates of retention and progression are low, particularly for certain groups. In doing so, we outline the fast-paced change our economy is experiencing, including the shift from manufacturing to services and the polarization of jobs into low- and high-skilled jobs, which has fundamentally changed the nature of work and conspired to make progression more difficult in many cases. The hourglass shape of the labour market means that certain workers are becoming trapped behind a bottleneck as it becomes ever more difficult for those in low-skill jobs to find stepping stones into higher-skilled work.

Finally, we consider policies that can encourage retention and progression. Such policies need to be tailored to the unique political economy of the UK – the 'Anglo-Social' model (Dixon and Pearce 2005). We argue that there are three areas that progressive policy-makers should be focusing on. First, skills – both 'hard' skills, such as numeracy and literacy, and 'softer' personal and social skills – are crucial in the Anglo-Social model. Entitlements to adult education and training need to be made more flexible and tied to the individual, not just employers. Second, improvements can be made in the way in which people are supported in accessing, retaining and progressing in their jobs by the government's employment support services. Third, there are questions about the nature of work itself. Can government do anything to promote career trajectories in public and private sector work, and to what extent does an expansion in the supply of skills need to be met with an expansion in employer demand?

Progressivism and progression

Why a chapter about labour market progression in a book about a new generation of progressive politics? We believe that progressive ambitions cannot be achieved without greater retention and advancement in the low-skill, low-paid labour market. There is a strong link between poverty and lack of retention and progression once someone has first moved into a job. Poor retention and progression unquestionably hinder government's pledge to end child poverty by 2020, and the progressive goal to provide a decent safety net for all.

First, the government is absolutely right to argue that work is the best route out of poverty. But, at the moment, it is by no means a guaranteed route. Almost one in three part-time workers and one in six full-time workers are poor (Bailey 2006). Almost half of children in poverty come from working households, and while persistent poverty (defined as living in poverty for three out of four years in a four-year window) has declined in recent years for children in workless households, it has remained constant for those in working households (Harker 2006). Moreover, as we discuss below, many individuals moving from Income Support and Jobseeker's Allowance into jobs churn in and out of low-paid work. Reducing rates of poverty through work therefore cannot just be about tax credits and moving people into jobs. We need a better understanding of what makes jobs sustainable and what allows people to progress into better-paid work. The potential impact should not be underestimated. If the rate of lone-parent job exits were reduced by half, to the rate of the non-lone-parent population, the 70 per cent employment target would be met without any increase in the number of lone parents entering work (assuming the work entry rate remains the same) (Harker 2006). And a 20 per cent reduction in lone parent exit rates could lift 44,000 children out of poverty (ibid.).

Second, improving retention and progression in the labour market for low-skill groups is a vital ingredient in improving social mobility. A socially just society is one characterized by social mobility. But as set out in Chapter 4, evidence shows that social mobility was lower in the UK for those born in 1970, compared with those born in 1958. Improving social mobility must be one of the key challenges for progressives over the next decade. This is a challenge often associated with compulsory-age school education. Of course, it goes without saying that education is hugely important in reducing the effect of place of birth and social class on life chances. But improving social mobility has to go beyond this: it also has to be about extending opportunities in adulthood. We need a lifelong model of social justice that caters for all individuals, including those who may have been unable or unwilling to take up opportunities while at school.

The extent of retention and progression

While the government has been successful in reducing unemployment and worklessness, and supporting some disadvantaged groups back into work, the story on retention and progression is a less positive one.

First, employment retention – the amount of time someone remains in employment, rather than remaining in a particular job or firm – is much lower for people moving off benefits into work than for the general population. Seven out of ten Jobseeker's Allowance (JSA) claims are from repeat claimants, who have previously moved into and back out of work (Harker 2006). Four out of ten people leaving JSA for a job return to benefits within six months.

So it is clear that static employment rates do not reveal the full picture: the move off benefits into work is often an unsustainable one. This is particularly true for lone parents and disabled people. Around one in ten lone parents leave work every year – twice as high as for non-lone parents (Harker 2006). Between 18 per cent and 20 per cent of lone parents leaving the New Deal for Lone Parents to go into work return to benefits within six months, 29 per cent return within a year, and 40 per cent within two and a half years (Evans et al. 2005).

Retention is similarly lower for disabled people, who are three times more likely to exit the labour market than non-disabled people – with this likelihood being significantly higher for the severely disabled (Rigg 2005). The government's 80 per cent employment aspiration will be almost impossible to achieve without a reduction in this low-pay no-pay churn.

Unfortunately, data on progression is much more limited than that on retention (Strategy Unit 2004). But as social mobility has declined, it appears that it is more difficult than it was 20 years ago for individuals to progress up the wage distribution into higher-skilled, better-paid work (ibid.; Dickens 1999). Not only are we facing historically high levels of income inequality (although post-tax and benefit income inequality has tentatively begun to decline since 2000, as outlined in Chapter 4), but it is also increasingly difficult to make the climb from the low to the high end of the distribution.

Again, it is particular groups who are finding it difficult to progress. The earnings trajectories of disabled people lag behind those for the non-disabled, with the median annual change in earnings 1.4 per cent lower than average for disabled men, and 0.6 per cent lower for disabled women, compared to non-disabled men and women respectively (Rigg 2005). The largest progression disadvantage exists for disabled men aged 25–49.

Women are also less likely to progress. Part-time jobs, largely the preserve of women, offer fewer progression opportunities: they are associated with lower rates of progression from low-paid to better-paid jobs (Pavlopoulos and Fouarge 2006). Even for women working full time, there is a significant gender gap for wage growth: on average, the pay of a woman working full time for ten years will be 12 per cent less than the equivalent pay for a man in the same situation (Manning and Swaffield 2005). About half of this gap can be accounted for by the different levels of pay associated with male and female choice of occupation, but the other half remains unexplained.

Why are rates of retention and progression so low for certain groups? Problems with retention can stem back to the original barriers to moving into a job, which do not automatically dissipate when someone moves off benefits and into work (Hoggart et al. 2006). Qualitative work for the Department for Work and Pensions (DWP) with low-income working families suggests that the same factors that make the initial move into work difficult also impede retention, and that these are particularly acute for disabled people and lone parents. Job sustainability early on was found to be related to the extent to which individuals could discern a financial gain and an increased standard of living as a result of moving into work; the extent to which they experienced psychological and emotional benefits; their own motivation to work and escape benefits; the adequacy of childcare arrangements; and whether they had the support of family and friends (Graham et al. 2005).

Once individuals have been in work for longer, factors that directly pertain to the nature of work become much more important in determining sustainability. The study found that people who found work 'stimulating', 'challenging', 'interesting' or 'varied' were more likely to sustain a job. Similarly, people's relationships with their colleagues and employers, and whether their job offered them progression opportunities, and fitted in with their other commitments and aspirations, were also important. Moreover, retention is clearly also a building block of progression. If individuals cannot sustain employment, the opportunities for advancement will be even more limited. But in addition, there are some fundamental shifts occurring in the labour market that change the nature of work and what it takes to progress, which we examine below.

The changing labour market

As outlined in Chapter 5, Britain's political economy is characterized by the flexible and deregulated labour markets associated with liberal economies, but with higher levels of social protection than in the US – what Dixon and Pearce (2005) call the 'Anglo-Social' model. Our political economy has shaped the way in which the labour market has responded to technological change and shifts in global economic activity. There have been two major shifts that have shaped the labour market in recent years: the move from a manufacturing-based to a service-based economy, and the impact of technological change on the nature of work.

The shift from manufacturing towards a service industry is well-documented and understood (see also Chapter 4). Britain now has one of the most service-oriented industrial economies in the world (Dixon and Paxton 2005). A number of factors have contributed to this change: higher productivity growth in manufacturing than in services (Rowthorn 2004); the effect of international trade as imports have replaced some domestic manufactured goods (Rowthorn and Coutts 2004); and rising gross domestic product (GDP), increased consumer spending and increasing female participation in the labour market, all of which have led to a greater demand for services (Hills 2004; Margo et al. 2006).

As Chapter 5 maps out, the result is an economy in which over 80 per cent of employment is predicted to be in the service sector by 2014 (Wilson et al. 2006). Moreover, the declining manufacturing sector has shifted its emphasis towards more highly specialized and skilled areas, such as aerospace, pharmaceuticals, electronics and biotechnology, which are less labour intensive and require a specialized skill set (Shah and McIvor 2006).

Across the whole economy, technological change has impacted on the nature of work itself (Goos and Manning 2004). As technology has become cheaper and more widespread, it has replaced employment in routine jobs that require precision, and are therefore relatively easily automated (ibid.). These jobs tend to be concentrated in the middle of the labour market. Jobs that are much more resistant to technological replacement are those that require hand–eye coordination, creative thinking or leadership – such as shelf-stacking or managerial roles. These jobs tend to be concentrated at the bottom and top of the labour market – jobs that are considered to be relatively low- or high-skilled.

The largest growth has been in high-skill jobs – from 30 per cent in 1984 to 41 per cent in 2004 (see Chapter 5). The percentage of low-skill jobs in the economy has declined slightly over this period from 38 per cent to 35 per cent, but the decline in mid-skill jobs has been most significant, from 31 per cent to 21 per cent. Thus the labour market has increasingly become polarized into an hourglass shape, with more jobs at the bottom and top of the skills distribution.

Organizations have adapted in response to changes in the economy and labour market. Gone are the days when employment success could be equated with long service, obedience and loyalty. The trend is for companies to reduce layers of middle management and to organize themselves around flexible, autonomous teams rather than hierarchies (Sennett 2006; Margo et al. 2006).

These shifts have important implications for progression in the labour market. As more and more jobs are service-related and technology replaces routine tasks, as hierarchies morph into looser structures and dilute established progression pathways, there is an emerging strand of thought that personal and soft skills – such as motivation, internal locus of control and self-esteem – are becoming increasingly important in relation to hard qualifications (Margo et al. 2006).

First, research using cohort data has suggested that the impact of non-cognitive abilities while young – personal and social skills and personality attributes – are becoming more significant in determining earnings later in life (Blanden et al. 2006). Employers are also increasingly becoming concerned about gaps in soft skills, such as customer handling and teamworking, particularly in lower-skilled work (see Chapter 5).

Second, the polarization of the labour market into a top-heavy hourglass means that many mid-skill jobs that people would have once used as stepping stones from low-skill to high-skill work have simply disappeared (Margo et al. 2006). 'Intermediate occupations' – administrative, clerical and secretarial professions and skilled trades – have declined in their share of the economy from 31 per cent in 1980 to 24 per cent in 2004, and are further expected to fall to 21 per cent by 2020. Certain groups are increasingly getting trapped behind this bottleneck in the hourglass.

Third, these changes have contributed to regional labour markets becoming increasingly diverse. It is impossible to ignore that issues of progression have a glaringly geographical dimension. For many individuals, their labour market opportunities are determined by where they live because the nature of the local labour market varies significantly from area to area.

As shown in Figure 9.1, high-skill jobs are mainly concentrated in London and the South East, which hinders progression for those living outside these areas. Geography matters most to the least-skilled as one of the most immobile groups in the population (Green and Owen 2006). People in low-paid work tend to interact with more localized labour markets, as low wages make commuting much less worthwhile. Adverse localized labour market conditions therefore impact much more on the low-skilled than their higher-skilled counterparts. In contrast, individuals in high-skill jobs are more likely to have longer commute times: the Oxford–Reading–London–Cambridge high-skill area in the South East has much longer than average commuting flows (ibid.). But this regional story is not unambiguously good news for London and the South East. London itself also has a higher degree of polarization of low- and high-skill jobs than elsewhere in the UK (Kaplanis forthcoming). It may actually therefore be harder to progress from low-skill to high-skill jobs in London than elsewhere.

Supporting people in achieving their aspirations

In the face of low retention and progression, and irreversible changes in the labour market, how can policy-makers better support people in achieving their aspirations? To some extent, we are constrained by our Anglo-Social political economy. The most fruitful areas for policy are therefore improving people's skills – both hard and soft – and improving the way in which people are supported in accessing, staying in and progressing in work. But there is also a growing role for policy in changing the nature of work, particularly in promoting more flexible, family-friendly working and in boosting employer demand for increased skills.

It should be stressed that improving progression is not a simple task. It is a long-term goal, and there are no quick fixes. A complex multitude of causes lies behind poor progression, including lack of retention. We do not yet have a good enough understanding of exactly how these causes interact and which are most important. This is partly because progression is more difficult to measure than labour market participation.

Improving progression is also closely related to individuals' own attitudes towards work and advancement. In-depth interviews with participants in the government's Employment Retention and Advancement demonstration programme reveal that people hold widely varying work orientations that affect their personal understanding of advancement

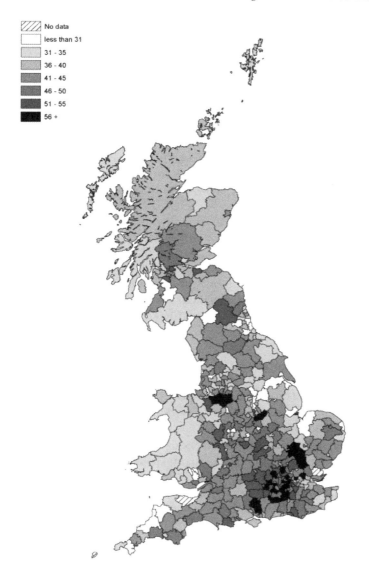

Figure 9.1 Percentage of working population employed in higher-skilled occupations, 2005

Note: Higher-skill occupations are Standard Occupational Classification (SOC) categories 1–3 (managerial, professional and technical occupations).

Source: Office for National Statistics (ONS) (2006).

(Hoggart et al. 2006). Many clients viewed advancement in terms of job satisfaction rather than the more traditional move up the career ladder – particularly those out of work. Some prioritized permanent, stable work; others (particularly lone parents) job satisfaction and a better work–care balance.

Interviewees fell into three groups with respect to attitudes towards advancement – some positively desired it, others were more ambivalent about it, and a third group were completely indifferent to it or rejected the idea of advancement altogether. These attitudes were influenced by whether individuals primarily valued work for the sake of work, were more focused on the financial benefits of working, or prioritized care for their children.

The first group were most likely to define advancement in terms of career progression; the second group as better pay, and the last group had more mixed feelings about advancement. Significantly, the interviews suggest that attitudes are not fixed over time. Participants who had successfully made the transition into work often developed a more positive view about advancement. This reinforces the theory that retention is a necessary (but insufficient) building block for progression.

Adult learning and skills

A lack of hard skills and qualifications is a significant barrier to progression. A study of progression out of low-paid work, using British Household Panel Survey data from 1991 to 2001, has found that higher levels of qualification were associated with increased likelihood of moving from low-paid to better-paid work (Pavlopoulos and Fouarge 2006). While one way of addressing this lack is through improving compulsory education for children and young people, it is not enough alone. A progressive commitment to social justice requires better opportunities for adult learners too.

The Labour government has increased resources for adult learning since 1997. However, the focus has increasingly been on two Public Service Agreement (PSA) targets to increase the number of people with basic skills and level two qualifications (the equivalent of five A*–C grades at GCSE level). While these targets have focused resources on adults with no or few qualifications, they have done so in a constrained way (Delorenzi 2007). They have led to a situation in which qualifications are commonly used as a way of certifying existing skills, rather than as a way of acquiring new ones. This is helped by the fact that the qualifications often do not include a requirement to learn anything new.

While adults working towards their first full basic skills or level two qualification (or level three for those aged 25 or under) receive full fee remission, individuals for whom other forms of provision are more appropriate are increasingly having to pay for them themselves; for example, those undertaking a level one or a partial level two qualification (ibid.). Although career development loans are available, these are repayable immediately after study at commercial interest rates – unlike the student loans available to students in higher education. So there is little flexibility with respect to qualifications. This is despite evidence that shows that the return to different qualifications varies widely, with level two qualifications having no discernable impact on earnings, while some other qualifications have much greater effects (Dearden et al. 2004). Much of the reason for the small effects of level two on pay will come down to employer use of these qualifications to certify pre-existing skills.

The main route for delivering adult learning is through employers in the Train to Gain programme. Train to Gain offers employers free access to advice from Skills Brokers, free funding of tuition for employees undertaking their first full qualification at the basic skills level or level two, and wage compensation for companies with fewer than 50 employees. The Leitch Review of Skills (2006) has reinforced this employer-led approach.

However, evidence from Train to Gain's predecessor, the Employer Training pilots, suggests that there can be problems involved with an approach that is solely employer-led, with little choice for individuals. There is a danger that some of the cost will be deadweight, with money going to pay employers for training that they would have provided anyway. In the pilots, deadweight costs were as high as 85–90 per cent (Abramovsky et al. 2005), which is why Train to Gain has a more explicit focus on 'hard to reach' employers. Unless they are married with a system that also ring-fences individual entitlements to adult learning, employer subsidies may simply help relatively advantaged groups: people in skilled occupations who already have many of the skills that a qualification certifies, rather than those who are out of work.

Yet we know that it is those out of work and in low-skill jobs who need the most help with training: those with the fewest qualifications have least opportunity to train at work (Delorenzi 2007). In 2004, just 12 per cent of employees with no qualifications had received training in the preceding 13 weeks, compared to 42 per cent of those educated to degree level; and only 30 per cent of inactive adults were current or recent learners in 2006, compared to around half of those in work (ibid.). Only around 7 per cent of parents participating in the New Deal for Lone Parents received any help with training (Bell et al. 2006) – despite the fact that four out of ten lone parents on income support have no qualifications (Harker 2006).

In order to reach all individuals, including those out of work, adult learning subsidies therefore need to be better targeted and more flexible, and should be better tailored to the individual, as well as being delivered through employer-linked entitlements (ibid.; Delorenzi 2007). A flexible entitlement should be created for all individuals without a level two qualification that would give all of them the equivalent of two years' full-time study, to be taken flexibly at any time. This would allow them to work towards a level two qualification by starting at entry level or level one, and to build up partial qualifications if most appropriate (Delorenzi 2007).

Expanding learning and training opportunities to everyone – not just those already in work – will mean integrating advice on how to make the best use of individualized entitlements into the role of Personal Advisers (PAs) in Jobcentre Plus, the government's employment service. Advisers should also continue to have a role in helping their clients to use their training entitlements for a period once they have moved into work. To ensure that individual skill needs are properly identified and met, the role of the PA would need to be considerably enhanced and upskilled, which we discuss in more detail below.

The emerging evidence of the importance of personal and soft skills in people's employment outcomes (Margo et al. 2006) suggests that there needs to be more research into how policy interventions can influence the development of these skills. Cohort data show that for those born in 1970, the effect of personal and social skills on later life chances was 33 times more important than for those born in 1958. The development of personal and social skills is also becoming more strongly related to parental income (ibid.). In the long term, policy needs to focus on developing these skills in young people, as Butler and Margo argue in Chapter 15.

How people access new opportunities

Sociologists have long argued that accessing work is not simply about raw skills and qualifications. It is also about the contacts and networks that people can call on in learning about new opportunities (see, for example, Granovetter 1995). And in a changing world where established career trajectories and progression ladders are becoming less common, these networks are becoming increasingly important to progression, but are unevenly distributed (Sennett 2006). Those in higher socio-economic groups are much more likely to have the 'cultural capital' that networks and contacts provide (ibid.).

One response has been to trial programmes that extend post-employment support for retention and advancement to disadvantaged groups through individual case management – along the same lines as the pre-employment support in welfare-to-work programmes. These programmes are being piloted and rigorously evaluated both in the US and the UK. The experimental evidence from the US on post-employment case management is limited and rather ambivalent, although it has been suggested that this has been due to less than optimal programme design rather than fundamental flaws in the model (Minoff et al. 2006). The Post-Employment Services Demonstration ran from 1994 to 1996, with case managers providing counselling and support, job search assistance and support service payments for work-related expenses. The evaluation found no impact on employment, earnings or welfare receipt – but it suggested that this might be due to limited contact between advisers and their clients and the lack of integration with any system of pre-employment support (ibid.).

A much larger-scale evaluation, the Employment Retention and Advancement demonstration, is now ongoing in the US, involving 15 different experiments across the US. Early results are only available from four, so it is impossible to draw definitive conclusions – but they are mixed. They suggest that some programmes can improve employment retention but that generating participation is difficult. However, one lesson that can be drawn is that post-employment support by itself is not enough to encourage progression: it needs to be better integrated with pre-employment services, education and training with greater attention given to the nature of the labour market itself (ibid.). The most positive evidence from the US is from those schemes in which pre- and post-employment support are fully integrated (Harker 2006).

In the UK, a similar evaluation – also called the Employment Retention and Advancement demonstration (ERA) – has been underway since 2003. It is targeted at three groups: jobseekers in the New Deal 25 Plus and New Deal for Lone Parents programmes, and low-income lone parents already in work. People taking part in ERA are offered additional support on top of what they receive through the New Deal: employment-related assistance from an Advancement Support Adviser (ASA) to help them find suitable work, solve work-related problems and advance in their jobs, and a tax-free retention bonus of up to £2,400 while in work. There are also additional funds for training and work-related emergencies. The UK pilot is therefore fairly well integrated into pre-employment support, training and additional financial support to encourage retention.

The final evaluation of the UK ERA is also still yet to report, but early evidence on retention and earnings progression is promising (Harker 2006; Dorsett et al. 2007). There are some very limited lessons that can be drawn from the early reports on implementation and attitudes.

While there are many similarities between the Personal Adviser (PA) job in the New Deal programmes, and the ASA job in ERA, the focus on progression requires a more proactive approach on the part of the adviser. A report on the early months of implementation found that ASAs expressed a lack of confidence in dealing with advancement issues (Hall et al. 2005). The fact that clients have very different work orientations suggest that the ability of ASAs to tailor their support to clients' attitudes and values, as well as their material and economic circumstances, will be key to ERA's success (Hoggart et al. 2006). This suggests that the role of the ASA will need to develop into a more highly skilled role than that of Personal Advisers, more akin to that of a recruitment consultant in the private sector.

However, as the integration of ERA into the New Deal recognizes, retention and advancement are goals that need to be incorporated into welfare-to-work programmes even while claimants are out of work and searching for work. This will require developing and evolving the New Deal programmes. As Lisa Harker (2006) has argued, we need to move from a work first to a 'work first plus' approach. This would continue to have a focus on moving people off benefits and into work, but with a more tailored approach that is sensitive to the employment needs and skills of each individual, and to the circumstances that may make sustainable employment difficult for them. Advisers would have more flexibility to decide whether it is appropriate for someone to move into the first job available, to continue searching for a job that is better suited to their progression opportunities, or to undertake full-time training prior to job entry (ibid.). They should also have access to a discretionary fund to help people meet the one-off costs of moving into work, as they currently do under ERA and Pathways to Work (see below). In this way, people would be supported in moving into work – but with a longer-term view to retention and advancement.

Evidence from both the UK and the US suggests that such an approach could pay dividends. In the UK, the government has been piloting Pathways to Work pilots for people in receipt of Incapacity Benefit (IB). These have been designed to offer a more personalized, tailored approach to supporting IB claimants into work, and to promote retention by recognizing the particular financial and other difficulties that disabled people may face in moving into work. Among other measures, they offer a more highly skilled adviser workforce, with specialist teams of trained IB Personal Advisers, Disability Employment Advisers and work psychologists; a return to work credit of £40 per week for the first year in work to encourage retention; and a package of in-work support, which may include mentoring, a job coach, occupational health support and financial support. It is too early to determine the effects of these pilots on retention, but early evidence suggests that the pilots are successfully increasing the number of people moving off IB (Blyth 2006), and increasing average monthly earnings (Adam et al. 2006).

The first job that someone moves into can also significantly affect retention and progression opportunities. A study of earnings progression in low-paid jobs in the US finds that it is not just employee characteristics that determine progression opportunities, but also certain characteristics of their employer (Andersson et al. 2005). More precisely, employment in higher-wage sectors of the economy – such as construction, manufacturing, transportation and health services – led to higher rates of advancement than employment elsewhere, as did working in large firms and firms with low turnover rates.

Job mobility from lower-wage to higher-wage employers in the same sector also generated higher wage growth over time than job retention – suggesting that while retention in *work* is key, promoting retention in the same low-paid job may not always be the right strategy.

Other US evidence also supports the claim that higher-wage work leads to more retention and progression (Rangajaran et al. 1998; Boushey 2002). Similarly, UK panel data show that progression out of low-paid jobs is more likely in certain sectors (Pavlopoulos and Fouarge 2006).

Perhaps unsurprisingly then, the most successful welfare-to-work programme in the 15 evaluated by the US National Evaluation of Welfare to Work Services was one in which applicants were encouraged to look for jobs that paid above the minimum wage and were more likely to offer long-term security, rather than take the first job available. Over the five years of the programme, participants worked 1.6 three-month periods more than control group members and earned about US$5,000 more on average (Hamilton et al. 2001). This programme also emphasized life skill, basic education and occupational training. In the UK, too, the Employment Zone pilots have found that good job matching was central to individuals sustaining work (Griffiths et al. 2005).

But incorporating the 'work first plus' approach into UK welfare-to-work programmes would cut against the grain of the targets against which their operational success is currently assessed (Hall et al. 2005; Bell et al. 2006). Currently, PAs are required to meet targets to move as many people back into work as quickly as possible, as befits the explicit goals of the New Deals. This may actually damage incentives to encourage retention: if a PA advises someone who successfully moves into work, leaves, rejoins the New Deal, and again moves into work, this counts twice towards their targets (Minoff et al. 2006).

If we are serious about incorporating retention and progression into welfare-to-work programmes, changing these targets to focus on retention and pay progression will be important (Leitch Review of Skills 2006; Work and Pensions Committee 2007). Targets need to be sensitive to the fact that taking the first available job may not always maximize someone's progression opportunities.

As early evaluations of the implementation of ERA have noted, delivering a more tailored approach that emphasizes retention and training as well as job entry will fundamentally change the role of the Personal Adviser. It will need to become a much more highly skilled and proactive job than it is at present. Advisers will need to be better trained, to proactively case-manage individual employment opportunities, and to match individuals to appropriate jobs that are more likely to result in retention and advancement.

The 'work first plus' model will also require advisers to work closely with employers to better understand the skills and qualities they are looking for. This will require PAs to develop better understanding of the local labour market and how it is likely to develop in the next ten years, and which skills people need to be encouraged to develop in order for jobs to be filled locally.

A resulting requirement may well be more resources for Personal Adviser training and salaries. But this should not be seen as problematic. If anything, it is entirely appropriate that the public sector acts as a showcase of best practice, leading the way in promoting greater progression trajectories for its own staff than it does at present.

The nature of work

Improving retention and progression will also require a focus on the nature of work itself. Here, we consider two areas: work–life balance, and the extent to which employers can be encouraged to upskill low-skill work and create more concrete 'career ladders'.

Difficulties in achieving work–life balance are a significant barrier to moving into work, and to retention and progression. In 2005, 58 per cent of Britons claimed to find their work stressful, and 66 per cent of these said it impacted on their home life (National Centre for Social Research 2005). Only 53 per cent believed they had the right 'work/life balance' (MORI 2005).

As discussed above, part-time work, largely the preserve of women, offers particularly poor progression opportunities. Carers may often be forced to choose between prioritizing their caring responsibilities and career advancement. Many women, when making the transition from full-time to part-time work, downgrade in their job (Connolly and Gregory 2007). This waste of skills harms both the individual and the economy. Hughes and Cooke examine these issues in more detail in Chapter 11. As they argue, the answer must partly lie in extending the right to flexible working to all employees. Employees should be required to advertise all jobs as part time, jobshare or flexitime unless there is good reason to do otherwise.

While the UK's political economy means that the emphasis on improving the supply of skills is the right one, we also need to tackle the low level of employer demand for skills to avoid a situation in which new skills are underused (Shah and McIvor 2006). One approach might be to encourage employers to build established career ladders within low-skill professions, akin to the promotion and development opportunities that are commonly available to employees in higher-skilled work. This is an approach that has been piloted in some areas of the US in professions such as long-term care and childcare (Fitzgerald and Wadia 2006). These programmes provide part-time education and training for workers, resulting in accredited qualifications and wage increases, and possibly advancement into higher positions on the career ladder. In some cases, new rungs on the career ladder are created to bridge the gap between positions; for example, between a certified nurse aide and a certified nurse.

The Early Childhood Education Career and Wage Ladder in Washington State brought progression and wider benefits. An evaluation of this programme found that the median hourly wages of childcare workers in participating centres increased compared to those at other centres, and that the quality of childcare also improved as staff motivation increased (ibid.). Similarly, the state of Kentucky provides grants to private sector employers to develop and implement career pathways that help to promote progression for low-skill employees (Holzer and Martinson 2005).

This is a relatively new area of policy and further work needs to be done to establish the effectiveness of these kinds of programmes, and their appropriateness for the UK. However, there is experience that can be built on. For example, the NHS has pioneered a 'skills escalator' approach which aims to promote retention and advancement (McBride et al. 2004). The government should consider rolling out structured career ladder programmes more widely within the public services and local government. In doing so, it would set an excellent example for the private sector.

Conclusions

Developing a better understanding of public policies that can promote retention and progression is fundamental to achieving the progressive vision of a society with equal opportunities and a decent minimum for all. As those engaged with public policy are increasingly realizing (see, for example, Harker 2006; Bell et al. 2006), it is becoming unsustainable to focus only on getting people into work at the expense of retention and progression. As we draw closer to the government's 80 per cent employment aspiration, achieving full employment will become more and more difficult with the traditional 'work first' approach alone. Instead we need a 'work first plus' approach, which combines job search with a more flexible, individualized entitlement to adult learning, adviser support on progression and retention, and policies that encourage employers to increase their demand for skills.

References

Abramovsky, L., Battistin, E., Fitzsimons, E., Goodman, A. and Simpson, H. (2005) *The Impact of the Employer Training Pilots on the Take-up of Training Among Employers and Employees*. Research Report No. 694. London: DfES.

Adam, S., Emmerson, C., Frayne, C. and Goodman, A. (2006) *Early Quantitative Evidence on the Impact of the Pathways to Work Pilots*. DWP Research Report No. 354. London: DWP.

Andersson, F., Holzer, H. and Lane, J. (2005) *Moving Up or Moving On: Who Advances in the Low-Wage Labour Market*. New York: Russell Sage.

Bailey, N. (2006) 'Does Work Pay? Employment, Poverty and Exclusion from Social Relations', in C. Pantazis, D. Gordon and R. Levitas (eds), *Poverty and social Exclusion in Britain: The Millennium Survey*. Bristol: Policy Press.

Bell, K., Branosky, N., Fitzgerald, J., Greenberg, M., Harkness, S., Hirsch, D., Minoff, E. and Wadia, A. (2006) *Staying On: Stepping Up: How Can Employment Retention and Advancement Policies Work for Lone Parents?* London: One Parent Families.

Blanden, J., Gregg, P. and Macmillan, L. (2006) *Accounting for Intergenerational Income Persistence: Non-cognitive Skills, Ability and Education*. London: Centre for the Economics of Education, LSE.

Blyth, B. (2006) *Incapacity Benefit Reforms: Pathways to Work Pilots Performance and Analysis*. DWP Working Paper No. 26. London: DWP.

Boushey, H. (2002) *Staying Employed After Welfare: Work Supports and Job Quality Vital to Employment Tenure and Wage Growth*. Washington DC: Economic Policy Institute.

Connolly, S. and Gregory, M. (2007) *Moving Down? Women's Part-Time Work and Occupational Change in Britain 1991–2000*. Oxford University Department of Economics Discussion Paper No. 302. Available at <www.economics.ox.ac.uk/Research/wp/pdf/paper302.pdf>.

Dearden, L., McGranahan, L. and Sianesi, B. (2004) 'An In-Depth Analysis of the Returns to NVQs Level 2'. Unpublished paper.

Delorenzi, S. (2007) *Learning for Life: A New Framework for Adult Skills*. London: ippr.

Dorsett, R., Campbell-Barr, V., Hamilton, G., Hoggart, L., Marsh, A., Miller, C., Phillips, J., Ray, K., Riccio, J., Rich, S. and Vegeris, S. *Implementation and First-Year Impacts of the UK Employment Retention and Advancement (ERA) Demonstration*. DWP Research Report No. 412. London: DWP.

Dickens, R. (1999) 'Wage Mobility in Great Britain', in P. Gregg and J. Wadsworth (eds), *The State of Working Britain*. Manchester: Manchester University Press.

Dickens, R. (2000) 'The Low Pay–No Pay Cycle: A Report for the Welfare to Work Team, HM Treasury'. Unpublished paper. London: Centre for Economic Performance, LSE.

Dixon, M. and Paxton, W. (2005) 'The State of the Nation: An Audit of Social Injustice in the UK', in N. Pearce and W. Paxton (eds), *Social Justice: Building a Fairer Britain*. London: ippr/Politico's.

Dixon, M. and Pearce, N. (2005) 'Social Justice in a Changing World: The Emerging Anglo-Social Model', in N. Pearce and W. Paxton (eds), *Social Justice: Building a Fairer Britain*. London: ippr/Politico's.

Evans, M., Eyre, J., Millar, J. and Sarre, S. (2005) *New Deal for Lone Parents Second Synthesis Report of the National Evaluation*. DWP Research Report No. 163. Sheffield: DWP.

Fitzgerald, J. and Wadia, A. (2006) 'The Poverty of Caring Work in the US', in K. Bell, N. Branosky, J. Fitzgerald, M. Greenberg, S. Harkness, D. Hirsch, E. Minoff and A. Wadia, *Staying On: Stepping Up: How Can Employment Retention and Advancement Policies Work for Lone Parents?* London: One Parent Families.

Goos, M. and Manning, A. (2004) *Lovely and Lousy Jobs: The Rising Polarisation of Work in Britain*. CEP Discussion Paper 0604. London: Centre for Economic Performance.

Graham, J., Tennant, R., Huxley, M. and O'Connor, W. (2005) *The Role of Work in Low-Income Families with Children – A Longitudinal Qualitative Study*. DWP Research Report No. 245. London: DWP.

Granovetter, M. (1995) *Getting a Job: A Study of Contacts and Careers*. Chicago: University of Chicago Press.

Green, A. and Owen, D. (2006) *The Geography of Poor Skills and Access to Work*. York: Joseph Rowntree Foundation.

Griffiths, R., Durkin, S. and Mitchell, A. (2005) *Evaluation of Single Provide Employment Zone Extensions to Young People, Lone Parents and Early Entrants*. DWP Report No. 312. London: DWP.

Hall, N., Hoggart, L., Marsh, A., Phillips, J., Ray, K. and Vegeris, S. (2005) *The Employment Retention and Advancement Scheme: Evidence from the Early Months of Implementation*. DWP Research Report No. 265. London: DWP.

Hamilton, G., Freedman, S., Gennetian, L., Michaelopoulos, C., Walter, J., Adams-Ciardullo, D., Gassman-Pines, A., McGroder, S., Zaslow, M., Ahluwalia, S. and Brooks, J., with Small, E. and Ricchetti, B. (2001) *National Evaluation of Welfare to Work Strategies. How Effective are Different Welfare to Work Approaches? Five-Year Adult and Child Impacts for Eleven Programs*. New York: Manpower Demonstration Research Corporation.

Harker, L. (2006) *Delivering on Child Poverty: What Would it Take?* A report for the DWP. London: TSO.

Hills, J. (2004) *Inequality and the State*, Oxford: Oxford University Press.

Hoggart, L., Campbell-Barr, V., Ray, K. and Vegeris, S. (2006) *Staying in Work and Moving Up: Evidence from the UK Employment Retention and Advancement (ERA) Demonstration*. London: DWP.

Holzer, H. and Martinson, K. (2005) *Can We Improve Job Retention and Advancement Among Low-Income Working Parents?* National Poverty Center Working Series 05-10. Michigan: National Poverty Center.

Kaplanis, I. (forthcoming) *The Geography of Employment Polarisation in Britain*. London: ippr.

Leitch Review of Skills (2006) *Prosperity for All in the Global Economy: World Class Skills Final Report*. London: HM Treasury.

Manning, A. and Swaffield, J. (2005) *The Gender Gap in Early Career Wage Growth*. Centre for Economic Performance Discussion Paper No. 700, London: Centre for Economic Performance, LSE.

Margo, J. and Dixon, M., with Pearce, N. and Reed, H. (2006) *Freedom's Orphans: Raising Youth in a Changing World*. London: ippr.

McBride, A., Mustchin, S., Hyde, P., Antonacopoulou, E., Cox, A. and Walshe, K. (2004) *Mapping the Progress of Skills Escalator Activity: Early Results from a Survey of Learning Account and NVQ Managers in Strategic Health Authorities*. Manchester: Manchester School of Management.

Minoff, E., Greenberg, M. and Branosky, N. (2006) 'Employment Retention: Evidence from the UK and the US', in K. Bell, N. Branosky, J. Fitzgerald, M. Greenberg, S. Harkness, D. Hirsch, E. Minoff and A. Wadia, *Staying On: Stepping Up: How Can Employment Retention and Advancement Policies Work for Lone Parents?* London: One Parent Families.

MORI (2005) *Observer* Election Research, 9 April.

National Centre for Social Research (2005) *British Social Attitudes: The 22nd Report*. November. London: Sage.

ONS (2006) *Annual Survey of Population*. Available at <www.nomisweb.co.uk/>.

Pavlopoulos, D. and Fouarge, D. (2006) *Escaping the Low Pay Trap: Do Labour Market Entrants Stand a Chance?* MPRA Paper No. 226. Munich: University Library of Munich.

Rangajaran, A., Schochet, P. and Chu, D. (1998) *Employment Experience of Welfare Recipients: Who Finds Jobs: Is Targeting Possible?* Available at <www.acf.hhs.gov/programs/opre/welfare_employ/post_employ/reports/employ_experiences/emp_experiences.pdf>.

Rigg, J. (2005) *Labour Market Disadvantage Amongst Disabled People: A Longitudinal Perspective*. London: CASE, LSE.

Rowthorn, R. (2004) 'The Impact on Advanced Economies of North–South Trade in Manufacturing and Services'. Paper presented at the First International Forum for Development, New York, 18 October.

Rowthorn, R. and Coutts, K. (2004) 'Commentary: De-industrialisation and the Balance of Payments in Advanced Economics'. Paper presented at the international conference on 'De-industrialisation and Industrial Restructuring', Seoul, South Korea, 5 December.

Sennett, R. (2006) 'Workers will carry on striking until they get a life', *Guardian*, 25 May.

Shah, H. and McIvor, M. (2006) *A New Political Economy: Compass Programme for Renewal*. London: Compass.

Strategy Unit (2004) *Designing a Demonstration Project: An Employment Retention and Advancement Demonstration for Great Britain Annexe 1 – The Justification and Evidence for Intervention*. London: Strategy Unit.

Wilson, R., Homenidou, K. and Dickerson, A. (2006) *Working Futures 2004–2014 National Report*. Warwick: Institute for Employment Research, University of Warwick. Available at <http://www.ssda.org.uk/ssda/pdf/Working%20Future%2020042014%20National%20R%20060215.pdf>.

Work and Pensions Committee (2007) *The Government's Employment Strategy*. Third Report of Session 2006–07. London: TSO.

Part 4
Community

10
Living Together: Diversity and Identity in Contemporary Britain

Alison Seabeck, Ben Rogers and Dhananjayan Sriskandarajah

Introduction

Many people who would describe themselves as 'progressive' feel that New Labour has betrayed progressive ideals of diversity, cosmopolitanism and anti-racism. They point to the government's tough talk and restrictive measures on asylum and immigration, its repeated criticisms of 'multiculturalism', and its understanding of and responses to Islamic extremism. Instead of welcoming outsiders, celebrating diversity and listening to minority grievances, many see a government obsessed with closing our borders, criminalizing asylum seekers, assimilating difference, unwilling to protect the interests of minorities, and oversimplifying the causes of terrorism.

Yet, as widespread as the betrayal sentiment may be, defences of Labour's record could and have been mounted from various directions. One route is to argue that Labour has not been as illiberal as the critics suggest. For example, since 1997, there has been a significant liberalization of several avenues of entry into the UK, especially in terms of work permits and the right of citizens of an enlarged European Union (EU) to come and work in the UK. It could also be argued that a party in government has to respond to public anxieties and real security threats in as effective a way as possible. Given that immigration and race have been among the top issues of public concern over the last few years, it would be political suicide to not act to reassure these anxieties. Similarly, in the face of new terror threats from within the UK, the government would be neglecting its responsibilities to the electorate if it did not do its utmost to prevent further atrocities such as the 7 July bombings in London.

Our aim in counterposing these two views on the government's record on immigration, integration and diversity is to highlight how contested and complex these issues are. Indeed, there is almost no policy area where you find greater or more visceral disagreement among progressives, or also less clarity of thinking, than this one. The left, in short, has found it hard to develop a compelling narrative on immigration, multiculturalism and cohesion. Yet there is no area where clear thinking and well-developed policies and practice are more important. Public concerns about immigration and race are at unprecedented levels – some 45 per cent of respondents to a poll in August 2006 identified these as important political issues facing the UK, more than for any other category of issues (Ipsos MORI 2007). Some argue that the two big challenges facing the UK over the next century are climate change and learning to live together as people of different races and faiths (Johnson 2006; Phillips 2006). What's more, the rate of social change – which many find so unsettling at the moment – is likely to continue as the large-scale movement of people in and out of the UK continues.

In this chapter, we attempt to outline what a social democratic policy framework for immigration, integration and identity might look like. We first look briefly at changes in Britain's demographic profile. Next we look at some of the best ways of tackling the policy challenges these throw up.

Growing diversity and the challenges it presents

There is no denying that Britain's ethnic profile is changing very significantly – and this is driven in large part by migration in *and* out of the UK. While Britons continue to emigrate in large numbers (some 200,000 left in 2005; see Sriskandarajah and Drew 2006), the UK has experienced high and sustained levels of net inward immigration in recent years (see Figure 10.1). This inward migration and higher fertility rates among some immigrant and minority groups have led to a doubling of the ethnic minority population within the UK in the last 25 years, from around 4 per cent in 1981 to 7.9 per cent in 2001, according to the Census. Moreover, the profile of Britain's new immigrant populations is very different from before. While the UK continues to attract large numbers of newcomers from 'old' Commonwealth countries such as Australia and New Zealand and from the rest of Europe, the last decade has seen rises in the numbers coming from 'new' Commonwealth countries (India,

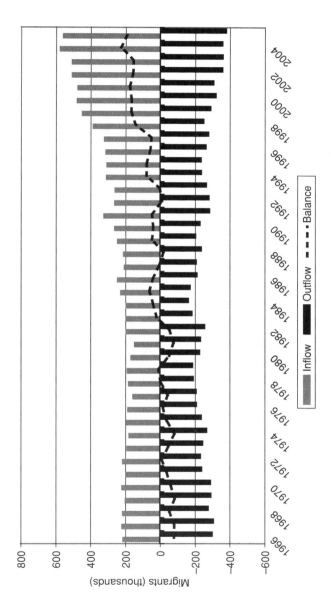

Figure 10.1 UK net immigration, 1966–2005

Source: International Passenger Survey.

Pakistan, the Caribbean, and so on) and from countries further afield such as Somalia, states of the former Yugoslavia, and the Philippines (see Figure 10.2). Since 2004, there has also been a dramatic rise in migrants coming from new EU member states. As a result of these increasingly diverse flows, places like London, which has absorbed almost half the migrants that have moved to Britain since 1991, and Slough, a town that has attracted relatively large numbers of new immigrants in recent years, are not just diverse – they are 'super diverse' (Vertovec 2006).

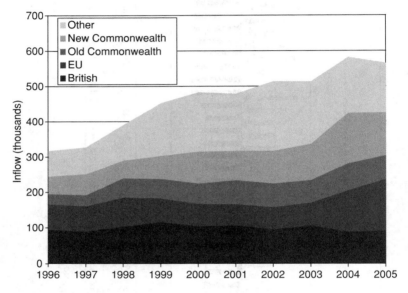

Figure 10.2 Migration to the UK by citizenship , 1966–2005

Note: EU data is EU15 for 1996–2003, and EU25 for 2004 and 2005.

Source: International Passenger Survey and Total International Migration, Office for National Statistics (ONS).

Immigration to the UK has, of course, been a positive thing for the UK. Immigrants have enriched our society in untold ways from a much-improved national cuisine to important global links. The economic contribution of immigrants is also significant. Immigrants have filled vacancies at both the bottom and top ends of the labour market, enabling the economy to expand and public services like the NHS to improve. Migrants are relatively strong net contributors to the UK exchequer, paying proportionately more in taxes and consuming less in terms of public services than the indigenous population (Sriskandarajah et al. 2005). The recent influx of migrants from the new EU member states has helped drive economic growth, keep down inflation and generate dynamism in some parts of the country. In the longer term, while by no means a panacea, high levels of immigration should help mitigate some of the problems posed by our ageing society.

Similarly, while many might bemoan the state of race relations in the UK, there is also plenty to be proud of. Britain has one of the most developed race equality *infrastructures*. Members of minority ethnic communities play prominent roles in society, from politics and business to sport and culture. Britain appears to be becoming a more tolerant place, as older generations who possessed what social scientists call an 'ethnic understanding' of national identity give way to those with a 'civic understanding' (Muir and Stone 2007). We should indeed acknowledge, the extent – impressive compared to many countries – to which Britain has succeeded in reimagining itself as a multicultural country. Witness the multicultural image that the country projected of itself in the successful bid to secure the 2012 Olympics, or the fact that the black athlete Kelly Holmes ranks alongside Margaret Thatcher and the Queen as Britons' most admired women (ICM 2004), or the fact that nearly two-thirds of all Britons think that 'multiculturalism makes Britain a better place to live' (BBC News 2005).

Yet it would be naive in the extreme to pretend that immigration or ethnic diversity are wholly unproblematic. Indeed, many of the challenges of managing migration and responding to growing diversity strike at the heart of the progressive project. Developing a coherent progressive position on immigration and diversity will require coming to terms with cross-cutting issues such as solidarity, deprivation, competition for scarce public resources, segregation and the rise of extremism. We touch on each of these challenges below.

A fundamental challenge for progressives relates to the possible tradeoff between diversity and solidarity (especially in the form of welfare state funding). This so-called 'progressive dilemma' (Goodhart 2004) raises the prospect that increasing diversity may undermine the very basis of support for a healthy welfare state. While we discuss the contested evidence for and against this thesis later, it is worth bearing in mind at the outset that how we respond to growing diversity matters for the entire progressive project.

While some migrant and minority groups are doing well, the correlation between socio-economic deprivation and potential socio-political exclusion among some ethnic minorities presents a particularly thorny second challenge. Some 69 per cent of Pakistanis and Bangladeshis in the UK live in poverty, compared to 19 per cent of the white population (Child Poverty Action Group (CPAG) 2004). Unemployment among Muslims is three to four times as high as among Christians (ONS 2004). Unemployment rates and economic activity rates among some new immigrant communities are also particularly worrying: nearly one in four Angolans in the UK are unemployed and a substantial majority of Somalis, Ethiopians and Albanians are economically inactive (Kyambi 2005). Improving the material attainment of these groups will be critical not just for the sake of greater equality but also for achieving better social cohesion.

The potential for competition between new immigrants and settled residents raises a third challenge for progressives. Some disadvantaged Britons, both white and non-white, may lose out, at least in the short term, in the competition that immigration brings to the labour market. Concerns about these impacts have led some commentators, including some from within the Labour party such as John Denham (BBC News 2006) and Frank Field (2006), to argue that the recent increases in immigration have pushed down wages and increased the strain on already stretched public services. The uneven spread of immigrants across the country raises a further challenge around the delivery of public services. The successful reception and integration of new migrants can often depend on how much experience of immigration an area has had previously but also on the capacity of local authorities and services to absorb new demands (ippr 2007). In some parts of the UK, newcomers are arriving in poorer areas that already have relatively large immigrant populations, thereby compounding problems of deprivation and exclusion. In other parts of the country, less used to immigration, the arrival of dispersed asylum seekers or migrant workers from an enlarged EU have caused tensions and created new challenges for service delivery.

There has been a lively debate on whether the UK is becoming more or less segregated by ethnicity in recent years (see Casciani 2006). While the academic literature on the question tends to disagree, depending on the methodology and scale used, there is no denying that at least in some parts of the UK people are living 'parallel lives' (Cantle 2005). Such segregation is often a healthy and expected outcome of newcomers clustering together but, in some cases, it may hinder the pursuit of social cohesion. Segregation may also result in tensions between communities, not just between white and other groups but among ethnic minorities – as the violent disturbances in the Lozells area of Birmingham in 2005, which saw clashes between Asian and black men, illustrated.

A fifth challenge relates to the rise of extremism, both in the form of the far-right and religious fundamentalism. While support for the far right in the UK has not been as strong as elsewhere in Europe, notably France and the Netherlands, the recent political victories of the British National Party in local elections does not bode well. Similarly, while people will disagree about the factors that have driven many young British Muslims to sympathize with or actively embrace the concept of *jihad* or 'struggle against unbelievers', few would deny that many young Muslims do feel deeply alienated from Western values and culture (Mirza et al. 2007; Garton-Ash 2007). Rising support for extreme political positions presents a clear threat not just to progressive ideals of inclusion and tolerance, but also to our democratic system through which progressives seek to effect change.

It is important to acknowledge, finally, that we are in some respects in uncharted territory and so need to be particularly vigilant against complacency. Liberal champions of recent immigration like to present it as just one more chapter in a long history of population movement into and out of this country (this way of framing things in fact goes back to William Defoe, writing in the early eighteenth century, but for a more recent example see Winder 2004). But it is arguable that immigration today is different in at least four respects. First, as already indicated, black and ethnic minority people are settling here in considerably greater numbers than ever before. Second, globalization in the form of cheap air travel and broadcast and communications technology, make it much easier for immigrants to retain ties with their communities of origin (Vertovec 2006). This is inevitably affecting processes of integration and mutual accommodation. Third, a much larger proportion of migrants are residing here on a temporary basis only. Fourth, at the same time local and national public opinion have become less accepting of authority, especially political authority, and in some respects more volatile. Policy imposed from above, even policy of the most impeccably progressive kind, will not be suffered by those subject to it (it is hard to imagine, for instance, Dutch voters rising up against the established political parties 30 years ago, in the way they have over the last few years). We live in new times. And we need new responses.

Ways forward

How should progressives meet the challenge of immigration and diversity? Given existing ethnic and racial diversity, and the strong principled and practical arguments, for welcoming further immigration, what sort of principles should guide progressive thinking and progressive policies in this area? In particular, how should we navigate our way between cosmopolitan liberals who would like the state and politicians to treat us all as culturally disembodied individuals, conservative nationalists who expect migrants to assimilate to the national culture, and radical multiculturalists? And what sort of policies and approaches look most promising when it comes to fostering cohesion on the ground?

The natural reflex for progressives will be to turn to material life. The pursuit of socio-economic equality, many will argue, is the tried and tested method of creating the conditions necessary for integration. There is no denying the importance of interventions to tackle the sort of deprivation discussed above or to protect the most vulnerable from adverse labour markets or poor experiences of public services. Improving social mobility among second and third generation immigrants may well be the most effective way of promoting their community's integration with British society. Yet we believe there is ample scope for progressives to move beyond the material and into the realm of identities and belonging.

It is certainly possible to overstate the importance of shared identities or origins to social democracy. Though David Goodhart's arguments (Goodhart 2004) are a welcome contribution to public debate and, in particular, a stimulating challenge to the left's tendency to embrace diversity in almost all its forms, he and others have probably exaggerated the role that cultural communality plays in underwriting public support for the welfare state. Countries like Canada and Australia have sustained relatively generous welfare states while embracing multiculturalism as official state policy, suggesting that perhaps the key factor distinguishing countries that do have more extensive welfare states from those (principally the US) that do not, is the existence or otherwise of strong labour movements and not 'diversity' (Banting 2006; Taylor-Gooby 2006).

But if some commentators may have overestimated the importance of shared cultures, there is also a tendency, more deep-rooted among progressives, to underestimate them and be blind to the dangers of celebrating and honouring 'minority' cultures and ways of life, and neglecting common understandings and identities. A more nuanced appreciation of the problems that can arise from diversity would have meant alarm bells going off in Bradford, Burnley, Oldham and elsewhere long before the outbreak of the disturbances of 2001. Similarly, it is arguable that today an unreflexive commitment to multiculturalism is blinding us to the problems that exist in public subsidy of translation and interpretation services, which have arguably gone past the point of helping migrants enter the national community and sometimes discourage them from doing so (Easton 2006). Something similar could be said of faith schools. We have been very good, as Ted Cantle argues, at building minority group consciousness, but less successful at building intergroup trust and shared identities (Cantle 2005).

Below we identify three key principles that should guide progressive policy in this area: fair treatment, respect for ethnic identities, and fostering shared identities at both the national and the local level.

Fair treatment

Social democrats have a principled commitment to social justice and public participation in democratic processes. But they also, characteristically, hope that social justice and democratic deliberation can provide a shared framework around which people of different backgrounds can unite – that where groups are fairly treated and fully engaged in collective decisions, ethnic and cultural tensions will diminish. But there are serious limits to this hope. Different groups understand social justice in different ways. And we are all naturally inclined to resent the beneficiaries of decisions that go against us, no matter how legitimate the decision-making process. There are also potential tradeoffs between the means by which decisions are made and their desired ends. An undue focus on process can sometimes have a detrimental impact on outcomes, especially where the resources being distributed are truly scarce.

Yet people of different backgrounds are much more likely to get along together where every effort is made to treat them fairly, and to demonstrate that they are being treated fairly. There is, in particular, as Nick Pearce indicates in Chapter 14, a growing academic literature that shows that people attach great value to fair procedures irrespective of whether the outcomes of such procedures are favourable to them.

Both the left and the right tend to acknowledge the importance of fairness, but they do so in a partial way. For the left, minority grievances are justified, while they see majority ones as tending to be an expression of xenophobia or prejudice. For those on the right it is the other way around – majority grievances are justified by state favouritism towards minorities, while minority grievances are based on prejudice against the national culture, its traditions and values. In fact there is a fair amount of prejudice on both sides – and this needs to be tackled directly. But both minority and majority grievances are not entirely founded on prejudice. Government and public services have a far from glowing record when it comes to equal-handed treatment of different groups or of engaging people affected by decisions in their processes. The decisions themselves are often far from fair. This naturally fuels resentment.

Four examples clearly demonstrate this. First, until recently, the dispersal and settlement of asylum seekers around the country occurred without any attempt to engage the host communities affected. Nor has government, local or national, been nearly active enough in challenging the 'myths' about the special treatment accorded to asylum seekers (Lewis 2005). Second, white working-class hostility to immigrants in the East End of London has been fuelled not just by xenophobia but by the conviction that these groups have been favoured over long-term residents; and this conviction has been fuelled in turn by a sense that housing policies – indeed, decisions about migration – were imposed on them from without (Dench et al. 2006): 'No one asked us.' Third, Alison Seabeck draws the same lesson from her years as a constituency adviser in Greenwich. Long-term residents were much less likely to object to immigration if they felt that their views had been heard and if the principles governing allocation were properly explained. Fourth, resentments that underlay the unrest in the Northern mill towns were traceable in part to the belief that the 'other side' was favoured by government – and a sense, shared by local people from all sides, that they were missing out on half a decade of national economic growth (Cantle 2005).

Britain's growing diversity and the threat of increased intergroup tension therefore give new life to old social democratic arguments in favour of fairness and participation.

Respect for minority identities

As important as social justice is, progressives also need to attend to issues of culture and identity – that is, to the extent that these are separable from issues of fairness at all. Many progressives are naturally wary of 'identity politics' of any form – they would rather politicians and the state limit themselves to promoting and honouring 'universal values' of, say, justice, democracy, tolerance, and stay out of the business of discouraging some identities and fostering others. They have a point at least insofar as there is an important role for government in actively promoting support for universal principles – through, for instance, the teaching of citizenship in schools and colleges. We would argue, in particular, that we do not do nearly enough to teach or promote principles of global citizenship and international democracy.

At the same time, identity is an extremely powerful political force, for good or ill. The way we understand and relate to others is determined in large part by our sense of who we are and who they are. And while there are limits to the extent to which public policy should or can shape identities – a sense of belonging cannot simply be imposed on people

– we neglect them at our peril (Muir 2007). It is often said that support for extremist politics, of either the religious or nationalist sort, has its roots, in part, in our failure to offer compelling non-extremist identities (see, for example, Fukuyama 2007). This, we believe, is broadly right.

As already indicated, one of the principles that should guide progressive policy-makers confronting the challenges of diversity is respect for minority ethnic identities. 'Multiculturalism', understood not as the fact of diversity but as policies and practices that display respect for minority cultures, gets a very bad press these days, with politicians and commentators falling over themselves to administer its last rites – moves that are made all the easier by the way 'multiculturalism' is defined in any way that suites the argument of its obituarists. There are, as we have already emphasized, dangers inherent in multiculturalism, as there are in all 'isms' – and very definite shortcomings in the form it has sometimes taken in the UK. Multiculturalism should not be permitted to allow groups to behave in ways that cannot be squared with liberal democratic values – though the question of what should and what should not be allowed is often hard to resolve in practice. We confidently draw the line at such things as forced marriages and female circumcision, but, for example, other subtler ways in which the subjugation of women is perpetuated the issue is less clear. Nor should multiculturalism be allowed to justify segregation.

But there are good reasons why we should respect the cultural differences that immigrants bring with them. Here we limit ourselves to two. First, culture is, as Bikhu Parekh has argued, part of someone's identity; respecting newcomers therefore involves respecting their culture. Second, minority cultures can enrich the horizons and deepen the self-understanding of the host culture (Parekh 2005). These are admittedly abstract arguments, and their implications, in practical terms, are far from clear. One sort of change on which liberals of a traditional kind and multiculturalists will agree is the need, as far as is feasible, for the country to stop favouring group-specific values and practices – to recast civic oaths and national ceremonies, say, in more multi-religious or secular form and make religious education less sectarian. Many multiculturalists, however, will go beyond this fairly minimal version of the position, and argue for active support for, or public recognition of, ethnic traditions and values represented in the country. They will point out, to begin with, that no country can ever erase altogether the cultural/ethnic imprint of its founding fathers or divest itself of its group-specific cultural biases (Kymlicka 1995; Miller 1995). National languages, the civic calendar, built heritage in the form of churches, civic buildings, and so forth, and the collections preserved in museums, libraries and archives, will inevitably be 'weighted' towards long-standing cultures and religions – they are likely to speak more to native groups than immigrant ones. In these circumstances, even-handedness dictates that we provide some public recognition to minority cultures and traditions. Indeed, the strictures we have been exploring above around the importance of fairness apply, arguably, to the distribution of 'recognition' as much as they do to other goods. As recent ippr-organized focus groups with white residents of Barking clearly showed, they feel that the state not only favours minority groups materially, but also does more to support their identities than it does to support white working-class identities. Immigrant groups have long claimed, fairly enough, that they are now part of the national story and want to be recognized as such. If we are going to continue as a nation to mark Christmas – and it is hard to imagine why we would want to expunge it entirely from national life, even if we could – then public organizations should mark other major religious festivals as well.

It is clear that here, too, we soon find ourselves confronted with hard cases. It is often difficult to draw the line between publicly recognizing an ethnic or religious identity and encouraging uncritical submission to it. Perhaps the best we can say is that as a general rule we should try to find ways of honouring and recognizing diverse cultures, while encouraging as much openness within them, and critical reflection on them as possible. If it seems appropriate to invite faith representatives to a public event, the invitation should go not just to elderly male religious leaders, but to a more representative selection of believers. If our public museums are to stage exhibitions that explore minority heritage, they should also ensure that a wide range of specialists and commentators are invited to take part in a discussion about their relevance. If we are going to teach school children about the major religions represented in our community, we should do so in a way that encourages them to reflect critically on the claims of each and all.

Practical arguments point in a similar direction. National culture will inevitably represent something of a barrier to most minority ethnic migrants. Our goal in the medium and long term should be to dismantle the barriers that can be dismantled, and help equip migrants and their children to negotiate or understand those – such as national languages and shared historical reference points – that remain. But in the shorter term, arguments based on social justice and integration suggest that we should recognize and support migrant cultures, by, for instance, subsidizing community groups and cultural events, providing some resources and services in translation (perhaps aimed particularly at minority ethnic women, for whom cultural barriers are often highest) and accepting that minority ethnic people will want to live among people of similar background – while guarding, of course, against the emergence of monocultural ghettoes. In our enthusiasm for promoting intergroup contact and building 'bridging social capital' we should not forget that group consciousness-raising and 'bonding social capital' can have value too.

Common belonging

We turn finally to the contribution that a sense of common belonging or shared identities and shared culture might make to community cohesion. Far too often, especially in recent years, public discussions on belonging focus on the extremes, on those who refuse to buy into the core values of society. As discussed earlier, this sort of political extremism is something that has to be tackled urgently. Yet this challenge should not distract us from the longer-term challenge of promoting interaction and sharing between the vast majority of the British population who do aspire to common belonging.

We begin with a progressive case for national identity as a source of common belonging before looking briefly at local identity. British progressives have tended to be wary of the nation state and its culture. Nations, it is often argued, foster conflict abroad and minority oppression at home. Patriotism, they argue, is just another word for chauvinism. Yet there are many reasons why progressives should take the claims of nationality seriously and seek to sustain a strong national culture. Put negatively, it has long been clear that nationalistic or patriotic sentiment is very deep-rooted, having again and again defied predictions of its demise (Berlin 1981). True, there is some evidence of a weakening national identity in the UK – not just a weakening of identity with Britain, as distinct from its constituent nations, but a weakening of felt-allegiance to Britain or its constituent nations (Muir and Stone 2007). Nevertheless, national identity remains a potent political force, as the recent rise in concern about migration, or the fever that surrounds the World Cup, indicates. Progressives should not allow conservatives and extreme nationalists to exploit what remains a deep-rooted identity to their own advantage.

Put more positively, nationality has, as Gordon Brown has argued, genuine progressive potential (Brown 2007). A common sense of nationality can provide an indispensable underpinning to the sort of liberal, tolerant and fair political order that liberals and multiculturalists value. Strangers, in short, are much more likely to honour the principles of social justice that liberals care about, or respect the minority groups that multiculturalists defend, if they feel bound by common ties of national culture – by a sense of shared history and geography. Social democracy requires solidarity not merely 'within groups, but across them, and this in turn depends upon a common identification of the kind that nationality – and perhaps nationality alone – can provide' (Miller 1995: 140).

But what, then, of the claims that national cultures are inherently uncosmopolitan and militaristic or that they necessarily discriminate against minority groups at home? Addressing the first of these, nationalist movements have often, of course, been expansionist and bellicose – but not always. Since the Second World War, liberal nation states have coexisted more or less peaceably. In fact, some nations (Sweden being an obvious example) define themselves partly by their internationalism. They take pride in their role as promoters of global peace and economic development.

The argument for the second of these claims – that national cultures are inherently discriminatory – is similarly doubtful. It is true, as we have already said, that no effective state can ever be entirely culturally neutral. At the very least, democratic civic life depends on shared languages – but languages to some degree always carry the culture of the people whose language it originally was (Kymlicka 1995). To some extent, then, the critics are right – but the discrimination they describe is avoidable. Indeed, their argument can be turned against them and in favour of policies that oblige or encourage all citizens, in the name of common belonging, to learn, as far as they are capable, the national language(s) and acquire some familiarity with the history of the nation, its customs and manners. Without this sort of knowledge, a shared sense of belonging will perish, and democratic political life and social democratic objectives will fail.

Yet the demand this places on minorities is hardly onerous – or at least not when minority cultural rights are respected in the way we have argued they should be. And it is to some extent matched by similar demands that the claims of liberal nationality make on the cultural majority. For if the goal of progressive nationality is a culture with which all groups can reasonably identify, then this requires that those from the majority culture also adapt, and give up on those aspects of national identity that exclude newer groups – or if not give them up, then reconceptualize them as aspects of their religious or ethnic identity, rather than their national identity. Requiring minorities to acquire some proficiency in the national culture does not seem unreasonable if – but only if – native citizens are willing to 'open up' national institutions and practices to newcomers and give a more inclusive cast to national narratives and symbols. It is reasonable to discourage the development of mono-minority cultural neighbourhoods, but only if every effort is made to prevent employers discriminating against minorities in the labour market, and promote minority presence in national life. It is right and proper to require Muslim schools to admit some non-Muslims and to provide a sympathetic overview of non-Muslim belief systems, but only if we require the same thing of Christian schools. This is the truth often articulated but not quite captured by the language of 'integration', that forging a shared sense of home requires a process of ongoing mutual adjustment (Parekh 2005). Integration is a two-way street. Earlier we argued that the obligation to respect minority cultures requires the state to shed those aspects of its national culture that exclude minority cultures. The argument we have been making in this sections points in the same direction, though this time the end is not so much to respect minority cultures as to sustain a national culture.

What does all this mean in practice? What sort of values and culture might bind us all together in our increasingly pluralistic societies, and what can we do to promote them? The first point to make here is that liberal or social democracy has the potential to be the best source of shared identity in a multicultural society like ours. A sense of national belonging cannot, however, be sustained by abstract values alone. It is nurtured through a sense of shared history and geography. Building a common sense of belonging, then, means not merely promoting support for 'democratic values' (as Gordon Brown is sometimes inclined to suggest), but elaborating a national culture or identity around these. Below we list a range of ways this can be done.

- Honouring democratic values in the history we teach and in the heritage we sustain. As a general rule, we in Britain have not tended to celebrate our democratic heritage – there are few public statues of democratic heroes, and we do not do much to commemorate democratic struggles. This needs to change. The national heritage organizations have recently run campaigns to save and celebrate industrial heritage, and English Heritage is leading a drive to protect and maintain England's churches. We need similar programmes for our democratic heritage. There is a strong case for investing more in our democratic built heritage and functioning civic buildings and spaces.
- While we may be culturally fragmented, there is scope for fostering greater shared cultural experiences. This might be done through

national institutions such as the BBC, but also through museums and galleries. Sport has become an enormously powerful carrier of national identity, and we need to continue efforts to make national sporting events more inclusive

- We need to be better at finding ways of making the social contract a reality that a citizen feels and recognizes – the principles of mutual respect and cooperation, and of shared rights and duties, that are the essence of democracy and so of progressive national identity. Here we suggest there are some fairly easy wins. We should be looking to turn the now wholly bureaucratic process of registering a child into a meaningful civic right – an occasion on which the parents, the extended family and the public, in the form of the state and its public services – affirm what they expect of each other and owe each other. We could similarly be looking at the sort of messages sent by other encounters we have with the state – whether it is paying taxes, doing jury service or voting (Cottam and Rogers 2005) – and at our ceremonial life more generally. As Francis Fukuyama (2007) has put it:

> American life is full of quasi-religious ceremonies and rituals meant to celebrate the country's democratic political institutions: flag-raising ceremonies, the naturalisation oath, Thanksgiving and the 4th of July. Europeans, by contrast, have largely deritualised their political lives. Europeans tend to be cynical or dismissive of American displays of patriotism. But such ceremonies are important in the assimilation of new immigrants.

We suggested earlier that social democrats have not always recognized the progressive potential of national identity. But they have arguably been even less sensitive to the value of shared local cultures or a shared sense of local belonging. Britain has a famously centralized state. Planning and regeneration and economic policy have done little to protect or foster individuality, with policy-makers slow to see the downside of allowing town centres to become 'clones' of one another (Simms et al. 2005). Yet research suggests that as many 'traditional identities', like class and party political identities, have declined in recent decades, so people's sense of local belonging remains strong – and that this is true across income and ethnic groups (Muir and Stone 2007). Of course, not all local identities are civic or inclusive – identifying strongly with an all-white or all-Asian neighbourhood can feed xenophobia. Yet most local identities, especially in multicultural areas, do not have a strongly ethnic aspect to them. Sir

Michael Lyons has recently been advocating that local government is about more than the delivery of local services – it is, or should be about 'place-shaping' (Lyons 2006). If he means creating shared local identities, he is right.

This has important, if often subtle, implications for local government policy across the board, from schools' admissions policy, through to the sort of cultural activity we fund, to the way we plan localities and design and maintain public places. Coming back to the issue of the uneven impacts of immigration around the UK, a renewed emphasis on local initiatives may be worthwhile but will require more responsive resource allocations to react to changing patterns in the movement of people.

Conclusion

We have here attempted to furnish an overview of some of the challenges posed by increasing diversity, and map out progressive approaches to them. Our basic argument is that long-standing social democratic commitments to democracy and social justice may well be important in tackling deprivation and exclusion among some communities. However, we believe that progressives need to do more than just this. They need to develop an identity politics that seeks to build a sense of common belonging while recognizing the claims of minority cultures. At a time when a growing number of people are becoming attracted to extremist identities – identities that threaten democracy itself – the fostering of meaningful and attractive versions of minority and national identity are extraordinarily urgent.

However, we end by stepping back from our discussion of substantive principles and policies and reflecting briefly on the sort of methods that should guide government activity in this area – on the question not of what government should do, but how it should do it. The point to be made here is that progress in promoting community cohesion will very much be a matter of spreading sensitivity across public agencies and promoting fairness and transparency in the system, rather than investing heavily in a narrow set of 'key policies' or building up an expert body of scientifically validated knowledge. It is important, of course, to identify particular political reforms and policy initiatives that should help promote better relations between Britain's many ethnic groups. We have argued for some of these here – notably turning the registration of a child into a civic rite, and doing more as a nation to celebrate our distinctly democratic heritage. Similarly, rigorous social science research has a role to play – it would be helpful, for instance, to know more about what shapes people's shared sense of local identity and what government can do most effectively to increase this. But what will really decide whether Britain develops into a country at ease with its ever-growing diversity, or falls victim to extremism born of intolerance, will be the extent to which politicians and public servants develop a more or less instinctive appreciation of the challenges before them, an intuitive feel for the values that should guide them, and the know-how to turn challenges into opportunities.

Over the last five years or so we have seen encouraging moves in the right direction. Central government, for instance, has recognized that the leading role in promoting better intergroup relations will often lie with local government, while seeking to encourage greater awareness of the challenges among local agencies and to build their capacity. The newly established Commission on Integration and Cohesion, with its explicit focus on local initiatives, will help in this process. Many cultural and heritage organizations have taken an active part in reaching out to minorities, promoting intercultural exchange and fostering a sense of common belonging. Enthusiasm for choice in schools and support for religious schools is being tempered by awareness of the importance of intergroup contact. But the sort of developments highlighted earlier – a rise in concern about immigration, support for extremist political movements, and the social exclusion of many minority ethnic people – suggest we still have a long way to go.

One of the fundamental challenges in all of this will be how to measure success. There is no Public Service Agreement (PSA) target to tell us whether we have devised the best interventions to respond most effectively to diversity. And there is unlikely ever to be one. Instead, we are left with some very thorny policy challenges that generate some bitter debates – is the government welcoming of outsiders; is New Labour interested in celebrating diversity; and do progressives understand social cohesion? Amid this contestation, however, emerges a moment in which the left can rethink how to marry progressive principles with concerns about fair treatment of all, respect for identities and the promotion of common belonging.

Acknowledgements

The authors are grateful to Laurence Cooley, Liz Forgan, Nick Johnson, Julia Margo, Rick Muir and Nick Pearce for their useful comments and suggestions. As always, final responsibility for what is said lies with the authors.

References

Banting, K. (2006) 'Ethnic Diversity and the Welfare State: A North American Perspective', in S. Delorenzi (ed.), *Going Places: Neighbourhood, Ethnicity and Social Mobility*. London: ippr.

BBC News (2005) 'UK Majority Back Multiculturalism'. BBC News Online, 10 August. Available at <http://news.bbc.co.uk/1/hi/uk/4137990.stm>.

BBC News (2006) 'New Call for EU Migration Delay'. BBC News Online, 15 August. Available at <http://news.bbc.co.uk/1/hi/uk_politics/4795595.stm>.

Berlin, I. (1981) 'Nationalism: Past Neglect and Present Power', in H. Hardy (ed.), *Against the Current*. Oxford: Oxford University Press.

Brown, G. (2007) Keynote speech to the Fabian Future of Britishness conference, 14 January. Available at <www.fabian-society.org.uk/press_office/news_latest_all. asp?pressid=520>.

Cantle, T. (2005) *Community Cohesion: A New Framework for Race and Diversity*. Basingstoke: Palgrave Macmillan.

Casciani, D. (2006) 'So Who's Right Over Segregation? BBC News Online, 4 September. Available at <http://news.bbc.co.uk/1/hi/magazine/5304276.stm>.

Cottam, H. and Rogers, B. (2005) *Touching the State: What Does it Mean to be a Citizen in the 21st Century?* London: Design Council.

CPAG (2004) *Poverty: The Facts*. London: CPAG. Available at <www.cpag.org.uk/ publications/extracts/PtheF5summary.pdf>.

Dench, G., Gavron, K. and Young, M. (2006) *The New East End: Kinship, Race and Conflict*. London: Profile Books.

Easton, M. (2006) 'Cost in Translation'. BBC News Online, 12 December. Available at <http://news.bbc.co.uk/1/hi/uk/6172805.stm>.

Field F. (2006) 'A State of Influx'. Comment posted on Comment is Free, 21 September. Available at <http://commentisfree.guardian.co.uk/frank_ field/2006/09/what_does_managed_migration_me.html>.

Fukuyama, F. (2007) 'Identity and Migration', *Prospect*, February.

Garton-Ash, T. (2007) 'The demagogic cliches of right and left can only make things worse', *Guardian*, 1 February. Available at <www.guardian.co.uk/Columnists/ Column/0,,2003319,00.html>.

Goodhart, D. (2004) 'Too Diverse?' *Prospect*, February. Available at <www.prospect-magazine.co.uk/start.asp?P_Article=12394>.

ICM (2004) *The People's Poll*. London: ICM. Available at <www.icmresearch.co.uk/ reviews/2004/UKTV-Endemol%20Nov%2004/TPP%20News%20Release.pdf>.

ippr (2007) *The Reception and Integration of New Migrants*. London: CRE.

Ipsos MORI (2007) *Long Term Trends: The Most Important Issues Facing Britain Today*. London: Ipsos MORI. Available at <www.mori.com/polls/trends/issues. shtml>.

Johnson, N. (2006) '"We're All In This Together": The Challenges of Diversity, Equality and Solidarity', *Renewal*, 14 (4): 18–25.

Kyambi, S. (2005) *Beyond Black and White: Mapping New Immigrant Communities*. London: ippr.

Kymlicka, W. (1995) *Multicultural Citizenship*. Oxford: Clarendon Press.

Lewis, M. (2005) *Asylum: Understanding Public Attitudes*. London: ippr.

234   *Politics for a New Generation*

Lyons, M. (2006) *National Prosperity, Local Choice and Civic Engagement: A New Partnership between Central and Local Government for the 21st Century*. London: Lyons Inquiry into Local Government.

Miller, D. (1995) *On Nationality*. Oxford: Oxford University Press.

Mirza, M., Senthilkumaran, A. and Ja'far, Z. (2007) *Living Apart Together: British Muslims and the Paradox of Multiculturalism*. London: Policy Exchange. Available at <www.policyexchange.org.uk/images/libimages/246.pdf>.

Muir, R. (2007) *The New Identity Politics*. ippr online working paper. London: ippr.

Muir, R. and Stone, L. (2007) *Who Are We? Identities in Britain 2007*. ippr online working paper. London: ippr.

ONS (2004) *Labour Market: Muslim Unemployment Rate Highest*. London: ONS. Available at <www.statistics.gov.uk/cci/nugget.asp?id=979>.

Parekh, B. (2005) 'Unity and Diversity in Multicultural Societies'. Lecture delivered at the International Institute for Labour Studies. Geneva: ILS. Available at <www.ilo.org/public/english/bureau/inst/download/1parekh.pdf>.

Phillips, T. (2006) Speech to the CRE Race Convention, 26 November. Available at <www.cre.gov.uk/Default.aspx.LocID-0hgnew0nu.RefLocID-0hg00900c002.Lang-EN.htm>.

Simms, A., Kjell, P. and Potts, R. (2005) *Clone Town Britain: The Survey Results on the Bland State of the Nation*. London: New Economics Foundation.

Sriskandarajah, D., Cooley, L. and Reed, H. (2005) *Paying Their Way: The Fiscal Contribution of Immigrants in the UK*. London: ippr.

Sriskandarajah, D. and Drew, C. (2006) *Brits Abroad, Mapping the Scale and Nature of British Immigration*. London: ippr.

Taylor-Gooby, P. (2006) 'Is the Future American? Or Can Left Politics Preserve European Welfare States from Erosion through Growing "Racial Diversity"', in S. Delorenzi (ed.), *Going Places: Neighbourhood, Ethnicity and Social Mobility*. London: ippr.

Vertovec, S. (2006) *The Emergence of Super-Diversity in Britain*. Centre on Migration Policy and Study (Compas) Working Paper 06-25. Oxford: Compas. Available at <www.compas.ox.ac.uk/publications/papers/Steven%20Vertovec%20WP0625.pdf>.

Winder, R. (2004) *Bloody Foreigners: The Story of Immigration to Britain*. London: Little, Brown.

11
Children, Parenting and Families: Renewing the Progressive Story
Beverley Hughes and Graeme Cooke

Out from behind closed doors – the rise of the politics of the family

The nature of childhood and family life are touchstone dilemmas of our time. How to be a good parent *and* earn a decent living? How to negotiate the freedoms and pressures of contemporary adolescence? Whether at the school gate, in the media or across the social sciences, few topics provoke such heartfelt debate. One explanation for this is that the pervasive insecurities of modern society often end up confronting us through their intensely personal impacts on families and local communities.

As the context of family life evolves, new claims and concerns move up the public agenda, reframing the relationship between government and families. This forces both progressives and conservatives to question traditional orthodoxies – as well as the very ways in which modern, enabling government is done.

The landscape of support for children and families has improved radically over the last decade, as a result of deliberate political choices. However, too many families still struggle too often in their everyday lives – with these struggles rooted in issues of time, money, relationships, support and skills, or more acute difficulties. Crucially, though, helping families thrive in the modern world requires more enabling government, not less public action.

The future agenda for children, young people and families is now fiercely contested political territory. This marks a welcome shift given that this is central terrain in shaping a more just, fair and equal society, in the vanguard of progressive politics. Therefore, in light of social change, political flux and emerging evidence, the time is right to ensure that progressive analysis and solutions genuinely address the everyday hopes and realities of modern family life.

Twenty-first-century families – new challenges for progressives

The idea of 'the family' as an institution headed by two married parents – one primary earner, one primary carer – still tends to be our default frame of reference. However, this family type only emerged during the late nineteenth century and the first half of the twentieth century, largely as a function of Britain's industrial society and entrenched through the Beveridge welfare settlement (Therborn 2004). As Margo, Sodha and Vance have set out in Chapter 4, the last 30 years have seen profound shifts in both family composition and working patterns. By 2004, just one-fifth of families could be described as 'nuclear' (that is, comprising two married and cohabiting parents where only one worked at least 16 hours per week (Lyon et al. 2006)). However, well-rehearsed headline trends – fewer marriages, increased cohabitation, more single parents and rising female employment (Babb et al. 2006) – fail to capture the complexity of modern family life (Williams 2004). The landscape of family policy is continually being reshaped by shifting cultural norms and attitudes, the contemporary politics of identity, gender and rights, and the impact of economic globalization on patterns of work and care (Bonoli 2004; Lewis and Giullari 2005; Taylor-Gooby 2005).

These profound changes provide the backdrop to current anxieties about 'twenty-first-century childhoods', encapsulated in the worrying increase in child mental health problems (Meltzer et al. 2000) and the prevalence of 'risky' behaviours among young people (Margo et al. 2006). Growing up and raising a family in a less certain society brings both new possibilities and new challenges. Hope and anxiety about parenting are nothing new, but are now openly debated with greater public scrutiny and rising expectations. Raising a family is a fundamentally intimate process, but we *all* have a shared interest in supporting its success.

Contemporary childhood is still underpinned by inequality. For many growing up in Britain today there is unparalleled prosperity, freedom and opportunity. However, those in the lowest socio-economic groups still face persistent disadvantage and injustice. A rising tide – driven by a strong social justice agenda – has not lifted all boats. Parents' access to money, time, choice and control – at home and at work – are neither equitably nor justly distributed. Alongside a traditional social democratic concern for poverty, work and education, 'quality of life' issues are increasingly significant, not least because the link between personal affluence and 'happiness' is far from clear cut (Layard 2005). Such dilemmas are often raised in the context of 'work–life balance', but pertain equally to questions of relationships, identity and belonging.

As social change reshapes the terms of political debate, so advances in social science confront policy-makers with increasingly sophisticated perspectives on family life. Research in psychology, neuroscience and child development provides an ever richer understanding of childhood, with parents and the family context a ubiquitously significant factor. While Labour has stabilized and begun to narrowly reduce the widening inequalities of the 1980s and 1990s, it is both self-evident and unacceptable that the socio-economic background of parents still powerfully shapes how well children do. Compared to a decade ago, we are also gaining a stronger grasp of the significance of parenting attitudes, styles and behaviours – framed by family contexts – and the impact of various policies aimed at supporting children and families.

So, a decade into a Labour government, has progressive thinking kept pace with this evolving story about contemporary family life?

Too often analysis from both left and right has started with questions about the 'structure' of the family, rather than the interests of the child. Two parents or one parent? Who is the breadwinner and who is the carer? Progressives have a proud tradition of championing tolerance and social liberalism. However, in standing up to narrow-minded moralizing and prejudice towards different family forms, some on the left have been guilty of a laissez-faire attitude towards family life. Coupled with the right's fatalistic narrative of moral and social decline, this has obfuscated a primary focus on the best interests of children and young people, while failing to realize the aspirations of adults as parents and individuals in their own right. Debate on the family among progressives has often taken place primarily through the prism of gender politics. However, focusing on what children need can highlight the potential for a mutually reinforcing relationship between the emerging fatherhood agenda and women's claims for domestic and economic equality.

Confronting the tensions in family policy: what do children and young people need?

Marriage and family structure – a partial story told from the wrong perspective

Family policy debate has long been dominated by competing claims about the merits of marriage compared with so-called 'non-traditional' family types. To summarize an often desperately polarized argument, some on the right have suggested marriage matters for everything, with others on the left appearing to counter that it matters for nothing. This decades-old dispute has invariably been more politically charged than child-friendly, with both sides tending to see marriage as a weathervane for wider social and moral mores.

There is strong evidence that growing up in an intact family with married parents is associated with a range of positive outcomes for children (Amato 2005; McLanahan et al. 2005). (Similar questions of marriage and public policy in the context of the increasingly challenging transition of young people to adulthood are addressed by Butler and Margo in Chapter 15.) Beyond the fierce debate about marriage, such findings are probably unsurprising and intuitive to most people. However, assuming the marriage certificate alone is not what makes the difference for children, the real question remains, what does? According to leading American research, the advantages of marriage for children are: a higher standard of living, more effective and cooperative parenting, better-quality family relationships, and fewer stressful or disruptive events (Amato 2005). While these are clearly advantageous for children, they are certainly not inevitable, less still essential, characteristics of marriages (Williams 2004; Gibson-Davis 2006). For example, though statistics point to the longer average length of this relationship form, marriage is more often a consequence of stability than its cause. Family structure does not determine child outcomes; rather, it seems that marriage is often a proxy for positive parenting approaches and family environments (Amato 2005; McLanahan et al. 2005).

Ultimately, debating the value of marriage for children is largely academic. The real public policy challenge is how to respond to the evidence. Voices on the right suggest marriage should be incentivized through the tax system and government rhetoric (Cameron 2006; Kirby 2005). The overarching progressive criticism of this argument is not that marriage is irrelevant, but that such an approach skews priorities by confusing means and ends. Our number one concern is what children and young people need – not the form of relationship between their parents, but its quality and stability. While the best marriages can provide hugely beneficial contexts for children, those characterized by hostility and conflict can be equally harmful (Stanley 2005). Also, it is misleading and fatalistic to suggest that children growing up with cohabiting or lone parents cannot, and do not, do well. What children need is not marriage itself but the love, stability, financial well-being and positive parenting that ideal marriages often provide – and it is fostering these attributes that public policy should focus on.

There are three simple but quite fundamental problems with a public policy agenda aimed at trying to persuade people towards marriage. First, there is absolutely no evidence it can work. The period in the 1970s, in which married couples were explicitly favoured in the tax system, coincided with the biggest rise in 'non-traditional' relationships during the last century. Ironically, rates of marriage have gone up and divorce down in recent years, at a time when some argue the benefits system 'encourages' people to be single parents. But are tax implications ever really paramount in the forming and breaking of adults' intimate relationships? Second, in the process of failing in its objective, a 'marriage promotion' agenda skews scarce resources towards already married parents, and away from children of cohabiting or single parents (who are twice as likely to be experiencing poverty) (Department for Work and Pensions (DWP) 2006a). Third, it is desperately partial in its scope and ambition. It has nothing to say, for example, about supporting positive parenting. Indeed, beyond a tax break and 'moral leadership', it offers no practical help with building strong, cooperative relationships around children. By focusing on the quality of family relationships – including the benefits of strong marriages – progressives can reframe a tired debate by starting with what children need: maximum stability and minimum disruption and conflict.

A policy agenda with these as its fundamental objectives would focus on three key areas. First, the promotion of engaged, active fatherhood and an emphasis on parental responsibilities as lying equally with both parents. Early paternal interest boosts children's development (Flouri 2005), tends to lead to sustained involvement throughout childhood (Goldman 2005), and is linked to greater stability in the couple relationship (Snarey 1993; Hohmann-Marriott 2006). Second, it should focus on the adoption of more holistic and preventative approaches to supporting healthy relationships – among married, cohabiting and separated parents. Powerful evidence links the quality of couple relationships to positive parenting and improved child outcomes – with positive 'emotional spillover' from one intrafamily relationship to others (Carlson and McLanahan 2005; Emery 1999). For example, mutually supportive couple relationships have been found to enhance both warm maternal parenting and positive paternal involvement (Bzostek et al. 2006; Reynolds et al. 2001). Unlike a tax break for married couples, practical support at the right time has been shown to have dramatic effects on the quality and stability of parental relationships (Cowan and Cowan 2002). Relationship type, of course, is far from the only factor affecting relationship stability. For example, a recent study found that the richest fifth of cohabiting couples are more likely to stay together than the poorest fifth of married couples (Benson 2006). Third, given that it is unrealistic to think all couple relationships will last for ever, we must help parents and children to manage family fracture in ways that minimize its emotional, practical and financial damage. Evidence suggests the way separation or divorce are handled determines their impact on children (Neale and Smart 2001; Smart et al. 2001). It is often the sudden changes in daily life that are most disruptive for children: a sudden drop in household income or moving house or school. Therefore, public policy should encourage and support families to manage such traumatic events as cooperatively and constructively as possible. Significantly, positive father engagement is associated with more regular post-separation contact and higher rates of maintenance payments – both of which are beneficial for children (Peters et al. 2004; Dunn 2005).

Progressives should not be indifferent to family structure, nor suggest that marriage is unimportant. Committed and loving family relationships are exactly what children need, and many parents provide this through marriage. Despite considerable socio-cultural change, marriage remains an aspiration and a positive choice for many. However, to use public policy or public money to signal that other family types do not – or cannot – provide supportive contexts for children is inaccurate, fatalistic and counter-productive. There is no evidence that the increasing diversity of relationships and family forms has diminished our yearning for commitment and connectedness (Williams 2004). The task for progressives is to focus on practical ways to promote parental responsibilities and strong couple relationships around children, managing the impact of separation and divorce where it occurs. In the final analysis, adult relationships are private and discretionary, while parental responsibilities endure and have a public dimension – and the role of government derives from this.

A holistic families policy – who parents are and what parents do

Our collective fixation with family structure has led us to neglect and obfuscate the significance of parenting attitudes, styles and behaviours, or 'what parents do'. In the experience of parenting and being parented, these are often what make the tangible difference. Also, by equating 'parent' with 'mother', we have drastically and damagingly underestimated the critical influence of fathers on their children's lives (Stanley 2005).

There are well-established links between 'who parents are' and how well their children do. Parents' social class, income, age and education are all found to be significantly related to their children's cognitive and non-cognitive development at age ten (Feinstein and Bynner forthcoming). A causal relationship between parental income and children's educational performance – which affects university entry and later labour market success – is a powerful driver of the intergenerational transmission of life chances (Blanden and Gregg 2004). Mothers who stay on in post-compulsory education are more likely to parent in ways which enhance their own children's learning (Feinstein and Duckworth 2006).

However, this pathway is far from straightforward. A mother whose own experience of education was positive is more likely to be actively engaged in her child's schooling, which we know has a major effect on attainment (Feinstein et al. 2004). Therefore the benefits a child derives from having a mother who was educationally successful herself are tied up in a bundle of positive approaches and endowments (Desforges with Abouchaar 2003). So part of the significance of family structure and social class lie in the ways they mediate, shape and contextualize parental attitudes, styles and behaviours. For example, both parents' education (structure) and parents' interest in children's education (process) are significant – and almost certainly do not operate independently of one another (Blanden 2006).

Recent research by ippr and others suggests the strength of the association between family income and children's non-cognitive development is heavily mediated by 'micro-level' processes – such as parental warmth and interest (Margo et al. 2006; Gregg et al. 2006). There is also a systematic association between the quality of the parent–child relationship and young people's subjective well-being (Quilgars et al. 2005). A recent Home Office study found that getting on badly with at least one parent more than doubled the likelihood of a young person engaging in anti-social behaviour (Wood 2005). US research investigating high levels of depression and substance misuse among the children of money-rich, time-poor parents suggests that the link between family income and non-cognitive development is complex and contingent (Levine 2006).

If public policy has failed to fully grasp or respond to the significance of parenting, we can look to the social sciences – especially psychology – for a sophisticated story about children's development. Advances in neuroscience (Dixon 2005) and attachment theory (Bowlby 2005) enhance our understanding of early brain development and the critical role of a primary carer in the early stages of life. As children grow, the importance of warm, consistent and assertive parenting is well established – especially in promoting social and emotional development and resilience against social class disadvantages (Amato and Fowler 2002; Johnson et al. 2006; Waldfogel 2006). However, challenging circumstances make positive parenting much more difficult (Seaman et al. 2006). For example, how much harder is parenting while coping with poverty, or being positively involved in your child's education if your own experience of school was poor? To what extent can positive parenting overcome entrenched social class disadvantages (Hango 2005)? Addressing questions such as these will increasingly be central to adopting the right progressive policies.

In reviewing the evidence, we see a picture of family life which, unsurprisingly, accords closely with our own everyday experiences. While no two families are the same, similar hopes, shared identities and common challenges cut across otherwise substantial divides. Our natural empathy for the happiness or pain of other families – no matter how little else we share – reflects the powerful sense of what it is to be a mother, a father, a brother, a sister. However, every family is unique, the product of constant interaction between context and experience, structure and agency. The task for progressive politics is to respond to this complex combination of commonality and diversity.

Social class creates the context for parenting and family life and so remains a potent determinant of children's outcomes. This makes core social democratic concerns – tackling poverty and inequality, narrowing the gap in school attainment and promoting full employment – as crucial as ever. However, inequality in children's well-being and life chances is driven by a dynamic interplay between social class and human action. A renewed progressive agenda must therefore combine sophisticated strategies to tackle traditional injustices with innovative approaches in new and fertile policy terrain.

As we deepen our understanding of how and why families are so significant for children – and the enabling role government and society can play – the danger for progressives may not be cries of 'nanny-statism', but accusations of knowing inaction.

The progressive agenda: responsible parents, enabling government, a family-friendly society

A progressive agenda starts with children at the centre, supported by positive, responsible parents, enabling government and a family-friendly society. Public policy should promote positive parenting and support parents to realize their aspirations for themselves and their families. A robustly child-centred approach is both right in itself, as well as offering a potential route through some of the difficult tensions and tradeoffs in family policy.

Good parenting represents a vital and valued contribution to society – just like entrepreneurship and public service – and we should do more to recognize this publicly. Equally, being a parent is a major responsibility which adults have a duty to live up to. It is a parent's job to bring up their child, though the vast majority express the desire for help at one time or another. Our approach to families is embodied in a progressive notion of rights and responsibilities, which fall fairly on all and bind society together around children. Government and society have a duty to create a context in which families can thrive; parents must meet their responsibilities to their children; while civil society – employers, charities, neighbourhoods and friends – has a role in shaping a family-friendly society. If we get the role of government and society right, the partnership between individual and collective contributions to parenting can be an empowering and enriching one.

Before addressing future policy terrain, it is vital to acknowledge two issues which pervade progressive family policy. First, ending child poverty is absolutely the number one progressive priority. How to accelerate progress towards this goal is the subject of ongoing debate (Harker 2006), with the tough but essential policy question being how to increase the incomes of poor households while also promoting sustainable, family-friendly employment. Second, we must fundamentally recast the current 'parent–mother' paradigm to recognize and mainstream the role of fathers across family policy (Stanley 2005). Progress on both of these is a prerequisite for any progress at all.

Parents at the heart of public services

If we believe that enabling government serves to bolster, not diminish, the liberty, agency and capabilities of families, the central question quickly becomes, how? How should our public and community services be organized so that they fulfil this purpose? Among a host of complex issues, two key themes emerge: first, embedding the indispensable role of parents throughout existing public services; and second, harnessing the expertise and experience of local community and kinship resources – alongside the public and voluntary sectors – to offer personal, responsive and empowering support to parents.

Too often the culture of our great national public services – schools, hospitals and social services – has been to support children almost independently of their parents and family. This has invariably been the product of the best child-centred intentions or because of practical difficulties. Occasionally it has been because professionals have seen some parents as uncooperative, obstructive or harmful. In place of an adversarial culture, we need a paradigm shift towards open and mutually reinforcing partnerships between families and public services focused around what children need. Strategies which recognize and enhance parents' own sense of capability and self-efficacy are likely to be far more effective and sustainable.

The 'Every Child Matters' agenda has focused on the importance of 'partnership' between agencies and professionals. A high priority for its next phase must be to embed fully the role of parents and families as integral, indeed primary, agents in local partnerships and strategies for children. Meaningful engagement with parents, recognizing the often crucial contribution of grandparents, and seeking whole-family solutions are often not easy options for practitioners. Therefore, government has a role in providing leadership and ensuring there are the time and resources for such work to take place. Equally, parents have a responsibility to cooperate with professionals who are trying to support their children.

Embedding parents as essential partners alongside public services will involve profound shifts in organizational and professional culture. For example, services may need to rethink how they assess needs and design packages of support. Professional language and ways of working will need to adapt so as to break down barriers and change attitudes – not least to facilitate the involvement of fathers as the norm rather than the exception. Such a cooperative culture between parents and services would also shape a far more favourable context for prevention and early intervention, with professionals working alongside families to support them in supporting their children. There is a role for local leadership, too, as in Manchester, where the city council is championing parents through a holistic and ambitious parenting strategy (Manchester City Council 2005). The model we envisage would position public services as mutually supportive partners alongside parents: 'more government' absolutely need not mean 'less parents'.

Alongside seeking more flexible and porous boundaries between public services and families, support for parents must go beyond traditional institutions. Progressives recognize that any parent may want help of some sort at some time – not just so-called 'problem families'. The only questions are: what support, when, how is it provided, and by whom? Historic underfunding and low priority mean that provision of parenting support remains patchy, with evidence of major unmet need (National families and Parenting Institute (NFPI) 2006; PricewaterhouseCoopers 2006). However, good practice exists – especially in the voluntary sector – and we are learning more about what works (Barlow et al. 2002; Department for Education and Skills (DfES) 2006a; Kendrick et al. 2000;

Moran et al. 2004; Sanders 1999; Sweet and Appelbaum 2004). A pilot of whole-family interventions has seen local complaints about anti-social behaviour either cease or significantly decrease in eight out of ten cases (Department for Communities and Local Government (DCLG) 2006a). Elsewhere, a combination of the internationally renowned 'Incredible Years' programme with SPOKES (Supporting Parents on Kids Education) has been found to result in more sensitive parent–child interactions, less harsh discipline and improved child concentration (Scott et al. 2006).

The diversity of family circumstances and needs requires a menu of flexible and personalized responses – empowering parents with the capabilities and resources to help them bring up their children. Children's centres and extended schools can be transformational institutions, providing bases for a diverse network of family support resources. Indeed, recent research shows that many Sure Starts are leading the way, demonstrating how responsive services can reach out and empower parents (Ball and Niven 2006; Williams and Churchill 2006).

Emerging models of parenting support are thus in the vanguard of refashioning more personalized public services. Many parents get practical help and emotional advice from friends and family – the kind of day-to-day support that often prevents serious problems occurring then growing (Linington 2006). But what about families who are more isolated? Filling this gap in informal support with an army of professionals would be neither appropriate nor effective. However, we could look to the Doula[1] movement, which is about experienced mothers providing non-medical, practical and emotional support to expectant and new parents. Harnessing the resources and expertise of local parents by promoting such local networks, alongside high-quality home visiting services in the first couple of years (Olds 2006; Cabinet Office 2006), would demonstrate a powerful partnership between personalized public services and innovative community action.

Civic activism of this kind is not, as many on the right would argue, a replacement for the state, but rather a complement to it. Enabling government does not 'crowd out' such community activity; it can help it to prosper by providing the spark and support for the collective endeavours of local people. Children's centres and extended schools, for example, can offer practical advice and assistance, helping groups of parents to support one another and access premises or resources (Williams

1. Meaning 'handmaiden' in Ancient Greek, the term 'Doula' was coined by Dana Raphael, a medical anthropologist, in her book *The Tender Gift*, which promotes the benefits of women teaching other women about mothering. The principle could equally hold for mutual support among fathers.

and Churchill 2006). We should learn from and significantly extend the Parenting Fund, which provides a central pot of money for voluntary and community groups to draw on to meet local needs. Another way to look beyond traditional institutions is to unlock the potential of new media and technologies. Online services have the potential to offer families information and signposting, as well as opportunities to share experiences and advice. Websites like netmums.com and the planned Parents Direct service, a single information hub, demonstrate the way forward.

Strengthening relationships, managing separation

It is the quality and stability of family relationships that make the difference for children, and while intimate adult relationships may end, parental responsibilities do not. Therefore the focus of government and wider society should be supporting parents to build and maintain strong, cooperative relationships around children.

Proposals for both parents to be registered compulsorily on the birth certificate mark an important step in recognizing the equally precious roles of mothers and fathers. Are there ways of further strengthening this notion of shared parental responsibility, providing a more solid foundation for future cooperation? Perhaps new parents – whatever their relationship status – could be offered the chance to make a public commitment to their partnership as parents, through a form of civic declaration? Beyond this, we must shape a culture of positive paternal engagement, both at home and with public services.

We should also take a quantum leap in our attitude and approach to relationship support. Historically, public policy has struggled to grasp and respond to the significance of emotional well-being. There is strong evidence that therapeutic support can have a marked impact on the quality of couple relationships (Cowan and Cowan 2002; McCarthy et al. 1998; Simons 1999). However, access to such support is severely restricted – both by a chronic undersupply of affordable services and continued ambivalence about the efficacy of therapeutic couple interventions. We should therefore establish a distinct Relationship Fund, with families able to draw down money themselves to purchase support services from an approved provider. Such a fund could champion the importance of happy, healthy relationships for our society; and draw together emerging evidence and best practice, while also registering providers to map services and ensure quality. Finally, engaging with fathers, supporting couple relationships and adopting whole-family perspectives must be mainstream aspects of professional training and development for the children's workforce.

In response to irreconcilable differences between couples, our approach must be to provide every opportunity for them to maintain as stable and cooperative a parental relationship as possible – with children's views and interests paramount throughout (in some circumstances it will not be in children's best interests for a particular parent to remain active in their lives – in cases of violence, abuse or neglect, for example). Ensuring strong links between relationship support and mediation services, and the new Child Maintenance and Enforcement Commission will therefore be essential. Such links would ensure a clear pathway for families from support in sustaining relationships, to opportunities for dealing consensually with the consequences of separation, through to mandated settlements and enforcement if all else fails. Negotiating agreements between themselves is exactly what most separating parents say they want the chance to do (DWP 2006b). Agreements between parents – which should look to consider emotional and practical as much as financial matters – could still be verified through court-backed 'Parenting Plans' or consent orders (Department for Education and Skills (DfES) 2006b).

Parental responsibilities must be seen as a non-negotiable act of citizenship. We are right to have the highest expectations of parents and to hold them to their responsibilities – financial, emotional and practical. Tough enforcement action is therefore legitimate and necessary, including considering deducting child support directly from the pay packet of non-resident parents. Maintenance payments are currently responsible for lifting around 100,000 children out of poverty, despite only 15 per cent of single parents on Income Support receiving any child support (DWP 2006c). We should allow resident parents on low incomes to keep a substantially greater proportion of child maintenance before it starts to affect their benefit entitlement – which would significantly reduce child poverty. This would also encourage non-resident parents to pay up, knowing that their child, not the taxman, will reap the benefits (Harker 2006).

Working and caring – shaping a family-friendly society
Ask parents what would make life easier and they invariably talk about time, money, choice and control. Despite our society becoming richer and more technologically advanced, balancing the competing pressures of family life is still far from easy. Complex family lives, and often fragile and fragmented employment patterns, mean that finding time and space for family while building a career and making ends meet can be a tough task. Increasing numbers of parents are also caring for elderly relatives, while extended transitions to adulthood mean that many young people

still live in the parental home well into their twenties. Such profound changes are rooted in long-term macro-shifts in the economy, culture and aspirations. However, the nature of the political response and the role of government are deeply contested.

Voices from both right and left suggest we should try to halt or reverse changes in work and family patterns – because of their links to increased poverty risks and job insecurity or supposed 'moral and social decline'. But the economic and family structures of the 1950s and 1960s cannot be remade, and these aspects of modernity have also heralded many liberating and emancipatory trends. However, in seeking to enable citizens to cope and thrive in the modern world, progressives cannot be indifferent to the underlying structures and contexts which shape their capabilities.

Progressives seek to enable families to make the choices that are right for them, but recognize that such choices are fundamentally framed by people's particular circumstances. Extensions to childcare, parental leave and flexible working rights have helped more families balance their working and caring responsibilities. However, the challenge now is to ensure that all families are able to 'activate' these and further such entitlements. The notion of 'parental choice' is, of course, far more complex than the expression of a rational, personal preference (Lewis forthcoming). People's choices are invariably interdependent, with a complex ripple of impacts and a range of cultural and emotional factors at play. The capacities of families to exercise 'choice' are unevenly distributed and severely constrained for many. Compare, for example, the choices facing a single or disabled parent, with limited skills, little family support and mounting personal debt, with those of an affluent, professional couple in a stable relationship with friends and family close by. Crucially, it is only progressive politics which understands that enabling meaningful parental choice for all requires positive action.

It is increasingly impossible to combine 'working like a man' with 'caring like a woman'. Rather than provoking a wider refashioning of gender roles, rising female employment has, in practice, often resulted in women having two jobs: a new professional one, plus the old domestic one. On average, twenty-first-century dads are spending more time with their children than ever before – with many expressing a desire to be more actively involved (Equal Opportunities Commission (EOC) 2006a). However, gender divides in family life remain deeply embedded in our cultural psyche. In the end these are challenges for society, with progressive government an agent of positive change.

We must reimagine the 'ideal worker', away from the fantasy of someone with no commitments other than work, and balance this with a notion of the 'ideal parent', held in the highest esteem for valuing and prioritizing this role. Current proposals for parity between full-time caring and paid work in accruing pension entitlement point towards further ways of publicly recognizing the contribution of parents to society. Many parents want to work and the vast majority have to. However, they rightly baulk at sacrificing their family life in order to earn a living. The goal of progressive politics is to help families negotiate this balancing act, avoiding negative tradeoffs between time and money, both of which are vital commodities for children.

Labour's focus on supporting more parents to work, and boosting family incomes through the national minimum wage and tax credits, has helped take 700,000 children out of poverty. Moving forward, we need a more nuanced approach to work, money, time and parenting. More time does not automatically mean happier families or improved outcomes for children. It is the quality of parenting and relationships that really counts. However, the extra challenges of parenting while constantly stressed or worried about making ends meet are well known (Wilson 1974; Orthner et al. 2004). Also, for most of us, family time has an intrinsic, unquantifiable value. Therefore our notion of 'choice' must be sufficiently flexible to help parents meet their aspirations to spend more time with their children, as well as fulfilling other responsibilities on which society depends.

We must shape the flexible labour market in the interests of families, resisting the trend towards what Richard Reeves has described as 'economy-friendly families' (Reeves 2005). The government is committed to legislating for a full year of paid maternity leave, six months of which will be transferable to fathers. However, research into early child development, parental aspirations to care for their children, and the gendered impact of current work–life balance policies, suggests that progressives must go further. Short-term priorities, to enable more fathers to support their young children, should be doubling the length of paid paternity leave to a month (Stanley 2005) and progressively increasing the rates of maternity and paternity pay – currently only around two-thirds the level of the minimum wage – so that caring for young children is a realistic option for all families.

As children grow, starting nursery then school, their parental needs change and they benefit from greater interaction with the world around them. At this point, many parents will want, and need, to work, but will strive for this to tessellate with family life. Therefore, the existing 13 weeks of parental leave should be paid, the right to request flexible working should be extended to all employees, and all jobs should be advertised as part time, jobshare or flexitime, unless there is a sound business case not to. It is unacceptable for family-friendly employment to be an option only for those parents, often women, who downshift in pay and status or have an exceptionally high labour market value. 'Work–life balance' is simply unobtainable for many low-income families, for whom the impact of low pay, job insecurity and long or atypical working hours bite hardest (Dean and Coulter 2006). Driving up the quality of childcare while keeping the cost to parents down is also critical for boosting children's outcomes and widening parental choices about working and caring (Stanley et al. 2006).

Making more time for families also means ensuring parents do not have to work all hours to make ends meet. Low wages often make a part time or shorter working week unaffordable. Despite repeated increases in the minimum wage, half of children experiencing poverty live in households where at least one adult works (Harker 2006). Therefore we must go further in ensuring that parents doing a decent week's work earn a 'living wage' through their pay packet to support their family. Finally, closing the gender pay gap would end the travesty of women having to work more hours to take home the same as men, helping to break the traditional division of labour within families (DCLG 2006b).

Tensions between working and caring are also often implicated in relationship breakdown. It is clearly easier to combine raising children and earning a living where these tasks are shared by two mutually supportive adults. Enabling families to have the time to parent positively is therefore an important part of supporting parental relationships. There is strong evidence that the stresses and strains associated with long hours and low pay – for example, where parents work and care in 'shifts' and still struggle to get by – can be damaging to family relationships (Ghate and Hazel 2002; Barnes et al. 2006). Poverty is a cause of fractured families as well as a consequence. Lone parents often face a much tougher task in finding time to parent as well as time to earn – another reason for raising our expectations of non-resident parents, both to pay up and to contribute practically and emotionally.

Progressive politics for families

The last decade has seen a revolution in the prominence of children and families within our political discourse. In the wake of major policy and delivery progress, and against the backdrop of shifting cultural, economic and demographic realities, all the political parties are now trying to show off their family credentials (EOC 2006b). A decade ago the public endorsed Labour's commitment to reverse both the scandalous rise in child poverty and a philosophy of active neglect towards children and families. The challenge now is to deepen the progressive agenda, by taking action to try to ensure every family is properly supported and every child's potential is realized. This means showing how an effective combination of enabling government and civic action enlarges, not diminishes, liberty, community and opportunity. It can be done by reorientating children's services to embed the integral role of parents; trailblazing personalized and responsive approaches to supporting parents in their communities; adopting a proactive and realistic approach to family relationships and parental responsibility; and genuinely enabling all parents to make the choices about working and caring that are right for them and their children.

Progressives cannot be complacent. There is an alternative story about families and the role of government that is told by the political right. This proclaims that what families need is for government to get out of their way: that liberty advances when the state withdraws; that charities, community groups and individuals themselves will meet the needs of families, if only government would 'get off their backs'. This is a meagre vision of a minimal government, confined to rescuing the so-called 'underclass' from their individually caused, pathological failings. It is a recipe for a passive and fatalistic agenda, constraining both individual liberty and collective well-being, as power, choice and autonomy, inequitably distributed, remain the preserve of the few. Progressives must confidently, optimistically and openly expose these fallacies.

Parenting is an intensely special and personal task, but it has profound public impacts. We must raise the stakes and change the terms of the debate: supporting and valuing parents, while making sure they live up to their responsibilities in return. We cannot measure or define a 'happy family'. However, we know that strong relationships, the right support at the right moment, and enough time and money are universally important. Each family is unique – and none of us has a recipe for getting it right. However, in the end, we know that when families thrive, the whole of society benefits, and children and parents can know alike a precious good that cannot be bought or sold.

References

Amato, P. (2005) 'The Impact of Family Formation Change on the Cognitive, Social and Emotional Wellbeing of the Next Generation', *Marriage and Child Wellbeing*, 15 (2). Princeton: Brookings.

Amato, P. and Fowler, F. (2002) 'Parenting Practices, Child Adjustment and Family Diversity', *Journal of Marriage and Family*, 64.

Babb, P., Butcher, H., Church, J. and Zealey, L. (2006) *Social Trends 36*. London: ONS.

Ball, M. and Niven, L. (2006) *Outreach and Home Visiting Services in Sure Start Local Programmes*. National Evaluation of Sure Start. London: HMSO.

Barlow, J., Parsons, J. and Stewart-Brown, S. (2002) *Systematic Review of the Effectiveness of Parenting Programmes in the Primary and Secondary Prevention of Mental Health Problems*. Oxford: Health Services Research Unit, University of Oxford.

Barnes, M., Bryson, C. and Smith, R. (2006) *Working Atypical Hours: What Happens to Family Life?* National Centre for Social Research. Available at <www.natcen.ac.uk/natcen/pages/publications/research_summaries/NC132_Working.pdf>.

Benson, H. (2006) *The Conflation of Marriage and Cohabitation in Government Statistics – A Denial of Difference Rendered Untenable by an Analysis of Outcomes*. Bristol: Bristol Community Family Trust.

Blanden, J. (2006) *Bucking the Trend: What Enables Those Who Are Disadvantaged in Childhood to Succeed in Later Life?* DWP Working Paper No. 51. London: DWP.

Blanden, J. and Gregg, P. (2004) *Family Income and Educational Attainment: A Review of Approaches and Evidence for Britain*. CMPO Working Paper Series No. 04/101. Available at <www.bris.ac.uk/depts/CMPO/workingpapers/wp101.pdf>.

Bonoli, G. (2004) 'Modernising Welfare States. Explaining Diversity in Patterns of Adaptation to New Social Risks'. Paper presented at the 2nd ESPAnet Annual Conference, Oxford.

Bowlby, J. (2005) *Making and Breaking of Affectional Bonds*. London: Routledge.

Bzostek, S., Carlson, M. and McLanahan, S. (2006) *Does Mother Know Best? A Comparison of Biological and Social Fathers After a Non Marital Birth*. Working Paper No. 27. Center for Research on Child Wellbeing, Princeton University.

Cabinet Office (2006) *Reaching Out – An Action Plan on Social Exclusion*. London: TSO.

Cameron, D. (2006) 'The Best is Yet to Come'. Speech to the 2006 Conservative Party Conference.

Carlson, M. and McLanahan, S. (2005) *Strengthening Unmarried Families: Could Enhancing Couple Relationships Also Improve Parenting?* Working Paper No. 02-16-FF. Center for Research on Child Wellbeing, Princeton University.

Cowan, P. and Cowan, C. (2002) 'Strengthening Couples to Improve Children's Wellbeing', *Poverty Research News*, 3.

DCLG (2006a), *Anti-Social Behaviour Intensive Family Support Projects*. Housing Research Summary No. 230. London: TSO.

DCLG (2006b) *Government Action Plan – Implementing the Women and Work Commission Recommendations*. London: TSO.

Dean, H. and Coulter, A. (2006) *Work–Life Balance in a Low-Income Neighbourhood: Preliminary Findings Report*. London: LSE.

Desforges, C., with Abouchaar, A. (2003) *The Impact of Parental Involvement, Parenting Support and Family Education on Pupil Achievement and Adjustment: A Literature Review*. DfES Research Report No. 433. London: TSO.

DfES (2006a) *Parenting Support – Guidance for Local Authorities in England*. London: TSO.

DfES (2006b) *Parenting Plans: Putting Your Children First – A Guide for Separating Parents*. London: TSO.

DWP (2006a) *Opportunity for All – Eighth Annual Report 2006*. London: TSO.

DWP (2006b) *Future Policy Options for Child Support: The Views of Parents*. London: TSO.

DWP (2006c) *A Fresh Start: Child Support Redesign – The Government's Response to Sir David Henshaw*. London: TSO.

Dixon, M. (2005) *Brave New Choices: Behavioural Genetics and Public Policy*. Discussion Document. London: ippr.

Dunn, J. (2005) 'Daddy Doesn't Live Here Any More', *The Psychologist*, 18 (1).

Emery, R. (1999) *Marriage, Divorce, and Children's Adjustment*. California: Sage.

EOC (2006a) *21st Century Dad*. Equal Opportunities Commission. Available at <www.eoc.org.uk/pdf/21st%20_century_dad.pdf>.

EOC (2006b) *Sex Equality and the Modern Family: The New Political Battleground*. London: Equal Opportunities Commission. Available at <www.eoc.org.uk/pdf/ICM.pdf>.

Feinstein, L. and Bynner, J. (forthcoming) *The Benefits of Assets in Childhood as Protection Against Adult Social Exclusion: The Relative Effects of Financial, Human, Social and Psychological Assets*. London: Centre for Research on the Wider Benefits of Learning, Institute of Education.

Feinstein, L. and Duckworth, K. (2006) *Are There Effects of Mothers' Post-16 Education On the Next Generation?* London: Centre for Research on the Wider Benefits of Learning, Institute of Education.

Feinstein, L., Duckworth, K. and Sabates, R. (2004) *A Model of the Inter-Generational Transmission of Educational Success*. London: Centre for Research on the Wider Benefits of Learning, Institute of Education.

Flouri, E. (2005) *Fathering and Child Outcomes*. London: John Wiley & Sons.

Ghate, D. and Hazel, N. (2002) *Parenting in Poor Environments: Stress, Support and Coping*. London: Jessica Kingsley Publishers.

Gibson-Davis, C. (2006) *Family Structure Events on Maternal and Paternal Parenting in Low Income Families*. Working Paper 2006-30-FF, September. Center for Research on Child Wellbeing, Princeton University.

Goldman, R. (2005) *Fathers' Involvement in their Children's Education*. London: National Family and Parenting Institute.

Gregg, P., Macmillan, L., Propper, C. and Washbrook, E. (2006) *Decomposing the Income Gradient in Child Outcomes*. CMPO. Available at <www.bris.ac.uk/depts/CMPO/events/workshops/family/gregg.ppt>.

Hango, D. (2005) *Parental Investment in Childhood and Later Adult Well-Being: Can More Involved Parents Offset the Effects of Socioeconomic Disadvantage?* CASE Paper No. 98. Available at <http://sticerd.lse.ac.uk/dps/case/cp/CASEpaper98.pdfplace/>.

Harker, L. (2006) *Delivering on Child Poverty: What Would it Take?* Report for the DWP. London: TSO.

Hohmann-Marriott, B. (2006) 'Father Involvement and Union Dissolution in the United Kingdom and United States', Pennsylvania State University. Paper presented at the Fourth Conference of the European Network for the Sociological and Demographic Study of Divorce, Florence, Italy.

Johnson, G., Cohen, P., Chen, H., Kasen, S. and Brook, J. (2006) 'Parenting Behaviours Associated with Risk for Offspring Personality Disorder During Adulthood', *Archives of General Psychiatry*, 63: 579–87.

Kendrick, D., Elkan, R., Hewitt, M., Dewey, M., Blair, M., Robinson, J., Williams, D. and Brummell, K. (2000) 'Does Home Visiting Improve Parenting and the Quality of the Home Environment? A Systematic Review and Meta Analysis', *Archives of Disease in Childhood*, 82.

Kirby, J. (2005) *The Price of Parenthood*. London: Centre for Policy Studies.

Lader, D., Short, S. and Gershuny, J. (2006) *The Time Use Survey 2005 – How We Spend Our Time*. London: ONS. Available at <www.statistics.gov.uk/articles/nojournal/time_use_2005.pdf>.

Layard, R. (2005) *Happiness: Lessons from a New Science*. Liverpool: Penguin.

Levine, M. (2006) *Ready or Not, Here Life Comes*. New York: Simon & Schuster.

Lewis, J. (2001) 'The Decline of the Male Breadwinner Model: Implications for Work and Care', *Social Politics* (8). Oxford: Oxford University Press.

Lewis, J. (forthcoming) 'Families, Individuals and the State', in D. Piachaud, J. Hills and J. Le Grand (eds), *Making Social Policy Work*. London: Policy Press.

Lewis, J. and Giullari, S. (2005) 'The Adult Worker Model Family, Gender Equality and Care: The Search for New Policy Principles and the Possibilities and Problems of a Capabilities Approach', *Economy and Society*, 34.

Linington, S. (2006) *Where do Parents Turn for Advice? An Overview of Research Findings*. London: National Family and Parenting Institute.

Lyon, N., Barnes, M. and Sweiry, D. (2006) *Families with Children in Britain: Findings from the 2004 Families and Children Study*. DWP Research Report No. 340. London: TSO.

McCarthy, P., Walker, J. and Kain, J. (1998) *Telling It As It Is: The Client Experience of Relate Counselling*. Newcastle: Newcastle Centre for Family Studies.

McLanahan, S., Donahue, E. and Haskins, R. (2005) 'Introducing the Issue', in 'Marriage and Well-being', *The Future of Children*, 15 (2). Washington DC: Brookings Institute.

Manchester City Council (2006) *Positive and Responsible Parenting in Manchester – A Strategic Approach*. Manchester: Manchester City Council.

Margo, J. and Dixon, M., with Pearce, N. and Reed, H. (2006) 'Raising Youth: Family Matters', in *Freedom's Orphans: Raising Youth in a Changing World*. London: ippr.

Meltzer, H., Gatword, R., Goodman, R. and Ford, T. (2000) *Mental Health of Children and Adolescents in Great Britain*. London: TSO.

Moran, P., Ghate, D. and Van der Merwe, A. (2004) *What Works in Parenting Support? A Review of International Evidence*. Policy Research Bureau, DfES Research Report No. 574. London: TSO.

Neale, B. and Smart, C. (2001) *Caring, Earning and Changing: Parenting and Employment After Divorce*. CRFKC Working Paper No. 24. Leeds: CRFKC.

NFPI (2006) *The Power of Parenting TV Programmes – Help or Hazard for Today's Families?* London: National Families and Parenting Institute/Ipsos MORI.

Olds, D. (2006) 'The Nurse–Family Partnership: An Evidence-Based Preventive Intervention', *Infant Mental Health Journal*, 27 (1).

Orthner, D., Jones-Saupei, H. and Williamson, S. (2004) 'The Resilience and Strengths of Low Income Families', *Family Relations*, 53.

Peters, E. H., Argys, L., Howard, H. and Butler, J. (2004) 'Legislating Love: The Effect of Child Support and Welfare Policies on Father–Child Contact', *Review of Economics of the Household*, 2 (3).

PricewaterhouseCoopers (2006) *DfES Children's Services – The Market for Parental and Family Support Services*. London: PricewaterhouseCoopers.

Quilgars, D., Searle, B. and Keung, A. (2005), 'Mental Health and Well-Being', in J. Bradshaw and E. Mayhew (eds), *The Well-being of Children in the UK*, 2nd edition. London: Save the Children.

Raphael, D. (1955) *The Tender Gift*. New York: Schocken.

Reeves, R. (2005) 'The Family Comes First', *Management Today*, 8 April.

Reynolds, J., Harold, G. and Pryor, J. (eds) (2001) *Not in Front of the Children? How Conflict Between Parents Affects Children*. London: One Plus One Marriage and Partnership Research.

Sanders, M. (1999) 'Triple P-Positive Parenting Program: Towards an Empirically Validated Multilevel Parenting and Family Support Strategy for the Prevention of Behaviour and Emotional Problems in Children', *Clinical Child and Family Psychology Review*, 2 (2).

Scott, S., O'Connor, T. and Futh, A. (2006) *What Makes Parenting Programmes Work in Disadvantaged Areas?* York: Joseph Rowntree Foundation.

Seaman, P., Turner, K., Hill, M., Stafford, A. and Walker, M. (2006) *Parenting and Children's Resilience in Disadvantaged Communities*. York: Joseph Rowntree Foundation/National Children's Bureau.

Simons, J. (ed.) (1999) 'High Divorce Rates: The State of the Evidence on Reasons and Remedies', Vol. 2 (Papers 4-7), Research Series No. 2/99, Lord Chancellor's Department. London: HMSO.

Smart, C., Neale, B. and Wade, A. (2001) *The Changing Experience of Childhood: Families and Divorce*. Cambridge: Polity Press.

Snarey, J. (1993) *How Fathers Care for the Next Generation: A Four Decade Study*. Cambridge, Mass.: Harvard University Press.

Stanley, K. (2005) *Daddy Dearest? Active Fatherhood and Public Policy*. London: ippr.

Stanley, K., Bellamy, K. and Cooke, G. (2006) *Equal Access? Appropriate and Affordable Childcare for Every Child*. London: ippr.

Sweet, M. and Appelbaum, M. (2004), 'Is Home Visiting an Effective Strategy? A Meta-Analytic Review of Home Visiting Programs for Families with Young Children', *Child Development*, 75 (5).

Taylor-Gooby, P. (ed.) (2005) *New Risks, New Welfare – The Transformation of the European Welfare State*. Oxford: Oxford University Press.

Therborn, G. (2004) *Between Sex and Power: Family in the World 1900–2000*. London: Routledge.

Waldfogel, J. (2006) *What Children Need?* Cambridge, Mass.: Harvard University Press.

Williams, F. (2004) *Re-thinking Families*. London: Calouste Gulbenkian Foundation.

Williams, F. and Churchill, H. (2006) *Empowering Parents in Sure Start Local Programmes*. London: National Evaluation of Sure Start.

Wilson, H. (1974) 'Parenting in Poverty', *British Journal of Social Work*, 4 (3).

Wood, M. (2005) *Perceptions and Experience of Antisocial Behaviour: Findings from the 2003/2004 British Crime Survey*. Home Office Online Report No. 49/04. Available at <www.homeoffice.gov.uk/rds/antisocial1.html>.

12
Crime and Punishment: A New Agenda

Nick Pearce

Introduction

It is a commonplace among liberal commentators, and even some of the government's strongest supporters, that Labour has got it wrong on crime. At best, it is argued, Labour has responded uncritically to public fear and anxiety; at worst, it has pandered to authoritarian popular sentiment with a cavalier disregard for liberal norms. 'Authoritarian, populist and punitive': it is a charge sheet that would be familiar to almost every Home Secretary, Conservative and Labour, since Roy Jenkins held the post in the liberal 1960s (although Douglas Hurd may be considered an exception, and it is worthy of note that he was a Conservative).

Yet in headline terms, Labour's record on crime looks good. Crime has fallen substantially, the number of police officers has increased, and more offences are being brought to justice. A whole new architecture for tackling youth crime has been erected, and a major reform of prison and probation services is underway. Even the public's fear of crime – notoriously higher than the level of crime itself – has fallen over Labour's decade in power. On hard facts alone, the government appears to have a good record on crime reduction.

Moreover, Labour can make a good case for having been tough on the causes of crime. It has reduced child poverty, invested in urban regeneration programmes, and significantly increased treatment services for those whose crimes are driven by drug addictions. Most importantly, it has presided over a strong and stable economy with relatively high rates of employment and a minimum wage, all of which have contributed significantly to lower crime rates.

So is unpopularity then simply the fate of Home Secretaries, whether Labour or Conservative, as they navigate the Scylla of liberal metropolitan sentiment and the Charybdis of an insatiable public authoritarianism? Or has Labour's home affairs agenda truly been mixed – effective in parts but incomplete or plain wrong in others?

In this chapter, I first set out why progressives should care about crime as much as they do about other areas of social policy such as education and health. I then examine Labour's record on some key issues of crime and justice, before turning substantively to what a future reform agenda might consist of, on the assumption that it needs to have a reasonable chance of appealing to centre-left politicians. In essence, I set out to answer the question of whether politicians in the UK can pursue a more progressive home affairs agenda without suffering at the ballot box.

What is progressive about cutting crime?

The shift in Labour's position on crime in the early 1990s, symbolized by the famous soundbite 'tough on crime, tough on the causes of crime', is widely acknowledged to have been an astute and successful political strategy. Whatever the actual content of its policy platform, no political party can afford to appear indifferent to crime or ineffective at tackling it. Although public attitudes to crime are complex and sometimes irrational, the maintenance of social order will always be a core public concern. A political party without credible or persuasive answers to the problems of crime and disorder places itself at an enormous electoral disadvantage.

To take a robust stance on cutting crime is not simply a matter of electoral tactics, however. It is sometimes argued that law and order are essentially right-wing issues, of central interest to social conservatives but tangential to the real business of progressive governance. This argument is often based on the sociologically naive view that crime is straightforwardly reducible to poverty, rather than a specific field of policy intervention in its own right whose causal interactions with other socio-economic domains are, at the very least, complex. Yet it also reflects a more fundamental failure to recognize that the experience of crime is a profound social injustice. Social and liberal democrats consistently employ the language and concepts of social justice when speaking about education, health or welfare policies, but rarely address crime and disorder in similar terms. This is a serious mistake. When viewed from the perspective of social justice, crime looms much larger on the terrain of progressive politics.

A few facts serve to illustrate this point. On average, people living in households with an income of less than £10,000 a year are 1.6 times as likely to be mugged, 1.3 times as likely to be burgled and 4.2 times as likely to be feel 'very unsafe' walking alone after dark as those living in households with an income of more than £30,000 a year. Looking at inequality in terms of area shows similarly pronounced differences: people living in the most deprived neighbourhoods are, on average, 2.5 times as likely to be mugged, 2.5 times as likely to burgled and 2.6 times as likely to be 'very worried' about being physically attacked as those people living in the least deprived neighbourhoods (Dixon et al. 2006: 12).

Crime is therefore distributed highly inequitably across social classes. Furthermore, its impact is amplified by repetition and disadvantage: victims of crime are more likely to suffer serious spillover effects if they are poor, in bad health, living in social housing, unemployed or inactive, living alone or without savings, or if they have been victimized before. Those on low incomes have fewer resources to protect themselves from crime, more to lose from experiencing it, and far fewer options for getting away from it. Even if they do not directly experience harm, the fear of crime may debilitate them and the communities in which they live. Crime therefore translates directly into substantial inequality in well-being and life chances (ibid.: 21–30).

There are some important qualifications to this broad argument. Crime is highly structured not just by social class, but also by gender and race, and these specificities may be ignored by public authorities at the cost of serious injustice, as the long history of domestic violence and the more recent experience of the Stephen Lawrence inquiry demonstrate. In addition, being a victim of crime is also one of the strongest predictors of being an offender, and the overlap is considerable as far as young men are concerned. The lens of social justice therefore cannot be pointed at a discrete category of 'deserving' victims. Finally, protection from crime and the prosecution of offenders are necessarily universal activities, since the state's monopoly of legitimate violence extends across all the citizens within its territory. Every citizen is entitled to make calls on the police and criminal justice system, and all are potentially subject to their purview. For these reasons, a social justice approach to crime cannot simply mimic the selectivity or exclusive targeting prevalent in other social policy areas.

These caveats notwithstanding, there is an abundance of normative reasons and empirical evidence to substantiate the claim that crime should matter more to egalitarians than has historically been the case, and therefore that a political focus on crime reduction amounts to more than the protection of a weak right flank by centre-left parties interested in winning elections (the 'security in security' strategy).

Many of Labour's critics would readily assent to this argument; indeed, perhaps find it sufficiently obvious to require little elaboration. But they would claim that Labour's policy response to the problems of crime and disorder has been the wrong one, focused on illiberal and ineffective reforms to the criminal justice system, and accompanied by a rhetoric that feeds a public appetite for 'tough' action that will never be satiated. What truth is there in these criticisms?

Crime and punishment: what has Labour achieved?

Reducing crime

A report from the Prime Minister's Strategy Unit leaked to the press over Christmas 2006 provides a useful place to start in assessing Labour's record on crime. The report – written to inform one of a number of policy reviews – gives a private and therefore relatively candid assessment from within the centre of government of its own successes and failures (Strategy Unit 2006).

The report starts by noting the overall achievements: increased resources, combined with legislative and administrative policy reforms, have led to a steady reduction in crime and the fear of crime since 1997. The report registers 'particular success' on reducing volume crimes, such as burglary, car theft and violence, and a fall since 2001 in public perceptions of anti-social behaviour. Since peaking in 1995, crime measured by the authoritative British Crime Survey (BCS) has fallen by 44 per cent, with falls in burglary of 59 per cent, vehicle theft of 80 per cent and violent crime of 43 per cent (Walker et al. 2006). It records improvements in the efficiency and effectiveness of the criminal justice system, and in the performance assessments of police forces. All of these claims are properly supported by empirical data.

But the report goes on to dig below these headline indicators. It argues that 80 per cent of the measured fall in crime since 1997 is attributable to economic factors – a highly plausible claim, given that the downward trend in crime accompanied the pick-up of economic growth in the mid-1990s, and was a trend shared with many other Western countries, notably the US. Since 2001, when growth in the UK jobs market began to tail off, the crime rate has fallen much more slowly, and now appears to have stabilized. Less benign economic and demographic circumstances may put upward pressure on the crime rate in the future.

It is also arguable – although the Strategy Unit report does not make this point – that Labour has been targeting the wrong kinds of crime. Its targets (expressed as Public Service Agreements between HM Treasury and the Home Office) have largely focused on high-volume crimes, such as burglary and vehicle theft, rather than those that cause most harm. As researchers at the Institute for Public Policy Research (ippr) have noted:

> there is good reason to think that while we have seen a dramatic fall in the volume of crime over the last decade, we have not seen as dramatic a fall in the impact of crime. According to one set of Home Office figures, (figures which are admittedly speculative and experimental), the total volume of crime fell by 20 per cent between 2000 and 2003/04, but the total cost of crime fell at just over a third of that rate – by just seven per cent ... this suggests that a substantial proportion of the fall in crime over the past decade may be due to reductions in less serious offences that do not have a large impact on people's lives. (Dixon et al. 2006: 41).

Taken together, these arguments suggest that the government has in large part targeted crimes that a combination of economic growth and situational crime prevention measures, such as better locks and disabling devices installed by manufacturers, would have done much to reduce anyway. It can also be argued that burglary has declined largely because the bottom has fallen out of the stolen goods market, whereas street robbery has increased because personal items such as mobile phones and iPods are valuable. Interestingly, theft of bicycles has not decreased by as much as car crime, because they are harder to secure.[1] In contrast, a social justice perspective would have shifted the government's focus towards the crimes that cause the most harm, and to the people (and the places in which they live) most affected by them. It would have targeted impact, rather than volume. However, it is worth noting that domestic violence – a particularly harmful crime that has historically been neglected – has fallen in recent years.

Although the government has moved some distance in this direction in recent years (the 2004 Spending Review set the Home Office a target of reducing the volume of crime by 15 per cent between 2002/03 and

---

1. I am indebted to John Graham for these observations.

2007/08, but supplemented this with a subsidiary objective of reducing crime 'further' in high-crime areas), it has done so tentatively rather than systematically.

Punishment

Perhaps the most revealing section of the Strategy Unit report is that which graphically illustrates crime reduction interventions on a spectrum from prevention to enforcement. It concludes rather starkly that 'much of the focus of recent policy has been on enforcement and punishment, though effectiveness is likely to be greatest for preventative interventions' – a conclusion reached by many criminologists and public authorities over the years (Strategy Unit 2006). It notes in passing that there has been no step change in the number of crimes resulting in a conviction or caution (less than 3 per cent) and that there has been 'heavy investment' in punishment.

Investment is a misnomer in this context. It simply means the cost of a large increase in the number of people sent to prison. Since 1997, the number of people in prison in England and Wales has risen from 61,000 to over 80,000 (the prison population in November 2006 was 80,500). It is set to rise further to nearly 100,000 by 2013 on current trends. This is not the result of conscious policy. No Labour Home Secretary has echoed Michael Howard's conviction that 'prison works'. Indeed, most of them have publicly repeated the formula that prison should be reserved for serious and dangerous offenders, while in private struggling with how to keep a lid on rising numbers. Meanwhile, the prison population has increased largely as the unintended consequence of other factors: an increase in average sentences from 20 to 30 months; the use of community sentences to substitute for fines, rather than as an alternative option to incarceration; and deteriorating recidivism rates. As penal reformers never tire of pointing out, Britain tops the per capita incarceration league in Western Europe, while 67 per cent of prisoners are caught reoffending within two years.

On this score, the government's critics are undoubtedly right. Labour has presided over big increases in incarceration, in part fuelled by how judges have responded to the prevalent political rhetoric in sentencing decisions. The pressure on the prison population, combined with the rapidity of its turnover (50,000 people a year are now sent to prison for less than six months), has made it incredibly difficult for the Prison Service to make effective use of the resources that Labour has ploughed into basic skills education, drug treatment and Cognitive Behaviour Therapy programmes for prisoners – all of which have received substantial funding increases in an effort to improve rehabilitation rates. Instability for prisoners, high turnover and overcrowding seriously inhibit the planning and sustained delivery of these interventions.

In sum, Labour can take credit for a sustained fall in crime, even if the primary responsibility for that achievement rests with the Treasury rather than the Home Office. But this overall reduction masks significant inequalities in the impact of crime, and at the same time we have witnessed an unplanned, unnecessary and ineffective increase in incarceration.

Public attitudes to crime

What about public attitudes to crime? Has Labour been successful at responding to public fears about crime, or has it missed opportunities to shape a new progressive consensus on law and order?

Although the fear of crime has dropped since 1997, two-thirds of the public still believes that crime is increasing, not falling. As with other public services, people are more likely to believe things are better in their local area than they are nationwide (42 per cent of people believe crime is getting worse in their local area, compared to 63 per cent who believe it is getting worse nationally (Walker et al. 2006)). Yet opinion poll surveys regularly record high levels of public concern with crime and anti-social behaviour – concern which has risen relative to other issues as the economy has improved, although law and order has always come behind both education and health as an issue upon which people have chosen how to vote during Labour's period of office.

The main drivers of this perception gap between the fear of crime and the reality of its incidence lie in underlying socio-economic factors such as the employment status and educational achievement of individual respondents, low levels of social trust, the public association of crime with everyday acts of anti-social behaviour and, of course, media presentation of criminals and criminal acts: tabloid readers are twice as likely as broadsheet readers to believe that crime is rising (ibid.). Fear of crime – a close cousin of the belief that it is rising, not falling – is closely correlated with lack of trust in others, poor educational attainment and unemployment (Dixon et al. 2006: 5–36).

Polls and surveys also record strong and largely enduring support for the death penalty, longer prison sentences and other authoritarian responses to crime. While more liberal attitudes prevail among the better-educated and the better-off, authoritarian views towards crime are widespread among the public. Britain does not appear to be witnessing a secular trend towards more progressive views on crime and punishment as it has on issues of sexuality, personal morality or the environment. Indeed, social liberalism may actually encourage punitive attitudes to crime, as people insist that the remaining social rules establishing clear limits to behaviour should be strictly enforced (Tyler et al. 1997: 108). In the US, support for the death penalty has risen substantially since the mid 1960s, at precisely the time when social mores first began to liberalize.

Yet public attitudes are not straightforwardly authoritarian. A more complex story is told by social psychologists and criminologists. Although studies repeatedly find that the desire for retribution is powerful and universal, to the extent that it may be considered a basic human instinct, it is not a uniformly expressed emotion (ibid.). It is held most strongly by those socialized from an early age into authoritarian norms, those on low incomes, the elderly and the poorly educated. And it varies to the extent that people evaluate the motives and morals of offenders, and the types of crime they commit. Vengefulness is felt most forcefully for crimes that shatter the symbolic moral order of a group (child abuse, for example), but far less so for crimes of a material nature, such as burglary. The intentions of the criminal also matter, as does his or her level of remorse.

Furthermore, disjunctions in responses to crime appear between the macro- and a micro-level. In one US study, for example, when asked in the abstract whether the death penalty should obtain for murderers of policemen, 66 per cent agreed. But when asked to evaluate an individual case of such murder, support for the death penalty fell to 15 per cent (Ellsworth 1978). Information sources also matter. When people are presented with information on criminals and their crimes by professionals in public authority, their attitude is considerably more liberal than when they receive it from the media. Deliberation on policy alternatives and involvement in community court and case conferencing processes also predict more liberal and less punitive attitudes (Hough and Park 2002; Rogers 2005).

In the UK, surveys and research studies conducted for the Esmée Fairbairn Rethinking Crime and Punishment (RCP) project found much more complexity and potential malleability in public attitudes to crime than opinion polls register (Allen 2004). Two findings were of particular interest. First, attitudes towards sentencing discriminated significantly in respect of drug users. Almost everybody, including tabloid readers, took the view that drug addicts should be treated, rather than punished. Second, the RCP studies found considerable public support for crime prevention strategies focused on improving parenting and working intensively with children at risk. In contrast, they found that the public were sceptical of the rehabilitative efficacy, if not the legitimacy or desirability, of prison sentences.

Other evidence supports the argument that public perceptions of crime are heavily determined by the behaviour of young people in public spaces, and the messages this behaviour sends about value socialization within families and the wider community. Tom Tyler and Robert Boeckmann's study (Tyler et al. 1997) of attitudes to California's 'three strikes' policy found that fear of crime as a social problem predicted support for the policy and for a general punitiveness, but a stronger predictor was depth of concern over the lack of moral socialization of teenagers in the family and the growth of gang culture (social values – that is, whether the person is predisposed to dogmatic and/or authoritarian attitudes – also predicted support for the 'three strikes' initiative and general punitiveness).

Public concern with how young people behave in visible public arenas and the signals that it sends about the wider moral state of the community also feature strongly in survey data on anti-social behaviour, and in research on neighbourhood incivilities and police reassurance programmes in the UK (Margo et al. 2006; Wood 2004; Bottoms 2006; Tuffin et al. 2006). Large numbers of people take offence, and sometimes experience fear, at the sight of young people 'hanging around'. It signals to them a lack of social order, or the threat of disorder, even if their personal risk of harm is slight or non-existent (Innes et al. 2004). This perception of an association between young people and crime and disorder has been growing since the early 1990s (Margo et al. 2006).

Public attitudes towards crime are therefore not immutably authoritarian. People react to signals about the strength of the social order sent by the behaviour of young people in public spaces, an issue which is clearly amenable to policy intervention. They also discriminate between types of crime and the values and interests that these breach, and account for the motivations, intentions and moral posture of offenders, in particular by recognizing that drug addicts do not behave rationally. They become more liberal in their orientations when supplied with information from professionals rather than the media, and when they have personal involvement in case resolution in the criminal justice system. But they stand firm on basic social norms and react harshly to high profile and repugnant breaches of those norms.

A progressive policy agenda for crime reduction can therefore find moorings in public attitudes, although the task is a difficult and complex one. Opportunities to shape a progressive consensus on law and order, and to lead public attitudes in new directions, clearly exist in a number of very specific areas – for example, on how to deal with drug users, target children at risk of crime – and better involve people in the criminal justice system through restorative justice-style techniques.

In this regard, it is promising that policy reforms are increasingly focused at the local level. Since the determinants of public attitudes are highly sensitive to local context, and the factors that appear to shift public attitudes are dependent in large part on local actors, a renewed attention to local public authority–citizen interaction could reap significant rewards. More specifically, recent reforms to bring policing and low-level criminal justice activities closer to people in their neighbourhoods, coupled with an extension of structured activities for young people, offer potentially fertile ground for changing public discourse on crime in the UK. Such responses embed the potential for attitudinal change in local institutions. I examine these issues below.

A progressive home affairs agenda?

On the basis of the preceding analysis, I turn in this section to look at the building blocks of a new, potentially progressive home affairs agenda.

Social justice and democratic accountability

A progressive crime reduction agenda must first be based on the right policy objectives. To begin with, that means much more emphasis on social policy, rather than criminal justice. This is particularly important for young offenders, as I outline below. But insofar as crime reduction is concerned, policies should focus more heavily on crimes that cause the most harm and areas which suffer the most crime (I examine crime prevention separately below). Resources will always be necessary for both low-level crimes, at the one end, and intensive investigation and prosecution of high level, serious crimes, at the other. But in between these extremes, more taxpayer resources and the efforts of public bodies should be directed towards social justice priorities.

In practice this means targeting high-impact crimes, such as those causing violence to the person, repeat victims and areas of persistently high crime activity. Instead of a target for reducing the volume of crime, measured by percentages year-on-year, the government should establish a target for reducing the harm caused by crime, and within that overall target, a specific measure for closing the gap between the highest crime areas and the rest of the country.

Social justice in crime reduction also requires reforms to funding allocations. The police grant is determined by a national formula that uses a number of factors, such as population and deprivation levels, to allocate resources in response to need. It ensures that police forces in high crime areas are better funded. But the distribution of resources in proportion to need is limited in two important ways. First, there are floors and ceilings to the police grant, which act to stabilize funding for individual forces but skew the distribution at the top and bottom. Second, the government does not determine how police authorities distribute resources within their areas. This means that high-crime Borough Command Units can lose out to those with lower crime levels but more political clout.

At the same time, public policy should be reoriented towards more effective and accountable local action, rather than the current over-reliance on targets and a plethora of plans and performance indicators set in Whitehall. Since the 1960s (and arguably before then), successive governments have centralized powers for reducing crime in the person of the Home Secretary, creating a framework in which the police and other agencies have little incentive to respond to local priorities, and in which accountability at local levels is very weak.

In particular, the system of tripartite responsibility for policing between the Home Secretary, police authorities and chief constables is riddled with flaws. Police authorities are barely visible to the public, let alone accountable to them. In the name of operational independence, Chief Constables are in practice relatively impervious to scrutiny by police authorities, but at the same time increasingly find themselves subject to performance assessment and direction by the Home Secretary and Home Office units. Meanwhile, although the bulk of police resources is raised through national taxes, the local element, the police precept to the Council Tax, is levied by local authorities that have no responsibility for the level at which it is set, nor how it is spent. Aside from a limited number of mechanisms – local councillors who sit on police authorities and the activities of Crime and Disorder Reduction Partnerships for example – there are no structural relationships between elected local government and police forces.

Democratic accountability for policing and community safety is therefore weak, and this may help explain public dissatisfaction with 'crime and grime' issues. Recent reforms have sought to empower the public to hold the police to account, through neighbourhood beat meetings and a community right to 'call for action'. But the formal accountability structures for policing and criminal justice remain largely remote from local communities.

A number of reform options for strengthening accountability for policing and community safety have been canvassed:

- Direct election of police authorities or police commissioners. This would enhance the visibility and accountability of police force leaders, but at the expense of strengthening connections between elected local government and the police. It would meet considerable institutional resistance in local government, police forces and the Home Office.
- A transfer of policing and community safety outside London to upper-tier local authorities – metropolitan authorities, county councils and shire unitaries. This would improve democratic accountability and the 'connectedness' of local services but at the cost of a substantial increase in the number of police forces, which is probably untenable. An alternative way of framing this option would be to nationalize higher-level crime fighting and anti-terrorist activity in an expanded Serious and Organized Crime Agency – sweeping up powers that need a truly regional and national response – while localizing the rest in a larger number of forces accountable to upper-tier local government. This may be practicable but, again, it is also a remote prospect, for largely political reasons.
- Allow local authorities (district, unitary or borough) to set local community safety priorities, including those for local policing, and retain the Council Tax police precept for that purpose – the purchase of funding for policing with these resources according to agreed plans. National funding for police forces would be retained, but with a needs formula to ensure that high-crime areas received higher proportions of national resources. These reforms would be backed up with strengthened neighbourhood bodies and reforms to the operational accountability and visibility of police authorities.

The last of these options seems the most plausible. It goes with the grain of current reforms, but radicalizes them and brings local government properly into the frame on policing and community safety matters. It is neutral on the question of police force size (an issue which has received attention for largely managerial and arguably invalid reasons), and does not presuppose a new regional tier of accountability. The downside is that it preserves the role of police authorities in exercising responsibility for the vast bulk of police activity and resources. In the long term, it should be our ambition to allocate accountability for different levels of policing to local and national government, without the need for a quasi-quango body such as the police authority (with appropriate safeguards for preventing political interference in the operations of the police).

Tackling anti-social behaviour

More effective targeting and accountability would also improve the government's policies for reducing anti-social behaviour. One of the main concerns with these policies is their catch-all nature. The government defines anti-social behaviour very widely, as 'behaviour which causes or is likely to cause harassment, alarm or distress to one or more people who are not in the same household as the perpetrator' (cf. the original provisions of the Crime and Disorder Act 1998). Subsequent attempts to categorize or list what constitutes such behaviour have been equally broad, ranging from serious racial abuse, to joyriding and making hoax phone calls.

Given the breadth of this definition, it is perhaps unsurprising that a wide array of policy responses has been marshalled towards anti-social behaviour. Not all of these have been focused on enforcement, despite what critics allege. But the introduction of new Anti-Social Behaviour Orders (ASBOs) is a key instrument in the policy armoury, and these have been subject to vociferous criticism. ASBOs last for a minimum of two years, and breaching them is a criminal offence punishable by up to five years in prison. They can restrict the liberty of a subject over extensive periods of time and place, and specify these restrictions in considerable detail (including restrictions that do not bear on the actual content of the anti-social behaviour which gave rise to the order). A criminal standard of proof is required for an ASBO, but an interim order can be sought with less onerous obligations. After a slow start, the number of ASBOs issued has risen sharply in recent years.

Few people would deny that anti-social behaviour can cause utter misery to those who experience it. A lot of this behaviour is clearly criminal and can be prosecuted as such. But ASBOs have been adopted to tackle discrete problems with the criminal prosecution of anti-social behaviour, in particular the fact that it may be persistent, rather than one-off, and conducted by neighbours who intimidate and threaten victims when they seek redress from the police. ASBOs divert social disorder problems out of the courts – a practice common in continental jurisdictions – but only to the extent that they are not breached. When breaches occur, ASBOs can function to fast-track people who have not committed a crime into prison.

A social justice approach would retain the ability to deal firmly with anti-social behaviour but target ASBOs more clearly on its harmful forms, such as so-called 'neighbours from hell'. ASBOs are discredited when they are inappropriately used for trivial offences (albeit that this happens in relatively few cases), and the deprivations of liberty they impose are significant. Restrictions imposed on the liberties of offenders should be constrained to those that are proportionate to the anti-social behaviour in question. In addition, penalties for breaches of ASBOs should be restricted in the first instance to non-custodial sentences, minimizing the potential for civil orders to set off an escalating process towards incarceration.

The accountability framework for tackling anti-social behaviour might also be extended by strengthening community involvement in dispute resolution and case adjudication. This can be achieved through the creation of a new tier of Community Courts, Community Justice Centres, Restorative Justice and localized forms of case conferencing. These have demonstrated potential to strengthen community engagement in crime and justice, and bring low level crime and disorder into the emerging institutional framework of neighbourhood governance. The government is already rapidly extending their use (Rogers 2005).

The 'new parochialism'

Community-based, localized responses to crime and disorder now have considerable pedigree in the academic literature on crime reduction. The leading candidate for a theoretically rich, empirically substantiated theory of crime is the work of Robert Sampson and his colleagues on 'collective efficacy'. Collective efficacy refers to the ability of the community's members to exercise informal social control, to intervene when young people are truanting from school or committing acts of anti-social behaviour, or to mobilize in the defence of valued public goods, like a local fire station (Sampson 2004). Where a community displays strong collective efficacy, crime rates are lower. Structural disadvantage and concentrated poverty will predict weak collective efficacy, but other factors, such as rates of home-ownership, also appear to be important.

This stress on the resources of the community stands in marked contrast to the solutions proffered by theories of crime that have had most influence on policy-makers in the last decade or so: 'Broken Windows' and rational choice theory. Broken Windows asserts that small problems become large ones unless tackled, and therefore underpins zero-tolerance policing strategies. It is popular among policy-makers because it is deemed to account for the success of the New York Police Department in reducing crime in the 1990s. Sceptics point to the role of a new police crime statistics system and a booming economy to explain falling crime in the city. Other US cities that pursued the Broken Windows path had far less success, while alternatives, such as Community Policing in Chicago, were equally efficacious.

Rational choice theory is a term covering the basic methodological assumptions of a huge array of economic analysis and social science. In criminology, it draws policy-makers' attention to the putative cost-benefit analyses that criminals make, seeking solutions to crime that increase the costs and lower the benefits of crime, as well as the opportunities to commit it (for example, situational crime prevention). But although instrumental calculations are of course observed in criminal behaviour, their impact is relatively small, and researchers argue that deterrence strategies premised on changing the terms of the criminal calculation (that is, through the imposition of longer prison sentences) are both costly and of limited effectiveness, chiefly impacting on particular crimes, such as burglary and car crime, in areas where surveillance is possible (Tyler and Fagan 2006). They are of scant help in tackling crimes fuelled by non-rational behaviour, such as drink-related violence and theft for drug use. Moreover, they are largely silent on how to promote community capacity for cutting crime.

Promoting collective efficacy might seem too long-term for an impatient public, but its stress on community resources and the importance of interactions between public authorities and local citizens are also found in recent work on police reassurance programmes undertaken prior to the rollout of neighbourhood policing. As noted above, Martin Innes and his colleagues have demonstrated the importance of signals of crime and disorder – such as the presence of young people in public spaces – and how locally responsive policing can respond to public concerns about these issues, providing visible signals to the community that public authorities can promote social order. To be effective, the police need to listen to local residents' concerns and then act upon them. When they do so, a virtuous circle of community–police interaction and capacity can be created, in which community interventions ('collective efficacy') and police and/or local authority activities are mutually reinforcing (Innes et al. 2004; Bottoms 2006).

A 'new parochialism' in policing, signalled by the national rollout of neighbourhood policing, therefore has potential to address concerns about local social order that feed public anxiety about crime. Structurally, neighbourhood policing can be integral to the development of wider neighbourhood governance, the localization of justice for low-level crime and anti-social behaviour, and the development of new forms of purposeful activity for young people (although, of course, a focus on neighbourhood policing does not imply that intelligence-led policing, particularly for serious organized crime, is any the less necessary). There are tensions here between a social justice insistence on targeting high-harm crimes and persistent anti-social behaviour, and a focus on low-level incivilities that signal disorder to local communities. But with the right mix of resources, targets and accountability, they are not insurmountable: for example, neighbourhood police teams could be restricted to a core operational team in affluent areas but expanded in high-crime areas.

Crime and punishment: the use of prison and community sentences

Prison is an expensive and ineffective way of warehousing social problems. It should be used far less in Britain, and to greater effect. For that to happen, the effectiveness of non-custodial provision, and public confidence in its use, must improve. Diversion out of the criminal justice system is also critical for drug users and people with mental health problems (on the latter, see the excellent study by James et al. (2002)). This is the holy grail of penal reformers. Non-custodial sentences have lower reoffending rates than prison terms (53 per cent compared to 67 per cent), but their performance is getting worse, not better, and public awareness and understanding of them remain very low. So reform should focus on demonstrated methods of improving their effectiveness, and communicating their efficacy to the public.

Evidence suggests that the public respond best to strongly moral messages on non-custodial sentences. They wish to associate them with reparation, responsibility, hard work and discipline, and treatment of the causes of offending. They are not persuaded by instrumental reasons for alternatives to prison, such as lower costs, or by humanitarian concern for offenders (Allen 2004). Crucially, non-custodial provision lacks a clear 'brand'. The public aren't really sure what it consists of, whether it's happening and whether it makes any difference. In contrast, prison is very simple to understand.

These considerations suggest that high-visibility 'payback' sentences, possibly nationally branded, with objectives set by local communities, are a necessary if not sufficient condition for establishing greater public confidence in non-custodial provision.

In addition, sentencers need to place more trust in alternatives to custody. Research has consistently shown that sentencers use non-custodial options as alternatives not to prison but to other community punishments. This pushes more offenders up the sentencing tariff and thereby accelerates their entry into custody. A way forward out of this morass was proposed by the Audit Commission in its work on youth justice. It proposed a shift from 'vertical' to 'horizontal' or 'sloping' sentencing tariffs, by which it meant a move away from the practice of using a more punitive sentence if a previous one has not worked, towards a flexible system in which different community sentences can be imposed according to the circumstances of the case. This would halt the escalator effect of moving up the tariff towards custody. Sentence reviews would also be used more often to improve the effectiveness of community-based interventions (Audit Commission 2004).

The creation of the National Offender Management Service (NOMS) is a significant and important step forward in the capacity of the state better to manage the offender population. The involvement of private and community sector organizations in service delivery, providing for some contestability in provision, is also likely to have beneficial effects. But the most important issue is the level at which offender management services are integrated. NOMS will have regional commissioning structures, which are arguably too remote from the highly localized areas in which the majority of offenders live. If neighbourhoods are the site of efforts to engage communities in crime reduction, and the role of local government and its partners in community safety is to expand, some budgetary and commissioning decisions must be made at the local level. This is important both for non-custodial sentences, so that they can be truly responsive to local community aspirations, and for the integration of services for those leaving custody (research is unequivocal that employment and stable housing cut reoffending rates significantly, so offender management services have to be structurally integrated with job and housing services: see Social Exclusion Unit 2002).

Prevention: a radical shift

It is a social policy cliché that prevention is better than cure, and that early interventions are more cost-effective than corrective ones. Labour has indeed significantly expanded investment in services that seek to prevent crime, both for the specific needs of offenders (that is, drug treatment and basic education for prisoners) and for children and families at risk of becoming engaged in crime (for example, Sure Start, On Track, Youth Inclusion and Support panels and parenting classes). A new framework for protecting children and young people, and ensuring their well-being, has also been legislated into existence, integrating education and children' social services at local government level, while resources have been spent on voluntary sector organizations that work with children in disadvantaged areas (for an overview of the evidence in this area, and developments in policy in England and Wales, see Graham 2006).

Yet we still lack a coordinated, properly targeted but national service for children at risk of crime, particularly for those of primary school age. A recently published longitudinal study (Farrington et al. 2006) showed that the most prolific offenders start early, between the ages of 10 and 13, and have longer criminal careers than other criminals, lasting on average 13 years. Hence the authors argue that prevention resources should be aimed at those most at risk of prolific offending among the pre-school and primary school age children. Impulsiveness that leads to criminal activity can be addressed through Cognitive Behaviour Therapy, while other risk factors such as low school attainment require more established but nonetheless intensive interventions (such as Reading Recovery). Holistic programmes such as Multi-Systemic Therapy are of proven efficacy for those with the most complex needs, while other targeted parenting programmes of the kind outlined in the recent Social Exclusion Task Force report (2006) have also been shown to be effective.

In the long term, our aim should be to ensure that these multi-agency interventions are grouped into a coherent service, under the rubric of Children's Trusts, that reaches those children who are at risk of prolific offending (based on identifiable risk factors), perhaps from age three to ten: a 'Sure Start Plus' programme directed at keeping young children out of crime. The research evidence on public opinion cited above shows that such an intervention – presented explicitly as a government policy for reducing crime and disorder – would receive widespread support. It would also help shift more of the resources spent on young people towards those living in conditions of disadvantage in deprived areas.

For adult offenders, the analysis of public attitudes showed strong support for treating drug users, not punishing them. Resources for such treatment have been hugely expanded in recent years, to the extent that recruiting qualified staff to deliver them has become a problem. But treatment programmes still have low completion rates and patchy coverage, so we should consider switching monies earmarked for expansion of prison places into residential drug treatment centres, as proposed by the Rethinking Crime and Punishment programme. We should be bolder in expanding harm-minimization programmes and spreading the practice of GP prescription of heroin. This can reduce acquisitive crime considerably.

Conclusion

The Labour government can legitimately claim a number of successes in crime reduction over its term of office. It has taken crime and anti-social behaviour seriously, as issues of central concern to progressive politics. It has legislated for significant reforms to the youth justice system and the management of the adult offender population, and it has invested heavily in drug treatment services. Crime and the fear of crime have fallen. These are important foundations upon which to build in the future.

On the other hand, Labour has failed to shift public opinion in a progressive direction on crime and justice, despite the evidence that in areas such as drug treatment, structured activities for young people and action for children at risk of falling into criminal careers, there is fertile ground upon which to develop public support for preventative rather than punitive action. Public reassurance on crime and criminal justice is possible with a set of more progressive policy tools, as well as supporting policy discourses.

The priority for the next ten years should be to strengthen local capacity and accountability for reducing crime and punishing and rehabilitating offenders – guided by social justice considerations in the allocation of resources and the objectives set for public agencies. The police and criminal justice systems need to be made more democratically accountable at a local level, and responsive to neighbourhood communities. These structural reforms offer a platform, if not a guarantee, that public concern about crime can be improved without lapsing into authoritarian solutions.

Acknowledgements

The author would like to thank John Graham, Ben Jupp, Paul Maltby and Ben Rogers for their extensive and very helpful comments on an earlier draft of this chapter.

References

Allen, R. (2004) 'What Works in Changing Public Attitudes: Lessons from Rethinking Crime and Punishment', *Journal for Crime, Conflict and the Media*, 1 (33): 55–67.

Audit Commission (2004) *Youth Justice 2004*. London: Audit Commission.

Bottoms, A. (2006) 'Incivilities, Offence and Social Order in Residential Communities', in A. Von Hirsch and A. P. Simester (eds), *Incivilities: Regulating Offensive Behaviour: Studies in Penal Theory and Penal Ethics*. Oxford and Portland, Oreg.: Hart Publishing.

Dixon, M., Reed, H., Rogers, B. and Stone, L. (2006) *Crimeshare: The Unequal Impact of Crime*. London: ippr.

Ellsworth, P. (1978) 'Attitudes Towards Capital Punishment: From Application to Theory'. Paper presented at the Annual Meeting of the Society for Experimental Social Psychology, Stanford, Calif.

Farrington, D., Coid, J., Harnett, L., Jolliffe, D., Soteriou, N., Turner, R. and West, D. (2006) *Criminal Careers and Life Success: New Findings from the Cambridge Study in Delinquent Development*. London: Home Office.

Graham, J. (2006) *Youth Crime Prevention in England and Wales*. Available at <www. police-foundation.org.uk/files/POLICE0001/Articles/Canadian%20Institute. pdf>. Accessed 6 January 2007.

Hough, M. and Park, A. (2002) 'Public Attitudes to Crime and Punishment', cited in *Attitudes to Crime and Punishment: Results of a Deliberative Poll of Public Opinion, Rethinking Crime and Punishment*. Available at <www.rethinking.org. uk/publications/index.shtml>. Accessed 7 January 2007.

Innes, M., Hayden, S., Lowe, T., MacKenzie, H., Roberts, C. and Twyman, L. (2004) *Signal Crimes and Reassurance Policing*. Guildford: University of Surrey.

James, E., Farnham, F., Moorey, H., Lloyd, H., Hill, K., Blizard, R. and Barnes, T. (2002) *Outcomes of Psychiatric Admission through the Courts*. Home Office RDS Occasional Paper No. 79. London: Home Office.

Margo, J. and Dixon, M., with Pearce, N. and Reed, H. (2006) *Freedom's Orphans: Raising Youth in a Changing World*. London: ippr.

Rogers, B. (2005) *New Directions in Community Justice*. London: ippr.

Sampson, R. (2004) 'Neighbourhood and Community: Collective Efficacy and Community Safety', *New Economy*, 11 (2): 106–13.

Social Exclusion Task Force (2006) *Reaching Out: An Action Plan on Social Exclusion*. London: Cabinet Office.

Social Exclusion Unit (2002) *Reducing Re-Offending by Ex-Prisoners*. London: TSO.

Strategy Unit (2006) *Policy Review: Crime, Justice and Cohesion*. Available at <www. timesonline.co.uk/article/0,,2087-2517940.htmln>. Accessed 24 December 2006.

Tuffin, R., Morris, J. and Poole, A. (2006) *An Evaluation of the Impact of the National Reassurance Police Programme*. Home Office Research Study No. 296. London: Home Office.

Tyler, T. R., Boeckmann, R. J., Smith, H. J. and Huo, J. Y. (1997) *Social Justice in a Diverse Society*. Oxford: Westview Press.

Tyler, T. R. and Fagan, J. F. (2006) Legitimacy and Cooperation: Why do People Help the Police Fight Crime in their Communities? Columbia Law School Public Law & Legal Theory Working Paper Group, 06-99. New York: Columbia Law School.

Walker, A., Kershaw, C. and Nicholas, S. (2006) *Crime in England and Wales 2005/06*. Home Office Statistical Bulletin 12/06. London: TSO.

Wood, M. (2004) *Perceptions and Experience of Antisocial Behaviour: Findings from the 2003/2004 British Crime Survey*. Home Office Online Report 49/04. London: TSO.

Part 5

Power

13
Power Politics: Who Runs Britain?

Emily Thornberry, Rick Muir and Ian Kearns

Introduction: democratic politics and the progressive project

The demand for democratic empowerment has always been central to the progressive tradition. The movement for votes for women and the working class, for the secret ballot, for the democratization of the second chamber – all were seen as both a fundamental component of and as instrumental to the advance of progressive objectives.

First, the demand for political democracy is an essential component of the demand for social equality more generally. Democracy is founded on a belief in both freedom and equality. It is about freedom because it is based on the idea that only *we*, the citizens, know what is fundamentally in our best interests and so therefore we ourselves are much better qualified than even the most benevolent guardian to choose the laws under which we have to live. But it is also a fundamentally egalitarian demand: because we all have an equal right to that political freedom and self-government, we should all (at some significant level) have an equal say in political decision-making. The redistribution of power is therefore as much a component of the social democratic drive for equality and social justice as the redistribution of wealth or income (Dahl 1989: 85–105; Held 1994: 47).

Second, the democratization of our political institutions has also traditionally been seen by progressives as not only a component of, but also as instrumental to the broader democratization of society. Universal suffrage in the early twentieth century created a majority working-class electorate that many thought would deliver Labour political dominance and make the advance of social justice unstoppable (Foot 2006). While Labour dominance was not achieved (quite the reverse), it is undeniable that mass enfranchisement delivered the comprehensive welfare state that even Margaret Thatcher's government was unable to dismantle in its basic fundamentals. In this sense political democracy was instrumental to the advance of social justice, as well as being an inherent component of it. The consolidation, widening and deepening of political democracy has always, then, been fundamental to the progressive project.

Over the last decade Labour has implemented a number of substantial constitutional reforms that have further democratized our political system. The removal of most of the hereditary peers from the House of Lords has long been a fundamental demand of constitutional reformers. The establishment of the Scottish Parliament and the Welsh Assembly have gone a great distance in meeting a long-standing desire for self-government of the different nations within Britain. The introduction of the Human Rights Act and the Freedom of Information Act has given British citizens new legal tools for asserting their rights and holding their government to account. Across the whole range of measures, Britain unquestionably has a much more democratic political system today than it did ten years ago (Democratic Audit 2005: 5).

However, while these reforms have undoubtedly made the system more democratic, they have failed to revive democratic politics and have, if anything, run alongside a process of increasing political disillusionment and disengagement. As Greenberg and Lewis have pointed out in Chapter 3, British politics is in trouble. Election turnout is at historic lows, politicians are among the least trusted of any profession and political parties are facing a crisis of membership and activism. For very many people, politics itself has become a dirty word.

Why, then, have Labour's reforms failed to renew Britain's democracy? There are a number of possibilities. One is that the constitutional reform agenda is itself incomplete. The Lords remains unelected and therefore fundamentally unaccountable to the electorate at large; early moves towards electoral reform were quickly shelved and the executive remains ever powerful in a system with few of the checks and balances common to most modern democratic systems (Power Inquiry 2006).

However, while constitutional reform is a necessary component of any progressive programme for democratic renewal, this chapter will argue that this on its own is insufficient to match the scale of our current political malaise. The causes of low levels of political participation and disengagement run much deeper, requiring a fundamental change not just in our institutional arrangements but also in our broader political

culture. Moreover, we argue that we need to shift beyonᵢ
focus on redistributing power within the political system ᴀ
where power is operating beyond the control of democrat
People are less likely to participate not just because they fiɪ.
to access the political system, but also because politics is no loᵢ
vehicle through which many important decisions are made. In sᴜm, we
need not only to change the way our politics works in institutional and
cultural terms, but also to extend its reach.

Politics in trouble

The traditional forms of political participation in Britain are on the wane.
The most commonly noted evidence for this is the decline in electoral
turnout. As Greenberg and Lewis have shown in Chapter 3, election
turnout in 1997 was already at its lowest level since the Second World
War, at 71 per cent. Since then, however, we have seen a drop in electoral
turnout of an entirely different order, with just 59 per cent voting in
2001 and 61 per cent voting in 2005. There is a similar trend in local
elections, with turnout falling from an average of 43 per cent between
1973 and 1978 to just 36 per cent between 1990 and 1999 (Keaney and
Rogers 2006).

Electoral participation has also become increasingly skewed by class and
generational inequality. Whereas in 1964 the gap between the highest and
lowest income quintile in terms of voting in a general election stood at
7 per cent, it had risen to 13 per cent by 2005. Mori found that whereas
70 per cent of people in class AB (the highest earning group) voted in the
2005 general election, just 54 per cent of those in class DE (the lowest
earning) did so (Keaney and Rogers 2006). The younger generations are
also much less likely to vote than the older ones. Politicians have all had
the experience of knocking on a door and it being opened by a grown-up
son or daughter who sees the candidate's rosette and says 'Wait a second,
I'll get my mum.' Mori estimates that only 39 per cent of those aged
between 18 and 25 voted in the 2001 general election, compared to 75 per
cent of those over the age of 65. Moreover, this age gap has been growing
over time: whereas in 1970 there was an 18 percentage-point difference
between those aged 18–25 and those aged 65 or over being likely to vote,
by 2005 this had grown to an astonishing 40 percentage points (ibid.).

Like election turnout, party political participation has been declining.
Labour's membership more than halved from over 400,000 prior to the
1997 election to just 198,026 in December 2006 (BBC News Online
2006b). The Conservatives have also been losing members, with their

membership falling from over 1.5 million in the early 1970s to just 290,000 in early 2006 (Whiteley and Seyd 1999; *Daily Telegraph*, 7 January 2006). Whereas in the 1950s there were over 3 million party members in Britain, there are just over half a million today (MacTaggart et al. 2006). Underpinning this loss of members is a broader decline in identification with political parties. Those claiming to identify strongly with a political party fell from over 82 per cent of the population in 1964 to just 51 per cent in 2005 (Heath et al. 2007).

This matters because parties have historically been the main instruments for representing British voters, aggregating their views and interests into broad-based programmes and implementing these through Parliament. Moreover, parties still monopolize political power in this country, being the primary recruiting agency for the political class: councillors, Members of Parliament and government ministers make their way into positions of power through their respective parties. The internal health of the major parties is therefore of enormous importance to the representativeness of the political system.

Labour has responded to these trends with a number of constitutional reforms and electoral innovations to try to encourage greater political participation. It was hoped that devolution of power to Scotland, Wales and London, for instance, would bring political decision-making closer to those it affects and help stem the tide of disengagement. Moreover, it was hoped that the more proportional electoral systems used for the devolved legislatures would boost participation by giving voters greater choice and flexibility. Turnout for the London elections has stayed relatively steady between 2000 and 2004 – rising slightly from 34 per cent to 37 per cent. However, between the first and second elections in the devolved national assemblies, turnout declined by 10 per cent in Scotland and 8 per cent in Wales (Marshall and Williams 2003).

There have also been a number of initiatives to reform the way we vote: most notably by making postal voting easier, or even experimenting with all-postal ballots for local government elections in some regions of the country. While there is evidence that these innovations raise turnout in the pilot regions, all postal ballots have been undermined by allegations that they have widened the scope for electoral fraud (Electoral Commission 2004).

However, none of these reforms has been able to reverse the decline in formal political participation set out above. It is likely, therefore, that the causes of our current political malaise go much deeper and that much more fundamental reform is required if we are to reconnect citizens with politics.

What's wrong with our politics?

There are broadly speaking two kinds of explanation as tc
participation is declining, one that focuses on the design o
system, and another that focuses on the effects of wide
our society, affecting for instance participation in civic ...c and the
distribution of social power outside the political system. It is argued
below that to adequately explain the current crisis we need to consider
both the democratic deficits in Britain's constitution and the wider social
changes affecting the relationship between citizens and the state. In doing
so we depart from those who see further constitutional reform as being
sufficient to deliver democratic renewal on its own.

The political system

Popular disengagement from politics is clearly linked to widespread dissatisfaction with the way the political system operates. This is shown in
the growth of negative attitudes towards political institutions, and in
particular towards the political class. As Greenberg and Lewis outline
in Chapter 3, trust in politicians is extremely low, with just 18 per
cent of people trusting politicians to tell the truth. Moreover, this lack
of trust in the political profession also spills over into mistrust of the
major institutions at the heart of our democracy: just 27 per cent trust
Parliament, only 24 per cent trust the government and a mere 20 per
cent trust the European Parliament. Significantly, the British are more
mistrusting of their major democratic institutions than the average voter
in other European countries (Coleman 2005: 2).

Related to this lack of trust, YouGov found that 72 per cent of people
in 2003 felt disconnected from Parliament, with nearly half feeling 'very
disconnected'. When asked how 'in touch' people felt with their local
councillor or Member of Parliament, these political representatives came
well below other community figures such as local GPs and next-door
neighbours. Remarkably for an increasingly secular society like Britain,
people felt marginally more connection to the local clergy than they did
to their councillor or MP (ibid.: 2–5).

The recent Power Inquiry (2006) found evidence linking these negative
attitudes to a number of popularly perceived flaws in the political system.
There is a widespread feeling that our system shuts the average citizen
out between elections; 'We only see you at election time' is something
heard by candidates and party activists across the country. In 2003, 56 per
cent of people said that they had no say in what government does, and
overwhelming majorities of people agreed that ordinary voters should

.rave more influence over government decisions (Power Inquiry 2006: 73–7). In short, there is a desire for a system that allows greater input and citizen participation throughout the electoral cycle.

Another widely perceived flaw in the system is that people believe the two main political parties are too similar: the primary reason given by non-voters to the Power Inquiry for not voting was that it would make no difference because the main parties were much the same. Moreover, the Inquiry found that voters feel that the electoral system prevents them from expressing their authentic choice of party for fear of 'wasting' their vote. Given that in any seat generally just two parties have a chance of winning, voters are forced to vote for a 'lesser of two evils' rather than for the party that is closest to their political views (ibid.).

These popularly perceived flaws in the British political system clearly play a role in fostering the disconnection we have identified between citizens and politics. As a result, the Power Inquiry and others have rightly argued that we need to fundamentally redistribute power within our political system, opening it up to new channels of citizen participation. In particular, the Inquiry called for greater power for Parliament to hold the executive to account, a radical devolution of power to local government, elections to the House of Lords, lowering the voting age to 16, and giving citizens the right to initiate legislation and other formal political processes.

Reforms to widen access to power would be welcome, and later in the chapter we set out some priorities for a progressive strategy to democratize the political system. However, opening up our political system is just one part of any solution to Britain's current political malaise. We also need to address how changes in the nature of civil society and in the distribution of social power beyond the political system are undermining levels of citizen engagement.

Civil society and politics

The relationship between civil society and politics in Britain has changed in recent decades, partly because of changes in the kind of associational activity taking place in Britain's towns, neighbourhoods and workplaces. Organizational membership has declined with each succeeding generation, with the biggest fall occurring between the end of the Second World War and the baby boomer generation which followed. When a person born in 1946 was in their thirties, around 60 per cent of men and 50 per cent of women belonged to at least one organization. This decreased to just 15 per cent and 25 per cent for the 'baby boomers' born in 1958 and to just 10 per cent and 15 per cent for the post-baby boomer generation born in 1970 (Halpern 2005: 213).

This decline has been especially acute for those organizations most closely linked to formal political processes. For example, trade unionism, which always made up the social backbone of support for the Labour Party, has declined significantly since the 1970s. Whereas there were 13.2 million trade union members when Margaret Thatcher came to power in 1979, this had fallen to just 7.7 million in 2002 (Office for National Statistics (ONS) 2002). But this trend is also true of the women's groups, veterans' associations, trade organizations and the like that have played such a crucial role in Britain's civic culture. For example, membership of the National Federation of Women's Institutes fell by 46 per cent between 1972 and 2002 (Halpern 2005: 213). Church membership and attendance have also declined: between 1989 and 2002, Sunday church attendance fell by 31 per cent for the Church of England and by 49 per cent for the Roman Catholic Church (Christian Research 2006). Even those civic institutions that retain nominally political roles have lost any real connection with politics. One only has to visit one of the many Conservative or Labour clubs in towns around the country to discover how disconnected these social institutions have become from formal politics (BBC News Online 2007).

There is some contrary evidence which suggests that the membership of organizations has remained stable since the 1950s – and that the change we have seen in fact represents older forms of civic activism being replaced with new ways of getting involved (Halpern 2005: 212). Membership of new social movements, especially those linked to conservation and the environment, has increased dramatically since the 1970s. Political activism beyond 'formal' political institutions has also increased: the number of people who had signed a petition rose from 23 per cent in 1974 to 81 per cent in 2000; the number who had taken part in a demonstration rose from 6 per cent to 23 per cent, and the number who had boycotted a consumer good rose from 6 per cent to 17 per cent. Impressively, 50 per cent of British adults volunteer formally or informally at least once a month (Power Inquiry 2006: 41–54).

The Iraq war led to the largest single demonstration in British political history, with up to 2 million people travelling from all over the country to take part. Make Poverty History brought up to 250,000 people to the streets of Edinburgh to campaign on issues of debt, aid and trade, and engaged millions more who bought white wrist-bands to show their support. These figures have led some to argue that far from lower levels of civic activism being responsible for the collapse in political participation,

British citizens want to be engaged in democratic politics. They are simply prevented from doing so by an ageing and remote political system (see ibid.: 57–94).

The growth in new social movements is unquestionably welcome: these groups have brought issues to the table that were previously absent, such as the debts of developing countries, the natural environment, our built heritage, animal welfare and gay rights. However, there are a number of reasons for doubting that the growth of such activity provides a new army of potentially *political* activists that are out there, waiting to be engaged.

First, we should be cautious about interpreting rising group membership as a sign of growing civic activism. This is because many 'single issue' organizations (and especially those with the largest memberships) require a relatively light degree of commitment. Membership of the Royal Society for the Protection of Birds, the National Trust or Greenpeace merely requires a direct debit taken once a year from your bank account.

Second, the character of pressure group activity is very different from the character of politics. Whereas politics is essentially about collective deliberation aimed at reaching compromise between different demands and interests, pressure group activity is about pressing a set of demands, independently of the resource constraints (Crick 2005: 7). It is not the job of the 'single issue' group to look at the compromises and tradeoffs involved in running the country – that is for the politicians. Are the very many people who find pressure group activity of this sort appealing also likely to enjoy the messy world of political tradeoffs and compromises? Campaigning for a political party, for example, involves signing up to a whole package of policies, many of which one might disagree with. It is in that sense more demanding of one's political commitment than signing up to a pressure group (Russell 2005: 43).

Finally, these new forms of civic activism will not help to reconnect the working class with formal politics. Research has found that there was a growing class polarization in terms of associational membership between 1972 and 1999, with working-class men in particular becoming marginalized from civic activism (Halpern 2005: 216).

The limits of politics

Britain is faced with declining levels of political efficacy. People are less inclined than in the past to believe that politics or their participation in it will make a difference to their lives. The Power Inquiry reports, for example, that whereas in 1965, 70 per cent of people agreed with the statement 'The way that people decide to vote in local elections is the main thing that decides how things are run in this area', this had fallen to just 51 per cent in 1999. At the national level, the Inquiry found that in 2004, 40 per cent of people disagreed with the statement 'When people like me get involved in politics, they can really change the way the UK is run' (Power Inquiry 2006: 76–7).

While this finding is likely to reflect a lack of faith that ordinary people can affect decisions made through the political system, it is also likely to reflect a growing feeling that politics itself matters less. This was underlined by a recent BBC Radio Four poll which asked listeners who they felt was the most powerful person or institution in the UK. The top two places were taken by a bureaucrat (the President of the European Commission) and a businessman (Rupert Murdoch), while the Prime Minister came behind the Chief Executive of Tesco (BBC News Online 2006a).

While traditional democratic theory is founded on the idea that it is the nation state which makes the decisions under which we have to live, a number of contemporary trends have tested this assumption. One of the most commented on aspects to this is of course economic globalization: the breakdown of the system of international financial regulation brought in after the Second World War, alongside technological advance and the broader spread of neo-liberal economic ideas mean that nation states have much less control over big economic decisions. While some of the wilder predictions of globalization theory have not come to pass, it is clear that our elected representatives have much less autonomy than in the past to make key economic decisions such as setting interest rates or managing the level of unemployment (Garrett 1997; Boix 1998).

Moreover, new layers of international governance have taken on many of the old responsibilities of the nation state. Many of the laws under which we live are decided through international negotiations and treaties, agreed at one step removed from national Parliaments. Within the European Union, large parts of our lives, such as workplace and environmental regulations, are determined by European rather than national legislation. Even though we do have one directly accountable body at the EU level (the European Parliament), turnout in European elections is typically low and those elections are generally seen as a vote of approval or disapproval on the national government, rather than as a way of holding the European Commission to account. Therefore, while the institutions of governance are increasingly international in nature, our constitutional thinking has yet to catch up (Gamble 2007).

Finally, technological advances are constantly changing the way that we live, creating new risks and dangers for citizens. And yet as the questions we are asked become more and more complex, the media's handling of these questions can often be seen to be more simplistic. Compare, for example, the complex issue of genetically modified (GM) food, against a likely viewers' poll from a rolling news channel along the lines of 'Are you scared of GM crops? Yes or no.'

Decisions about these complex issues are moving further and further away from the reach of public debate. Increasingly, politicians have come to rely on experts to guide decision-making in these areas and in some cases have even delegated the decisions to committees of specialists. So, for example, decisions regarding which new drugs should be made available on the National Health Service are made by the National Institute for Health and Clinical Excellence (NICE). Those campaigning for new cancer drugs to be made freely available on the NHS are now told by ministers that they have no say in these decisions, which are based on clinical considerations and made by NICE.

In conclusion, while the democratic deficits in the political system play an important role in our current legitimacy crisis, it is not just our political institutions that need to change. If we are to restore people's faith in the value or relevance of politics, we will also need to foster a broader culture of political participation in civil society and address important questions concerning the broader distribution of social power.

An agenda for democratic renewal

Below we set out an agenda for change which is made up of three main imperatives for the progressive left: the need to radically change our political culture so that it reflects why politics is in the public interest, the need to redistribute power within the political system to increase participation and further social justice, and the need to extend the reach of politics into new social spheres so that power beyond the political system can be more effectively held to account.

Shifting the culture

Politics has become a dirty word, and yet we unquestionably could not function as a society without it. Politics is the way we manage conflicts between diverse interests, by providing for negotiation and compromise between them. The alternatives to it – anarchy would be one, authoritarianism would be another – are almost indisputably worse (Crick 2005: 7). Meg Russell argues rightly that in order for politics to function successfully, it requires a basic and widely understood agreement between politicians and the citizenry at large as to what politics is for and why it is valuable. It is in part our failure to do this that has led to our current political malaise (Russell 2005).

For example, the parties have started to write their manifestos and frame their election campaigns in response to focus group findings, aping the techniques of consumer marketing. Voters are asked what they want and then parties promise to deliver, rarely setting out the difficult tradeoffs and resource constraints that politics inevitably entails. Marketing of this kind generates expectations politics is simply unable to meet. We are promised major improvements in health care and education, on the one hand, while being promised that we will not have to pay higher taxes, on the other (Gordon Brown's 1 per cent increase in National Insurance in 2001 to pay for increased spending on the NHS was an honourable (and popular) exception). We are told we can reduce climate change, on the one hand, while being able to sustain our current carbon-dependent lifestyles on the other.

Consumerist expectations of what politics can deliver are bound to lead to disappointment. Unlike consumption, politics is not about the immediate fulfilment of individual demands or preferences – it is rather about deciding between competing views and interests and producing a fair and reasonable compromise between them. Unless our political culture reflects this essential truth, electoral competition will generate unrealizable expectations and the subsequent accusations of dishonesty will continue to corrode public confidence.

In another example, the culture of adversarialism in British politics undermines faith in the system because it too neglects why politics has value. Even when there is fundamental agreement between the parties, petty partisanship leads to political leaders impugning not just the policies of the other side, but their motives as well. One of the reasons the public doesn't trust politicians is because politicians themselves tell them that other politicians cannot be trusted. Take a couple of statements from either side. First Tony Blair, when Leader of the Opposition, confronting John Major at Prime Minister's Questions prior to the 1997 election:

> Has not this Parliament ended as it began, with the Government breaking their word? If the Prime Minister fails to have this report published, when everyone knows that he could, it will leave a stain on the character of his Government that will be erased only by a new Government with a fresh mandate, who will restore confidence in our public life for good. (Hansard, 20 March 1997)

Then the Conservative leader, Michael Howard, accusing Tony Blair of untrustworthiness and deception prior to the 2005 election:

> Tony Blair has lost the trust of the people. Most people no longer believe what he says. He came in with very high expectations. He tried to persuade people, he succeeded in persuading people – this was his great achievement – that he was a politician like no other that there has ever been. People feel completely taken in and deceived. (*Guardian*, 17 November 2004)

The result of this aggressive rhetoric is that the public ends up believing that all politicians are basically untrustworthy. In reality, both sides exaggerate the degree of 'sleaze' that exists in British politics for short-term electoral ends.

These dysfunctional tendencies in our political culture have a further consequence: we end up not so much with a political culture, but with an 'anti-political culture', in which almost everyone (including the politicians) agrees that politics is a bad thing. Hence we see the rise of populists like Robert Kilroy Silk and extremists like the British National Party (BNP), and also the tendency among even mainstream politicians to distance themselves from 'party politics'. Candidates in local and national elections end up emphasizing parochial local issues, depoliticizing their public profile to win votes. Overwhelmingly, political figures, with perfectly reasonable *political* opinions, end up saying things like 'This is not a party political point', as if making such a point were a bad thing in and of itself.

So how can we shift attitudes towards politics and foster a political culture that would encourage citizens to take up political activity? Attitudes take a long time to change – but change can start with institutional reforms explicitly aimed at enhancing those aspects of our political culture that operate in the public interest.

First, contrary to those who believe we should work around political parties, or simply let them wither on the vine, parties are central to successful democratic politics. This is because while single issue groups play an essential role in putting issues on the agenda, they cannot bring together conflicting view points and fashion them into a coherent and holistic programme for government. If the value of politics is in the reconciliation of conflicting interests, parties play a critical role in a representative system by aggregating the views of millions of their supporters into practicable strategies for change.

And yet our parties are losing members and voters are ceasing to identify with them as authentic representatives of their values or interests. There are a number of measures we need to take to renew our democratic political parties which will invest in the value they add to our politics, rather than in the dysfunctional aspects of their current behaviour. If parties' contribution to the public interest lies primarily in their representative aggregative role, then a priority should be to reconnect parties with voters at the local level. MacTaggart, Mulgan and Ali (2006) argue that if parties are to receive state funding it should not be for negative billboard advertising, for example, or even electoral campaigning in general, but rather for community-based activities to connect voters with the wider political process. So, for example, state funding should go primarily to local constituency parties and ward branches rather than national parties. This funding could be used by local parties to employ staff whose job it is to build up the local membership, to conduct community consultations such as petitions and street surgeries, or to organize public meetings to discuss local concerns. Such funding should also help parties restore their youth sections to get young people involved in party political activity in the communities where they live. Perhaps a condition of such financial support should also be that parties ensure their membership is as representative as possible, rewarding them for reaching out to women, members of black and minority ethnic groups and those currently most marginalized from the political system.

In addition to reforming party funding to encourage such civic activities, national parties should democratize their decision-making structures. One of the reasons given by the Power Inquiry for the collapse in party activism is the fact that party members feel they have little say in decision-making. Policy-making within the parties therefore needs to be decentralized, perhaps through more local and regional conferences which will be accessible to a wider range of members. Parties also need to give their members genuine decision-making authority through their annual party conferences, rather than using them as platforms for politicians to speak to television audiences. The selection of candidates should conform to basic democratic norms, with a top-down veto of locally selected candidates possible only in extraordinary circumstances. The Electoral Commission should be given the authority to ensure that parties operate in an internally democratic fashion – this function is too important to the health of our politics to remain largely unregulated as it is at present.

A second set of institutional changes that might shift our broader political culture in a positive direction would be to create new spaces for public involvement in deliberating over policy problems. One way of moving away from the consumerist political culture that is doing so much damage to the relationship between citizens and democracy would be to engage a much wider range of citizens in deliberating over complex problems. There are a number of ways this might be done, some of which have been piloted already in this country.

The most common such approach is the use of citizens' juries or citizens' panels to discuss complex issues facing either the country or a local town or neighbourhood. These panels are made up of a relatively small number of people selected at random so that they are likely to be representative of the population as a whole. These have already been used by local councils around the country and by national government, such as to debate whether to allow trials of GM foods in British agriculture or to discuss issues of rationing in the health service.

In recent years, voting in general elections has focused more on a clash of personalities than a clash of values or policies. This is worrying because it puts distance between voters and policies – members of the public vote for a personality, and begin to see policy as separate from their political engagement. Then when extremely contentious long-term issues facing the nation arise – like nuclear weapons or nuclear power stations – people do not feel connected to the decision that is taken; it becomes a decision made solely by the individual for whom they voted.

The government could begin to tackle this perception by introducing 'citizens' assemblies'. These are also made up of a randomly selected group of citizens, this time larger (up to 150), brought together to deliberate over issues of major national import. In the Canadian province of British Columbia, for instance, a citizens' assembly was set up to discuss how to best reform the electoral system (Rogers 2006). Of course, while such assemblies have benefits in terms of the time they allow participants to deliberate over the issues, they are weaker at engaging the wider population. This could be compensated for by televising their proceedings or, more ambitiously, submitting their recommendations to a referendum of the population at large. A word of warning, however: citizens must be confident from experience that whatever they decide will be acted upon. It can be even worse to engage people and then ignore their decisions than it is not to ask them in the first place; it is a fast-track to disillusionment and disengagement.

A further measure aimed at engaging citizens in deliberating over political problems is Participatory Budgeting (PB) – used extensively in Brazil, but also now in a large number of European cities. PB processes dedicate a proportion of a local council's budget to be allocated according to the decisions of ordinary citizens, whether in small neighbourl.. assemblies or in city-wide budgeting meetings. Typically, a smaller group of citizens is selected to monitor implementation throughout the year. While the proportion of the budget allocated to this process can be very small at first, experience from Brazil shows that over time this can be increased as citizens learn more about how the financial system works. Again, this is a model that has been piloted in a number of British towns, including Salford, Harrow and Newcastle-upon-Tyne, but if we are to develop a more deliberative political culture we need to extend this approach throughout local government. The recent local government White Paper could help act as a catalyst for this, in particular through its proposal to make public participation in decision-making a duty for most Best Value public authorities (Department for Communities and Local Government (DCLG) 2006; Community Pride Initiative/Oxfam 2005; Allegretti and Herzberg 2004; Baiocchi 2003).

One final set of reforms to encourage a healthier political culture and generate a shared understanding as to the value of politics would be to change the way in which the media operates. Given that direct communication between voters and their elected representatives is inevitably less regular than daily newspapers and 24-hour news, much of the communication between the public and politicians occurs via press and television. At present this prism through which politicians see voters and voters see politicians is highly distorted. The press in particular is engaged in a fierce battle for increased market share that encourages sensationalist headlines. Voters' views are presented in very simplistic terms, and politicians, if they are to secure the attention they crave, are encouraged to speak in slogans and soundbites. Even in the broadcast media, highly aggressive interviewing techniques frequently overstep the mark between legitimately holding politicians to account and treating them with disdain and contempt (Lloyd 2004).

So what could be done to foster a media culture that encourages citizens to engage with the political process? First, the rise of digital media is rapidly increasing the space for online interactivity and direct conversations between politicians, journalists and citizens. This is a positive democratic development, but as Stephen Coleman has argued, the government could do more in particular to ensure that online networks link deliberation among citizens to the social institutions that have a major impact on their lives, such as schools, local authorities and government itself. While these spaces should be kept free from management by these various authorities, it should be made clear to

engagement in such online networks will feed into the
ocess (Coleman 2006).
ill continue to get much of our information about
the television news and the press. The power of the
our political culture is such that serious consideration
en to regulation. Press freedom, when combined with
enormous power to frame the nature of public debate, brings with it
democratic responsibility. Media organizations should be required to
promote participation in and engagement with democratic politics and
to ensure accuracy in their reporting. They should help citizens deliberate
over complex questions, and make a commitment to avoid trivializing
complex issues.

Third, we should use new technologies to give citizens greater power
to shape the media. One approach is to encourage peer-reviewed citizen
journalism, such as OhmyNews (<http://english.ohmynews.com/>)
where stories are chosen on the basis of what readers, not editors, want.
A further possibility would be an 'Open Commission for Accuracy in
the Media' (Mulgan et al. 2005) to ensure accuracy in all mass media.
This could employ a reputation system that would allow members of
the public to report inaccuracies, view rulings of the Press Complaints
Commission and possibly even adjudicate on alleged inaccuracies.

To conclude, a successful agenda for democratic renewal needs to
move beyond the traditional agenda of constitutional reform and the
unfinished business of Labour's 1997 manifesto. It requires significant
changes to our national political culture, moving away from treating
voters like consumers and from needless adversarialism, towards a
functional politics which places collective deliberation over complex
questions at its heart.

Redistributing political power

Voters currently feel shut out of the political system, with real political
authority being exercised by most people just once every four to five
years in a general election. We therefore need to increase the space for
citizen participation in decision-making through new mechanisms of
direct democracy. In addition, we need to tackle the growing gap between
the affluent citizens who vote and the poorer citizens who do not. This
is of critical importance for the left if we are to prevent the democratic
system being captured by the middle classes, thus reinforcing broader
social inequalities. Both of these objectives require a fundamental redistribution of power within the political system.

Participation and representation: a new balance

In order to increase citizen participation in the system we need to open it up to new forms of direct democracy. Again, many of these models are currently being piloted around the country: giving social housing tenants control of estate management, introducing forms of participatory budgeting in town halls and giving local residents the power to decide how to spend large-scale regeneration funds. In expanding the use of such mechanisms, however, we need to be realistic: even in the famous Participatory Budgeting processes introduced in Brazil, turnout rarely exceeds more than 2 per cent of the population. In Britain there are 400,000 people who regularly participate on school governing bodies, in tenants' and residents' associations, and in regeneration bodies such as New Deal for Communities – around 1 per cent of the UK's population (Skidmore 2006). Simply setting up new participatory forums in and of itself is unlikely to deliver an upswing in political engagement. Most people simply have better or more pressing things to do with their time than spending it in political meetings.

Being realistic about the degree of public appetite for greater political participation, however, need not be a cause for pessimism. First, we should make the best use of those who do currently participate – those whom Paul Skidmore (2006) has described as the 'magic 1 per cent'. While recognizing that this activist minority are unlikely to be representative of the population as a whole, we should remember that these 400,000 active citizens are involved in a wide range of cross-cutting social networks. Many of them are active in more than one network and therefore help to link different communities together and share community information. By better using the 'magic 1 per cent' to help consult and interact with the wider community, we can in fact begin to involve a much larger pool of people in community governance.

Second, we should think much more carefully about how representative institutions and more direct mechanisms can complement each other. So, while participatory mechanisms provide for more direct citizen empowerment, they tend to involve relatively small numbers who are often unrepresentative of general opinion. The opposite is true of representative systems: they are remote from citizens, but have the legitimacy of a broader mandate. Both have their place, and the interesting question for progressives in the years ahead is not which is preferable, but rather how the two can fit together.

For example, Brazilian-style Participatory Budgeting allows citizens a large degree of control over a proportion of the budget, but this is balanced by local authority oversight. Ultimately, the municipal council can veto the PB section of the budget, although in general terms they would not do so because of its popular legitimacy. However, the council can also ensure, for instance, that social justice considerations are reflected in outcomes by dividing up the budget by neighbourhood according to social need prior to the participatory process. Another example would be the way that citizens' assemblies have been linked to wider processes – such as by putting their recommendations out to referenda. In these different ways we can ensure a healthy interplay between the need to encourage greater citizen involvement in decision-making and the need to ensure decision-making is not captured by unrepresentative minorities.

Third, we should also ensure that the political system is able to respond when a much larger group of people want to participate. While most people do not want to regularly attend civic meetings or sit on community bodies, they do want to get involved when an important issue arises that affects them directly. Any local councillor will tell you that when something important happens, such as a new proposal to build a supermarket in the local area, or a major flood, turnout at local meetings increases massively. It is at these times that a larger number of people need to have easily-accessible mechanisms to influence decision-making. We need to give people 'trigger' mechanisms so that when they want to get involved they can do so. For example, the Housing Association Bill, which one of this chapter's authors, Emily Thornberry, tabled in Parliament, proposed that housing association residents should be allowed to choose their estate management. While not necessarily performing management functions themselves, residents would be able to trigger an inspection of their services if they felt they had fallen below an agreed level. As a result, residents would be able to control their services without needing to be permanently involved. This is the broad vision expressed through the idea of 'community calls to action', as seen in the recent local government White Paper (DCLG 2006).

Beyond the current White Paper proposals, such calls could be used even more ambitiously, possibly by being given statutory bite. So, for example, if 5 per cent of the population sign a petition, they could secure a referendum on a particular proposal locally, or on a proposed piece of legislation nationally. Some countries allow citizens to revoke existing legislation by a referendum if enough signatures can be collected. These kinds of demand-based measures allow large numbers into the system when they want, and are therefore based on the recognition that most of us find the idea of 'permanent participation' unappealing.

Participation and social justice

How could power be redistributed within the political system to empower those currently least likely to participate? This is essential if we are to fulfil the social justice aims set out elsewhere in this volume: without political power being fairly spread, those who suffer most from current social injustice will go unheard.

First, we need to make sure that new participatory mechanisms include the most marginalized voices. We should ensure that Skidmore's 'magic 1 per cent' includes those from currently under-represented groups, through outreach work. This means investing resources in letting people know what's happening and how they can get involved, or in going out to consult those who are hardest to reach, through community development work, neighbourhood management and youth work.

Second, while many see the first-past-the-post electoral system for the House of Commons as vitally important in maintaining a strong constituency link for MPs, more proportional electoral systems could be used in other assemblies. Following on from the use of proportional representation (PR) in the devolved assemblies, reform of the House of Lords gives us an opportunity to bring PR to Westminster. There are probably as many ideas on Lords reform as there are MPs in the Commons, but one option would be to base the Lords' composition on the proportion of votes cast in a general election. This form of 'secondary mandate' would mean no votes were wasted in general elections.

Third, being serious about reducing inequalities in election turnout also means making it easier for everyone to vote. A straightforward way to achieve this would be to move elections away from a regular workday. The most obvious option is to have elections on Saturdays – but we could also consider holding them on Wednesdays, and making election day a bank holiday. An unusual day off in the middle of the week would draw attention to the election, and it would give more people the time to vote, yet without encouraging them to take the day as part of a long weekend.

Evidence reviewed by ippr also shows that making it a legal obligation to participate in the electoral process can dramatically affect levels of voter inequality. Not only this, but a recent study found that countries which have introduced compulsory turnout also tend to have more egalitarian social outcomes and, particularly, lower levels of income inequality (Chong and Olivera 2005). While it remains to be seen whether compulsory turnout could work in a British context, this evidence suggests that further research could be worthwhile.

Extending the reach of politics

Politics has become less relevant to people as power has shifted away from the political system and into alternative domains that are much less accountable to the average citizen. As a consequence, progressives cannot focus on reforms to the political system alone if we are to renew our democracy. We should also consider how to spread the reach of democratic politics, and with it models of participation and public accountability, into new social spheres. Where power has shifted, politics should follow (Gamble 2007).

First, the left should return to the question of economic power, how it is distributed and how it can be effectively held to account by ordinary citizens. Politicizing the economic realm means incorporating into the workplace and market place the basic democratic principle that as broad a range of people as possible should be involved in making important decisions.

So, for example, the workplace should not be a politics free zone. Indeed, there is a growing hunger in Britain for new ways of holding employers to account for their decisions. This is shown by the innovative work of London Citizens in the capital, which has successfully combined faith groups, unions and local community leaders in lobbying private sector employers to pay a living wage. These new forms of collective action, not just by workers in a particular workplace, but by civil society at large, have been remarkably successful through mobilizing moral pressure on employers (TELCO Citizens 2006).

In terms of what government can do, it should ensure that workers are properly consulted over the long-term strategic decisions facing their organizations (Coats 2007). It should also explore how employees can gain greater economic empowerment through asset ownership, and look at how employee-owned social enterprises could be expanded. The accountability of workers' pension funds is another element of this agenda, given their enormous power in the modern boardroom. For too long the left has been largely silent on these questions, despite the fact that we spend much of our lives at work and that power relationships in the workplace are fundamental to our autonomy and sense of citizenship. The public want to make sure their money is used by business in a responsible way, but monitoring pensions and investments is complex and time-consuming. The government's pension proposals should make it easier for people to have the pensions they want.

The government should act to ensure that all companies meet their wider environmental and social obligations. One of the authors of this chapter, Emily Thornberry, was contacted by over 300 constituents asking that the Companies Bill force companies to be environmentally and socially responsible. But it is not just Islington's 'chattering classes' that are concerned: nine out of ten people think there should be enforceable rules that stop companies damaging the environment (ICM poll for War on Want, 24–26 March 2006). We need to close the gap between what the public want from business, and what they are getting. We should go beyond the Companies Bill and ask companies not only to take account of the social and environmental effects of their activities, but, working with trade unions, to play their part in helping employees themselves to be environmentally and socially responsible at home and on the way to work. This would help to rebalance power towards the public, who currently feel that big business has too much power to do as it likes.

Politics could also be brought to bear in the marketplace through consumer empowerment. The rise of Fair Trade foods and recent customer pressure on supermarkets over GM products and their 'carbon footprint' show that Britain is in many ways an international leader in consumer-led pressure for greater corporate responsibility. For instance, collective action by consumers has enormous potential to force firms to adopt higher ethical standards with respect to employment or environmental behaviour. While much of this coordination currently comes from civil society and social movements, the government could help through much clearer regimes of information and statutory labelling.

A second site of power in which politics should play a role is that of the production, dissemination and use of knowledge and information. In particular, we should explore how the public could be involved in complex decisions regarding the use of new science and technology. While citizens and politicians will always to some extent rely on the advice of experts and specialists to make educated decisions, there are ways of enhancing public engagement in these areas. For example, the government's National Institute for Health and Clinical Excellence set up a citizens' panel to help it adjudicate over which new drugs to be registered for use in the NHS. Another key component of a programme for democratic renewal should be how to introduce elements of citizen participation and deliberation into important scientific and technological decisions, which often have a major moral component.

A vital area here is the ownership and control of the media. As Steven Lukes has argued, there is no aspect of power more significant than that which shapes our ideas and consciousness. Sociologists have long argued that power as ideological hegemony acts to 'frame' political and social debate by closing down certain options and favouring others, in the interests of those with the most power (Lukes 2005). Given the importance of such power, how the media is run and who controls it are of primary public importance. We are fortunate in Britain to have a highly regarded public service broadcaster in the BBC, which has a statutory duty to act in the broader public interest, rather than the interests of a private owner. A progressive media policy that would help to renew our democratic politics should prevent the concentration of ownership of press and television media organizations that exists at present.

Finally, we should explore new ways of holding international layers of governance more effectively to account. National parliaments, for all their faults, are still the most accountable institutions, commanding the largest popular mandate for making decisions. It is time to bring national legislatures back in, giving them a greater role in the scrutiny of international agreements signed by the executive on our behalf and in particular in the scrutiny of decisions taken at the European level. At Westminster, a new range of select committees should be established to scrutinize EU-level decision-making. Parliament could also be given the power to approve whether the country goes to war or the signature of foreign treaties, powers that currently reside in the hands of the Prime Minister and are therefore subject to little public debate.

Conclusions

In any democracy the legitimacy of a state's decision-making rests on the consent of its citizens to be governed in a particular way. Falling political participation, which has now reached an historic low, therefore puts the legitimacy of our democratic system at risk. In finding solutions to this crisis we have argued that there needs to be a major redistribution of power within the political system, to open it up to much greater direct citizen involvement in decision-making and to prevent our democracy reflecting, and reinforcing, the inequalities that exist in our society as a whole.

However, constitutional reform on its own is insufficient, because we need to tackle the wider causes of the current crisis, which lie in social changes affecting the nature of civil society and the distribution of social power in its broader sense. Any progressive agenda for democratic renewal will therefore also need to change our political culture so that it reflects what is valuable about politics, and extend the reach of politics into new areas of unaccountable power.

References

Allegretti, G. and Herzberg, C. (2004) *Participatory Budgets in Europe: Between Efficiency and Growing Local Democracy*. Amsterdam: Transnational Institute.
Baiocchi, G. (2003) 'Participation, Activism and Politics: The Porto Alegre Experiment', in A. Fung and E. Olin Wright (eds), *Deepening Democracy: Institutional Innovations in Empowered Participatory Governance*. London: Verso.
BBC News Online (2006a) 'EU boss "most powerful man in UK"', 2 February 2006, <www.bbc.co.uk/news>.
BBC News Online (2006b) 'Labour facing "membership crisis"', 26 December, <www.bbc.co.uk/news>.
BBC News Online (2007) 'Are political clubs still political?', 12 February, <www.bbc.co.uk/news>.
Boix, C. (1998) *Political Parties, Growth and Equality: Conservative and Social Democratic Economic Strategies in the World Economy*. Cambridge: Cambridge University Press.
Chong, A. and Olivera, M. (2005) *On Compulsory Voting and Income Inequality in a Cross Section of Countries*. Research Department Working Paper No. 533. Washington DC: Inter-American Development Bank.
Christian Research (2006) 'English Church Census 2005'. Available at <www.christian-research.org.uk>. Accessed 29 January 2007.
Coats, D. (2007) 'No Going Back to the 1970s? The Case for a Revival of Industrial Democracy', *Public Policy Research*, 13 (4).
Coleman, S. (2005) *Direct Representation: Towards a Conversational Democracy*. London: ippr.
Coleman, S. (2006) 'Digital Voices and Analogue Citizenship: Bridging the Gap between Young People and the Democratic Process', *Public Policy Research*, 13 (4).
Community Pride Initiative/Oxfam (2005) *Breathing Life in Democracy: The Power of Participatory Budgeting*. Manchester and Oxford: Community Pride Initiative/Oxfam.
Crick, B. (2005) *In Defence of Politics*. London: Continuum.
Dahl, R. (1989) *Democracy and its Critics*. New Haven: Yale University Press.
DCLG (2006) *Strong and Prosperous Communities*. London: DCLG.
Democratic Audit (2005) *War and Peace: Executive Democracy in Action*. Colchester: Human Rights Centre, University of Essex.
Electoral Commission (2004) *Delivering Democracy? The Future of Postal Voting*. London: Electoral Commission.
Foot, P. (2006) *The Vote: How it was Won and How it was Undermined*. London: Penguin Books.
Gamble, A. (2007) 'Constitutional Government in the 21st Century', *Public Policy Research*, 13 (4).
Garrett, G. (1997) *Partisan Politics in the Global Economy*. Cambridge: Cambridge University Press.
Halpern, D. (2005) *Social Capital*. Cambridge: Polity Press.
Heath, A., Martin, J. and Elgenius, G. (2007) 'Who Do We Think We Are? The Decline of Traditional Identities', in A. Park, J. Curtice, K. Thomson, M. Phillips and M. Johnson (eds), *British Social Attitudes: The 23rd Report – Perspectives on a Changing Society* London: Sage.

Held, D. (1994) 'Inequalities of Power, Problems of Democracy', in D. Miliband (ed.), *Reinventing the Left*. London: ippr.

Keaney, E. and Rogers, B. (2006) *A Citizen's Duty: Voter Inequality and the Case for Compulsory Turnout*. London: ippr.

Lloyd, J. (2004) *What the Media are Doing to Our Politics*. London: Constable and Robinson.

Lukes, S. (2005) *Power: A Radical View*, 2nd edition. Basingstoke: Palgrave Macmillan.

MacTaggart, F., Mulgan, G. and Ali, R. (2006) *Parties for the Public Good*. London: Young Foundation.

Marshall, B. and Williams, M. (2003) *Turnout, Attitudes to Voting and the 2003 Elections*. London: Electoral Commission.

Mulgan, G., Steinberg, T. and Salem, O. (2005) *Open Source Methods and Their Future Potential*. London: Demos.

ONS (2002) 'Trade Union Membership of Employees: By Occupation and Sex, 2002', *Social Trends*, 34. London: TSO. Available at <www.statistics.gov.uk/ STATBASE/ssdataset.asp?vlnk=7391>.

Power Inquiry (2006) *Power to the People. The Report of Power: An Independent Inquiry into Britain's Democracy*. York: Power Inquiry.

Rogers, B. (ed.) (2004) *Lonely Citizens. Report of the ippr Working Party on Active Citizenship*. London: ippr.

Rogers, B. (2006) 'Citizens Assemblies: Radical Common Sense', <www. opendemocracy.net>,15 November.

Russell, M. (2005) *Must Politics Disappoint?* London: Fabian Society.

Skidmore, P. (2006) 'Disengaged Democracy?', *Prospect*, 129, December.

TELCO Citizens (2006) *TELCO is Ten: A Proud History of Fighting for a Better Society*. London: TELCO.

Whitely, P. and Seyd, P. (1999) 'Slow Collapse', *Observer*, 5 October 1999.

14
Fair Rules: Procedural Fairness and the Reform of Public Services

Nick Pearce

Introduction

Debate about the reform of public services is dominated by arguments about how best to achieve desired outcomes, such as increases in educational attainment, lower hospital waiting times or more journeys taken by train. This seems obvious enough; after all, the public care about what public services deliver, not about how schools, hospitals or train companies go about their business. 'What works' is more important than how things work.

These common assumptions are buttressed by a considerable literature on how to achieve effective public service reform. A central claim of the dominant paradigm of public administration of the last 20 years, the New Public Management, is that central government should steer, not row, concerning itself with high-level outcomes, not the wherewithal of how services are delivered. Similarly, discourses on choice focus on how to make services responsive to individual users, through the creation of quasi-markets, individual budgets and other mechanisms. The 'howness' of procedures is given far less attention in this literature. If it merits study, it is usually only in instrumental terms, relating particular procedural strategies to the achievement of specified outcomes.

It is undeniable, of course, that outcomes matter, and for progressive reformers the distributional justice of those outcomes is of vital concern. We rightly care about social class gaps in education or health; these are social injustices that we seek to redress. We also care about ensuring that those who run our public services and the professionals who work in them are not subject to excessive interference in how they do their jobs. A focus on outcomes should – at least in theory – give them space and discretion for achieving their objectives.

But in focusing almost exclusively on outcomes, reform strategies may miss important insights about how the procedures that govern public services – and in particular their fairness – elicit particular responses from the public. These responses can condition trust in public services and determine how willing people are to cooperate with service providers, cooperation which in turn can be crucial to achieving the objectives of a service. The sense of 'fair rules, fairly implemented' therefore has important consequences for public service reform. Moreover, it may also help explain public attitudes to such issues as immigration and welfare state entitlements.

What do we mean by procedural fairness? For obvious reasons, procedural justice is a central concept in legal theory. It refers to how a trial or other legal process is conducted, rather than the outcome of a case. Procedural fairness may attest to rules that are followed with accuracy, impartiality and consistency, or alternatively to close judicial attentiveness to the individual merits or particulars of a case (Sunstein 2006). In both instances, however, the question of procedure, rather than outcome, is at stake.

Social psychological theories of procedural justice work with a similar definition but typically examine how individuals and groups perceive the fairness of procedures and the fairness of how they themselves are treated by public authorities and private organizations. Social psychologists have related these perceptions to the legitimacy of institutions and the trust in which they are held, and the consequences that these perceptions have for cooperation between institutions and individuals.

In political philosophy, procedural justice is associated with deontological ethics or the claim that the 'right' has priority over the 'good'. However, both procedural and distributive justice are often considered components of 'substantive justice', in contrast to the 'formal justice' of fairly implemented rules – what John Rawls termed 'justice as regularity'.

To avoid confusion, in this chapter I use 'procedural justice' and 'procedural fairness' interchangeably, and stick with the more common usage of the terms as meaning the fairness of rules and their implementation. I begin by examining some of the main findings of social psychological research into procedural justice, before turning to more recent strands of welfare economics concerned with so-called 'procedural utility'. I then look at three examples of public policy areas in which procedural fairness has been researched: policing, tax compliance and planning mechanisms for facilities that are unpopular in local communities. I relate procedural fairness to other central issues in contemporary public service reform strategies in the UK – choice, voice and personalisation – before concluding with a discussion of how to situate procedural justice within a pluralist set of objectives for public services.

Procedural justice: social psychological perspectives

In the 1970s, social psychologists began to develop theories of procedural justice to capture behavioural responses to different ways of resolving conflicts over resources and the allocation of goods and services. This 'third wave of justice research', as it has been described (Tyler et al. 1997), studied whether evaluations of the fairness of decision-making processes impacted on reactions to the outcomes of those processes, that is, to the question of who gets what. Researchers discovered that, counter-intuitively, people will accept outcomes that are negative or adverse for them personally if they believe that the manner by which they were arrived at was fair. For example, Thibaut and Walker's pioneering study (1975) of adversarial and inquisitional legal systems found that people choose dispute resolution mechanisms that they think will be fair and yield a fair outcome, rather than those that might stand them the best chance of winning. Similarly, they found that people are more satisfied with trial procedures that they experience as fair, regardless of the trial outcome.

Subsequent procedural justice research demonstrated that people care about the fairness of procedures in a wide range of settings: from trial procedures to arbitration mechanisms, performance-related pay at work and police–citizen interactions (Tyler 1990; Tyler et al. 1997; Tyler and Fagan 2006). Moreover, not only are people more satisfied with procedures they deem to be fair and more ready to accept their outcomes, but their loyalty and willingness to help the organization concerned also improve. Fair procedures and fair treatment generate loyalty and cooperation.

These responses can be mediated by prior experience. If people trust an authority, they are more likely to consider its procedures fair and to use fairness, rather than distributive concerns in arriving at judgements about its decisions. But this prior legitimacy can be a double-edged sword: if people trust an organization but then feel unfairly treated by it, they react more negatively to the outcomes of a decision. Loyal people can feel betrayed by unfairness (Tyler et al. 1997: 86).

A sense of control also appears to matter. Victims of crime feel that trial procedures are fairer when they have been given a chance to contribute their views to sentencing decisions. Employees will more readily accept the outcome of pay reviews if they have been offered the opportunity to put forward evidence of their performance. Fathers will more readily accept defeat in custody hearings if they think that they have been given a fair chance to present their case and articulate their feelings.

A comprehensive theoretical framework for understanding the fairness of procedures was devised by G. S. Leventhal (summarized in Tyler et al. 1997: 91). He offered six criteria for procedural justice:

- *consistency* – equal treatment across persons and time
- *bias suppression* – the avoidance of personal interest and/or ideological bias by public officials
- *accuracy* – utilizing up-to-date, accurate information and opinion
- *correctability* – the provision of opportunity for review, appeal or redress
- *representativeness* – ensuring that all citizens can be involved in decision-making and/or that a representative view has been taken of public views and values
- *ethicality* – decisions must conform to fundamental moral values or ethics.

These criteria or 'fair rules' have been found to be important in a number of experimental studies, particularly those rules that bear most heavily on the fairness of procedure: consistency, bias suppression, accuracy and ethicality. Other studies have added trustworthiness of the institution as an important criterion (for example, Tyler 1988).

People therefore appear to make sophisticated judgements about procedural fairness using multiple criteria. But judgements about procedural fairness may also reflect the use of a 'fairness heuristic'. Rather than make complex cost-benefit judgements about different outcomes, individuals may rely on a sense of whether the procedures were fair, trusting outcomes where fair procedures are believed to obtain. In ideological terms, framing outcomes with the fairness heuristic then becomes decisive. Socio-economic inequalities will appear just or unjust depending on whether people believe they result from fair chances.

Procedural utility

Economists have also recently begun to study procedural fairness in institutional settings. Their results challenge the view that individuals derive utility or satisfaction solely from outcomes, rather than the processes or conditions that lead to outcomes. Building on the earlier work of social psychologists, economic researchers have found that utility varies with the value individuals place on institutional allocative or decision-making processes rather than the substantive gains or losses these may produce (Frey et al. 2004; Benz 2005).

This 'procedural utility' is observable across a wide range of social and economic policy domains, from consumption behaviour, work organization and employment, to opportunities for democratic participation, the allocation of public goods and tax compliance. Taking employment as an example, research shows that people gain utility at work from non-pecuniary aspects such as independence, autonomy and an absence of hierarchy, and that employees will accept the outcomes of pay negotiations, restructuring plans, and mergers or acquisitions if they believe that fair procedures have been applied and they have been given an opportunity to contribute to them (Benz 2005).

Why is procedural utility important? One way of understanding the question is to address the impact of institutional decision-making on people's sense of self and the well-being they experience when they are treated fairly, given respect and offered the opportunity to exercise control in their lives. In other words, procedural utility or well-being may derive from a need for self-determination, understood as the need to experience autonomy in one's life, recognize oneself as a capable person exercising self-control, and in turn receive recognition and respect from others. As Matthias Benz puts it, 'procedural utility can be understood as the well being people gain from living and acting under institution-alised processes as they contribute to a positive sense of self, addressing innate needs of autonomy, competence and relatedness' (ibid.: 7). (An alternative reading of this evidence might be to connect the experience of procedural fairness to freedom in the republican sense of non-domination by arbitrary power; that is, that procedural fairness testifies to legitimate, non-arbitrary authority. This is an issue worth further exploration.)

A consistent theme of this research into procedural fairness is that individuals are not simply rational maximizers of self-interest, as orthodox economics has long taught. People often apply non-rational shortcuts – like the fairness heuristic – or place a value on procedures from which they stand to gain less personal reward. The orthodox view of 'Chicago Man' maximizing his or her utility from the outcomes of different socio-economic interactions simply cannot explain these findings.

Results such as these are broadly congruent with those from game theoretical studies of behaviour which repeatedly demonstrate that the majority of people are 'conditional cooperators', rather than altruists or egoists. In numerous studies, the phenomenon of 'strong reciprocity' has been observed, by which individuals cooperate if they perceive that each other's intentions are fair. Those who freeride are punished, while those who cooperate are rewarded. Once again, the perception of fairness is critical: while there are always a small minority who try to freeride on others' efforts, and another group who are consistently altruistic, the majority behave on the basis of reciprocal reward – 'something-for-something' – to mutual benefit (Ghintis et al. 2005).

Procedural fairness and public services: some examples

What are the policy implications of these research findings? To begin to answer this question, we can draw upon some public policy case studies from research into procedural fairness.

Fair policing

Criminologists have shown that levels of crime in a neighbourhood are strongly related to the 'collective efficacy' of the community. Collective efficacy refers to the ability of the community's members to exercise informal social control – to intervene when young people are truanting from school or committing acts of anti-social behaviour, or to mobilize in the defence of valued public goods, like a local fire station (Sampson 2004).

Collective efficacy foregrounds the importance of self-regulatory models of social order, in contrast to instrumental or deterrence models. The latter explain levels of crime according to the calculations potential criminals make of the costs and benefits of criminal activity; that is, will I get caught and how severe will the punishment be? Such instrumental calculations can indeed be observed in criminal behaviour, but their impact is relatively small and researchers argue that deterrence strategies premised on changing the terms of the criminal calculation (that is, through the imposition of longer prison sentences) are both costly and of limited effectiveness, chiefly impacting on particular crimes, such as burglary and car crime, in areas where surveillance is possible (Tyler and Fagan 2006).

In contrast, self-regulatory models of social order examine the resources within a community (its levels of collective efficacy, in turn related to, but not solely causally determined by, socio-economic disadvantage), and its social norms. To the degree that the community has both the resources and values necessary to regulate itself, interventions from the police and other agencies become less necessary. Trust and cooperation within communities and between police and the local community become salient considerations for police force effectiveness where crime necessitates intervention. Public authorities find it very difficult to enforce the law unless they receive the cooperation of those they serve, while their effectiveness is improved when local communities report crimes and assist with investigations.

How does procedural fairness impact on crime and policing? Procedural justice research asserts that local people trust the police and cooperate with them when they are perceived to be legitimate and fair in how they treat individuals (whereas cooperation within a community appears to depend instead on identification with the community). In a panel study of police–citizen interactions in New York, Tyler and Fagan (2006) found that a crucial factor in people's willingness to cooperate with law enforcement activities was the legitimacy in which the police were held, which in turn derived from the perception of the justice of the force's procedures and whether it treated individuals fairly. Public evaluations of police effectiveness were not irrelevant, but after controlling for them, legitimacy judgements remained shaped by procedural justice assessments. Prior legitimacy also counted, as those who viewed the police as legitimate before interacting with them were more likely to report that they were treated justly and received a favourable outcome afterwards.

This research suggests that the police may remain distrusted – even when their effectiveness in cutting crime has improved – if their procedures are considered unjust or they are held to be discriminatory or unfair in their dealings with individual members of the public. The 2005 Citizenship Survey provides evidence of a strong correlation between trust and perceptions of discrimination: 28 per cent of those who did not trust the police 'at all' thought that the police would treat them worse than people of other races, compared to 3 per cent of those who trusted the police 'a lot' (Department for Communities and Local Government (DCLG) 2006). This is also a plausible reading of why the Metropolitan Police Force has not substantially increased its public standing, particularly among the Afro-Caribbean community, despite falling crime in London. The cumulative effect of the Stephen Lawrence case, the racial profile of stop-and-search statistics and other more recent incidents, has been to create a 'fairness deficit' for the force that has undermined its legitimacy.

Tax compliance

Rather like explaining why people vote, orthodox economics has always found it difficult to account for why people pay their taxes so readily.

After all, the chances of being caught and the severity of punishment appear low, while the monetary benefits of tax avoidance are high. If taxpayers were applying the standard cost-benefit calculus, tax evasion would be much higher than is the case in the UK and elsewhere.

Procedural fairness gives a new perspective on tax compliance. First, taxpayers will respond positively in a systematic way if treated with respect and dignity by tax officials. In a study of a sample of Swiss cantons, Feld and Frey (2002) found that taxpayers experience higher utility when treated respectfully, rather than as 'subjects' of tax investigations, and pay more tax as a result. Second, opportunities to contribute to tax policy matter. Mattias Benz cites experimental studies that have 'investigated how democratic participation rights affect people's willingness to pay taxes … [which] … have shown that individuals evade less taxes if they have the possibility to vote on tax measures' (Benz 2005: 18). Third, tax evasion will vary by the perception of how others are behaving. If evasion is perceived to be widespread, people will be more likely to cheat, and vice versa. Fairness and reciprocity are better predictors of actually observed behaviour than material incentives or disincentives. Indeed, some researchers have found that people actually contribute less tax when the penalties for evasion are advertised, but more when they are made aware of the high rates of compliance by others (Kahan 2005).

NIMBYs

Another example of the inadequacy of standard cost-benefit outcome analyses is that of NIMBY (Not In My Back Yard) responses to government proposals for siting unpopular facilities like waste incinerators or asylum seeker reception centres in local communities. As the aggregate benefits of such proposals outweigh the costs, the standard answer to NIMBY complaints is to redistribute some of the rewards to affected communities – through fiscal compensation schemes or the grant of new public facilities like health centres.

Yet a common reaction to such proposals is increased hostility, not less. In an experimental study, Frey and Oberholzer-Gee found that the offer of compensation substantially reduced the proportion of people willing to accept a nuclear waste storage facility (from over 50 per cent to less than 25 per cent) in their local community (cited in Kahan 2005: 352), and these results appear to mirror the experience of a number of US and Canadian states. This is because compensation schemes, while they may have a role to play, are often perceived as bribes. People place much higher value on the procedural fairness of the initial decision to allocate the facility to their community. Have they been singled out for unfair burdens? Were they properly consulted? Did they get a chance to air their views? Crucially, was the allocation process fair?

In summary, these three examples demonstrate that the procedural fairness of public services can strongly determine (a) how users perceive those services, (b) the utility or satisfaction they derive from them, (c) the trust in which a service is held, and (d) the willingness of the public to cooperate with service providers. Individuals care about the 'how' and not just the 'what'. Moreover, they make judgements based on fairness and reciprocity criteria, not pure self-interest. Policies that rely on standard assumptions about the rational maximization of outcome utility by service users may simply fail, miss their target, or crowd out other-regarding actions and civic virtues.

Issues for public service reform

If procedural fairness is important, how might it find its place in strategies for the reform of public services? Procedural fairness is already a governing ideal of public services to the degree that public administration in a liberal democracy conforms to basic norms of formal justice between free and equal citizens: service providers must not unfairly discriminate between individuals, officials must not exhibit bias, and decisions must be taken impartially and consistently. In recent years, a number of reforms have been enacted in Britain – such as the Race Relations Amendment Act 2000 and the Equality Act 2006 – which strengthen formal procedural fairness in this sense of the term. But procedural fairness in a practical, substantive sense is largely absent from discussion in the dominant approaches to public service reform, such as 'choice', 'voice' and 'personalization'.

Choice and fairness

The relationship between choice and distributive fairness in service outcomes is the subject of considerable policy debate. Proponents of extending choice in public services argue not only that it drives up standards by putting competitive pressure on providers, but that it enhances social equity in access to services and their utilization. Choices currently only available to the middle class will improve services for lower socio-economic groups, as long as they are accompanied by measures to ensure effective equality in their use: the provision of information, advice, travel-to-service support, and restrictions on providers' ability to select users ('cream skimming'). This equalization of access and use, it is argued, will ensure greater equality in outcomes (Le Grand 2006; Prime Minister's Strategy Unit 2006).

Empirical evidence for these assertions is patchy, however (for an overview, see Prime Minister's Strategy Unit 2006), and there is considerable distance to travel between theoretical models of well-functioning choice markets and the practical reality of service delivery on the ground. In the UK context, it is perhaps safest to assert that choice can enhance distributional equity, under certain circumstances, but that the jury is still out.

But what about procedural fairness? Is it possible that choice can enhance perceptions of the fairness of services, or might the cut and thrust of competition undermine them? Given the earlier remarks about the importance of control and the exercise of agency to procedural utility, we would expect the extension of choice in public services to enhance user satisfaction. Evaluations of pilots of choice-based lettings (CBL) in social housing provide interesting evidence on this point. Overall, clients in the pilots appeared to believe that CBL increased transparency and openness, and reduced the scope for unfairness and/or discrimination by officials making housing allocations. One study found that 'customers tended to welcome the transparency of CBL. Consumer feedback indicates that the pilots achieved their aim of establishing more open, transparent and simple systems that are perceived to offer choice' (Office of the Deputy Prime Minister (ODPM) 2004b).

Drilling further down, the perception of fairness depended on a number of variables: pre-existing attitudes to the council, the behaviour of staff, whether clients understood the allocation criteria, and the efficiency of the 'front end' of the application process. Where allocation priorities were well-advertised and understood, the perception that staff could make unfair or corrupt decisions diminished, and vice versa (OPDM 2004a).These findings are congruent with what we would expect from earlier social psychological research on procedural justice. In principle, well-designed choice systems may then enhance perceptions of 'fair rules, fairly implemented'.

However, outcomes also mattered in the pilots. The perception of the overall fairness of CBL was heavily dependent on whether housing need was met. Those who had little or no hope of moving home felt that the system was unfair, by definition (reflecting again the importance of agency and self-determination). Hence, while choice improved the procedural fairness of the allocation mechanism, fairness perceptions still depended on whether the substantive promise of choice was delivered – in this case a function of housing supply.

This is an important finding, for a number of reasons. First, it suggests that there are limits to how far procedural justice promotes satisfaction with services if basic or pressing needs are not met; at the very least, it demonstrates the interdependency in practical contexts of the 'how' and 'what'. Second, it reminds us that the distributive equity of choice policies is critically dependent on capacity. Can choice promote equity in conditions of supply constraint, whether of units of social housing, popular school places, or hospital beds? Finally, it points towards the importance of wider considerations – how do citizens decide which public services are important and whose needs do they take into account? These are ultimately questions which are fundamental to democratic governance.

Voice and fairness

One response to these dilemmas is to argue that citizens should be given greater opportunities to deliberate upon public policy choices and the design and delivery of services. Enhanced 'voice' can improve public understanding of the tradeoffs and tough choices that exist in public services, and moderate unrealistic expectations of service delivery. It can enhance the sense of power and control people feel over the services they fund and embed other-regarding, civic perspectives into their decision-making.

Collective democratic deliberation therefore has intrinsic value, as the expression of self-government among free and equal citizens. It also advances procedural justice to the degree that it increases effective political equality in decision-making. It may also increase procedural utility. Frey and Stutzer (cited in Benz 2005: 16) found that citizens in Swiss cantons with extensive opportunities for participation in representative and direct democratic mechanisms had higher levels of reported life satisfaction. The measured procedural utility was three times higher for citizens with political participation than for foreigners living in the same jurisdiction who lacked those rights. Opportunities for political participation enhanced people's sense of self-worth and self-determination.

As noted above, social psychological studies of procedural fairness also register the importance of 'voice' in individual case proceedings – the opportunity to be heard and to contribute – and the inclusion of representativeness criteria in popular assessments of procedural justice. Closed, inaccessible decision-making processes score badly in procedural fairness terms, whatever the outcomes.

In practice, whether 'voice' arrangements satisfy these ambitions varies considerably. Low levels of participation, interest group capture, spurious populism and weak deliberative capacity may all undermine the experience and efficacy of participatory mechanisms. There is now an extensive literature on these practical questions, as democratic theorists have sought to model, test and review empowered participatory governance (see in particular the work of Archon Fung, <www.archonfung.net>).

This caveat notwithstanding, improvements to citizen 'voice' in public service reform may both increase procedural justice and user utility, and enrich public debate over the normative values and practical governance questions that shape public services. Schematically, procedurally fair and democratically accountable public services would tend to be: information rich; open in policy design to deliberation and engagement, and in delivery to regular citizen review; normatively guided by procedural justice; and implemented according to the tenets of fair treatment.

Personalization

How does procedural justice relate to the personalization of public services? It is conceivable that the insistence of procedural fairness on the equitable, consistent and impartial application of rules may conflict with the personalized attention and tailored sensitivity that are increasingly considered central to successful public services. Strict procedural rigour might restrict personalized differentiation and produce satisfaction with services at the expense of their efficiency, effectiveness or long-term sustainability.

In his discussion of legal and administrative decisions, Cass Sunstein (2006) posits two interpretations of procedural fairness: the most familiar one derived from the ideal of the rule of law that requires clear rules, properly propagated and understood, with safeguards to ensure their protection in the real world; and an alternative, that states that fairness consists of attending to the particularities of each case, weighing the evidence and characteristics of each situation carefully. His argument is that the choice between these two alternatives (or better, poles on a continuum) will depend in large part on costs and the potential for error. If we could attend to the particulars of each case without extra cost, we would do so on grounds of accuracy and responsiveness. But in so doing, we might open up more areas of decision-making to the risks of arbitrariness, bias or inequality that greater discretion brings with it. Moreover, service users and providers would have to spend more time planning their actions to cope with contingency in the absence of clear rules.

Clearly, much hinges on context. Public services which require large volumes of bureaucratic case processing and strict equity between recipients, such as social security benefits systems, are better suited to rule-bound procedural fairness (although even here, users benefit from personal advisers and detailed examination of their needs). Public services which require close attention to individual needs, aptitudes and aspirations, and which depend critically on co-production, such as education, may be better served by personalization. Resource costs will also be a key factor. While competition between service providers may help drive down unit costs, the expansion of personalized services may necessitate increased investment, driving up resource requirements.

One way of addressing these tradeoffs is to focus on entitlements to public services. For example, personalized primary education could offer catch-up literacy teaching to children falling behind the rest of the class (such as the Every Child a Reader programme now being rolled out in English schools). This catch-up provision would meet differentiated needs, assessed and addressed through personalized attention, but the entitlement to it would be national, meeting the foundational requirements of procedural justice.

Some questions and caveats

I have argued that a focus on procedural fairness offers important new insights for the reform of public services, and that attention to the modalities of 'fair rules, fairly implemented' can yield fruitful evidence for public service improvement. But big ideas have proved fatal for public services in the past, so I conclude this discussion with some questions and caveats.

First, public services have plural objectives. Inter alia, we look to them to advance the cause of social justice, to help us secure economic prosperity, and to promote environmental sustainability. Procedural fairness must therefore find its place in a complex and overlapping set of goals. In particular, we should resist the idea that maximizing satisfaction, utility or happiness – whether derived from procedures or not – should be the overarching aim of public policy. Utilitarian ambitions of this kind suffer numerous conceptual problems, well-attested to in the academic literature. In addition, there may be tradeoffs between procedural utility, distributive justice and other principles of social justice, for which housing policy offers a good example. Do we prioritize basic housing need, the sense of fairness of housing allocation, or the distributive justice of who gets what housing?

Second, public services face new challenges posed by the increased diversity of society. Does procedural fairness offer shared common ground for resolving resource disputes and other tensions? Research suggests that a commitment to procedural fairness is cross-cultural, and cross-national studies have shown that the fairness of a society matters more for its level of social trust than its homogeneity (see, for example, You 2005). Countries with high levels of procedural and distributive fairness (that is, with democratic institutions, probity in public administration and relatively equal income distributions) have higher levels of generalized interpersonal trust ('social trust'). Diversity declines in salience as countries become more equal and more democratic. The perceived fairness or unfairness of ethnic relations in a society – related in turn to levels of discrimination, income inequality and political participation by minority groups – is more important than diversity per se.

These are important conclusions, and they buttress the liberal claim that societies can make ground rules stick, despite diversity of belief, practice and cultural custom. But we need further research to understand whether improved procedural fairness helps mitigate substantive resource concerns. To use the housing example again, would community relations improve if housing allocations are perceived to be fairer, or will only substantive restrictions on the access of non-citizens to housing satisfy residents? In addition, a commitment to 'thin' procedural justice may not generate the thicker civic bonds and forms of belonging that sustain the group identities necessary for social interaction (Pearce 2004).

Third, public services are under increasing pressure from rising expectations. Some of those expectations represent wholly legitimate demands for better services. But others are simply unrealistic, such as the widespread view that the National Health Service should provide all drugs and treatments. Bolstering procedural fairness in decision-making might therefore increase the legitimacy of rationing decisions and take the heat out of some of the controversies that surround constraints on service delivery. By the same token, however, there is a danger that procedural fairness could become an excuse for bureaucratic, unresponsive service delivery: a charter for a 'job's worth' attitude writ large. So it is important once again to register that procedural justice must be nested in wider reform strategies for securing high quality public services.

Finally, as noted earlier, differentiations in service delivery – whether of entitlements, or forms of transactions with government officials, and so on – can undermine the public sense of procedural fairness. Procedural justice might better be served by universalism, since universal services and social security benefits can lay claim to stronger public understanding and political support. But the fiscal reality in the UK is such that means-testing will remain a necessary part of an affordable welfare state and it is inconceivable that universalism will be extended beyond a limited number of key areas (early years education and elements of the post-Turner pensions reform, for example).

Moreover, the ubiquity of 'strong reciprocity' in public behaviour and attitudes may lead fairness criteria towards differentiated sanctions and rewards in public services and the welfare state. We therefore need to address which public services are best suited to procedural fairness in its different guises; that is, whether as a set of rules for universalism, or as means of regulating and legitimating differentiated or personalized service delivery, or a vehicle for fair deliberation over 'lumpy' collective goods.

These are all issues for further research and discussion. But these considerations notwithstanding, the insights generated by the research of social psychologists, economists and behavioural scientists into procedural justice, utility and fairness have important implications for public services. They not only address the importance of the 'how' as much as the 'what', but seriously challenge the simplicities of orthodox views of human agency that still inform public policy in a number of areas. They merit wider, deeper attention in public service reform debates.

References

Benz, M. (2005) *The Relevance of Procedural Utility for Economics*. University of Zurich Institute for Empirical Research in Economics, Working Paper No. 256.

DCLG (2006) *The 2005 Citizenship Survey: Cross Cutting Themes*. London: TSO.

Feld, L. P. and Frey, B. S. (2002) 'Trust Breeds Trust: How Taxpayers are Treated', *Economics of Governance*, 3: 87–99.

Frey, B. S., Benz, M. and Stutzer, A. (2004) 'Introducing Procedural Utility: Not Only What But Also How Matters', *Journal of Institutional and Theoretical Economics*, 160 (3): 377–401.

Ghintis, H., Bowles, S., Boyd, R. and Fehr, E. (2005) *Moral Sentiments and Material Interests: The Foundations of Cooperation in Economic Life*. Cambridge, Mass.: MIT Press.

Kahan, D. (2005) 'The Logic of Reciprocity: Trust, Collective Action, and Law', in H. Ghintis, S. Bowles, R. Boyd and E. Fehr (eds), *Moral Sentiments and Material Interests: The Foundations of Cooperation in Economic Life*. Cambridge, Mass.: MIT Press.

Le Grand, J. (2006) *'Equity and Choice in Public Services'*, Social Research, 73 (2): 695–710.

ODPM (2004a) *Applicants' Perspectives on Choice-Based Letting*. Housing Research Summary 207. London: ODPM.

ODPM (2004b) *Piloting Choice Based Lettings*. Housing Research Summary 208. London: ODPM.

Pearce, N. (2004) 'Diversity vs Solidarity: A New Progressive Dilemma?' *Renewal: A Journal of Labour Politics*, 12 (3).

Prime Minister's Strategy Unit (2006) *The UK Government's Approach to Public Service Reform: A Discussion Paper*. London: Cabinet Office.

Sampson, R. (2004) 'Neighbourhood and Community: Collective Efficacy and Community Safety', *New Economy*, 11 (2): 106–13.

Sunstein, C. R. (2006) 'Two Conceptions of Procedural Fairness', *Social Research*, 73 (2).

Thibaut, J. and Walker, L. (1975) *Procedural Justice: A Psychological Analysis*. Hillsdale, NJ: Lawrence Erlbaum.

Tyler, T. R. (1988) 'What is Procedural Justice? Criteria Used by Citizens to Assess the Fairness of Legal Procedures', *Law and Society Review*, 22: 301–55.

Tyler, T. R. (1990) *Why People Obey the Law: Procedural Justice, Legitimacy and Compliance*. New Haven: Yale University Press.

Tyler, T. R, Boeckmann, R. J. Smith, H. J. and Huo, J. Y. (1997) *Social Justice in a Diverse Society*. Oxford: Westview Press.

Tyler, T. R. and Fagan, J. F. (2006) *Legitimacy and Cooperation: Why do People Help the Police Fight Crime in Their Communities?* Columbia Law School Public Law & Legal Theory Working Paper Group, 06-99.

You, J-S. (2005) *Corruption and Inequality as Correlates of Social Trust: Fairness Matters More than Similarity*. Working Paper No. 29, Hauser Center for Nonprofit Organizations and JFK School of Government, Harvard University.

15
Freedom's Orphans: Raising Youth in a Changing World

Dawn Butler and Julia Margo

In early 2006, a judge at the Old Bailey released CCTV footage of a gang of youths in South London beating and kicking a homeless man. In an orgy of violence that was likened to scenes from *A Clockwork Orange*, the gang attacked eight people, finally killing one of them. As they assaulted their victims, one of the gang, teenager Chelsea O'Mahoney, videoed the scenes on her mobile phone. Born into a working-class family of heroin addicts, O'Mahoney would watch her parents inject at the age of one. By her third birthday, she would wander the streets of South London alone. And in adolescence, the most powerful influences on her life were not adults but other children just like her – abused and brutalized teenagers. At first glance, O'Mahoney might appear as nothing more than yet another sad casualty of poor parenting and neglect. But we would argue that, more than this, she is a product of our time, one of many teenagers orphaned not merely by her parents but by the broader forces of social change.

In Britain the state of our teenagers – their behaviour, attitudes and educational achievements – have come under increasing scrutiny. Academics, practitioners and commentators – even the Archbishop of Canterbury – are now engaged in an extensive debate about the younger generation. In part, this debate expresses familiar themes from the repeated bouts of moral panic about the state of youth that have taken place in the UK and elsewhere for at least half a century, and probably longer. But there are also real and historically specific issues at stake in contemporary debates that cannot be dismissed as the moral hand-wringing of disgruntled adults. For example, British teenagers are more likely to drink and take drugs than their European counterparts, and at earlier ages. They are more likely to have engaged in underage sexual activity (38 per cent of our 15-year-olds are sexually active) and less likely to use a condom (in 2006 one-third did not). Thus British teenagers are more likely to become teenage parents and to contract sexually transmitted infections such as chlamydia and herpes. British youths – hooded or otherwise – are apparently so feared by adults that last year 1.5 million Britons considered moving home to escape teenagers who 'hung around' outside their homes, and 1.7 million are scared to go out at night (Margo et al. 2006).

During 2006, ippr analysed evidence from across the world and survey data spanning the last three decades in an attempt to uncover the true story of what has happened to youth in contemporary Britain. This research has shown that over the last 30 years, deep-seated changes to the family, to local communities, to public services and to the economy have combined to cause deep inequalities in the transition to modern adult life, leaving increasing numbers of young people incapable of growing up safely and successfully. Although some of these trends have impacted on all young people, and not just the most disadvantaged, a clear 'socialization gap' has emerged between children from deprived backgrounds and their better-off peers.

Social change

From the post-war period to the mid 1970s, the pathways young people followed from childhood to adulthood were relatively straightforward. Young people in working-class areas could expect to leave school and go straight into work, settle down and have a family. For the majority of young people, leaving school was swiftly followed by getting a job, usually involving some form of apprenticeship (at least for boys) (Ferri 1993). Relatively few continued on to higher education – just 3 per cent in 1950 – and for those that did, stable employment soon followed. But in the 1970s and 1980s, the post-war patterns of work and family life, rooted in industrial economic structures, underwent profound change. As youth labour markets collapsed under the pressures of rapid deindustrialization, it became increasingly difficult to move directly into work, and rising unemployment set school leavers in direct competition with more experienced workers in the hunt for jobs (Bynner et al. 2002). Young people, particularly the disadvantaged, were decreasingly able to rely on formal organizational structures to guide them straightforwardly into work, and were more dependent on their own 'agency' and motivation (Margo et al. 2006).

In many parts of the country, we have failed to replace what many see as the basic building blocks of post-war socialization into the adult world, such as marriage and stable family life, predictable employment and community institutions, with any coherent alternative. Yet the very aspects of social change that have undermined the way young people are socialized into adulthood have contrived to make personal social skills more important to young people's life chances. Consequently, thousands of young people are caught in the double bind of being less well-prepared for a more demanding world. Recent research using two large surveys following young people born in 1958 and 1970 has shown that in just over a decade, personal and social skills became 33 times more important in determining relative life chances – for example, predicting whether individuals would be successful in work, in relationships and in their social lives. Most importantly for us, this measure also captures the capacity of young people to control their behaviour, to communicate and to socialize successfully with people. At the same time as these socio-economic trends were taking place, young people from less affluent backgrounds became less likely than their more fortunate peers to develop these skills (ibid.).

Basic psychological theories about child development claim that an individual's 'personal and social development' – their acquisition of social skills – is associated with interaction with adults (talking, playing or spending time with them), or participation in 'positive socializing activities' such as sport, art, drama and other educational, long-term activities where children have the opportunity to interact with other adults and children in secure settings (Erikson 1950). These activities enable young people to learn from adult role models about what is appropriate in terms of behaviour and values, and of course what is inappropriate. Although the evidence shows that the role of the community, the school and extra-curricular activities are crucial in a young person's development, the role of parents is of course vital.

This is where it becomes problematic: in modern Britain, survey data reviewed later in this chapter has shown that not all children spend much time with their parents, and that there are huge social class differences in children's early life experiences (Margo et al. 2006) with richer parents more able to ensure that their children are engaged in positive socializing experiences when not at home, and poorer parents less able. So, for example, richer parents are more able to ensure their children are cared for by dedicated adults when not with a parent (nannies, au pairs, and so on). They are also increasingly able to purchase activities and obtain access to institutions that can enhance children's personal and social development. The average parent now spends more than £9,300 on their child's hobbies by the time they are 21 and another £6,700 on their other leisure and recreational pursuits (Liverpool Victoria 2005; Maxwell et al. 2006). But children from less advantaged backgrounds are much more likely than their richer peers to spend their free time away from parents or teachers 'hanging out' with friends or watching TV (60 per cent of British teenagers spend more than four nights a week with their mates, compared to just 16 per cent in France (Margo et al. 2006)). 'Peer socialization' of this kind is what Chelsea O'Mahoney experienced. Left to their own devices, poorly socialized children can have a very bad effect on each other's behaviour and morality. US research shows that moving a child from a school where few of their peers take drugs to one where many do, significantly increases the likelihood that they will become drug users (Bearman and Brückner 1999).

The reasons for rising peer socialization in the UK are intuitively obvious. Changes to families, such as more parents (especially mothers) working, rising divorce, cohabitation and single parenthood, have undermined the ability of families to spend time with young people – and this has been experienced particularly markedly by those from less advantaged backgrounds who cannot 'supplement' time with parents with other positive socializing activities. This situation is exacerbated by relatively static gender roles within the family. Women's greater labour market participation has not been matched by an increase in men's participation in unpaid household or caring work.

Changing families

In an international context, these trends in work, family life and structures – in combination with cultural idiosyncrasies – mean that British children spend less time with their parents than in most comparable European countries (Bradshaw et al. 2006). In 2003, just 67 per cent of 15-year-olds in the UK ate with their parents around a table several times a week – a lower proportion than any other country in Europe apart from Finland (Organization for Economic Cooperation and Development (OECD) 2006). It is difficult to act as an influential role model for your child if you barely see them. British teenagers consistently complain about the lack of time they spend with their parents, and there are decisive links between the amount of time spent with parents and anti-social behaviour, drug and alcohol use.

Many people have argued that the root of youth anti-social behaviour is a breakdown in families, and progressives have often found it difficult to engage in debates concerning marriage (see Hughes and Cooke, Chapter 11, for a fuller account). Research using the Millennium Cohort Study has shown that, controlling for other factors, children of cohabiting couples do worse than those of married couples (Benson 2006). This is largely because of the increased risk of separation for cohabiting couples. Marriage simply tends to be more stable and secure. This has been taken to suggest that marriage promotion is the answer. But this response, while intuitively attractive, simply will not work. First, divorce, cohabitation and single parenthood are economically and culturally driven trends and thus unlikely to reverse. We cannot start telling couples they must marry or cannot divorce, and financial incentives are unlikely to work: the introduction of the Married Couples Allowance in the 1970s famously coincided with the largest move away from marriage that century. Second, focusing support on traditional family types regardless of need skews much-needed resources towards those who need them less (as lone-parent families tend to be most in need of financial support), and is unnecessarily morally prescriptive – telling people how they should live, rather than enabling them to choose. And research (reviewed more thoroughly in Chapter 11) consistently shows that children growing up in non-traditional family forms can succeed if warmth, stability and consistent parenting are also present. So family policy needs to acknowledge the significance of both family structure and parenting processes and support all families to develop the parenting processes that are most effective, rather than penalize single-parent families.

If the UK is to respond to changes to families it must do so in its own way. We will never become like Italy, with its highly religious culture dictating strong nuclear and extended families, but we could become a bit more like Sweden, where families are better supported by the state so that they spend comparatively more time with their children and less time at work. But responding to family changes will be only one part of the solution: it is not only parents who spend less time with children in modern Britain, but adults in general.

'Paedophobia'

Adults in Britain are apparently more scared of young people and consequently less likely to discipline them than adults in other countries. For example, only 36 per cent of Britons would intervene if they saw youths graffitiing public property or being noisy and rowdy outside their home. Elsewhere in Europe this figure rises to 65 per cent (ADT Europe 2006). Many have argued that this is due to low levels of social trust in the UK. As crime rates rose through the 1980s and early 1990s, most measures of social trust fell, but as crime rates fell from their mid 1990s apex, social trust appeared to rise – so this does not entirely explain it. Looking at another measure of social trust – collective efficacy – is more informative. In 2005, levels of collective efficacy – the ability and willingness of local residents to intervene in youth violence and anti-social behaviour – were strongly related to disadvantage; 92 per cent of those in the most affluent areas said local people would intervene if they saw children spray-painting graffiti, compared to 58 per cent of those in the most deprived areas (Kitchen et al. 2006). If this pattern has held over the last few decades, it seems clear that children from more advantaged communities would have experienced greater levels of intervention from their neighbours and other adults than those from more disadvantaged communities. As the impact of communities became more important, this would have meant a growing divide between the socialization experiences of the best- and worst-off.

Changing patterns of internal and external migration have also altered the demographic make-up of many communities, again impacting on the way adult society socializes the young. Using the same indicators as before, in 2005, people from minority ethnic groups were much less likely to say that people in their community would intervene if a child was rude to an adult or if a group of children were spray-painting graffiti than those from a white background.

Consumed childhood

Just as important as these developments in leisure activities is the related phenomenon of rising consumerism, and young people's increasingly unmediated interaction with it. Today's young people spend increasing amounts of time thinking about, and purchasing, consumer goods, and are a large consumer market in their own right – the total net worth of the child-orientated market comes to an estimated £30 billion a year (Childwise 2005; Mayo 2005). These figures are striking. But perhaps the best indicator of young people's growing immersion in unmediated consumerism has been the year-on-year increases in pocket money since records began in the late 1980s, which have consistently outstripped inflation. Seven- to eleven-year-olds are now worth nearly £20 million a year and have become an increasingly lucrative target audience for unscrupulous advertisers eager to harness the 'pester power' of an increasingly brand-aware group of young consumers – 31 per cent of boys and 44 per cent of girls claim that they 'could not go for a whole week without spending any money' (Halifax 2006). With 80 per cent of 13–16-year-olds now shopping with their peers rather than parents, children are also taking greater control over making spending decisions, a trend that is viewed as unwelcome by many parents, 84 per cent of whom stated in 2004 that there was too much marketing directed at children (National Family and Parenting Institute (NFPI) 2004).

The advertising industry is becoming increasingly sophisticated and aggressive in its targeting of young people. More than a century after Coca-Cola's first celebrity spokesperson appeared in an advert, and 55 years after the first toy was advertised on television, public fascination with unscrupulous advertising has led to a plethora of undercover media exposés (Mayo 2005). Recent examples include an internal brief from Walker's crisps, which explicitly aimed to make children think 'Wotsits are for me. I am going to … pester mum for them when she next goes shopping'; a job advert for a senior researcher in Kellogg's 'kids brands' division, which asked potential applicants to prove that they can spend 'time understanding kids, finding out what interests them … and appreciating the realm of pester power'; and, perhaps most damningly, an undercover report exposing the agency behind a recent Fruit Winders campaign boasting that their strategy had 'entered the world of kids in a way never done before' and managed to 'not let mum in on the act' (Freedland 2005). Worryingly, contemporary British children seem to be more enmeshed in consumerism than even their US counterparts. In 2006, children in Britain were more brand aware and less satisfied with what they saw as the limited amount of money they had to spend. Some 66 per cent of British children said they 'like clothes with popular labels', compared to 52 per cent of US children; and 46 per cent of British children said the 'brand name is important', compared to 40 per cent of US children (Mayo 2005). This is perhaps because British children's access to advertising is unprecedented.

In 2005, eight in ten children aged five to sixteen had a TV in their room (Childwise 2005), and over half had a personal video recorder or DVD to go with it. And around one in five children – nearly 1.5 million young people (Government Actuary's Department (GAD) 2005) – have access to the internet in their own room (Livingstone and Bober 2005). This raises familiar concerns around young people's access to inappropriate content, including explicit sexual imagery: 57 per cent of children reported having come into contact with online porn; most of it accidentally, such as in the form of pop-ups, and one in four had received pornographic spam. Although around half of all parents with internet access had some kind of blocking in place to stop their children viewing certain types of websites in 2006 (Ofcom 2006), just 7 per cent of parents were aware that their child had received sexual content through this form of media (Livingstone and Bober 2005).

There is emerging evidence of a connection between rising consumerism and rising depression among young people. Researchers have found that being part of commercial culture results in children becoming more materialistic, more depressed, more anxious, and more prone to frequent headaches, stomach aches and boredom. The greater the involvement of children in consumerism, the more likely they are to suffer depression, anxiety and stress-related physical discomfort (Schor 2004).

One persuasive strand of thinking explains the impact of childhood consumerism in terms of its impact on children's perceptions of their identities. The central idea is that children are becoming more dependent on brands to give them a sense of what aspirations, values and possessions are important and acceptable – that brands are beginning to powerfully dictate social hierarchies in a way formerly done by communities and parents, effectively making value judgements about what is appropriate in terms of lifestyle and normative behaviour (Martens et al. 2004). Most attention has been focused on the role of the media and advertising in promoting obesity. The Royal College of Physicians reports that obesity doubled among two- to four-year-olds between 1989 and 1998, and trebled among six- to fifteen-year-olds between 1990 and 2002 in the UK. Hastings et al.'s recent (2003) systematic review for the Food Standards Agency concluded that 'Food promotion is having an effect, particularly on children's preferences, purchase behaviour and consumption. This effect is independent of other factors and operates at both a brand and category level.' There is an unsurprisingly distinct lack of social responsibility in media companies in the way they cater to stockholders over children (Steyer 2003). The British Medical Association, responding to the government's White Paper, *Choosing Health: Making Healthier Choices Easier* (November 2004), has recommended an outright ban on advertising foods to children in the UK. This goes a crucial step beyond the White Paper, which suggested a voluntary period of modification of advertising foods to children, giving food advertisers until 2007 before reconsidering the question of a ban. In Sweden, most notably, a ban is already in force, and was implemented relatively smoothly.

The effect of the media on children is not confined to obesity. Only a handful of studies have examined sexual content in the media and its impact on teenagers, but they all show that there is an impact. In the absence of effective sex education, the media have become one of the leading sex educators of children and teens today. In a recent study of nearly 1,800 teenagers, teens' viewing of sexual content led to a doubled risk of earlier sexual initiation (Collins et al. 2004). In addition, numerous studies in the US and Europe have shown a link between media coverage of suicide and subsequent increases in suicides among teens (Gould et al. 2003).

This demonstrates the need to take the relationship between the media and children's mental health and wider development extremely seriously. It is vital that an up-to-date understanding of mental health problems is placed at the heart of our approach to the media's relationship to young people. Adding weight to this concern is the finding that the negative impact of growing childhood consumerism is disproportionately experienced by young people from disadvantaged backgrounds. Unmediated interaction with consumerism compounds the disadvantages poorer children face, particularly in altering their relationships with and expectations of their parents. Research shows that the more children and young people bought into consumer culture, the more negative they were about their parents, and the more likely they were to fight and disagree with them (Schor and Holt 2000; Schor 2004). Recent empirical research shows that children from the poorest social groups are the most interested in consumer and materialist concerns. They are more likely than their wealthier peers to say that brand name is important, more likely to favour clothes with popular labels and more likely to wish their parents gave them more money to spend (Mayo 2005).

Children's ever-earlier engagement with consumerism is reflected across the broad scope of their lives, as adolescence extends ever further into childhood. Contemporary youth live accelerated lives, as milestones – physical, emotional and social – are passed at younger ages. Over the last 50 years, the average age of first sexual intercourse has fallen from 20 for men and 21 for women in the 1950s, to 16 by the mid 1990s, and the proportion of young people who are sexually active before the age of consent has risen from less than 1 per cent to 25 per cent over the same period (Wellings et al. 2001). There are also indications of the physical ageing process happening earlier. Scientists tracking changes in the onset of menarche (puberty) in girls over the past 100 years have found it has fallen by about three years (Whincup et al. 2001; Gluckman and Hanson 2006). And these physical changes have been accompanied by cultural shifts in similar directions. Pundits point to the proliferation of sex tips for teenagers in youth magazines, and health and beauty spas for ten-year-old girls as evidence that children are exposed to and expected to navigate adult concerns at younger stages in their development (Schor and Holt 2000; Schor 2004; Mayo 2005).

Rising affluence has been important, but technological change has also underpinned many of these trends. The proliferation of mobile phones (in 2006, 49 per cent of children aged eight to eleven and 82 per cent of those aged 12–15 had their own mobile phone (Ofcom 2006)) in combination with increased internet use has meant that many young people are increasingly able to control their own social lives at younger ages, planning their leisure activities independently of adult supervision.

Rethinking youth policy

The evidence presented here shows that if we want to ensure that the younger generation is adequately socialized into the norms of behaviour in our society, we need urgently to rethink our policy approach to youth. The solution lies in strategies to reinvent our civic spaces so that they are more 'child-friendly' and enable adults and children to mix; to enhance 'collective efficacy' – the capacity of residents to intervene in the precursors of youth anti-social behaviour; to support families in spending more time with their children; and to ensure that when young people are not with their parents or at school, they are cared for by responsible adults in secure environments – at least some of the time.

Supporting families

The single most important factor in the development and socialization of young people is their immediate family. In this area policy needs to recognize the importance of hard factors – such as income, poverty and time off work – and softer factors – such as parenting skills and experience, support and advice. The government has made welcome improvements in many areas related to these goals, and in Chapter 11 Hughes and Cooke have set out recommendations in the areas of childcare provision, parental leave and flexible working, and engaging fathers and supporting families through parental separation. The analysis here gives additional weight to the importance of such policies.

It is vital that policy supports all family types, but in particular it must address the issue of teen parenthood in order to ensure the next generation benefits from a secure start in life. Research systematically shows that teenage pregnancy is associated with worse outcomes for both mother and child, reduced likelihood of parents staying together and reduced likelihood of sustained, positive paternal engagement (Margo et al. 2006; Teenage Pregnancy Unit 2006). Children of younger mothers are more likely to face all the negative aspects of parenting – disengaged fathers, poverty or low parental income, to name just a few. To this end we would recommend that statutory Personal, Social and Health Education, including learning about sex and relationships, in the last year of primary school is now essential and that different forms of contraception, including long-term options, should be made more available to young people (Department for Education and Skills (DfES) 2006).

Protecting childhood

We should not so readily tolerate a state of affairs in which children are schooled into consumption as early as possible in their development. The approach adopted in the mid 1990s in Sweden, which has uncompromisingly banned advertising aiming to capture the attention of children of primary school age (Swedish Department of Culture 1996: 844), should be implemented in Britain. Of course this is a politically contentious issue. But it would be a popular move among the public. Research outlined in NFPI (2004) shows that an overwhelming majority of parents – 84 per cent – consider there to be too much advertising to children. The challenge is to respond to considerable vested interests in the advertising industry, which appears to maintain the delicate position of publicly claiming that such advertising does not affect children's development, while simultaneously persuading clients that it represents a worthwhile investment.

This position has been easier to maintain due to a lack of convincing, holistic evaluations looking at the impact of advertising on young people's development. Previous research has tended to be siloed, looking at the 'effectiveness' of a particular campaign or the impact of advertising on a particular behavioural outcome, such as childhood obesity (Livingstone and Helsper 2006). Perhaps unsurprisingly, therefore, these studies have found little support for banning advertising – critics often cite high childhood obesity levels in Sweden as evidence that advertising bans simply do not change behaviour. Yet this simplistic assessment misses the big-picture point that the impact of advertising is cumulative and cultural; we need to look in the round at the psychological and developmental impact of advertising on young people. The evidence highlighted in this chapter shows clearly that current practice is having a severely detrimental effect, particularly on the most disadvantaged.

Proscribing advertising would have a clear benefit, as well as sending out a positive message about the kind of society we would like Britain to be.

Investing in positive activities for young people

While the family is key to improving child outcomes, what older children do when they are not at home is equally important. Every child should be able to enjoy socializing with their peers, and should have the freedom and choice to do so. Putting restrictions and limits on teenagers would be unfair and pointless (unless, of course, they are causing harm to others). But adult society does bear a responsibility to young people to ensure that they are able to socialize in secure and stable environments; even, or especially, when not with their parent or primary carer.

The extended schools agenda as set out in *Youth Matters* (DfES 2006) will aim to provide a range of services and activities, beyond the school day, to help meet the needs of children, their families and the wider community. The government wants all schools to offer access to core services by 2010. A varied 'menu' of activities will be offered, such as homework clubs and study support, sport or music tuition. This approach is to be welcomed. However, a key challenge will be engaging the most disadvantaged young people in structured activities.

There are difficult questions here about how far to compel young people to take part in such activities. The current approach is based on making positive activities attractive enough to the most disadvantaged, rather than relying on legal or regulatory measures. Opening up opportunities has been seen as sufficient. But recent analysis (Margo et al. 2006) has shown that the young people who would benefit most from structured activities are those least likely to attend.

The challenge for policy in this area is twofold. First, it is to promote the provision of those activities which best facilitate positive youth socialization, without undermining young peoples' right to choose how they spend their 'free' time. This will require an alternatively nuanced approach to voluntary sector funding and the current extended schools rollout. Second, we must ensure that all young people have genuine opportunities to participate. In the current climate, the best evidence shows that this will require elements of compulsion within an overall package of user choice.

Supporting communities in developing collective efficacy

If we are to tackle 'paedophobia' it is also essential that we consider how best to use public space in a way that is beneficial for both children and adults, and that we provide adults with the tools and confidence to tackle youth anti-social behaviour. First, localities should provide a range of public spaces and amenities where young people can mingle with peers and adults securely. This would involve changes to planning and regulation policy that are somewhat beyond the remit of this chapter (see Margo et al. 2006 for a fuller account). But a vital step towards 'opening up' the public realm must involve tackling local disorders – graffiti, vandalism, litter and decay – and crime that can make an area unsafe (in Chapter 12, Pearce considers a range of measures to tackle such civil disorders). We feel that more crime prevention funding should be directed towards 'constructive' measures that make crime harder to commit by designing the built environment to encourage constant use by residents (better lighting and more open design, for example), rather than the current 'defensive' strategies, such as installing CCTV, which do little to deter crime in the first place. Building the capacity of citizens to participate in maintaining the security of their local area is no easy task. But there are models of community engagement projects in other countries that could be trialled here. For instance, in New Zealand, Safer Community Councils – groups of representatives from local businesses, police, schools, and so on – convene regularly to discuss issues relating to the local civic order (Margo et al. 2006).

These ideas and recommendations would go some way in improving the life chances of today's young people. However, we have not yet addressed the issue of young people already at risk of social exclusion because of their behaviour. In particular, we must consider how to better support young offenders.

Supporting young people in the criminal justice system

We consider here policies to divert first-time young offenders away from custody; strategies to deal with mentally ill offenders, and more general changes to the criminal justice system to improve the lot of young offenders.

Currently, local authorities do not audit the needs of young adults in the criminal justice system and therefore do not know what kind of services they require. The Barrow Cadbury Commission (Barrow Cadbury 2006) recommends that Transition to Adulthood teams (T2A Teams) should be established in every local criminal justice area to take responsibility for young adults in the criminal justice system. These teams would measure the effectiveness of local services in education, employment, housing and health. The Commission also recommends that young adults convicted of first-time or minor offences should be diverted away from the criminal justice system wherever possible through the use of conditional cautions or the extension of youth offender panels. We would support this recommendation, but, further to this, would argue that an incentive structure should be built into rehabilitation programmes for young offenders. In this system, first-time young offenders could opt to take up a training or educational course from a 'menu' of options which should be provided within the local area. These should be courses, programmes and activities that are known to provide beneficial development opportunities (as above) for young adults. Completion of such a course should allow a young offender freedom from further punishment and a clean criminal record. Non-completion would entail criminal record and possible further punitive measures. Young adults in custody should also be given a chance to take part in learning programmes and gain the skills they need and qualifications that are comparable to those in mainstream education. The Offender Learning and Skills Strategy, produced by the DfES, should highlight how the educational needs of young adults differ from those of older adults and younger people.

Dealing properly with young people with poor mental health is absolutely key to a progressive strategy for youth offenders. Each Primary Care Trust should have a strategy for young adults with mental healthcare needs. One response, supported by the Barrow Cadbury Commission, is an open access 'one-stop shop' for young adults, with advice and advocacy workers on housing, independent living skills, the criminal justice system, education and careers advice (Barrow Cadbury 2006). The Department of Health, the Department for Education and Skills, the Department for Work and Pensions and the Home Office should provide joint funding to establish a pilot model offering support services for young adults. These should include access to a personal adviser who is able to help the young person navigate the support networks that are open to them.

The National Offender Management Service (NOMS) with the Department of Health should consider how young adults with mental health problems can be identified and diverted away from custody where possible. There should be joint training between Youth Offending Teams and the NOMS in recognizing the full range of learning difficulties in young adults. Regional Offender Managers should commission good practice work for all young adults with learning difficulties.

Protocols on transition between youth and adult services should be developed at local level by Drug (and Alcohol) Action Teams. Prison drug treatment teams should work with the NOMS, the Department of Health and the National Treatment Agency to find the best way of working with young adults with drug problems in the criminal justice system.

References

ADT Europe (2006) *Anti-Social Behaviour Across Europe*. London: ADT. Available at <http://adt.co.uk/cc4471AD-Great-Britain.pdf>.

Barrow Cadbury (2006) *Lost in Transition*. London: Barrow Cadbury.

Bearman, P. and Brückner, H. (1999) *Peer Effects on Adolescent Sexual Debut and Pregnancy: An Analysis of a National Survey of Adolescent Girls*. Washington DC: National Campaign for the Prevention of Teen Pregnancy, April.

Benson, H. (2006) *The Conflation of Marriage and Cohabitation in Government Statistics – A Denial of Difference Rendered Untenable by an Analysis of Outcomes*. Bristol: Bristol Community Family Trust.

Bradshaw, J., Hoelscher, P. and Richardson, D. (2006) 'An Index of Child Well-Being in the European Union', *Social Indicators Research*, 78 (1): 1–45.

Bynner, J., Elias, P., McKnight, A., Pan, H. and Pierre, G. (2002) *Young People's Changing Routes to Independence*. London: Joseph Rowntree Foundation, <www.jrf.org.uk/bookshop/eBooks/184263108X.pdf>.

Childwise (2005) *ChildWise Monitor Trends Report 2005*. Norwich: Childwise.

Collins, R. L., Elliott, M. N., Berry, S. H., Kanouse, D. E., Kunkel, D., Hunter, S. B. and Miu, A. (2004) 'Watching Sex on Television Predicts Adolescent Initiation of Sexual Behaviour', *Pediatrics*, 14 (3): 280–9.

DfES (2006) *Youth Matters*. Green Paper. London: TSO.

Erikson, E. H. (1950) *Childhood and Society*. New York: Norton.

Ferri, E. (1993) *Life at 33: The Fifth Follow-up of the National Child Development Study*. London: National Children's Bureau.

Freedland, J. (2005) 'The onslaught', *Guardian*, 11 October.

GAD (2005) *Current National Projections (2004-based)*. London: TSO. Available at <www.gad.gov.uk>.

Gluckman, P. and Hanson, M. (2006) 'Evolution, Development and Timing of Puberty', *Trends in Endocrinology and Metabolism*, 17 (1): 7–12.

Gould, M., Jamieson, P. and Romer, D. (2003) 'Media Contagion and Suicide Among the Young', *American Behavioral Scientist*, 5 (46): 1269–84.

Halifax (2006) *Halifax Pocket Money Survey*. London: HBOS.

Hastings, G., Stead, M., McDermott, L., Forsyth, A., MacKintosh, A. M., Rayner, M., Godfrey, C., Caraher, M. and Angus, K. (2003). *Review of the Research on the Effects of Food Promotion to Children* (Final Report). London: Food Standards Agency.

Kitchen, S., Michaelson, J., Wood, N. and John, P. (2006) *2005 Citizenship Survey. Active Communities Topic Report*. London: DCLG.

Liverpool Victoria (2005) *Cost of Raising a Child is £166,000* (Press Release). Annual Cost of a Child Survey. Liverpool: Liverpool Victoria.

Livingstone, S. and Bober, M. (2005) *UK Children Go Online: Final Report of Key Project Findings*. London: LSE.

Livingstone, S. and Helsper, E. (2006) 'Does Advertising Literacy Mediate the Effects of Advertising on Children? A Critical Examination of Two Linked Research

Literatures in Relation to Obesity and Food Choice', *Journal of Communication*, 56 (3): 560.

Margo, J. and Dixon, M., with Pearce, N. and Reed, H. (2006) *Freedom's Orphans: Raising Youth in a Changing World*. London: ippr.

Martens, L., Southerton, D., Scott, S. (2004) 'Bringing Children (and Parents) into the Sociology of Consumption', *Journal of Consumer Culture*, 4 (22): 155–82.

Maxwell, D., Sodha, S. and Stanley, K. (2006) *An Asset Account for Looked After Children*. London: ippr.

Mayo, E. (2005) *Shopping Generation*. London: NCC.

NFPI (2004) *Hard Sell, Soft Targets?* London: NFPI.

OECD (2006) *OECD Factbook 2006 – Economic, Environmental and Social Statistics*. Paris: OECD.

Ofcom (2006) *Media Literacy Audit: Report on Media Literacy Among Children*. London: Ofcom. Available at <www.ofcom.org.uk/advice/media_literacy/medlitpub/medlitpubrss/children/children.pdf>.

Schor, J. (2004) *Born to Buy: The Commercialized Child and the New Consumer Culture*. New York: Scribner.

Schor, J. and Holt, D. (2000) *The Consumer Society: A Reader*. New York: New Press.

Steyer, J. P. (2003*) The Other Parent: The Inside Story of the Media's Effect on Our Children*. New York: Atria Books.

Swedish Department of Culture (1996) *Radio and TV Law*. Stockholm: Swedish Department of Culture.

Teenage Pregnancy Unit (2006) *Teenage Pregnancy: Accelerating the Strategy to 2010*. London: TSO.

Wellings, K., Nanchahal, K. M., Macdowall, W., McManus, S., Erens, B., Mercer, C., Johnson, A., Copas, A., Korovessis, C., Fenton, K. and Field, J. (2001) 'Sexual Behaviour in Britain: Early Heterosexual Experience', *Lancet*, 358: 1843–50.

Whincup, P., Gilg, J., Odoki, K., Taylor, S. and Cook, G. (2001) 'Age of Menarche in Contemporary British Teenagers: Survey of Girls Born between 1982 and 1986', *British Medical Journal*, 322: 1095–6.

Part 6

The World

16
A Greener Shade of Red

David Miliband

Previous chapters in this volume have shown that while many of the problems that Labour was elected to overcome in 1997 have been tackled, new issues have emerged. This means we need to broaden and deepen the progressive project. In this drive to broaden and deepen our progressive offer, the environment will be important. At the next election, I believe climate change will become a threshold issue. All political parties will have to prove their competence on climate change alongside the economy, public services and crime. Until now, the debate has focused on 'who cares' about the environment. Soon it will move on to the question of 'who can deliver'. In this chapter, I argue that climate change would be held back by both traditional deep green or conservative traditions. Progressives are best placed to tackle climate change, but only if we can rethink our ideas about the role of markets and the state, social justice, and the role of Europe.

My argument is this. First, the case for action has become overwhelming. The science is unambiguous and economic analysis suggests that the cost of business as usual will be between 5 and 20 times more than the cost of cutting greenhouse gas emissions (Stern 2006). Second, the practical solutions to tackle climate change while enhancing our standard of living and economic growth exist. We can transform the productivity with which we use natural resources, rather than having to force citizens here and in the developing world to reduce their aspirations. Third, the policies required to stimulate a UK energy revolution are possible, but they will challenge all political parties, and will require progressives to re-examine our traditions. Fourth, the government has done a lot to decouple economic growth from carbon and greenhouse gas growth, but we need to look at how our approach to markets, to social justice and to empowerment can be taken forward if we are to go further and build the low-carbon economy that is essential.

Science

We are now close to a scientific consensus on climate change. The climate is changing, and it is man-made. We are, as Tim Flannery points out, 'the weathermakers' (Flannery 2005). The scientific journey began nearly two centuries ago with the great French mathematician, Jean-Baptiste Fourier. By analysing the incoming energy from the sun and the outgoing energy from radiation, he calculated that the earth should be a block of ice – frozen solid at 5 degrees Fahrenheit. Fourier hypothesized that something in the atmosphere must be acting like the glass in a greenhouse – letting sunlight in, but trapping it – what he called 'the greenhouse effect' (Fleming 1999).

In the 1890s, a Swedish chemist, Svante Arrhenius, took up this theory. Arrhenius predicted that CO_2 levels would double over 3,000 years if coal-burning continued at the same pace, and this would bring a hotter climate. In fact, being a Swede, he advocated more coal-burning as he thought it would bring better weather (Arrenhius 1908).

But although theories of global warming have a long history, it is only in my lifetime that the huge uncertainty over climate science has begun to clear. Thirty years ago, scientists still disagreed about whether the earth was warming or cooling. Since the millennium, the debate about climate change has begun to shift: from whether it is happening, to how fast we need to move to stop it. The facts are increasingly clear, as outlined in the government's 2006 report on climate change:

- Atmospheric carbon dioxide (CO_2) levels are now higher than at any time for at least the last 740,000 years. Atmospheric CO_2 is now around 40 per cent higher than before the Industrial Revolution.
- This has resulted in a rise in temperature at the earth's surface of 0.7 degrees Centigrade in the last century, almost certainly unprecedented in human civilization, and caused by human activity.
- The rise in temperature is likely to be partly responsible for the current rise in extreme weather in terms of heatwaves, droughts, storms and floods. All of the ten warmest years since 1850 have occurred since 1990. Arctic sea ice in summer has already thinned

by about 40 per cent in the last 50 years. Climate change is a short-term issue.

- A doubling of pre-industrial levels of greenhouse gases is very likely to commit the earth to an eventual global temperature rise of between 2 degrees and 5 degrees Centigrade. This will push many of the great ecosystems of the world to irreversible decline. Even if the temperature rises by only 2 degrees, 15–40 per cent of species will face extinction.
- The effects will be not just on nature but also on people. More than 30,000 deaths were caused by the 2003 European heatwave. In future, declining crop yields and reduced fish stocks from ocean acidification could leave hundreds of millions of people without the ability to produce or purchase sufficient food. Melting glaciers could reduce dry-season water supplies to one-sixth of the world's population. Rising sea levels could result in tens to hundreds of millions more people flooded each year (HM Government 2006).

The science presents a stark warning. The debate is increasingly moving from whether it is desirable to tackle climate change to whether it is affordable.

Economics

Climate change is the classic example of market failure. The cost of greenhouse gases does not accrue to the people, businesses or nations that generate them. The polluter does not pay. Those who fail to pay for it cannot be excluded from enjoying its benefits and freeriding on those who do pay. But unlike many other public goods, such as air pollution, climate change is global in reach, long term in gestation, and bound with uncertainty in terms of the precise scale, location and speed of its impacts. The report by Sir Nicholas Stern into the economics of climate change is beginning to reverse the economic debate. His conclusions are clear:

- The financial cost of mitigating climate change will be far less than the cost of dealing with the effects. You don't have to be an altruist to care about climate change.
- Early and gradual action will be far more cost-effective than sudden and late action. Early action is affordable, late action is not.

- Action by individual nations or continents need not lead to a loss of competitive advantage for firms, particularly if we act at the European level.
- The answer to market failure is not to obliterate markets but to make markets work. Climate change is soluble if we begin to apply a 'polluter pays' principle in each and every product and service we buy (Stern 2006).

A UK energy revolution

The science and economics highlight the case for action. The positive news is that the practical and technological solutions exist to tackle climate change. Becoming a low-carbon economy will involve every part of the energy chain in change: from the electricity generators who own power stations; the National Grid and the distribution network operators who own the wires that feed electricity into our homes; the electricity suppliers who sell us energy; the fuel suppliers who sell us gas, to the end-users themselves – consumers and business.

Our future energy system will be based on three changes – what could be called a '3D energy revolution'. The first change is to decrease demand: the most cost-effective route to a low-carbon economy is to increase energy efficiency and reduce demand. This is often a win–win for consumers and the environment. To achieve this, we need to fundamentally change how energy companies work. Imagine a world where your energy company makes money by reducing your energy use rather than increasing it; where it actively seeks out the most cost-effective energy savings rather than waiting to be approached by customers; where it offers you a personal carbon audit that identifies energy savings in your home, your travel and your lifestyle; and where it pays the upfront cash needed to make savings, and even arranges for the improvements to be made from accredited suppliers. This world is not as far away as some people think. Essentially it involves a new business model for energy suppliers. They generate value by working with consumers and enabling them to change their behaviour rather than pure cost-cutting. These organizations, known as Energy Service Companies, are beginning to emerge. For instance, Woking Council has created an Energy Services Company through a public–private partnership. As a result, it has reduced its own energy use by nearly half and cut its own CO_2 emissions by over three-quarters between 1991 and 2004 as a result of decentralizing its energy supplies (Mayor of London 2006).

The second change is to decarbonize the supply of energy – the shift from high-carbon to low-carbon energy. Some 90 per cent of energy currently comes from high-carbon sources – coal, gas and oil; 8 per cent comes from nuclear and 2 per cent from renewables. Unless this mix changes dramatically in the twenty-first century, we will not reduce emissions. In future, electricity and heat must increasingly be generated through low-carbon fuels such as wind, wave, solar, biomass, carbon-capture and storage, and, if necessary, nuclear. Transport must be powered by low-carbon technologies, initially biofuels and hybrids, but in the long term, electric motors and hydrogen fuel cells.

The third change is decentralization. Since the opening of the world's first thermal power station in London in 1882 by Thomas Edison, the trend over the past century has been towards increasingly centralized power generation. Scale economies have driven the construction of large power stations and the transmission of electricity through a national grid. But in some countries, with the emergence of new technologies we are increasingly seeing more decentralized and distributed power generation – from combined heat and power stations serving a community, to individual citizens producing energy through solar or wind power and selling their energy back on to the grid. Around 60 per cent of energy is typically wasted as unwanted heat by centralized generation – more than enough in total to heat every UK home. In the next 30 years, we could see the same transformation in energy production that we have seen in computers over the past generation – with a growing reliance on small computers connected via a network rather than a traditional mainframe. For instance, a large proportion of energy in Denmark and the Netherlands is produced on a decentralized basis – a transition that took around 20 years.

This 3D revolution in energy has the potential to help us to live within our environmental limits; not at the expense of well-being and quality of life, but in pursuit of it.

Politics

The case for action is clear, and the solutions exist. The question is whether we can develop and secure support for the policies that will drive investment in a 3D energy revolution domestically and interna-tionally. The political challenge is domestic and ideological as well as international and technological. The political leaders in this country now agree that climate change is a big issue – but if we are honest, it is a massive challenge to the policies and practices of every political party:

- It is a challenge to the right because although there is a conservationist tradition at the heart of any party that calls itself 'Conservative', it is incompatible with a belief in free markets, a minimal state and Euroscepticism.
- It is a challenge to the left because although there is a red–green tradition, climate change requires us to rethink how we approach questions of production and distribution.
- It is a challenge to the way we do politics because it calls for real rather than rhetorical solidarity with people around the world and people not yet born; real rather than rhetorical acceptance that governments and markets have both failed to find the answers to this problem, and real rather than rhetorical engagement with the need to mobilize people to help tackle the problem.

The remainder of this chapter considers how we may overcome this political logjam.

The limits of deep green

Although the roots of the green movement stretch back centuries, it was in the 1960s and 1970s that modern environmentalism took off. The publication of Rachel Carson's *Silent Spring* in 1962 warning of the impact of pesticides on the bird population, and the Club of Rome's *The Limits to Growth* a decade later, along with James Lovelock's Gaia thesis in 1979, catapulted environmental concerns into the mainstream of political debate (Dobson 1995).

While there is huge diversity and debate within the green movement, environmentalists became associated with challenging our interest in economic growth and material progress, and advocating a return to simpler living, personal sacrifice, and spiritual rather than material progress. This gave the movement a deep but narrow appeal. By exaggerating the tradeoff between economic dynamism and environmental protection, between human welfare and nature, the politics of the environment failed to gain the legitimacy needed to make it a governing idea for a major party.

Arguing for zero growth, particularly to rapidly industrializing developing countries, plays to the worst fears of India and China – that climate change is an excuse to cement the existing disparities in wealth and power. If we are to gain a consensus both here and abroad that climate change is soluble, it has to be an ally of aspiration, progress and economic growth. Zero growth is impractical and immoral. That is why climate change must enter mainstream political parties rather than remain within a separate green culture. The Stern Report shows it is pro-growth to be pro-green; but equally, unless we are pro-growth, especially for developing countries, we will not end up being pro-green. Changes in energy technologies and the structure of economies have reduced the responsiveness of emissions to income growth, particularly in some of the richest countries. With strong, deliberate policy choices, it is possible to 'decarbonize' both developed and developing economies on the scale required for climate stabilization, while maintaining economic growth in both (Stern 2006).

The limits of blue–green

If deep green is no answer, what of conservatism? The truth is that there is a tradition on which Conservatives can call, but it is a commitment to conservation of the status quo – or a return to the status quo ante – not radical change to meet a new threat. Zac Goldsmith has said: 'I consider myself a conservative as opposed to a radical' (*Guardian* 2005). The problem is that climate change is about managing radical change – a transition that will challenge established routines and institutions. In reality, climate change challenges the very basis of conservative thinking:

- It challenges the idea of national sovereignty over decision-making. Climate change is the defining example of interdependence and the need to pool powers in international institutions.
- It challenges conservatives' attachment to free markets. Markets work when the price of goods reflect their value. But climate change is the defining example of market failure – where the price does not reflect the cost to the environment. The need to account for the interests of future generations trips up even thoughtful free marketeers.
- It challenges conservatives' dogmatic distrust of the state. Climate change cannot be addressed by purely voluntary action alone. It requires the power of the state – to regulate and tax, to subsidize if necessary, and to define and enforce property rights. This is why David Cameron's language of social responsibility cannot deliver the substance of national action – it is simply not enough to implore greater responsibility from individuals for a problem that needs organized collective action.

Red–green: why climate change is a social justice issue

I believe, therefore, that it is plausible to argue that unless parties of the centre-left address climate change, it will not be addressed. It is a progressive project to use government to shape markets – and that is vital in the battle against climate change. It is a progressive project to put social justice at the heart of politics – and an equitable balance of rights and responsibilities as the defining test of a civilized society. And it is a progressive project to recognize the importance of internationalism in an age of interdependence. However, red–green must be more than a marriage of convenience. We need to show that red and green traditions can challenge but ultimately enhance each other.

The vision of New Labour in 1997 got a lot right. It has helped to rehabilitate collective action and reframe debates about the economy, public services and national culture. But that vision is no longer sufficient for the present day, when the science has moved on, when popular concerns have moved on and when progressive ambitions have also moved on.

With regard to climate change, there are reasons to be proud of progress. In respect of greenhouse gases, they are down by 8 per cent since 1997 while the economy has grown by more than 25 per cent, but carbon dioxide emissions are up just over 1 per cent (*Independent* 2006). Policies like the Climate Change Levy were pushed through against a lot of opposition. But equally, I believe there are four areas where we especially need to up our game. The symptoms of global warming are environmental, but the causes go to the heart of economic, social and foreign policy, and even our vision of democracy itself.

Political economy

First, climate change requires a different vision of political economy. As Gordon Brown has set out, in 1997 we made economic stability and high employment our top priorities (Brown 1997), but now we need a third ambition, to redress the imbalance between the natural resources we consume and the natural capital we reinvest; a kind of 'golden rule' to ensure that we do not mortgage the futures of our children in an unsustainable ecological debt. That is the significance of the Climate Change Bill (HM Government 2007) – a reform that ensures that the UK is the world's first country with a legislative timetable for becoming a low-carbon economy.

As many businesses, including the Confederation of British Industry (CBI) have said, we need to give certainty not just about public finances and low inflation, but also about the carbon-priced environment in which we want business to operate. This means leading the economy, not just managing it. In 1997, we said we wanted to extend the power of choice and voice that exist in the private sector to public services. Today, we need to extend market mechanisms to public goods. We need to put a price on carbon dioxide and use the power of the market to find the lowest cost emissions.

A decade ago we said we wanted to raise labour productivity; we also introduced the idea of Best Value to improve the efficiency, equity and effectiveness of local services, and we regulated to protect labour standards – signing the Social Chapter and the minimum wage. Now we must revisit these issues from a different perspective. We should focus as much on today's scarcity issue – natural resources – and commit to raising natural resource productivity. We should always build in the need to tackle climate change when we commission and provide services. And regulation must focus on environmental standards, from zero-carbon homes to phasing out energy-inefficient light bulbs and appliances, with the UK acting as the champion of reformed EU regulation.

In 1997, we focused on macro-economic stability and active labour market policy. Old-style industrial policy, sector by sector, was condemned as micro-management. But like Eastern Europe after the Cold War, we are now a 'transition economy'. The lessons are clear. Too much government and you stifle the power of the market; too little, and you have a free-for-all.

A low-carbon economy will have a new market at its heart: a market in carbon, with the vast majority of the economy covered by carbon trading. Getting there will require a mix of measures: regulation, tax, subsidy, planning, procurement, the transformation of markets – all to accelerate change. It will require a stronger role for government as leaders of change – helping the complex system of public and private organizations that affect our travel, housing and waste – adapt to a new economy. And it will require a new confidence – not to pick winners, but to transform markets so that they price out the high-polluting losers.

Social justice

The second area where climate changes tests our capacity for new thinking is in respect of social justice. This will test us philosophically and politically. Most theories of justice have as a prerequisite an assumption of reciprocity – a community of justice. But extending this to future generations in developing countries, distant in both time and space, involves no reciprocity. Theories of social justice have therefore often struggled to grapple with intergenerational injustice. John Rawls's famous 'veil of ignorance' (Rawls 1971) asked us to consider what position we would take if we did not know which of the current living generations we were born into. Climate change requires us to thicken the veil and consider how we should act if faced with the possibility of being born far into the future. The Bruntland Report, published 20 years ago, provides the foundation: sustainable development is that which 'meets the needs of the present without compromising the ability of future generations to meet their own needs' (Bruntland Commission 1987).

Without a clear theory of how environmental burdens and rewards can be shared fairly between nations and generations, we will not secure a global deal between developing and developed countries, and we will not sustain the moral authority to drive change at home. We take as our starting point 'common but differentiated responsibilities'. In essence, this means recognizing that developed countries need to show leadership, to help bridge the gap between high-carbon and low-carbon paths of development, and to support the adaptation to the climate change already happening due to industrialized countries' emissions. In return, it means that developing countries must recognize the need to play their part in developing low-carbon economies.

But climate change will also challenge our notion of social justice domestically. The application of a 'polluter pays' principle involves distributing resources based not just on need but on desert; a recognition that resources should be linked to fulfilling citizenship responsibilities. So while in 1997, our conception of citizenship was social, economic and political, today it must also be environmental. Just as in 1997, we developed a New Deal for the unemployed (Department for Work and Pensions (DWP) 2004) – and provided more help, training and financial rewards conditional on people taking up work opportunities – today we must look at providing more help and incentives for people to save energy and recycle in return for citizens sharing responsibility with the state for maintaining the environment. Just as in 1997, we introduced political citizenship education into schools, today we must think how our education system can nurture environmental citizenship, and how our schools can become exemplars of energy efficiency and micro-generation.

EU – Environmental Union

Third, New Labour was right to challenge the Euroscepticism that had dogged both the major parties. But today the European project has stalled: the constitution rejected, its *raison d'être* in question. Now is the time to recognize that in an interdependent world we need a Europe that works, based on a new mission for the EU – taking the carbon out of the Single Market. We must be prepared to make the case for a powerful EU in return for institutions that are more transparent and more accountable. So what would a new EU – an Environmental Union – focus on?

It would agree to a 30 per cent cut in greenhouse gas emissions by 2020. It would extend the European Union Emissions Trading Scheme to aviation, and potentially to surface transport; it would link the scheme to emerging carbon markets to form the basis of a global trading scheme, and it would secure its long-term future as the biggest delivery vehicle of our 2020 and 2050 targets.

It would use the size of the single market and intra-European trade to ensure higher environmental standards without competitive disadvantage, whether through mandatory tradable emissions standards for car manufacturers, tougher energy ratings for products, or regulating out of existence high-polluting electrical equipment and household appliances.

It would reform the Common Agricultural Policy and refocus the programme on environmental public goods rather than subsidizing food production. It would develop a major technology and R&D programme aimed at supporting innovations in energy and transport, and transferring innovations to developing countries. And it would use the power of negotiating as a single block to forge an ambitious post-2012 international framework.

If we do so, the prize is bigger than many imagine. Reducing the dependence of the world economy on oil is at the heart of the Middle East peace challenge. Preventing climate change would avoid the disastrous migrations and conflicts over natural resources. Creating a robust Global Carbon Market would see more transfers from North to South than the development policies of all of Europe put together. Climate change is a security issue, a migration issue and a development issue.

New politics

Finally, climate change will challenge our way of thinking about politics. Our conception of politics has too often been Whitehall- and Westminster-based. It has allowed management to have a greater role than mobilization; governing, not campaigning. It has been based on active government but not active enough citizens. Climate change shows how outdated this is as a model. People want to do their bit to tackle climate change. They don't want the dilute and remote influence of lobbying their representatives through the occasional tick in the ballot box. They want to be players, not just spectators. However, they lack the information on what changes in their lives would make a difference, they get confused by the welter of contradictory messages on what car to buy or whether offsetting makes any difference; but, most of all, they worry that their actions will not be reciprocated by others either here or abroad, and therefore won't make a difference.

We can only tackle this sense of powerlessness by creating a unique combination of collective action through the state, and individual action through markets. Government must create the framework – establishing through legislation the pathway to a 60 per cent reduction in carbon emissions by 2050. Government must show we are doing our bit directly in achieving this, whether this is ensuring that all new homes are zero-carbon, making the government estate carbon-neutral, or factoring in sustainability into public procurement. But government must also create the tools for others to take action.

The implications are most far-reaching in the idea of personal, tradable carbon allowances, about which the Department for Environment, Food and Rural Affairs (Defra) published an issues paper in early 2007 (Roberts and Thumin 2007). Around 44 per cent of all emissions are by individual households, most of which come from four transactions: electricity and gas in our homes, and car and air travel (Retallack 2006). Under a Personal Carbon Allowance (PCA) system the government would define the overall carbon budget and allocate carbon allowances to each individual or household in a fair way. Individuals, through their own actions and through trading, would find ways of living within these limits: those who are environmentally thrifty would be financially rewarded; those who aren't would pay.

PCAs combine scientific evidence, government embodiment of collective will, and individual initiative. This is what the renewal of a progressive agenda on the environment needs to be about. If we are to engage citizens in tackling climate change, we must be prepared to show that radical problems need radical solutions; we must create a link between everyday politics and Westminster politics.

Conclusion

Climate change will not be tackled by 'social responsibility' alone. It requires government to deepen the role of markets. Climate change is incompatible with isolationism and Euroscepticism; it is a global problem that requires commitment to act within Europe and international institutions. We will not secure an international agreement without a commitment to apply social justice to the distribution of resonsibility between generations and nations.

But while the left is best-placed to address climate change, it does not hold a monopoly. The environmental movement is a growing force in civil society, searching for a home in mainstream politics. To win the argument for a socially just response to our environmental problems we need more than policies. We must make it a defining mission for the progressive project – something that recruits and inspires the next generation of progressive thinkers and practitioners. We must never fail to remember that climate change is about people, not just nature; a social issue, not just an environmental one. Former US Vice President Al Gore's recent film *An Inconvenient Truth* warned us convincingly of a 'planetary emergency'; in fact, it is also a warning of a humanitarian crisis, and one to which we must be ready to lead the response.

References

Arrhenius, S. (1908) *Worlds in the Making: The Evolution of the Universe*. New York: Harper & Row.

Brown, G. (1997) Speech to the Confederation of British Industry, 20 May. Available at <www.hm-treasury.gov.uk/newsroom_and_speeches/speeches/chancellorexchequer/speech_chex_200597.cfm>.

Bruntland Commission (1987) *Our Common Future*. Oxford: Oxford University Press.

Carson, R. (1962) *Silent Spring*. New York: Houghton Mifflin.

Dobson, A. (1995) *Green Political Thought*. London: Routledge.

DWP (2004) *Building on New Deal: Local Solutions Meeting Individual Needs*. London: TSO. Available at <www.dwp.gov.uk/publications/dwp/2004/buildingonnewdeal/mainreport.pdf>.

Flannery, T. (2005) *The Weather Makers: The History and Future Impact of Climate Change*. Melbourne: Text Publishing.

Fleming, J. (1999) 'Joseph Fourier, the "Greenhouse Effect", and the Quest for a Universal Theory of Terrestrial Temperatures', *Endeavour*, 23 (2): 72–5.

Guardian (2005) 'True-blue green'. Interview with Zac Goldsmith, 3 December.

HM Government (2006) *Climate Change: The UK Programme 2006*. London: HMSO.

HM Government (2007) *Draft Climate Change Bill*. London: Defra.

Independent (2006) 'With a little bit of goodwill, we can still stop', 30 September.

Lovelock, J. (1979) *Gaia: A New Look at Life on Earth*. Oxford: Oxford University Press.

Mayor of London (2006) 'Submission to the Energy Review'. Available at <www.london.gov.uk/mayor/environment/energy/docs/energy-review-response.rtf>.

Meadows, D., Meadows, D., Randers, J. and Behrens, W. (1972) *The Limits to Growth*. New York: Universe Books.

Rawls, J. (1971) *A Theory of Justice*. Cambridge, Mass.: Harvard University Press.

Retallack, S. (2006) 'Against the Climate Pornographers', article for TomPaine.com. Available at <www.tompaine.com/articles/2006/08/15/against_the_climate_pornographers.php>.

Roberts, S. and Thumim, J. (2007) *A Rough Guide to Individual Carbon Trading: The Ideas, the Issues and the Next Steps*. Report to Defra by the Centre for Sustainable Energy. London: CSE.

Stern, N. (2006) *Stern Review: The Economics of Climate Change*. London: TSO. Available at <www.hm-treasury.gov.uk/independent_reviews/stern_review_economics_climate_change/stern_review_report.cfm>.

17
A New Agenda for International Development

Hilary Benn

What should a progressive political approach to international development in the twenty-first century look like? I think it should focus on increased engagement, multilateralism, good governance, country ownership and, where appropriate, ethical intervention. Although I write as a Labour minister, this chapter is not about party politics. It is about the broader goal of global justice, sustainability and better quality of life for all.

These may seem like naturally progressive aims. But it is in fact only recently that a truly global perspective has entered mainstream progressive thought and practice. Before the Universal Declaration of Human Rights in 1948, it was only states – and not individuals – that had rights in international law. And even then leading social justice theorists were notably silent on international issues for decades after this. John Rawls's classic text, *A Theory of Justice*, makes no mention of duties beyond national borders and even his later work, *The Law of Peoples*, is relatively sanguine about the extent of such obligations (Rawls 1971, 1999).

In more recent years, philosophical debate has taken a markedly more international focus (Mepham 2005). Philosophers such as David Miller and Michael Walzer have emphasized the importance of shared nationality, culture and community in determining the limits of our obligations (Walzer 1983; Miller 2000, 2005), while others – such as Brian Barry, Peter Singer, Charles Beitz and Thomas Pogge – have argued that our moral obligations to developing countries are far more demanding (Barry 1973; Singer 2002; Beitz 2000; Pogge 2002). Whatever position you take on these questions, the very existence and urgency of these debates shows that in the twenty-first century it is no longer ethically tenable to look merely inwards.

Nor is it practical. The world is becoming far more interdependent as what happens in one country rapidly and profoundly affects others (Held 2004, 2006; Giddens 1990; Buchanan 2000; United Nations Conference on Trade and Development (UNCTAD) 2005; Moore and Unsworth 2006). Conflict in Africa impacts on Britain through migration and asylum, and reduced trade and proliferation of disease, and can provide cover for terrorists or organized criminal groups (Department for International Development (DfID) 2006a; Djankov et al. 2005; World Bank 2003), for example. Rapid industrialization in developing countries and continued high emissions from developed countries pose a serious threat to climate stability, which will affect us all (Stern 2006). And at a more ideological level, many argue that the increasingly glaring gap between rich and poor countries is creating a sense of 'global rancour', encouraged and utilized by political extremists to foster disaffection and resentment against the West, with obvious damaging consequences (Mepham 2005; Halliday 2004; Burke 2003; Kilcullen 2006). So for prudent as well as moral reasons, progressive internationalism is vital.

A progressive consensus on international development?

It is now ten years since Labour established the Department for International Development and Clare Short published the first of her two development White Papers, asserting that Britain had a 'moral duty' to help the world's poor and to strive for a 'more just world' (DfID 1997). Britain's work in international development since has already contributed much to the progressive cause: it has not only had an impact on global poverty reduction – the DfID estimates that British aid now helps 5,000 people out of poverty every day (Benn 2006a) – and made a profound difference in areas as diverse as humanitarian assistance, United Nations (UN) reform, trade, global and national governance, conflict, education, disease prevention, economic growth and security (DfID 2006a), but it has also helped to frame the debate about international development in more progressive terms.

There is now a consensus across the political spectrum that aid is effective and should be increased and that the government should take account of the impact on global poverty of a broad range of policies, from international trade to climate change. No one in mainstream politics advocates repealing the International Development Act (which places poverty elimination at the heart of the DfID's work and ensures that development assistance may not be used for other purposes, such as encouraging procurement contracts for UK companies), cutting aid – as the Thatcher administration did throughout the 1980s – or making it legal again for British companies to pay bribes. The mood has now changed.

Perhaps the best example of popular support for this new consensus was 2005's Make Poverty History campaign, in which millions wore a white wrist-band to signal their commitment to fighting global poverty and hundreds of thousands marched in the streets before the summit of the British presidency of the G8 (Make Poverty History 2006). This was progressive politics at its best: people making clear demands while giving politicians the legitimacy, urgency and backing to make unprecedented financial commitments (DfID 2006b). Compared to the protests in Seattle a few years before, it was clear that the mood had profoundly altered; there is now a largely constructive and positive view about the capacity and willingness of governments to act internationally to promote global justice. But for the progressive cause to succeed, there is of course more to be done. It would be naive to simply assume that contemporary agreement about international development's importance is here to stay.

Nor should we assume that a progressive view of international development is entrenched in British policy-making. A distinctively progressive approach should be founded on a commitment to global social justice (Mepham 2005; Pearce and Paxton 2005; Chapter 18, this volume). This places a concern for inequality at its heart, both between countries and within them, and extends beyond a narrow focus on income and poverty towards a fuller understanding of human capabilities: it is concerned with what people can become, what they can achieve and the human rights to which they are entitled (Vizard 2001; Sen 1999). As such, this puts a strong emphasis on inclusion, voice and community. In practical terms, it means a commitment to democracy, fair multilateralism and the autonomy of developing countries to determine their development priorities (Maxwell 2005; DfID, 2006a; Mepham 2005). So what are the challenges to a distinctively progressive view of international development in future?

Three challenges for progressive internationalism

Three fundamental questions should shape our thinking in this area:

- Is our model of development right for the changing world we live in? While the business of international development will always be poverty reduction, we need to ensure that our approach is suited to the modern world, the changing balance of global power and the changing nature of poverty. For example, as the developing world becomes more urban (UN 2003), poverty is likely to become more urban too, creating new challenges for donors and governments alike. And it may also become more geographically concentrated: by 2030, sub-Saharan Africa alone could be home to more than half of the very poorest people in the world – nearly twice the proportion of today (World Bank 2007). Over the past decade we have made good progress in fighting poverty but will need to continue to reassess our approach: thinking about the issues of the role of the state, national autonomy, political models and sector priorities (DfID, 2006a).

- How can we maintain public support for a progressive approach – are there better ways of ensuring and demonstrating the effectiveness of our work?
- Should we alter our approach to foreign policy more generally, particularly given our experiences in recent years, to be even more explicitly focused on development? Is development quite simply the best long-term foreign policy?

These three questions underpin the arguments in the rest of this chapter, and in the following sections I look at the changing aid landscape and the challenges this will create, and set out policy implications in the areas of governance, climate change, conflict and security. In conclusion, I turn to the issues of sustaining public support and the future of Britain's broader international role.

The new aid landscape

More diverse donors

Perhaps the most fundamental global change over the coming decade will be a gradual shift in economic and political weight. There is one real superpower today, the US, with a larger economy than Japan, Germany, China, the UK and France put together (International Monetary Fund (IMF) 2006), and a higher defence budget – at $471 billion a year (Department of Defense (DoD) 2007) – than the next 25 highest spenders combined (Central Intelligence Agency (CIA) 2005).

Although the US will continue to be by far the world's dominant national economy over the next two decades, this pre-eminence is likely to start declining. Asia will play an increasing role in global growth, with China overtaking Japan as the world's second largest economy in around ten years; the EU will also remain an important bloc, at about the same size as the US (Foreign and Commonwealth Office (FCO) 2006). Regional integration in South-East Asia, Africa and South America is also likely to continue, although at varying paces (ibid.). And Brazil, South Africa, India and other large developing countries will become increasingly significant global players.

This represents an enormous opportunity for the world's poor. Thanks to rapid economic growth in Asia, the number of people across the world living on less than $1 a day is set to halve by 2015 and there are now over 75 million more children in primary school than in 1990 (World Bank 2006a; United Nations Educational, Scientific and Cultural Organization (UNESCO) 2006). Aid, alongside countries' own efforts, is working (DfID, 2006a; Clemens et al. 2004). It is now clearer than ever that sustained and shared economic growth is quite simply the fastest way to reduce global poverty (DfID, 2006a). But these global trends also mean that progressives will have to change their approach international development.

There has been a significant degree of convergence and agreement between donors over the past decade, at least in rhetorical terms. The Paris Agenda for aid effectiveness (based on five principles: partner country ownership; alignment with partners' development strategies; donor harmonization; managing for results, and mutual accountability (Organization for Economic Cooperation and Development (OECD) 2005)), and what Maxwell has called 'the meta-narrative' in policy approach (Maxwell 2005) – focusing on the Millennium Development Goals (MDGs), with special concern for poorly performing and failed and failing states and the importance of untying aid – have underpinned many countries' approaches to international development. Yet as we look to the future, there are signs that this consensus may be increasingly difficult to sustain; a central progressive challenge for the next decade in international development is to ensure its survival and expansion.

Put simply, the donor world is becoming larger, far more diverse and more bilateral (Shafik 2006; Klein and Harford 2005). This is something we should celebrate. It represents countries moving from being recipients of aid to donors themselves – perhaps the ultimate proof that development really works. Indeed, the growth in donor activity over the past decade has been astonishing, reaching more than $100 billion in 2005, more than double the volume of 1997 and triple that of 1985 (OECD 2006). There are now more than 40 bilateral donors, 26 UN agencies and 20 global and regional financial institutions, and the most recent round of replenishment of the International Development Association (IDA) at the World Bank included 40 countries, compared to 18 in 1964 (Klein and

Harford 2005). At the same time, private financial flows to developing countries – including foreign direct investment, remittances and other private flows – were, at $491 billion in 2005 (World Bank 2006b), nearly five times official development assistance (OECD 2006). In total, it is estimated that there are more than 1,000 financing mechanisms (Kaul and Conceicao 2006). Yet as well as providing enormous benefits, this complexity will also create significant challenges for a progressive approach (Rogerson, 2005; Rocha Menocal and Rogerson 2006; Burall et al. 2006).

There are two main issues here. The first is the relatively familiar challenge of coordination between like-minded donors, albeit on a larger scale. This really matters: for countries with limited civil service capacity, responding to a plethora of individual donors' reporting requirements can severely constrain their ability to get on with the job of governing. For example, between 2003/04 and 2006/07, the Government of Uganda had to deal with 684 aid instruments and associated agreements for aid coming into the central budget alone (Burall et al. 2006) – hence the importance of the Paris Agenda (OECD 2005). A progressive response should be to continue to argue for increased harmonization and multilateralism – providing aid through multilateral channels such as the World Bank, global funds and the European Union (EU).

The second challenge is a more political one: the emergence of a different kind of donor altogether. China's current approach in Africa is a good example, providing finance for development on very different terms to those favoured by more traditional donors, with less emphasis on human rights or good governance (Wild and Mepham 2006). China can play a hugely positive role in Africa, not least in sharing its success in reducing poverty domestically. (Between 1990 and 2001, the number of people living in poverty in China fell by 165 million, while the number living in poverty in Africa rose by 77 million (ibid.).) But its increased engagement arguably changes the context for all donors.

One implication is that the 'carrots' and 'sticks' available to donors focusing on poverty reduction, good governance, corruption, the MDGs, human rights and upholding international obligations will alter as other sources of finance become more available. Britain's role in response should be twofold: first, to advocate to new and emerging donors the long-term advantages of the approach we are taking; a more stable world is after all in all our interests, at least in the long term – and that depends on effective states committed to poverty reduction. Second, we should better equip poor countries to manage their own aid flows strategically: the need to get donors to come behind a country's own plans and systems will become critical in complementing efforts by donors for harmonization.

The growing importance of global public goods and fragile states

Just as the donor landscape changes, the development challenges we face in the world will also evolve. In all countries, we should focus on increased sustainable growth and improved public services – particularly in the areas of education, health, water and sanitation, and 'social protection' (DfID 2006a). But the way we work towards these needs to be sensitive to the needs of individual developing countries.

Five priorities for progressives stand out. First, we will need to focus more on global public goods, particularly avoiding disastrous climate change, building global capacity to respond effectively to humanitarian emergencies and diseases such as HIV and AIDS, and improving global governance and trading systems.

Second, in stable developing countries where prospects of progress are good, but where aid is likely to remain a large proportion of gross domestic product (GDP) for some time, such as Tanzania or Rwanda, we should focus on good governance – building the capacity of governments to be accountable, capable and responsive (see below) (DfID 2006a) – while remaining sensitive to countries' ability to absorb increased volumes foreign aid (Foster and Killick 2006).

Third, in countries such as India, China, Brazil, Botswana and others which are becoming decreasingly dependent on aid as a proportion of GDP and experiencing strong growth – the '0.2% club' (Maxwell 2006) – technical assistance and sharing experiences in running a successful economy and effective state institutions will be paramount in continuing to reduce poverty. These countries will also rightly demand a more equal relationship with developed countries, focusing on issues beyond traditional development concerns (Messner and Humphrey 2006).

Fourth, in fragile states, particularly those in sub-Saharan Africa where few, if any, of the MDGs are likely to be met by 2015 without much faster progress (DfID 2006a), we should focus on preventing and ending conflict, finding political solutions to entrenched disputes, reducing corruption and improving governance.

Fifth, in countries where poverty reduction has been so dramatic that our aid is no longer appropriate, we should close our development programmes, celebrate success and engage in a different form of relationship.

Each of these challenges will require a firm commitment to multilateralism. And it is increasingly clear that the European Union must take a leading role in development, albeit with reform to improve cooperation and effectiveness (DfID 2006a).

Global public goods

Tackling climate change

Left unchecked, we know for certain that climate change will kill millions of people, most of whom live in the developing world, and many of whom are yet to be born (Stern 2006). And the wider effects of climate change – conflict over resources, especially energy, and hugely increased pressure on land use and migration, for example – will exacerbate many other existing problems (DfID 2006a). Any effective response will require, without doubt, concerted international action; no country can act alone. A stable climate is therefore perhaps the archetypal public good. Even if Britain's emissions were reduced to zero tomorrow, the growth in emissions from China would compensate for this in just two years (Blair 2006).

Crucially, the Stern Review showed that the world has the capacity to prevent disastrous climate change (Stern 2006); rather than a question of ability, it is now one of commitment. This makes climate change one of the most important issues for development policy over the next decades (DfID 2006a). This is why the Stern Review was so important. It changed the debate from being about resignation or panic to being about practical action. As David Miliband argues in Chapter 16, for too long we have allowed the language of inevitability and impossibility to dominate environmental politics. The diplomatic job here, however, is substantial, in convincing political, academic, economic, business and community leaders across the world of its findings, relevance and implications.

The best long-term solution to climate change depends on a properly working global carbon market, and hence on multilateral political agreement and action (DfID 2006a). A global carbon market would in itself foster enormous technological progress and substantial changes to the way we all live our lives, in Britain and developing countries. For Britain, the benefits of moving early towards a green economy should be clear – in terms of global justice, for reasons of energy security, for the competitive advantage of moving first and developing new technologies, and for political reasons too, in demonstrating to those more reluctant than us that it is possible to cut emissions.

The most obvious imperative for developing countries to tackle climate change, particularly in focusing on adaptation, is to prevent unnecessary deaths from disease, famine and other climate related changes, and to avert the serious economic impact that climate change will cause (ibid.). We need to continue to find ways to help these countries adapt, through better planning of infrastructure, research into appropriate agricultural techniques, and other efforts (ibid.). But we should also recognize the enormous potential of an effective global response through carbon markets to benefit developing countries.

For countries that are currently classed as poor, the potential revenues from selling environmental services to countries currently classed as rich would almost certainly dwarf current official development assistance in terms of the benefits accruing to developing countries. It is important to understand that a carbon market is not merely a clever way of transferring financial resources from the developed to developing world: it involves a much more profound recognition of the economic value of previously undervalued assets, such as rainforest, biodiversity, low carbon economies and clean beaches.

Creating an effective market to do this will not be easy, nor will it in practice work out as simply as we would like it to, but we should not be pessimistic. Given sufficient political will and effort, with vocal public support, it is often surprising how quickly institutions can change. Indeed, the bicentenary of the abolition of slavery this year should remind us how what was once accepted can be overturned by political conviction and effective campaigning. As we look to the future we need our concern for climate change to run through everything we do.

Global governance and trade

Climate change is just one example of the increasing importance of global public goods and fostering progressive institutions and systems that can respond effectively. But there are many others. Although we would not design the international governance system in its current form if starting from scratch (Woods 2006; Burall et al. 2006), we should be optimistic about the prospects of multilateralism to respond to these challenges – if our global institutions undergo considerable reform.

To remain relevant, global governance institutions must better reflect the economic and political realities of the contemporary world, rather than that of 1945. A progressive system would give far more voice and weight to developing countries; just a few rich countries should not expect to shape priorities in the way they have in the past. Progressives should continue to push for a fairer balance of power in UN reform, through an expanded Security Council, and for progress on consolidation towards the 'four ones' within countries: a unified UN presence based around a single programme, with one leader, one office and one budget

(DfID 2006a). The UN should also focus its activities on preventing and responding to conflict, helping fragile states and reacting to humanitarian crises, and developing international agreements and standards.

Progress on trade will also be central: if Africa enjoyed the same share of world exports today as it did in 1980, its exports in 2005 would have been $119 billion (in constant 2000 dollars) higher (United Nations Development Programme (UNDP) 2005). In practical terms, both the EU and the US must move on agriculture; the former to offer greater access, and the latter to reduce distorting domestic support (DfID 2006a; Brown 2007; Mepham and Lorge 2005). But any deal must also be sensitive to the needs of countries at different levels of development: many countries will need 'special and different treatment' to protect vulnerable farmers from surges in food imports, for example (DfID 2006a). These are not quick projects and will require sustained political will (Burall et al. 2006). But nor are they impossible.

Improving national governance: the progressive approach to development

These global efforts must be accompanied by progressive politics in countries. Our goal should be to help countries achieve sustainable and shared economic growth: this is without doubt the 'exit strategy' for aid (DfID 2006a). And this also means a flourishing private sector.

Yet a strong private sector cannot develop in a vacuum. Domestic and foreign investment rely on macro-economic stability, good infrastructure, appropriate and clear regulation – things that can only be achieved by capable, responsive governments (ibid.). And efforts to fight disease, particularly HIV and AIDS (Benn 2006b), and improve education, health and livelihoods – all essential for economic growth as well as valuable in their own right – depend on effective public services.

This is why we should focus on helping countries to improve their governance. Although there are advocates of avoiding government systems whenever possible and providing services and goods directly to poor people (Easterly 2006), it is my firm belief that we should work with and through countries' governments whenever possible. We should focus on helping to improve countries' own systems, fostering states that are accountable to their people, responsive and capable (ibid.). This is a long-term task rather than a short-term quick fix.

A central part of this approach to governance is to provide resources directly to countries through their central budgets – a strategy known as budget support – while offering technical assistance to strengthen the civil service and public services. (Our approach to deciding when budget support is appropriate should be based on a 'quality of governance' assessment. See DfID 2006a for more details.) Working with countries' own systems helps strengthen them (ibid.; Kauffman, 2004). The alternative – creating parallel donor systems within countries – risks encouraging talented people to leave public services to work for international donors, and undermines national capacity.

Fostering better governance is not a simple task, nor is it a short term one. Accountability, legitimacy, transparency, an effective civil society and strong private sector, some central elements of democratic structures and an effective civil service with the right capacity and skills to deliver and administrate public services and regulatory functions, are all important (DfID 2006a). But it can be done: Botswana, Ghana and Tanzania have all strengthened their public institutions in recent years. Rwanda, Mozambique, Vietnam and Cambodia have successfully rebuilt their countries after devastating conflicts, through effective state mechanisms. And East Asian countries such as Malaysia and South Korea have shown that good governance can foster rapid economic growth and lift millions out of poverty in just a few decades (ibid.).

In most cases, strong political leadership, economic growth and a vibrant private sector were the main factors encouraging change (McLeod 2005). Accountability is at the heart of this: where it is good, audit institutions and parliamentary committees scrutinize public expenditure and government achievements. Courts help prevent corruption. And beyond the formal structures of the state, civil society organizations give citizens power, help poor people get their voices heard and demand more from politicians and government (ibid.).

Where there is demand for good governance, where states are focused on tackling poverty, promoting rights and democracy and building effective public services, donors can play an important and relatively uncontroversial role. This needs to be backed by donors 'putting their house in order' too, addressing domestic policies that create perverse incentives for developing countries or their political elites (Mepham and Lorge 2005; Moore and Unsworth 2006). But where state failure is widespread and the internal demand for governance is poor due to a lack of basic infrastructure and rights, the question of what actions are legitimate on the part of donors is a more complex one.

An historical analogy may be useful here: imagine if Millicent Fawcett, Emmeline Pankhurst and the early suffragettes had been sponsored in their fight for universal suffrage in Britain by the government of another foreign power. Would this have helped their cause, or made it more difficult to garner public and private support? In contemporary development, donors face a similar difficulty. It is useless to pretend that development and governance are not deeply political, yet progressives can feel a very real tension about intervening in foreign countries. The key lies in a detailed understanding of the internal politics of each case.

In future, we will need to think more broadly about the incentives that will really work for developing countries, and what we can realistically offer – based on a real understanding of the causes of poor governance within countries, particularly how to alter the huge incentives available to existing elites. In practice this will mean work to legitimately influence the internal political economy of countries (rather than trying to create incentives ourselves) through increasing transparency, access to information, a free media and opportunities for international trade.

A good example of this approach is the Extractive Industries Transparency Initiative (EITI), which encourages governments to make public the payments they receive from oil, gas and mining companies, and companies to make public the payments they make to governments (DfID 2006a; Moore and Unsworth 2006). This enables people to see how resources are being used, and to check there is no corruption.

So, too, other measures such as enabling a developing country's voice in international negotiations, access to concessional or grant finance, support to build domestic capital markets, securing private investment or offering membership of global groups, should also be part of a progressive approach. We should draw lessons here from the 'long campaign' by the EU to encourage Greece, Portugal and Spain into modern democratic rule in the 1970s, and the Balkans and much of Central Europe in the 1990s (Moore and Unsworth 2006). But when conflict is endemic or state failure severe, more radical action may be necessary and legitimate.

Conflict and state failure: when is progressive intervention legitimate?

The current crisis in Darfur is one of the world's major tragedies. But despite its scale, it is just one example among many that show how damaging conflict can be. Indeed, during the 1990s, half the countries where life expectancy, income and education went backwards had experienced violent conflict (United Nations Millennium Project (UNMP) 2005), and of the 34 countries currently furthest from reaching the MDGs, 22 are in the midst of – or emerging from – violent conflict (ibid.). Although the number of conflicts has fallen in recent years (by 40 per cent since the early 1990s (Human Security Centre (HSC) 2005)), as we look to the future it is possible that mounting pressure on natural resources and energy security through climate change may reverse this trend (DfID 2006a). And as countries free from conflict race ahead of those mired in it, it is also apparent that the world's poor will be increasingly concentrated in fragile, conflict-affected states. By 2010, as many as half the world's poorest people could be living in states that are experiencing or at risk of violent conflict (DfID 2007).

The fundamental question here is one of legitimacy: when is it acceptable for one state to intervene in another's affairs, and when is it feasible to do so? The last two years have seen significant progress on this issue, as the UN has recently endorsed the concept of a 'responsibility to protect' – the idea that sovereign states have a responsibility to protect their own citizens from avoidable catastrophe, but that when they are unwilling or unable to do so, that responsibility must be borne by the broader community of states (International Commission on Intervention and State Sovereignty (ICISS) 2001). This is undoubtedly the right approach: the greatest legitimacy for intervention in a nation state's affairs comes from a multilateral decision.

The challenge for progressives across the world is to ensure that the UN has the political will to put this into practice. And it also requires countries to invest in the necessary capacity to better protect civilians in acute crises – enough troops, police and civilian personnel, with appropriate equipment and the right kind of training – linked to a political strategy for ensuring that people are protected when international forces leave.

We should also focus on preventing conflict occurring in the first place. A progressive response to conflict should be based on three strands: a greater emphasis on preventing violent conflict in the long term by tackling its underlying causes, such as land disputes, and in the short term by supporting local, national and international mechanisms to manage and resolve disputes peacefully; making development work more 'conflict sensitive'; and making our international response to armed conflict more effective by building the capacity of international and regional organizations and civil society to manage conflicts better (DfID 2007).

If, as in Darfur, this requires us to develop imaginative new ways of funding and organizing a military presence, we should rise to this challenge. There is now a strong case for an increased Central Emergency Response Fund (CERF), pooled funds at the country level, a stronger United Nations Office for the Coordination of Humanitarian Affairs (OCHA) and clusters to come together to look like 'one UN' on the humanitarian side. And it is also worth noting that many in the development community are now calling for a standing UN military force to be maintained for rapid deployment. This is an issue that will need to be considered carefully in future.

Security and development

Security is a theme running through many of the chapters in this book, and through much of contemporary progressive thought. It is undoubtedly a long-term challenge, but it needs both a short- and a long-term response. Traditional international development work can in practice do relatively little in the short term; with regard to the longer term, however, development assistance may turn out to be one of the most effective approaches we have at our disposal. Yet somewhat paradoxically, seeing development uniquely as a tool through which to counter security threats may in fact be the least effective way to achieve change.

International terrorism often feeds on an ill-defined sense of global injustice (Halliday 2004; Burke 2003; Weber et al. 2007). As leading counter-insurgency theorists argue, in the current Iraq and Afghanistan insurgencies there is little evidence of those carrying out terrorist activities working towards any clearly defined goals other than disruption – there are no discernible attempts to create permanent liberated areas or replicate state capabilities, for example – and as such these insurgencies can be best understood as states of 'being, not doing' (Kilcullen 2006: 4).

This analysis suggests that security will only be achieved in the end through 'soft' approaches, including disaggregating each terrorist network and avoiding terms that reinforce the conception of terrorism as a global, united movement (ibid.). Economic development and cultural exchange, albeit reinforced by harder responses when necessary in the short term, should be central to our strategy. The Cold War ended, eventually, because of cultural and economic shifts, not because one side outfought the other.

This is why we should be wary of overstating the contribution that development can make to counter-terrorism in the short term. Quick Impact Projects – such as improving roads, distributing food or providing police uniforms in Afghanistan (Hansard 2006) – are undoubtedly important for garnering goodwill, and are effective in their own right, but are no panacea (DfID 2006e). And there is a real danger in seeing development work as a political tool in the short term. The reason we care about international development is not an instrumental one: Britain's development work is, and should continue to be, motivated by a deep-rooted concern for global justice and the belief that we can and will continue to make a difference.

Of course, we must also recognize that the 7/7 London bombings were carried out by British-born Muslims, raising a crucial question about how we communicate with minority groups in the UK about our foreign policy, particularly our development work. Some people might be surprised to learn that we currently support work in more than 30 countries with significant Muslim populations, spending more than £1,000 million in 2004/05 (DFID, 2006c). To take just two examples: in Pakistan, as well as responding to the October 2005 earthquake and continuing to provide support, we have helped over 70,000 women to support their families and increase their incomes, and over 35,000 women to be elected to posts in local councils; and in Bangladesh we are helping to provide 17 million children with free primary education (DfID, 2006d).

Fostering better awareness of development work, particularly among diaspora groups is not easy. But it is one we are starting to take on and must develop further; one which will become more important, not only for security reasons but also because better engagement with those who have strong links to developing countries, through family or other ties, helps us to be more effective in what we do.

Maintaining public support for internationalism

In the end, Britain's development work depends on sustained public support. It may be that 2005 marked a high point of public awareness to which it will be difficult to return: the challenge now is to ensure that what we do in development lives up to public expectations. This is why development awareness is so important; as well as making a difference in the wider world, we have an obligation to report both success and setbacks. This means communicating effectively, addressing people's real and legitimate concerns and making clear the benefits that British development work brings to millions of people around the world in ways that resonate.

Progressives should talk less about money spent, and more about the practical difference aid makes in countries. After all, we all care far more about things changing than about processes. Yet there is a widespread if somewhat understandable reluctance on the part of many of those in the development community to talk about the impact of development work, largely due to worries about measurement and evaluation. It is, after all, far easier to measure how much has been spent on a project, or who it was given to, than to identify how many people it has taken out of poverty or how many lives it has saved. This is particularly true of efforts to improve governance. What donors do is just one part of a complex process and attributing success to any particular activity is fraught with difficulty. But as we look to the future, rigorous evaluation and showing the difference that has been made will become much more important. Social policy in the developed world has undergone a radical transformation in the last decade, partly as a result of technological and statistical advances that have made evaluation much easier (Mulgan 2005).

Development needs to follow in these footsteps, fast, if progressives are to defend our approach to governance and improve our ability to use aid more effectively by learning from past experience. Demonstrating that aid works will become increasingly important over the next decade, as aid volumes rise and public scrutiny increases. And central to this will be responding to what is perhaps the most common public concern: corruption. There is undoubtedly a widespread perception that aid funds are particularly vulnerable to being siphoned off en route to those who need them. We currently take many steps to ensure that our funds are adequately protected and reach those for whom they are intended (DfID 2006a). But in future, closer vigilance and awareness will almost certainly be necessary to ensure public support.

We should also encourage people to support development in their private efforts. One of the most important features of the Make Poverty History campaign was its message that individual action can make a substantial difference. In modern Britain, political participation has expanded to the private realm, and people are expressing their political preferences in many areas of their lives (Dixon and Paxton 2005): buying Fair Trade and switching to green energy suppliers are just two examples of this. People will be more likely to maintain their support for government action if they are also involved in private efforts – the challenge is to link the two effectively. The reward would be not only sustained support for international development, but also deeper roots to progressive politics.

A progressive internationalism for the twenty-first century

The final point I want to make in this chapter is a broader one, concerning the political case for a more progressive internationalism, based more centrally on development. I think that the great global political issue of the twenty-first century will be the battle between nationalism and protectionism, on the one hand, and multilateralism and shaping globalization in our own interests, on the other. The world could go either way in the face of the rapid change we see all around us. Making the case for development – and for all the benefits it brings – is one of the ways we can sustain a multilateral world.

It is clear that the most popular element of Labour's foreign policy has been our international development work and our efforts to prevent conflict around the world. Britons still see Britain as a potential force for good, and, when questioned, the people I talk to have an enormous amount of goodwill for the difference Britain's international development work is making. From climate change to UN reform to fighting for debt cancellation, the British voice is consistently a leading one. So as we look to the future, it seems clear that there is an appetite for a foreign policy that is explicitly centred on development. Placing global justice at the heart of everything we do beyond our shores is not just the moral thing to do, it is also the right thing for the future safety and security of our world.

References

Barry, B. (1973) *The Liberal Theory of Justice*. Oxford: Clarendon Press.
Beitz, C. (2000) *Political Theory and International Relations*. Princeton: Princeton University Press.
Benn, H. (2006a) '5,000 People Lifted Out of Poverty Every Day'. Speech to the Labour Party Annual Conference, Manchester, 27 September.
Benn, H. (2006b) World AIDS Day speech at the London School of Economics, 30 November. London: TSO. Available at <www.dfid.gov.uk/news/files/Speeches/benn-world-aids-day2006-speech.pdf>.
Blair, T. (2006) Comments at launch of Stern Review. London: TSO.
Brown, G. (2007) Speech at the Confederation of Indian Industry, Bangalore, 17 January. London: TSO.
Buchanan, A. (2000) 'Rawls' Law of Peoples: Rules for a Vanished Westphalian World', *Ethics*, 110.
Burall, S. and Maxwell, S., with Rocha Menocal, A. (2006) *Reforming the International Aid Architecture: Options and Ways Forward*. Overseas Development Institute Working Paper No. 278. London: ODI.
Burke, J. (2003) *Al-Qaeda – Casting a Shadow of Terror*. London: I. B. Tauris.
CIA (2005) *World Factbook*: Rank Order – Military Expenditures – Dollar Figure. Available at: <www.cia.gov/cia/publications/factbook/rankorder/2067rank.html>.
Clemens, M., Radelet, S. and Bhavani, R. (2004) *Counting Chickens When They Hatch: The Short-Term Effect of Aid on Growth*. Washington DC: Center for Global Development.
DfID (1997) *Eliminating World Poverty*. London: TSO.
DfID (2006a) *Eliminating World Poverty: Making Governance Work for the Poor*. London: TSO.
DfID (2006b) *G8 Gleneagles One Year On* London: TSO.

DfID (2006c) *DfID's work with Muslim Communities.* Unpublished mimeo. London: DfID.

DfID (2006d) *Quick Facts About DfID's Success.* London: TSO.

DfID (2006e) *Quick Impact Projects: A Handbook for the Military.* London: TSO.

DfID (2007) *Preventing Violent Conflict.* London: TSO.

Dixon, M. and Paxton, W. (2005) 'The State of the Nation: An Audit of Social Injustice', in N. Pearce and W. Paxton (eds), *Social Justice: Building a Fairer Britain.* London: ippr/Politico's.

Djankov, S., McLeish, C. and Ramlho, C. (2005). *Regulation and Growth.* Washington DC: World Bank.

DoD (2007) *National Defense Budget Estimates for FY 2007.* Available at <www.dod. mil/comptroller/defbudget/fy2007/fy2007_greenbook.pdf>.

Easterly, W. (2006) *The White Man's Burden: Why the West's Efforts to Aid the Rest Have Done So Much Ill and So Little Good.* New York: Penguin.

FCO (2006) *Active Diplomacy for a Changing World: The UK's International Priorities.* London: TSO.

Foster, M. and Killick, T. (2006) *What Would Doubling Aid Do for Macroeconomic Management in Africa?* Briefing Paper. London: Overseas Development Institute, April.

Giddens, A. (1990) *The Consequences of Modernity.* Cambridge: Polity Press.

Halliday, F. (2004) *Terrorism in Historical Perspective*, OpenDemocracy.net.

Hansard (2006) *Supporting Documentation: Summary of UK Funded Quick Impact Projects in Helmand Province.* 1 November: Column 513W. London: TSO.

Held, D. (2004) *Global Covenant: The Social Democratic Alternative to the Washington Consensus.* Cambridge: Polity Press.

Held, D. (2006) 'Reframing Global Governance: Apocalypse Soon or Reform!', *New Political Economy*, 11 (2), June.

HSC (2005) *Human Security Report: War and Peace in the 21st Century.* Oxford: Oxford University Press.

ICISS (2001) *The Responsibility to Protect: Report of the International Commission on Intervention and State Sovereignty.* Ottawa: International Development Research Centre.

IMF (2006) *World Economic Outlook Database.* New York: IMF.

Kaul, I. and Conceicao, P. (2006) *The New Public Finance: Responding to Global Challenges.* New York: Oxford University Press.

Kauffman, D. (2004) 'Human Rights and Governance: The Empirical Challenge'. Unpublished mimeo. Washington DC: World Bank Institute.

Kilcullen, D. (2006) 'Counterinsurgency Redux', *Survival*, winter. London: Institute of Strategic Studies.

Klein, M. and Harford, T. (2005) *The Market for Aid.* Washington DC: World Bank.

Make Poverty History (2006) *2005: The Year of Make Poverty History.* London: Make Poverty History.

Maxwell, S. (2005). *The Washington Consensus is dead! Long Live the Meta-narrative!* Overseas Development Institute Working Paper No. 243. London: ODI. Available at <www.odi.org.uk/publications/working_papers/wp243.pdf>.

Maxwell, S. (2006) *What's Next in International Development? Perspectives from the 20% Club and the 0.2% Club.* Overseas Development Institute Working Paper No. 270. London: ODI. Available at <www.odi.org.uk/publications/working_ papers/wp270.pdf>.

McLeod, D. (2005) 'Review of Drivers of Change Country Study Reports'. Unpublished mimeo. London: DfID.

Mepham, D. (2005) 'Social Justice in a Shrinking World', in N. Pearce and W. Paxton (eds), *Social Justice: Building a Fairer Britain*. London: ippr/Politico's.

Mepham, D. and Lorge, J. (2005) *Putting our House in Order: Recasting G8 Policy towards Africa*. London: ippr.

Messner, D. and Humphrey, J. (2006) 'China and India in the Global Governance Arena', *IDS Bulletin*, 37 (1): 107–14.

Miller, D. (2000) *Citizenship and National Identity*. Cambridge: Polity Press.

Miller, D. (2005) 'What is Social Justice?', in N. Pearce and W. Paxton (eds), *Social Justice: Building a Fairer Britain*. London: ippr/Politico's.

Moore, M. and Unsworth, S. (2006) 'Book Review Article. Britain's New White Paper: Making Governance Work for the Poor', *Development Policy Review*, 2006, 24 (6): 707–15.

Mulgan, G. (2005) 'Going With and Against the Grain: Social Policy in Practice since 1997', in N. Pearce and W. Paxton (eds), *Social Justice: Building a Fairer Britain*. London: ippr/Politico's.

OECD (2005) *Paris Declaration on Aid Effectiveness: Ownership, Harmonisation, Alignment, Results and Mutual Accountability*. Paris: OECD. Available at <www.oecd.org/dataoecd/11/41/34428351.pdf>.

OECD (2006) *Net ODA from DAC countries from 1950 to 2005*. Paris: OECD. Available at <www.oecd.org/dataoecd/43/24/1894385.xls>.

Pearce, N. and Paxton, W. (eds) (2005) *Social Justice: Building a Fairer Britain*. London: ippr/Politico's.

Pogge, T. (2002) *World Poverty and Human Rights: Cosmopolitan Responsibilities and Reforms*. Cambridge: Polity Press.

Rawls, J. (1971) *A Theory of Justice*. Oxford: Oxford University Press.

Rawls, J. (1999) *The Law of Peoples*. Cambridge, Mass.: Harvard University Press.

Rocha Menocal, A. and Rogerson, A. (2006) *Which Way the Future of Aid? Southern Civil Society Perspectives on Current Debates on Reform to the International Aid System*. Overseas Development Institute Working Paper No. 259. London: ODI, January.

Rogerson, A. (2005) 'Aid Harmonisation and Alignment: Bridging the Gap Between Reality and the Paris Reform Agenda', *Development Policy Review*, 23 (5): 531–52.

Sen, A. (1999) *Development as Freedom*. Oxford: Oxford University Press.

Shafik, N. (2006) 'Summer Reflections on the Role of Aid in an Increasingly Complex World'. Unpublished mimeo.

Singer, P. (2002) *One World: The Ethics of Globalisation*. Princeton: Yale University Press.

Stern, N. (2006) *The Economics of Climate Change*. London: TSO.

UN (2003) *World Urbanisation Prospects, the 2003 Revision*. New York: UN. Available at <www.un.org/esa/population/publications/wup2003/2003WUPHighlights.pdf>.

UNCTAD (2005) *Trade and Development Report 2005: New Features of Global Inter-dependence*. New York: UNCTAD.

UNDP (2005) *Human Development Report 2005*. New York: UNDP.

UNESCO (2006) *Education for All Global Monitoring Report*. Paris: UNESCO.

UNMP (2005) *Investing in Development: A Practical Plan to Achieve the Millennium Development Goals.* New York: UNMP.

Vizard, P. (2001) *Economic Theory, Freedom and Human Rights: The Work of Amartya Sen.* London: ODI.

Walzer, M. (1983) *Spheres of Justice.* London: Martin Robinson.

Weber, S., Barma, N., Kroenig, M. and Ratner, E. (2007) 'How Globalization Went Bad', *Foreign Policy*, January/February.

Wild, L. and Mepham, D. (eds) (2006) *The New Sinosphere: China in Africa.* London: ippr.

Woods, N. (2006) *Global Economic Governance.* London: ippr.

World Bank (2003) *Breaking the Conflict Trap – Civil War and Development Policy.* Washington DC: World Bank.

World Bank (2006a) *Global Economic Prospects: Economic Implications of Remittances and Migration.* Washington DC: World Bank.

World Bank (2006b) *Global Development Finance 2006: The Development Potential of Surging Capital Flows.* Washington DC: World Bank.

World Bank (2007) *Global Economic Prospects 2007: Managing the Next Wave of Globalization.* Washington DC: World Bank. Available at <www-wds.worldbank.org/external/default/WDSContentServer/IW3P/IB/2006/12/06/000112742_20061206155022/Rendered/PDF/381400GEP2007.pdf>.

18
Securing the Future

Sadiq Khan and Leni Wild

After a decade of Labour government, there is a pressing need to re-examine and refresh the UK's approach to international security policy: to identify how the global security environment is changing and the new security challenges this creates for the UK. This chapter focuses on four particular challenges. First, there is the issue of terrorism, a subject that has been at the very top of the international political agenda since 11 September 2001, and whose salience was dramatically and tragically reinforced for Britons by the 7 July 2005 bombings in London. Second, there is the threat posed by the proliferation of weapons of mass destruction (WMD), particularly in the hands of unstable regimes or terrorist groups. We also address briefly the proliferation of conventional weapons and conventional arms control. Third, the chapter addresses the UK's involvement in major international military operations in Iraq and Afghanistan and considers the options available to the UK in each case. Fourth, there is a set of issues about when, where and how the UK should intervene in other countries to help prevent war crimes or massive human rights violations – what has become known as the 'responsibility to protect' agenda. There is one hugely important security issue – climate change – that is not considered in detail in this chapter. This is because the issue is addressed so comprehensively by David Miliband in Chapter 16.

In the four areas identified, the chapter will touch on some features of UK policy over the last decade, looking at those aspects of the government's approach that have been effective and progressive, as well as other instances in which UK policy has been much less so. Important lessons can be learnt from the successes and failures of recent foreign policy decisions. But the main focus here is forward-looking: to outline feasible policy responses to these security challenges, consistent with a commitment to progressive values. The chapter also addresses ways to strengthen multilateralism and how to make UK decision-making on security policy more accountable, legitimate and coherent.

The changing global security environment

It is important to start by reflecting on the changing global security context and what that implies for the future of UK security policy. Traditionally, security threats to a country like the UK were seen to emanate from other states – the Soviet Union, for example, during the period of the Cold War. Large and militarily capable states are still significant players in the international system. While Russia and China do not appear to pose any immediate threat to the UK or its allies, it is not inconceivable that they might do so at some point in the future, depending on how they develop over coming years and decades. But an approach to security policy that focuses purely on a traditional understanding of power is no longer adequate. This is because the concept of power itself is much more complex and multidimensional than previously recognized. If by power we mean the ability to shape the outcomes we want, then there are clearly several aspects to this. Power encompasses military force and economic strength, but also what the American political scientist Joseph Nye has called 'soft power' – getting others to do what we want because of the attractiveness of our economic and social systems or our values (Nye 2004). These softer forms of power have acquired growing importance in a world where the technological, information and communications revolutions are dispersing power away from states while at the same time empowering individuals and sub-national groups to play a larger role in global politics (ibid.).

The traditional approach to security policy was also oriented around dealing only or primarily with 'threats deliberately directed by a human hand' (Ikenberry and Slaughter 2006). But in a world that is simultaneously more interdependent and fragmented than ever before, countries face major new threats that are the outcomes of complex processes rather than being directed at us by a hostile state. These include climate change, resource scarcity, the spread of infectious disease, the risk of nuclear accidents and HIV/AIDS. These issues may be relatively new ones for the international security agenda, but they can hardly be dismissed as secondary concerns. For example, more people have now died from HIV/AIDS since the early 1980s than have been killed in all the world's armed conflicts since 1945 (Heinecken 2001). And although hard to calculate with precision, vast numbers of people have also died, and will die in the future, as a consequence of the droughts, desertification, hurricanes, floods and water scarcity that are some of the consequences of global climate change (Gore 2006).

Interdependence also blurs the distinction between domestic and global security threats. The young men responsible for the terrorist bombings in London in July 2005 were not foreigners but British citizens, although their extremist beliefs and actions were influenced by global and not merely national ideas and events. Similarly, health pandemics like SARS (severe acute respiratory syndrome), the drugs trade, international criminal gangs and environmental threats like climate change do not respect territorial boundaries. Both national action and international cooperation are required to help tackle them.

There are two broad conclusions that progressives should draw from this brief analysis. First, when thinking about security, we should be as or more concerned about the safety of people living within states as we are about the security of the state itself from external attack. This is known as a 'human security' approach, as opposed to a more traditional state-centred approach to security (Axworthy 2003). Second, achieving this more comprehensive concept of security has far-reaching implications for the way we seek to advance security objectives and the balance between military force and other policy instruments in trying to do so (Commission on Human Security 2003; Barcelona Report 2004; Clarke 2007). These points will be illustrated throughout this chapter.

Tackling terrorism

The threat posed to UK citizens by terrorist groups is a very real one. The attacks in London in July 2005 killed more than 50 people and injured hundreds more. A number of other attempts to carry out atrocities in the UK over the last two years have been foiled. Dealing with this threat obviously requires highly effective policing and intelligence policies. But by themselves these responses are unlikely to be sufficient. It is important to see action against terrorism in a wider context.

In recent years, the UK has linked its anti-terrorism policies – and its foreign policy more generally – far too closely to that of the Bush administration, including to the US's so-called 'war on terror'. Under this slogan, the US has introduced sweeping new restrictions on civil liberties and detained thousands of 'terrorist suspects' without access to lawyers or the prospect of a fair trial, in clear violation of international humanitarian law and the Geneva Conventions. It is estimated that since 11 September 2001, some 100,000 people have been detained without trial, primarily but not exclusively in Afghanistan and Iraq (Rogers 2006). There is further evidence that some of the individuals detained in this way have been tortured and subject to other forms of cruel and inhumane punishment (Brody 2006). Another dimension to this policy has been the practice of extraordinary rendition: the process of detaining and transferring terrorist suspects to third countries, beyond the reach of normal legal processes and safeguards, for the purposes of interrogation. Some of these individuals have been transferred via UK airports, although the UK government has been reluctant to acknowledge this or to condemn this totally illegal practice (Mepham 2006).

Not only have these policies led to human rights abuses for the individuals concerned, weakened the moral credibility of the US (and its UK ally) and damaged the international norm against the use of torture, they have also increased hostility towards the West, particularly among parts of the Islamic world. Indeed, over the last six years, terrorist incidents have gone up, not down (Rogers 2006). Al-Qaeda or like-minded individuals and groups have perpetrated at least 30 major attacks over this period: they include Karachi and Sinai (three times each), Bali, Jakarta and Istanbul (twice each), Islamabad, London, Madrid, Riyadh, Tunis, Casablanca and Mombasa (ibid.).

A progressive UK government should be advocating a more comprehensive and nuanced approach to reduce the risks of terrorism. In the UK, strategies for countering terrorism should work with, and avoid alienating, the very communities whose cooperation is so essential to defeat the terrorist threat (Omand 2006). It is important, for example, that policing in areas with a significant Muslim community should be fair and be seen to be fair, and avoid creating an environment in which all British Muslims are treated with suspicion or are stereotyped – a danger highlighted by the UK's most senior Muslim police officer, Assistant Commissioner Tariq Ghaffur (cited in Blick et al. 2006).

The UK should ensure that its policies to address terrorism are consistent with international human rights standards. While we recognize that it may be necessary for UK citizens to accept some reduction in their privacy in particular circumstances, surveillance for anti-terrorism purposes should take place within a robust legal and human rights framework and with adequate accountability and oversight of the security and intelligence agencies (Joint Committee on Human Rights 2006). Internationally, there should be greater emphasis on enhanced cooperation between governments, police forces and intelligence agencies to detect and apprehend terrorist suspects, and a more vigorous effort to curb their access to sources of finance: money that is used to sustain their terrorist networks and operations (Brown 2006).

Nationally and globally, there needs to be a much more sophisticated and sustained attempt to understand the motivations of those who carry out these actions and the national and global factors that contribute to religious and political extremism. Contemporary jihadism should not be seen primarily in cultural or religious terms (Roy 2004; Kepel 2004). On the contrary, it is more accurately understood as a product of what the French writer Olivier Roy calls 'deterritorialized' Islam, 'in which individual Muslims find themselves cut off from authentic local traditions, often as uprooted minorities in non-Muslim lands' (Roy 2004). This explains why so many 'jihadists' have not come from the Middle East but have rather been raised (like the 9/11 conspirator Mohammed Atta) in Western Europe. The long-term problem is thus 'one of better integrating people who are already in the West, and doing so in a way that does not undermine the trust and tolerance on which democratic societies depend' (Fukuyama 2006). Any strategy will need to look much more closely at the process of radicalization within the UK and abroad. This could include for example, examining the trigger factors that contribute to radicalization, and possible government or community-level responses to them. While this strays beyond the remit of this chapter, there are also issues here about education and the role of radical preachers.

However, there is also a foreign policy dimension to the growth of extremist Muslim forces within the UK. A leaked letter from Michael Jay, the then Permanent Under-Secretary at the Foreign Office, stated that UK foreign policy was a 'recurring theme' in the Muslim community, 'especially in the context of the Middle East peace process and Iraq'. The letter continued: 'this seems to be a key driver behind recruitment by extremist organizations' (Campbell and Aglionby 2005). US intelligence agencies have further highlighted the radicalizing consequences of the Iraq war and the 'war on terror'. To draw attention to this is emphatically not to excuse terrorism; it is to understand the factors that fuel extremism and how to reduce the vulnerability of the UK and other countries over coming years. To give one concrete example of what we mean, progress towards a resolution of the Israeli-Palestinian question could help to eliminate one important source of hostility towards the West in parts of the Islamic world. An equitable two-state solution to this conflict would be right in its own terms, but it could also prevent Islamic extremists from misusing the Palestinian cause to garner support for their own more radical agendas in the future.

As Hilary Benn argues in Chapter 17, terrorism often feeds on an ill-defined sense of global injustice. International action to help tackle real injustice – poverty, inequality, repression and human rights abuses – will have little impact on the die-hard fanatics that run al-Qaeda and associated movements. However, it could help to reduce the appeal of extremist movements to others who may be susceptible to them. Building on its considerable achievements in this area over the last decade, the UK should continue to work for a strengthened global effort to combat poverty, repression and injustice, alongside support for state-building and good governance. Increased resources should be allocated to these efforts. This will not be a short-term panacea for addressing terrorism, but it should be part of a longer-term strategy for creating conditions in which moderate politics and liberal values are more likely to thrive (Mepham 2006).

Preventing proliferation

A second critical focus for UK security policy should be the issue of nuclear, chemical and biological weapons proliferation. In recent years, India and Pakistan have both become declared nuclear weapon states. Israel is also known to possess nuclear weapons, though it refuses to formally confirm this. The other five states with nuclear weapons capabilities are the US, Russia, China, the UK and France. North Korea is also believed to have developed a nuclear weapons capability, though it is unclear how advanced this programme really is and it remains the subject of international negotiations (see below). And there is a tense standoff between the international community and Iran about its nuclear ambitions. In addition, there is the fear that terrorist groups might soon be able to obtain and use chemical, biological or nuclear weapons or threaten to do so in order to secure particular political objectives.

A progressive UK government should commit to strengthening the international non-proliferation regime, including by providing additional resources to the International Atomic Energy Agency (IAEA), and working to enhance the Chemical Weapons Convention (CWC) and the Biological and Toxin Weapons Convention (BTWC). It should also advocate intensified dialogue with countries like North Korea and Iran.

In the case of North Korea, diplomacy appears to have secured something of a breakthrough. At the time of writing (early 2007), North Korea has taken a first step towards eventual disarmament by promising to shut down its nuclear reactor at Yongbyon and to readmit international inspectors from the IAEA, in return for millions of dollars worth of aid.

This was the outcome of six-party talks involving both North and South Korea, the US, Japan, Russia and China. While the nature of the North Korean regime raises legitimate concerns about its adherence to the terms of this agreement (it has reneged on agreements before), this nevertheless represents an important advance for multilateral diplomacy and creates the prospect of North Korea's denuclearization. The alternatives – military action against North Korea or punitive economic sanctions that might have brought about the implosion of the regime – were certainly much higher risk and no more likely to be successful.

By contrast, there is growing international alarm about Iran's nuclear ambitions and the response that this might trigger on the part of the US and Israel. Three years of talks between the EU3 – Britain, France and Germany – and the Iranians have come to nothing, and selective UN sanctions have been imposed because of Tehran's non-compliance with the IAEA. These sanctions are likely to be intensified because of Tehran's refusal to meet a UN Security Council demand that it suspend its enrichment of uranium.

In recent months, senior figures in Washington and Tel Aviv have openly speculated about a military attack on Iran to prevent its acquisition of a nuclear bomb. While serious political pressure is required to try to deny Iran a nuclear capability, a progressive UK government should use all of its diplomatic influence to help dissuade the US and the Israelis from embarking on such a reckless course. A military strike on Iran would be unlikely to end Iran's nuclear programme (given the steps the Iranians will have taken to conceal it). By strengthening hardliners in the regime, and rallying Iranian public opinion behind their government, it may actually intensify Iran's efforts to acquire the bomb. It could also be a stimulus to nuclear proliferation across the region as a whole, with countries like Saudi Arabia, Egypt and Turkey seeking to obtain a nuclear capability. A military strike would massively destabilize the region, destroying any remote prospect of the Iranians cooperating with the US and the UK on policy towards Afghanistan and Iraq. Moreover, the Iranians would be well-placed to hit back at the US and Israel, through support for Hizbollah in Lebanon and Hamas in the Palestinian Territories.

What is the alternative? There are no easy answers here, but it may be that some kind of 'grand bargain' is required, in which the Iranians commit not to acquire nuclear weapons if the US promises not to attempt to bring down the regime, linked to agreements on trade and investment (Mepham 2007). Economic sanctions may have a part to play in shifting Iranian calculations, but direct US-Iranian talks remain the key to this. From the Western side, the Iranians should be expected to end their inflammatory statements about Israel (Supreme Leader Ali Khamenei already appears to have taken steps to rein in President Mahmoud Ahmadinejad), and halt its destabilizing activities in Iraq and Lebanon. A progressive UK government should be advocating precisely this kind of approach.

But where does all this leave UK policy on nuclear weapons? The UK has had a nuclear capability for the last half-century. During this time the world has changed dramatically, as has the original context in which the nuclear bomb was acquired. Since 1997, the government has taken steps to reduce the UK's nuclear arsenal. The UK now has the smallest stockpile of nuclear warheads among the recognized nuclear states; it is the only country to have reduced to a single deterrent system, and it has proposed a further 20 per cent reduction in the number of operationally available warheads over the next few years. This would reduce this stockpile to no more than 160 (see Blair 2006). While this capability is unlikely to deter terrorist groups, the government suggests that it may influence the actions of governments that might sponsor terrorists and that it serves as a general 'insurance policy' in an unstable and insecure global environment (Browne 2007).

A progressive UK government should honour its obligations under the Nuclear Non-Proliferation Treaty (NPT) regime, which requires existing nuclear powers to further reduce the size of their own nuclear arsenals at the same time as it obliges non-nuclear powers to refrain from acquiring a nuclear capability. And it should do much more to address the problem of 'loose nukes' – nuclear materials that are subject to inadequate controls and which might be transferred illicitly to terrorist groups.

In this context, it is worth highlighting some issues relating to conventional arms control. Over the last decade, the UK has taken steps to tighten UK controls over conventional weapons transfers, including small arms. But the UK still licenses military equipment to states that are listed as 'major areas of concern' in the Foreign and Commonwealth Office's annual report on human rights. This includes Saudi Arabia, Columbia and Russia. Although we recognize that there is a legitimate arms trade, we believe that there should be a presumption to deny arms export licences for countries that violate human rights on a large scale (Mepham and Lorge 2005). Progressives should also campaign for the establishment of an International Arms Trade Treaty, setting high common standards governing arms transfers, as well as tighter controls over arms brokers and traffickers.

There is an important and related discussion on the types of weapons that it should be legally permissible to export and use. The Ottawa

Convention of 1997 was an international agreement to ban the use of anti-personnel land mines – and the 1997 Labour government was a strong supporter of the Convention. But landmines are not the only weapons that cause exceptional suffering to innocent civilians. Cluster munitions also fall into this category. These are air-dropped or ground-launched shells that eject multiple small submunitions (Goose 2006). Various international non-governmental organizations (NGOs) as well as the United Nations have called for cluster bombs to be outlawed. We argue that the UK should show international leadership in ending UK use of these weapons and pushing for an international agreement to limit and ultimately outlaw their use altogether.

Next steps in Afghanistan and Iraq

The UK is currently involved in major military operations in Afghanistan and Iraq, alongside the US and a number of other states. Policy towards these two countries will continue to constitute huge security priorities for the UK over the next few years. The UK currently has around 6,000 troops in Afghanistan, the vast majority of them in Helmand province in the south of the country, serving as part of a North Atlantic Treaty Organization (NATO) mission. In Iraq, UK troop numbers are set to fall to around 5,000 by the end of May 2007.

Following the 9/11 attacks on the US, the international intervention in Afghanistan (whose government, the Taliban, was providing sanctuary to al-Qaeda) commanded widespread international support and was generally seen as internationally legal and legitimate. It hardly needs to be said that US-UK military action in Iraq was much more controversial and divisive, with many more people – in the UK and internationally – disputing the legality and wisdom of this intervention. Again, as is well-known, the Iraq war has hugely damaged the credibility and international standing of the UK government, particularly in the Middle East and the wider Islamic world, but also more broadly.

However, our aim here is not to rehash the arguments of the past. Major mistakes have been made in respect of both countries, particularly Iraq. But we do not conclude from this that the UK or the wider international community should simply walk away. Opponents and supporters of military action in both cases should be able to agree that the UK has a moral duty and a strategic interest in helping Afghanistan from falling once more into the hands of the Taliban and also in helping to stabilize Iraq.

In the case of Afghanistan, while the Taliban government was deposed very quickly in 2001, establishing effective government across the country has been much more difficult. Although much of the country is relatively peaceful and despite progress with reconstruction and development in the north and west of Afghanistan, there has been a serious worsening of the security situation in the south and the south east, with a resurgent Taliban carrying out suicide bombings, assassinations and other forms of violence on an almost daily basis.

Progress here will require a revised international response including additional troops for the south, but also a new focus on the wider political context. By itself, military force will not deliver a stable government in Afghanistan that commands sufficient public support. Indeed, heavy-handed US-led counter-insurgency operations and the civilian casualties they create may even help the Taliban to attract new recruits. Alongside a more discriminate military strategy, there needs to be greater investment in infrastructure and the creation of livelihood opportunities for ordinary Afghans (Grono and Nathan 2006). This should be complemented by a greater international focus on supporting the rule of law in Afghanistan and the building up of government capacity, as well as action to better protect human rights.

A new approach is required in Iraq too. While there are no good options left, it is very clear that the continuation of the US's current strategy is a recipe for disaster. This was the central message of the Iraq Study Group, whose main recommendations are broadly sensible and offer a possible way forward for Iraq (Iraq Study Group 2006). Although UK ministers warmly welcomed this report (suggesting that its approach was close to the government's own thinking), the Bush administration has largely dismissed the report's proposals, including the suggestion that the US open a dialogue with Iran and Syria in an attempt to help stabilize Iraq.

A progressive UK government should be making two core arguments in relation to Iraq. First, there is no military solution to the problems facing the country. In the right circumstances, international forces can play a role in helping the Iraqi army and police to ensure greater stability in the country – and withdrawing those forces overnight might make things worse not better. But to suggest that the Iraqi government can defeat the insurgency through a stepped-up military campaign is fanciful (International Crisis Group 2006). Second, and by implication, there needs to be a more concerted international effort, one that involves key regional states, to reach a new political accommodation between Iraq's various communities. This accommodation will necessarily have to revisit the country's constitution, whose provisions are regarded as profoundly unfair by many of Iraq's Sunni community. It will also need to reach agreements on the distribution of revenues from oil, gas and other natural resources, and a deal on the nature of Iraq's federal system.

Furthermore, at a later stage, the UK policy community should conduct a far wider discussion on the policy and practical mistakes surrounding the Iraq conflict. One option would be to establish an Iraq Study Group-style panel for the UK, to bring together policy experts and academics as well as practitioners from the field (but this would be retrospective and not forward-looking). This Group would not be a formal inquiry as such, but would present a forum for lesson-learning and policy analysis. Another option would be to establish a more formal inquiry, along the lines of the Franks Committee of Privy Counsellors which looked at the Falklands conflict. However, the mandate of such a committee would need to be clearly defined to limit its investigation to UK policy on Iraq (it could not, for example, assess US policy decisions). Whatever format was adopted, timing would be crucial, as it would clearly be difficult to assess policy decisions if operations were ongoing.

The responsibility to protect

A fourth critical area of UK security policy is when, where and how the UK should intervene in cases of war crimes or gross human rights abuses overseas. There is clearly a link here between this debate and the previous discussion on interventions in Afghanistan and Iraq, although in neither case were humanitarian concerns the primary reason for intervention. Despite this, there are some generic lessons about international interventions that can be drawn from the Iraq and Afghanistan cases that have relevance to interventions undertaken for more explicitly humanitarian purposes.

The best single attempt to address this issue has come in the work of the International Commission on Intervention and State Sovereignty (ICISS), whose influential report, *The Responsibility to Protect*, was published in 2001. ICISS has sought to reconceptualize the notion of sovereignty, arguing that this is no longer unconditional but rather dependent on countries' upholding various responsibilities, not least to protect their own people 'from avoidable catastrophe – from mass murder, rape, starvation' (ibid.). Where states are unable or unwilling to discharge this duty, ICISS has suggested that this responsibility must be borne by the wider community of states (ibid.).

The Commission has suggested that the responsibility to protect embraces three specific responsibilities. First, there is a 'responsibility to prevent' ... to address 'both the root causes and direct causes of internal conflict and man-made crises' which put populations at risk. Second, there is a 'responsibility to react' ... to respond to 'situations of compelling human need with appropriate measures ... including in extreme cases military intervention'. Third, there is a 'responsibility to rebuild' ... to provide, particularly after a military intervention, 'full assistance with recovery, reconstruction and reconciliation, addressing the causes of the humanitarian crisis the intervention was designed to halt or avert' (ibid.).

The Commission was right to say that 'prevention is the single most important dimension of the responsibility to protect' (ibid.). There are obvious benefits in reduced human suffering, if conflict can be defused at an early stage. Conflict prevention is also cost-effective (Carnegie Commission1997). This reinforces the argument made earlier in this chapter that increased investment is needed in so-called 'soft' forms of security policy, such as development, support for good governance, human rights and the rule of law. Such investment can significantly reduce the risks of armed conflict (ibid.).

But while prevention is always preferable, there will be exceptional cases where military intervention is necessary. The cases of Rwanda in 1994 and Sierra Leone in 2000 are obvious examples. We also believe that only a properly mandated and authorized international force will be capable of ending the appalling atrocities that continue to be carried out in Darfur (Mepham and Ramsbotham 2006).

The Commission has suggested that all of the relevant criteria for judging the appropriateness of military intervention can be summed up in six criteria: right authority, just cause, right intention, last resort, proportional means and reasonable prospects (ICISS 2001). If military intervention is to be justified as a response to massive human rights violations, it is essential that this action be lawful and legitimate. But even where appropriate international legal authority has been granted, an intervention could be counter-productive if military force is used disproportionately and indiscriminately, leading to substantial civilian casualties. Before an intervention is undertaken for humanitarian reasons, it is therefore critical to consider very carefully the last of the ICISS criteria: that of reasonable prospects. Governments have many policy instruments for pressuring rights-abusing states to curb or end their abuses. The ultimate option of military force may be justified, but it should not be used if it would cause more human suffering than it would be likely to alleviate.

As a champion of this agenda internationally, the UK needs to think more profoundly about the 'how' of intervention, looking at issues around mandates, rules of engagement, training, and the relationship between the military and civilians (Holt and Berkman 2006; Mepham and Ramsbotham 2006). It is also essential to think through what follows an international intervention. The international community needs to provide much greater support for political processes and peace-building initiatives in the countries concerned, so that over time, civilian protection can be guaranteed without an external security presence.

Strengthening multilateralism

In each of these four areas, a progressive UK government should be advancing fresh thinking along the lines suggested here. But in almost none of these cases can the UK's security interest be pursued wholly independently. On the contrary, in a globalized world the pursuit of the UK's interests will invariably require working closely with other states, and stronger global institutions, to tackle the great majority of security issues that impact beyond the boundaries of the nation state.

The UK's closest security relationship is with the US. While any UK government will want a constructive relationship with the Americans (regardless of who occupies the White House), many believe the UK has been greatly damaged by the closeness of its relationship with the Bush administration. Nor is it obvious that this fealty to the US has brought much by way of tangible benefits for UK security. It may have made the UK less, not more, secure. In the coming years, we suggest that the UK government should be prepared to adopt a less uncritical approach to US policy, and be ready to disagree more frequently where US policy is damaging to UK security interests or contrary to progressive values (Gamble and Kearns 2007). This is not about picking fights with the US or rupturing relations with it. On the contrary, it is about revising the terms of that relationship in a way that works better for the UK.

A progressive UK government should also be championing more effective common positions within the EU on foreign policy. This does not mean a single EU foreign policy on all issues, nor should it ignore the important differences that may exist between the UK and other member states of the EU. But the UK and others in the EU often share similar interests regarding the major global challenges and the UK can potentially achieve more by acting through the Union than on its own; for example, towards China, Russia or the Middle East (Grant 2007).

There is an important ongoing role for NATO, too. The NATO mission in Afghanistan is a crucial test. Failure there would raise serious question marks about the viability of the Alliance. Success in helping to stabilize the country would send a powerful signal of the enduring value of NATO in the projection of security beyond the borders of its member states. A progressive UK government should strongly support such a role.

In addition, a commitment to strengthened international cooperation and effective multilateralism requires a deeper process of engagement with emerging powers, like China, India, Brazil and South Africa. As Gordon Brown highlighted in a speech in India in January 2007, 'The post 1945 system of international relations is not yet broken, but it is urgently in need of modernization and reform' (Brown 2007). One small but important step might be to enlarge the G8 grouping of countries, so that these new powers become members of it.

The debate about the future of multilateralism is too often reduced to an exclusive discussion about UN reform. Progressives are rightly committed to a strengthened and reinvigorated United Nations, with an overhauled Security Council, and a stronger UN role in relation to human rights, development, the environment and peace and security. But we also recognize that multilateral governance is broader than this. As Francis Fukuyama has argued:

> There is a great deal of global governance in the world today that exists outside the orbit of the United Nations and its allied agencies; everything from bank settlements to communications protocols to safety standards to internet domain names is set by new and often complex institutions that escape traditional definitions of international cooperation. (Fukuyama 2006)

A progressive UK government should welcome this diversity of global bodies and institutions, rather than imagining that a single institution is appropriate for dealing with all of the world's problems. At the same time, it should work to ensure that global bodies are more open, transparent, accountable and representative, and that poorer countries in particular have a more significant say in how they function (Woods 2006). These more accountable and effective global institutions also need to be complemented by a strengthening of the international rule of law (Held 2007).

Security policy and public accountability

Advancing the kind of security agenda outlined here has implications for the way in which the UK government makes its security policy. There are three particular aspects to this that we address here: accountability to Parliament, legitimacy and public support for security policy, and policy coherence.

If Parliament is to be given a more significant role in relation to security policy – something that we support – then there will need to be reforms to the 'Royal prerogative' powers. The historical evolution of these powers has meant that the UK government does not require permission from Parliament to declare war or sign treaties. Traditionally, UK governments have justified the use of the Royal prerogative by arguing that ministers are held to account in Parliament through the doctrines of collective and individual responsibility. We believe that this argument is no longer tenable. As it stands, the system of ministerial accountability to Parliament is simply too broad and retrospective to ensure parliamentary accountability over the executive (Burall et al. 2006).

Arguably, the vote on the Iraq war in 2003 set a precedent. Gordon Brown has indicated that 'while there must be scope for emergency action, it is right that, in future, Parliament, not the executive, should make the final decisions on matters as important as peace and war' (Brown 2006). Enshrining this principle in statute would be an important step, but we would go further. The UK Parliament and relevant Select Committees should be given an enhanced role in scrutinizing the nation's security policy, particularly international operations involving British troops (Wild and Williams 2007).

We also believe that it is important that UK security policy should be legitimate and, so far as possible, command public support. Progressives should favour and help to foster greater public debate on major security issues, not just in Parliament but across society as a whole. One small but significant way of doing this would be to encourage more discussion of these issues within schools (see Khan 2006). More broadly, it is important to help build a greater public consensus about the UK's security interests and priorities, and that should involve drawing on the expertise of think tanks, universities, NGOs and others. (An ippr Commission on National Security in the 21st Century, chaired by George Robertson and Paddy Ashdown, began work on producing a comprehensive UK national security strategy in April 2007. It is expected to produce its final report in early 2009.)

UK security policy should also be more coherent. Conflicts between departmental objectives are a common occurrence. But unless this process is managed effectively it can lead to highly inconsistent policies being pursued by the UK government as a whole. A positive attempt to join up policy across departments emerged in 2001 with the establishment of the Conflict Prevention Pools. The Pools are jointly run by the Foreign Office, the Ministry of Defence and the Department for International Development, and aim to enhance the UK's contribution to conflict prevention and management – in Africa specifically, but also in the rest of the world. Although an important step forward, the Pools have been criticized as lacking sufficient resources and effective procedures for ensuring consensual outcomes and effective policy-making (see Austin et al. 2003). It is too early to say whether the UK Post-Conflict Reconstruction Unit (established at the end of 2004) will surmount these barriers more effectively, though it has a remit to do so. Cross-departmental initiatives of this kind should be promoted strongly to help ensure a more holistic approach to policy-making on international security issues by the UK.

Conclusion

In this chapter we have assessed the changing global security environment and what this means for UK security policy. We have also identified four priorities for UK policy and suggested how a progressive UK government should try to deal with them. We have also made recommendations for strengthening multilateral institutions and reforming UK policy-making on security issues. By adopting a more multidimensional and coherent approach to security, and by working with others and through global institutions, a progressive UK government would be better-placed to enhance the security of British citizens and to help contribute towards a more stable and secure world over the next decade.

Acknowledgements

The authors would like to thank Nur Laiq for her useful background research for this chapter, and Alan Hunt, Julia Margo, David Mepham, Greg Power, Andrew Puddephatt and Paul Williams for their comments on earlier drafts.

References

Austin, G., Brusset, E., Chalmers, M., Pierce, J. (2003) Evaluation of the Conflict Prevention Pools. Synthesis Report. Commissioned by the DfID. Available at <www.dfid.gov.uk/aboutDFID/performance/files/ev647synthesis.pdf>.

Axworthy, L. (2003) *Navigating a New World: Canada's Global Future*. Toronto: Alfred A. Knopf.

Barcelona Report (2004) *Study Group on Europe's Security Capabilities: The Human Security Doctrine for Europe*. European Union, 15 September. Available at <www.lse.ac.uk/Depts/global/Publications/HumanSecurityDoctrine.pdf>.

Blair, T. (2006) Parliamentary Statement on Trident, 4 December. Available at <www.number-10.gov.uk/output/Page10532.asp>.

Blick, A., Choudhury, T. and Weir, S. (2006) *The Rules of the Game: Terrorism, Community and Human Rights*. York: Joseph Rowntree Reform Trust/Democratic Audit, November. Available at <www.jrrt.org.uk/>.

Brody, R. (2006) 'The Road to Abu Ghraib: Torture and Impunity in US Detention', in K. Roth, M. Worden and A. D. Bernstein (eds), *Torture: Does it Make us Safer, is it Ever OK?* New York: The New Press/Human Rights Watch.

Brown, G. (2006) 'We Will Always Strive to Be on Your Side'. Speech to the Labour Party Conference, 25 September. Available at <www.labour.org.uk>.

Brown, G. (2007) Speech at the Confederation of Indian Industry, Bangalore, 17 January.

Browne, D. (2007) Speech at Kings College London, 25 January.

Burall, S., Donnelley, B. and Weir, S. (2006) *Not in Our Name: Democracy and Foreign Policy in the UK*. London: Politico's.

Campbell, D. and Aglionby, J. (2005) 'Leak puts foreign policy role in fuelling extremism under scrutiny', *Guardian*, 29 August. Available at <www.guardian.co.uk>.

Carnegie Commission (1997) *Preventing Deadly Conflict – Final Report, Carnegie Commission on Preventing Deadly Conflict*. Washington DC: Carnegie Commission.

Clarke, M. (2007) 'Rethinking Security and Power', in D. Held and D. Mepham (eds), *Progressive Foreign Policy: Future Directions for the UK*. Cambridge: Polity Press.

Commission on Human Security (2003) *Human Security Now*. New York: Commission on Human Security.

Fukuyama, F. (2006) *After the Neo-Cons – America at the Crossroads*. London: Profile Books.

Gamble, A. and Kearns, I. (2007) 'Recasting the Special Relationship', in D. Held and D. Mepham (eds), *Progressive Foreign Policy: Future Directions for the UK*. Cambridge: Polity Press.

Goose, S. (2006) 'Presentation to the meeting of the Military and Technical Experts at the Convention on Conventional Weapons (CCW): Cluster Munitions, Explosive Remnants of War, and CCW Protocol V'. Available at <http://hrw.org/english/docs/2006/08/31/global14169.htm>.

Gore, A. (2006) *An Inconvenient Truth: The Planetary Emergency of Global Warming and What We Can Do About It*. London: Bloomsbury.

Grant, C. (2007) 'Europe's Global Role', in D. Mepham and D. Held (eds), *Progressive Foreign Policy: Future Directions for the UK*. Cambridge: Polity Press.

Grono, N. and Nathan, J. (2006) *Not Too Late for Afghanistan*. International Crisis Group, 17 August. Available at <www.crisisgroup.org/home/index.cfm?id=4349&l=1>.

Heinecken, L. (2001) 'Living in Terror: The Looming Security Threat to Southern Africa', *African Security Review*, 10 (4).

Held, D. (2007) 'Multilateralism and Global Governance: Accountability and Effectiveness', in D. Held and D. Mepham (eds), *Progressive Foreign Policy: Future Directions for the UK*. Cambridge: Polity Press.

Holt, V. and Berkman, T. (2006) *The Impossible Mandate? Military Preparedness, the Responsibility to Protect and Modern Peace Operations*. Washington DC: Henry L. Stimson Center.

ICISS (2001) *The Responsibility to Protect*. Ottawa: International Development Research Centre. Available at <www.dfait-maeci.gc/iciss-ciis>.

Ikenberry, J. and Slaughter, A-M. (2006) *Forging a World of Liberty under Law: US National Security in the 21st Century*. Princeton: Princeton University Press.

International Crisis Group (2006) *After Baker-Hamilton: What to Do in Iraq*. Middle East Report No. 60. Available at <www.crisisgroup.org/home/index.cfm?id=4580&l=1>.

Iraq Study Group (2006) *The Way Forward – A New Approach. The Report of the Iraq Study Group*. New York: Random House.

Joint Committee on Human Rights (2006) *Counter-Terrorism Policy and Human Rights: Prosecution and Pre-Charge Detention*. 24th Report of Session 2005–06. HL Paper 240, HC 1576.

Kepel, G. (2004) *The War for Muslim Minds: Islam and the West*. Cambridge, Belknap Press.

Khan, S. (2006) 'Being a British Muslim'. Speech to Fabian Conference on Britishness, 3 July. Further details available at <www.sadiqkhan.org.uk/news/july/03_07.htm>.

Mepham, D. (2006) *Changing States: A Progressive Agenda for Political Reform in the Middle East*. London: ippr.

Mepham, D. (2007) 'The Middle East – A New Agenda for UK Policy', in D. Mepham and D. Held (eds), *Progressive Foreign Policy: New Directions for the UK*. Cambridge: Polity Press.

Mepham, D. and Lorge, J. (2005) *Putting our House in Order: Recasting G8 Policy towards Africa*. London: ippr.

Mepham, D. and Ramsbotham, A. (2006) *Darfur: The Responsibility to Protect*. London: ippr.

Nye, J. S. (2004), *Soft Power: The Means to Success in World Politics*. New York: Public Affairs.

Omand, D. (2006) 'Security Dilemmas', *Prospect* magazine, December.

Rogers, P. (2006) 'The War on Terror: Past, Present and Future', OpenDemocracy.net, 24 August. Available at <www.opendemocracy.net/media/article>.

Roy, O. (2004) *Globalised Islam: The Search for a New Ummah*. New York: Columbia University Press.

Wild, L. and Williams, P. (2007) 'Redesigning Foreign Policy', in D. Mepham and D. Held (eds), *Progressive Foreign Policy: New Directions for the UK*. Cambridge: Polity Press.

Woods, N. (2006) *Power Shift: Do We Need Better Global Institutions?* London: ippr.

19
The European Project Renewed

Martin Rhodes

Introduction

No book on the future of the progressive agenda would be complete without reference to the European Union (EU). Yet there has been little overarching consensus within the wider British progressive movement about the future direction of the EU, or the normative assumptions that should underpin it. This chapter aims to fill that gap. In so doing, it avoids some well-trodden territory. It does not ask, for example, whether Blair fulfilled his potential as a European leader, whether Britain's behaviour towards Iraq damaged our standing in the EU or whether the British government should have held a referendum on membership of the euro. These questions are now largely irrelevant to the future of the Union. And because this is covered by David Miliband in Chapter 16, it does not examine the potential for reform of the EU's emissions trading scheme or targets for reductions in greenhouse gases. Rather, it argues that the EU's core problem is that it lacks legitimacy – both 'input legitimacy', related to the democratization (or lack of) of the EU, and 'outcome legitimacy', related to effective policy implementation – and proposes new and more forward-looking ways of overcoming this legitimacy gap. The recommendations focus on four related domains: Europe's economy, its 'social dimension', its political system and its relations with the world.

Europe's policy dilemmas: why the EU should do less and do it better

Although it is tempting to start with an argument for deeper integration (partly as a stimulus to progressive economic and political reform in some newer member countries), in reality Europe badly needs a pause in the integration process if it is to re-legitimize the European process. The core problem confronting the European project is that it lacks core legitimacy, in large part because its remit has become too wide and opaque.

Since the 1990s, the European project has been underpowered and overextended, as certain communities of political and policy elites have attempted to drive it forward without the requisite financial and institutional resources. In lieu of a hard-to-achieve intergovernmental bargain on establishing a hierarchy of priorities and finding the means to deliver them, the EU has seen the proliferation of objectives and ambitions under the Lisbon programme, and the arrival of a new phase of multi-level policy-making via horizontal and vertical 'coordination' (Sapir 2006).

Unfortunately, although predictably, the latter has delivered little by way of results. In both internal and external policies, the EU faces a recurrent 'conditionality' problem: influencing the domestic policies of member states outside areas of core European competency can be as hard as changing the politics of non-member states via the instruments of the European Neighbourhood Policy (ENP). The consequent 'capabilities gap' is potentially far more damaging for the credibility and legitimacy of the EU than the so-called 'democratic deficit' (Majone 2006), and there was little in the Constitutional Treaty to address this issue.

Problems of increased but unmet expectations are created as the EU's declared policy goals become increasingly ambitious (most notably, but not only, in the Lisbon programme to make Europe the world's foremost knowledge-based economy), while the resources and institutional capacity for meeting them remain wholly unequal to the task (Creel et al. 2005; Majone 2005, 2006).

For progressives, confronting this legitimacy gap – by focusing only on those policy areas that the EU can influence – will be essential. And although it is somewhat beyond the remit of this chapter, climate change represents a key example of a policy area that, if tackled by the EU properly, could enable it to acquire the 'outcome legitimacy' that it needs. Another key aspect will be reorientating the EU's limited financial resources.

Economic Europe: real and imagined challenges

In the economy, the EU is constrained by having much of its resources tied up by intergovernmental bargains of the past (especially in the Common Agricultural Policy (CAP) and the Structural Funds), the

Economic and Monetary Union's (EMU) Stability and Growth Pact also places limits on the reform capabilities of its member states. Contrary to popular claims (Scharpf 2000a), 'globalization' is much less important here than the demands of successfully managing the transition in these economies from manufacturing to service sector employment, under conditions of budgetary austerity. Within the context of the current macro-economic monetary and fiscal framework it is necessary to redefine the Lisbon programme, making more incisive use of the 'open method of coordination' (OMC), especially in education reform, and to discontinue unproductive interventions in member state employment policies, developing instead new means of promoting human capital growth, and research and development.

Europe is still coming to terms with the consequences of implementing the Single Market Programme, which, launched in the mid 1980s, aimed to remove barriers to the intra-European mobility of goods, services, labour and capital. The EU is also still in a period of experimentation with EMU, which, in providing a single European currency that reduces the cost of cross-border transactions, introduced new constraints for national policy-makers. These developments, alongside the ongoing process of enlargement and the perceived ramifications of 'globalization', have contributed to perceptions that Europe has entered a new period of turbulence and instability. But there is no evidence of the feared 'race to the bottom' in social spending, or that increased trade and capital flows are undermining European welfare states (Dixon and Pearce 2005).

Indeed, except for those countries where spending had risen to excessive levels in the 1980s and left them dangerously exposed in a period of much greater uncertainty than today, there has been little sign of retrenchment, and social outlays have continued to grow (Castles 2004). And despite concerns, there is little hard evidence that domestic jobs in high-wage European countries are being relocated on a significant scale to the low-wage regions of the East and South (Konings and Murphy 2004).

In fact, contrary to the impression given by the publicity surrounding the Lisbon programme, Europe 'as a whole' does not face especially severe problems of employment, economic growth or even innovation. Ireland, the UK and the Scandinavian economies perform well on most if not all indicators. The economic malaise is concentrated, instead, in certain core Eurozone countries (notably France, Germany and Italy) that are experiencing low levels of employment, relatively low levels of growth and, in some instances (Italy and Greece) very high levels of public debt. The latter countries, in particular, are caught in a vicious circle of reduced productivity and competitiveness, and downward pressure on the welfare of their citizens.

The Lisbon agenda and its 'coordination processes' are now widely regarded to have failed. Put in place to provide a joint, pan-European response to Europe's multiple challenges (slow growth, high unemployment, inadequate training and education systems, and insufficient investment in research and development and the assets required by the 'knowledge society'), Lisbon and its policy innovations have few teeth and even fewer resources. They aimed too high, tried to do too much, and sought to include too many policies and countries within its ambit.

This is especially true of the 'European Employment Strategy', the most ambitious and institutionally well-grounded of Europe's OMCs. It is also true of its less well-developed equivalents in the critical areas of research, innovation and education. There is considerable uncertainty among economists as to where the 'real' problem lies, especially in debates over why Europe's productivity levels and living standards lag behind those of the United States – the standard benchmark of unfavourable comparisons (see, for example, Daveri 2004). The macro-economic regime of EMU is important here, for, as revealed by recent research (for example, Soskice 2007), by reducing the scope for national reflation and focusing competition on unit labour costs, EMU has helped to subdue the performance of economies with high non-wage labour costs and highly skilled workers.

If public spending is restricted by the Stability and Growth Pact, private consumption is constrained by the pressures of competition. In the coordinated market economies of France, Germany and Italy, given high and difficult-to-reduce non-wage costs, firms have been holding down wages to compete, and workers with the highly specific, firm-related skills have increased their savings to insure against the risk of unemployment. These countries' growth dynamics are quite different from those of Europe's liberal market economies (the UK and Ireland), where generic skills are more easily transferable, non-wage labour costs are lower and private consumption is higher.

Reform capacity is also restricted in the continental economies. Budgetary constraints combine with and reinforce worker hostility to change in precisely those countries where further reform to product and labour markets is required – especially in reducing levels of employment protection in favour of 'person protection'; that is, assisting workers' transitions from one job to the next and cushioning that process with unemployment insurance.

Many economists (for example, Boeri 2005) argue that competition – especially in product markets – will gradually force these systems and their workers to adjust. But market-induced reforms take time and cost money. The danger in the meantime is that political conflict will increase, and that the consensus on the role of 'Europe' in promoting reform will be an early casualty.

This analysis points to two obvious conclusions. First, the Lisbon agenda, as others have argued, needs to be refocused and given more clout, especially by restructuring the EU budget and through a reassessment and redeployment of the OMCs. Second, Eurozone fiscal policy needs to be made more flexible, and used to reward and facilitate reform in countries where resistance to change is the greatest. Regenerating growth and raising tax revenues from that growth will also help accomplish structural reform (Hughes et al. 2004). Although the challenges are considerable, these two reforms can be linked to give the EU both more effectiveness and credibility – and thereby also enhance the legitimacy of the project.

Regarding the EU budget, agricultural spending through the Common Agricultural Policy (CAP), amounting to just under 50 per cent of the budget, is the single biggest obstacle to progressing the Lisbon agenda. The figures are astonishing, and just one fact explains why the EU is so ineffective as a policy actor outside its core regulatory functions, rendering all other arguments superfluous by comparison: support for French, German and Italian farmers alone accounts for half of CAP spending and a quarter of the entire EU budget.

The Sapir Report (Sapir et al. 2004) recommended a transformation of Europe's budget and its existing funds (the CAP and different structural funds) into three new funds, more closely tailored to its current needs: a Growth Fund (to promote R&D and cross-border infrastructure); a Convergence Fund (to be allocated to low-income countries – a substantial shift from present structural-fund focus on 'poor' regions, including those in rich countries); and a Restructuring Fund (that would shift resources from farm subsidies and income support to a more general programme for redeploying manpower) (see Pelkmans and Casey 2004 for a sympathetic critique). The success of all other EU economic growth and adjustment initiatives hinges on such reform, and yet the political will to tackle the issue is distinctly lacking.

There are numerous proposals as to how to transform the budget and the funds, given predictable opposition from veto players (in both governments and interest organizations) who will fight to preserve the status quo (Blankart and Kirchner 2003; Gros and Miscossi 2005, Baldwin 2005). But mobilizing support for any type of reform would require the investment of considerable energy in pan-European alliance-building and intergovernmental bargaining. The domestic politics of extensive budgetary reform would also be intense and, in some countries, potentially explosive, especially in those countries that are the largest current recipients of agricultural funding.

As for the pre- and post-Lisbon OMCs, the Sapir Report argued that the OMC should be restricted to those areas where there is no alternative, due to subsidiarity constraints and the absence of core EU competencies; for example, labour markets, taxation, welfare, education, innovation and R&D. But there was no detailed consideration as to how the OMC could be made more effective.

The fact is that the circumstances under which policy influence and transfer can work are few, in the absence of coercion or strong material incentives (Citi and Rhodes 2007). But education policy, especially at the university level, and human capital development in general present two areas in which a reinforced system of OMC policy transfer could work, and there are good reasons for focusing efforts here. First, raising skills levels would contribute powerfully to achieving the Lisbon employment target of 70 per cent, even in the absence of labour market reform (Gros 2006). Second, promoting adult education and on-the-job learning can achieve relatively short-term success in increasing a country's human capital endowment (Ederer 2006).

Moreover, as recent research confirms (for example, Schleicher 2006; Jacobs and Van der Ploeg 2006; Lambert and Butler 2006), without such reforms to higher education there can be no sustainable improvement to Europe's systems of research and innovation. As they currently stand, the post-Lisbon research and innovation and education coordination programmes are among the weakest of the OMCs. Even if reinforcing them means facing problems stemming from the diversity of member states, and the difficulties of implementing pan-European initiatives across them, there is, at least, the potential for economies of scale and the facilitating force of cross-border externalities in research, innovation and education that do not exist elsewhere.

Thus there are obvious economies of scale to warrant the Europeanization of innovation promotion through the creation of a single patent for the EU – a Community Patent – under the jurisdiction of a European Patent Court: the fact that, to date, initiatives to do so have failed is arguably due to the protectionism and vested interests at work in national patent industries (Van der Horst et al. 2006). The externalities of improving R&D spending – in both quantity and quality, and from both private and public sources – stem from the fact that there can be cross-border spillovers into productivity gains from one country's R&D investments to the next (Keller 2004; Ederveen et al. 2005). Without such reforms the Lisbon strategy is bound to fail.

As for the contribution that a reformed European fiscal policy could make towards facilitating structural change, the reform paradox in these countries derives from the fact that EMU-related public spending constraints and cuts only make reforms harder to achieve – reforms like more liquid capital markets and more fluid labour markets, sustainable public finances and a recalibration of welfare states. The problem is not that the European Central Bank (ECB) has been too conservative in its monetary policy, as argued by those who believe that Europe's problems can be explained by EMU and the ECB's ostensive inflation obsession. In fact, EMU has had growth-enhancing effects: it has delivered historically low interest rates and removed exchange rate costs from cross-border transactions. Moreover, monetary policy can only have short-run benefits; it cannot deliver long-term growth (Alesina and Giavazzi 2006). However, new public investment is restrained in some of the core Eurozone economies by the Stability and Growth Pact, and, as argued above, competition-driven wage moderation among their firms has contributed to lower private consumption growth.

André Sapir (2006) argues that the supply-side reform required by those economies can more easily be delivered by national politicians when accompanied by monetary expansion (to offset its effects on aggregate demand) and fiscal relaxation (to compensate the losers). But he provides little indication of the ways in which those reforms can be implemented, given the Eurozone economies' veto-heavy policy systems and, in particular, the still-powerful position of national trade union confederations within them.

One can imagine a way forward as follows. Coeuré and Pisani-Ferry (2005) propose a sustainability and growth pact, under which each country should present a plan with three components: a fiscal plan, which would target the government's net value (GNV) – this is the difference between its total assets and financial liabilities – and describe how the GNV value would be met; a reform plan, which would be like the Lisbon-related national reform programmes, but with a stronger link to budgetary policy; and a contingency plan, which would describe how budgetary policy would respond to positive or negative shocks (for example, an increase in tax revenues or recession). The Coeuré–Pisani-Ferry scheme could be linked to national reform pacts that could help to overcome the vetoes that bedevil distributive politics in most Eurozone economies.

Pontusson (2005) has suggested, for example, that government–union pacts could exchange wage moderation for fiscal stimulation. But one could go further and include labour market and pensions reforms, which are otherwise notoriously difficult to achieve. Such fiscal incentives would be permitted if GNV allowed scope for an increase in public spending, and prior commitments to reform by a range of policy actors convinced Eurozone finance ministers of the credibility of the government's reform plan. Of course, this raises the issue of precisely what kind of reforms to pursue, and whether the OMCs (especially the European Employment Strategy) still have any role to play here. This brings us to Europe's 'social dimension'.

'Social Europe'? The future of the EU's social dimension

A long tradition of analysis of Europe's various types of welfare system has revealed some by now very well-known features of 'social Europe'. The continental and southern European systems suffer from the worst efficiency and sustainability problems, related primarily to low levels of employment and high levels of passive benefit spending. Benefits tend to be proportional to earnings and financed through social security contributions, which impact heavily on non-wage labour costs. Benefit replacement rates are generous and benefit duration tends to be long. Employment protection is high – though for a decreasing core of workers on permanent contracts.

The Anglo-Irish systems are quite sustainable at present levels of expenditure and enjoy high levels of employment, but also suffer from high levels of inequality. The UK is a higher social spender than Ireland, and spending growth has recently been higher than the EU15. Wage subsidies also supplement the incomes of low-paid workers and their families, and a minimum wage in the UK and national wage agreements in Ireland help to prevent the proliferation of 'working poor'. Benefits – which are flat rate – are modest, and social protection tends to be targeted and means-tested, and replacement rates low. Public and family services are less developed than in Scandinavia and the continental countries. Levels of employment protection are low.

The welfare states of Central and Eastern Europe (CEE) are minimal and low-income, and some are heavily biased towards pensions, but given typically low employment rates, apart from the very low-spending Baltic countries, their sustainability at present levels is in question. Hungary, Poland and Slovakia are among the worst employment performers in the

EU, while Slovenia, the Czech Republic, Estonia and Latvia are close to France and Germany.

Only the Nordic systems manage high levels of both equity and sustainability – primarily because their expensive and universal systems of social protection and redistribution are underpinned by very high levels of employment and education. Besides generous replacement rates, these systems offer a wide array of public social services beyond health and education. Employment protection is not high or extensive in these systems, but generous, though short-duration, unemployment benefits, together with active labour market programmes, encourage and sustain high levels of both male and female employment. Public sector employment is also extensive (Esping-Andersen 2002; Ferrera et al. 2001; Hemerijck et al. 2006).

The social dimension to Europe involves European legislation on minimum employment and working standards agreed intergovernmentally in the Council of Ministers, an expanding body of European Court of Justice (ECJ) case law, framework agreements between European trade unions and employers' organizations and, more recently, the OMC. The latter marks a major departure from the standard 'community method' of policy-making in seeking to influence member state policies via 'soft methods' of policy transfer across a wide range of issues, from employment policy through to social exclusion, pensions and education.

Over time, the emphasis of the Commission has switched from legislation to social agreements, and then to the OMC, in order to avoid the vetoes of certain groups of member states to a more fully developed European social dimension. But, in the process, the legitimacy and effectiveness of intergovernmental agreements, and legislation and the backing of ECJ jurisprudence have been lost, even if that older mode of policy-making is still extant, though harder to use, in a Europe of 25 member states with very different social systems and levels of economic development (Rhodes 2005).

Although the main new instrument to emerge from the Lisbon Summit in 2000, and valuable, perhaps, as a means of diffusing awareness of the challenges facing European economies and the gaps between the EU's reform ambitions and achievements, the OMC has proven to be weak in practice. This is due to its overwhelming reliance on elite deliberation and experimental methods of benchmarking and peer review.

If the EU truly wishes to resolve its core employment problems and make serious inroads into poverty and social exclusion, then there are two obvious directions to take. The first concerns combating the tendency for the core Eurozone economies – Germany, France and Italy – to re-regulate their labour markets by following the path of least resistance: leaving the core, mainly male and unionized workforce heavily shielded by high levels of employment protection, and creating a growing 'periphery' of underprotected, part-time and temporary workers with little potential to move into more secure, merit-based career paths.

The key lessons in terms of policy transfer from the Nordic economies to the continental economies are, first, that higher rates of employment will underpin higher levels of welfare. The second is that, in addition to active labour market policy, higher rates of employment can be achieved by the following: lowering the level of job protection to increase employer flexibility in favour of greater employee support through retraining and promoting employability; and shifting resources from the apprenticeship-based, vocational-type training that predominates in the continental countries to enhanced levels of transferable industrial skills training and general education. (France, Italy and Germany are currently placed eighth, tenth and thirteenth, respectively, out of thirteen, on the European Human Capital Index, compared to Sweden, Denmark, the UK and the Netherlands in positions one through four) (Pontusson 2005; Ederer 2006).)

Although there have already been moves in this direction, there also needs to be a faster, general (rather than targeted) shift from payroll taxes as the major source of funding for social security, which weigh heavily on employment costs in these countries (especially for smaller, lower-productivity, service sector employers) to general income taxation. This would help stimulate demand for lower-skilled labour and would also render the welfare state more distributive, because income taxation tends to be more progressive than payroll taxes (Scharpf 2000b; Pontusson 2005).

Achieving such changes may prove easier in some countries than in others. In Italy, where unemployment compensation is low, and high levels of job protection a poor functional equivalent, a 'social pact' (backed up, perhaps, by reformed European fiscal policy incentives, as discussed in the previous section) could trade job protection for more unemployment spending. Where unemployment protection is already quite high (for example, Germany and France), and where trade unions tend to defend payroll taxes as less susceptible to erosion than income taxes, more imaginative solutions will be required (Pontusson 2005).

A second obvious step for the EU to take – this time in combating poverty and social exclusion – is to focus on putting a floor under family and child poverty. Even the supporters of the social policy OMC (OMCincl) (for example, Daly 2006) have to admit that the practical outcomes are few, and can only provide evidence, for instance, of an increase in NGO participation in policy deliberation (a process result rather than a policy outcome) in their search for tangible consequences.

It would be far better to concentrate on one core ambition instead, or at least establish a list of priorities that could be approached via the more standard Community method of EU legislation, with the most politically feasible course of action that has the greatest potential impact at the top. This would have the advantage of promoting clear divisions between supporters and opponents, among and within the member states and in the European Parliament, and of being amenable to the same kind of Commission-led coalition-building that produced successful European social policy initiatives in the past (Rhodes 2005). The initiative may initially fail; but, unlike the amorphous and publicly invisible OMCincl, it would at least have the potential for identifiable success, and would ultimately acquire the democratic legitimacy and credibility to be derived from the EU's tradition of hard law policy-making.

A basic income for Europe's children is an obvious candidate. It already has considerable support among social policy experts and in European Commission circles as the key to both social inclusion and investment in the future of the knowledge economy (Commission of the European Communities (CEC) 2005). A strategy for dealing with childhood deprivation with a 'child basic income' (CBI) has been proposed and its effects simulated by Levy et al. (2006). They argue for setting a CBI as a proportion of national median household income, financed by a flat tax, set for the EU15 with a common rate applied everywhere, levied on all non-benefit income, including pensions. They show that a flat tax of 2.3 per cent would fund a CBI set at around 20 per cent of median income, and would at least halve child poverty in all countries except Italy and the UK. The outcomes would improve in line with a higher flat-tax level. Note that a single-rate flat tax is proposed by its advocates for reasons of simplicity and lower incidence than alternatives on government, employer and taxpayer administrative costs. It should not be confused with right-wing proposals for a regressive flat-rate income tax.

The distributive dimension of the flat-rate tax/CBI would be important, transferring between generations and across countries. Careful monitoring of welfare spending in those countries that would make the major gains would be important to avoid any substitution of CBI spending for national social spending. But this problem has long been controlled for (though not always successfully) in the deployment of the EU's structural and existing social funds. And a CBI proposal could also be assessed alongside other modest EU tax proposals – some suggesting a modification of the current system of national contributions (for example, Tsoukalis 2005: 136–7) – and included in a reorganization of Europe's budgetary spending allocations and structural funds, as recommended earlier.

Europe in the world

The current period features major security and developmental challenges to the EU's east, in its immediate south-west, and in the Middle East and North Africa. With the emergence of a militant Islamist terrorist threat, external and internal security issues have become intertwined, as have key dimensions of defence, foreign, security and aid policies.

Moving forward with common European foreign, security and defence policies conforms to the strong and consistent support of European publics for such initiatives. Regardless of traditional national, sovereignty-based resistance, this combination of external threat, public support and the potential for realizing considerable scale economies makes the foreign, defence and security domains the most susceptible of European policy areas to a new phase of enhanced integration.

There is much debate about whether Europe should exert 'hard' military power abroad or emphasize 'soft' civilian power via aid and trade promotion, with much criticism of the former (for example, Sangiovanni 2003; Manners 2006). This debate is entirely misconceived: the EU already combines both forms of power, but is unable to use either adequately.

Regarding 'hard' power, arguments about whether Europe should 'go it alone' militarily (as suggested by Jacques Chirac after the early divisions with the US over the invasion of Iraq) or remain the 'handmaiden' of the North Atlantic Treaty Organization (NATO) in the military dimension of the transatlantic relationship (for example, Cameron and Moravcsik 2003) are similarly misconstrued. The transatlantic alliance is already in better health than several years ago. The EU has begun to make itself a more effective partner in that alliance, and a new relationship and division of labour with the US and NATO will, of necessity, be found.

But the real issues that Europe confronts are instead those of rationalizing its military, security and intelligence apparatuses; creating a unified defence budget; and developing an efficient industrial defence market to generate gains from trade and economies of scale and reduce the costs from duplicating R&D. Despite the disparaging remarks attracted by the emerging 'Brussels military-industrial simplex [sic]' (Manners 2006), and apart from the other benefits mentioned below, the latter could eventually play a major role in boosting demand for European research in theoretical and applied science.

As for the EU's 'soft' or 'transformative' power, this is an area replete with European policy hubris and journalistic catchphrases of the 'Americans are from Mars, Europeans from Venus' variety. Celebrations of Europe's 'civilizing' mission and 'normative' power by Euro-idealists (for example, Leonard 2005) ignore the failure of EU civilian power and means of persuasion in preventing the Yugoslav tragedy of the 1990s, play down the evident shortcomings of the Barcelona process for development and democratization in the Euro-Mediterranean region, and are largely based on the success of Eastern enlargement and its accompanying democratization and economic transformation in the former Soviet satellite states.

Of course, the promise of real membership played a major role in the latter (Vachudova 2005), and is one that cannot be extended much further beyond the current 25, plus Romania and Bulgaria. And one should not forget that not all core members of the EU15 (notably France) were natural 'enlargers' in the first place: they had to be won over by persuasion and package deals from an alliance of states led by the UK and Germany. Nor should one forget the critical role played by NATO in Eastern enlargement and democratization, especially, but not only, in reforming civil-military relations (Epstein 2005). Ultimately, there were real interests driving enlargement, not just a belief in bringing the East back into the democratic fold. There are real interests, as well, rather than a simple and superior 'civilizing mission', in Europe's relations with countries further to its east and to its south.

Beginning with 'hard' power, a coordinated defence/industrial policy makes sense for numerous reasons. While market pressures are pushing European states towards greater defence industry integration, both within Europe and beyond Europe's borders, budgetary pressures across the EU also require a rationalization of expenditure, more competitive procurement markets and an avoidance of the waste created by duplicate defence spending.

Until recently, Europeans have been deeply divided on the politics of defence-related industrial policy. But that protectionism is now strongly challenged: national governments are no longer necessarily the biggest purchasers of systems and components originating in their own countries; cross-national defence industry integration is increasingly the norm; states now prefer to foster quality and price competition at the expense of supply self-sufficiency; and firms are seeking to survive by increasing their global market shares rather than political favouritism (Epstein 2006).

These trends present an opportunity for the EU to reduce overcapacity, increase competitive efficiency and diminish costs. The biggest (and politically most achievable) gains are likely to be made through a combination of defence market liberalization within the EU – by modifying or abolishing Article 296 – and replacing national procurement agencies with an EU procurement agency (Schmitt 2003; Hartley 2006). It should be noted that the projected gains and savings of these two policy initiatives alone are in the billions of euros (currently, some 180 billion is spent annually by the EU on defence). Such savings would allow more spending on some of the other critical areas of policy need mentioned above (education and child poverty foremost among them) and/or reducing the Eurozone's large budget deficits that create a drag on growth. Defence industry integration could also provide the material base for a uniform and enforceable arms export code, would endow the EU with increased bargaining power vis-à-vis the US, and enhance its capacity to defend its territory at home and interests abroad.

A number of such initiatives have already been undertaken. Regarding procurement, Germany, France, Italy and the UK created the Organization for Joint Armaments Cooperation (OCCAR) in 1996 to improve the efficiency of collaborative projects. OCCAR manages a number of joint European projects, including the A-400M transport aircraft, a combat helicopter and air defence and anti-tank missile programmes. 1998 saw two further steps forward, when these countries, plus Sweden and Spain, signed the Letter of Intent (LoI) aimed at facilitating the cross-border restructuring of the defence industry, ensuring the security of supply and information, and harmonizing export procedures, and all 15 EU member states agreed to the terms of an EU Code of Conduct on arms sales. The European Aeronautic Defence and Space Company (EADS) was created by France, Germany and Spain the following year. The European Defence Agency (EDA) was created in 2004 to develop defence capabilities in crisis management, to promote arms cooperation, to strengthen the EU's military-industrial complex and to create a more competitive market in defence equipment. In 2005, France called for an EDA-backed procurement code to better exploit the EU's equipment market (for example, there is a need for 10,000 new armoured fighting vehicles but some 23 existing programmes to develop them) (Epstein 2006; Hartley 2006; Allen and Smith 2006).

These initiatives do not yet add up to a coherent political and economic response to present challenges and opportunities. Article 296 presents a major impediment to defence market competition and the realization of scale economies in defence procurement. With respect to the LoI, states still try to cling to the premise of national autonomy on issues such as 'security of supply'.

The EU Code of Conduct on arms exports is impressive on paper, but is not legally binding regarding arms sales and proliferation on the part of European member states. It is not clear, for example, that a key feature of the Code – bilateral consultations on export licences that have been denied – has had any real effect on 'undercutting', that is, the practice whereby an EU state steps in to fill a contract that another has rejected on the grounds of proliferation, human rights or terrorist risk (Epstein 2006).

The EDA has a small budget (€20 million), has only 80 staff and has encountered numerous turf battles in its early years of operation. And most of the organizations with which it has to coordinate, such as OCCAR and the LoI, operate outside of any stable EU institutional framework (Howarth 2004). Pursuing these policies will contribute to the success of other European efforts within the ambit of the new European Security and Defence Policy (ESDP). These include the development of a European military capability for crisis management, peace-keeping and rescue missions, the most concrete manifestations of which have been the 2003 launch of the European rapidly deployable force of 100,000 personnel; the development by 2005 of 18 'battle groups', with the aim of being able to conduct two operations simultaneously and within five days of a Council decision; and the establishment by Spain, France, the Netherlands, Italy and Portugal, in 2005, of a *gendarmerie* force, headquartered in Italy, that can be deployed to fill the gap between military operations and reconstructions in unstable theatres (Allen and Smith 2006; Alber et al. 2006).

Shifting our focus towards the 'soft' power complements of these developments, two further initiatives must now be pursued to consolidate the EU's civilian crisis management (CCM) capabilities. The first, and most important, is the creation of a European civilian expert reconstruction corps, referred to in most discussions, since the concept was launched in the mid-1990s, as a 'European civil peace corps' or ECPC, though it has nothing in common with the American Peace Corps of young volunteers. The ECPC would enhance the EU's capacity to act in CCM by replacing the current and fragmented system of coordinating consultant or specialist non-governmental organizations (NGOs) with a common service or corps of expert volunteers, to be linked to a European Peace-building Agency, and managed by the Commission, member states, specialist organizations, or a combination of all three. Two feasibility studies, Gourlay (2004) and Robert et al. (2005), have both found in the ECPC's favour. The second initiative, much closer to the US Peace Corps in inspiration, was set out in the draft Constitutional Treaty (Article

III-223) as a 'European Voluntary Humanitarian Aid Corps' (EVHAC) 'to establish a framework for joint contributions from young Europeans to the humanitarian actions of the Union'. In developing its own version of a humanitarian corps, the EU has a major opportunity to extend its 'soft' power abroad, to bring home the practical dimension of European 'values' to young Europeans (already the most 'European' of the EU's citizens), and to enhance public recognition of what the EU can achieve through a broader set of international and humanitarian interventions.

Turning now fully to the EU's 'soft' power capacities, a careful examination of EU influence beyond its borders reveals, first, the same capabilities gap that one finds with the new generation of internal integration policies. This is compounded – in both cases, it should be noted – by the EU's skewed budgetary and protectionist agricultural policies. For, if farming subsidies and income support prevent a redeployment of funding to 'new economy' priorities, agricultural protection is also a formidable obstacle to the fulfilment of the EU's development and 'Neighbourhood' agendas in the south (Dodini and Fantini 2006). Second, the experience of Europe's aid and trade policies demonstrates similar mistakes to those made by international organizations and the development industry over decades: top-down, technocratic agendas for change, linked to vague and sometimes contradictory conditionality requirements, and driven primarily by commercial interests within the EU.

What is clear from wider experience is that trade alone will not work in spreading the norms and institutions underpinning democracy and the extension of human rights to the Middle East and the wider Mediterranean. Analysts of US trade deals in the region note that they tend to underpin rather than undermine pre-existing social and political arrangements, while conditional trade and aid risk producing hostility, and unconditional aid threatens to do little more than entrench already powerful and self-serving elites – and thereby undermine the prospects for peace and prosperity (Moore and Schrank 2003).

Some (for example, Dearden 2003; Gavin 2005) have argued in favour of creating an OMC for the region that would encourage the socialization of local elites in European norms via 'policy learning'. But, as Kelley (2006: 51) observes, the ENP countries have extensive human rights abuses, no democracy, are poor and feature few of the domestic political conditions (including political competition) that were critical for the success of enlargement to the CEE countries, let alone the conditions for policy transfer and norm diffusion that exist in the older EU member states but where OMCs have still achieved little.

Improving the influence of the EU's 'soft' power beyond its borders requires a different kind of change – and one, first, within its own frontiers. Breaking down protectionism in agriculture and textiles and opening EU markets in those sector's products would make a great deal of difference, both to EU leverage over the domestic democratic and the human rights policies of its partners, and to those countries' economic prospects. But the EU cannot 'buy' democratic convergence; that of the CEE countries was encouraged by the prospect of full EU membership – a prize that is not on offer in the Euro-Med region, and perhaps not even in other Eastern countries.

Another major change required is to the kind of domestic policies promoted. A core target of financial assistance should be education policies, not the kind of projects that provide markets for European producer interests. Regional institution building is a further critical step, thereby promoting a common market among the countries of the region, stimulating trade and economic activity across their own borders, and helping them to attract foreign investment.

And, as with the development programmes of the international organizations and NGO-supported aid efforts worldwide, a shift must be made away from the top-down policies and aid flows to developing country governments, which have proven so disappointing in their outcomes to date, towards bottom-up assistance for local infrastructure projects, and for human capital and micro-finance promotion (Easterly 2006).

Finally, and this applies equally to the non-democratic countries to the EU's east, a major investment must be made in promoting civil society organizations and pro-democracy, grassroots social movements (Emerson and Noutcheva 2005; Raik 2006). As noted above, successes in EU development policy in the past have occurred in precisely those areas where efforts were targeted at local projects and where civil society was involved. And that is precisely where the attention of future aid and development programmes should be focused.

Political Europe

As for the political dimension of the EU project, the increasing recourse of the EU to deliberation and referendums hit a dead end with the rejection of the draft Constitutional Treaty by France and the Netherlands, and the discrediting of these methods of 'popular democracy'. But careful consideration should be given to the reasons why the French and Dutch rejected the Constitutional Treaty, and to the more general views held by European publics of the EU and what it should be doing.

By focusing more closely on issues where the EU can truly make a difference to people's lives, one form of legitimacy – 'outcome legitimacy' linked to effective policy implementation – can be enhanced. 'Input legitimacy' – gained from democratizing the EU – is more difficult, given the gulf that still exists between fragile and poorly coordinated Euro-parties and nationally embedded political ideologies and opinion. More limited reforms are required here, including enhancing the European Parliament's influence over the selection of the Commission President and Commissioners, and strengthening the links between national Parliaments and the EU institutions.

Good arguments (Moravcsik 2002) have been made that the present institutional architecture of the EU is perfectly democratic, given the limited range of policy areas that fall under its remit, the links between national governments and representation in the European Council, and the powers that now accrue to the European Parliament after a number of reforms that extend the co-decision procedure. Crombez (2003) makes a parallel argument: that the EU's policies are not undemocratic, as such, and that the composition of its institutions is not inherently less democratic than those of the US, a more fully-fledged federal system. But, unlike Moravcsik, Crombez argues that there may be a lack of transparency and an excess of delegation in the EU, pointing to the fact that, while Parliament is directly elected, requiring one step of delegation, the Council requires two: voters vote for national Parliaments and the latter delegate powers to national ministers, who also become Council members – one step of delegation too far from national publics. Crombez recommends two changes to correct this defect: open Council meetings and the direct election of the Commission President, who can then nominate the other Commissioners. Alternatively, the Commission could be appointed by the Parliament.

Many arguments have been made in favour of a system with a more direct involvement of the Parliament, either by giving MEPs the power to elect the President (perhaps from a slate proposed by the council) and/or the entire College of Commissioners, or the election of the President by national MPs or a combination of national MPs and MEPs (see Smith 2004 for a survey) or through some kind of conciliation procedure (Crum 2005). But negotiating a path between too much politicization and too little under current institutional arrangements would counsel in favour of restricting the election of the President to the European Parliament, but from a slate proposed by the Council, and perhaps also of including a public debate on a presidential manifesto and Commission mandate, as proposed by Hix (2006: 24). This would not turn the European institutions into the equivalents found in a democratic nation state, or in a fully-fledged federal system. But the EU is currently neither, and there is little to be gained by politicizing its institutions and decision-making system as if it were. Given the limits on the EU as a source of influence and inputs into the core policy issues of interest to member state voters, and given that its Parliament has no powers to tax and spend, to initiate legislation or to form a government, politicization, as Bartolini (2005; 2006) persuasively argues, may well generate excessive hopes and expectations that will only be frustrated, and 'widen the gap between normative expectations and reality'.

Conclusion: renewing the project

This chapter began by arguing that renewing the European project should not involve new, grand schemes of deepening and widening, but should proceed by doing less and doing it better. The recommendations made in its subsequent sections have, therefore, been rather modest – but they will certainly not be controversy-free. So what reforms should the British government press for, for the next ten years?

The overriding need at this stage in the EU's evolution is an acknowledgement by its elite of the limits to integration in a Europe of 25 member states, and a much greater degree of honesty in communicating those limits to the European people. One feature of the Constitutional Treaty's rejection by the French and Dutch was a large degree of misunderstanding about what the EU does and what it can do. By presenting their publics with grandiose projects, with little real impact on their lives, while also using the EU's more important and significant innovations (especially EMU) as a scapegoat for their own problems, Europe's politicians have created a crisis of credibility and legitimacy that need never have existed.

Europe is in imminent danger of becoming a giant with feet of clay, and the substitution of fantasy for realism among European policy analysts has played a part in that outcome. As repeated many times above, rectifying Europe's core problems requires, first, revisiting the bargains of the past, and recasting them for the immediate future. It is to that project that the work of Europe's policy analysts should be dedicated.

Achieving that task politically will be extremely difficult, and the present political architecture of the EU may not be up to it. But, if one thing is clear from the French and Dutch votes, it is that such issues should not be dealt with by treaties and referendums. Nor will expanding the

EU's deliberative forums or politicizing its decision-making system help. Such steps will only increase the problems of gridlock and exacerbate the system's 'decision-trap' tendencies. Renewing the project requires some rather unfashionable remedies instead: firm Commission leadership and coalition-building among member states and across the European institutions; a new generation of European leaders with the courage to recast the bargains of their predecessors via intensive intergovernmental bargaining; and the will to provide the EU with the collective goods and resources it so obviously needs, but of which it has been deprived by connivance between the politicians and powerful lobby groups of its member states.

It is to be hoped that this goal can be achieved within the present institutional architecture, perhaps with minor modifications. After all, that system provided Europe with the Single Market and EMU. It should not be beyond its powers to endow the European project with a more solid foundation of material resources and normative legitimacy.

References

Note: web references correct at December 2006.

Alber, A., de Boisgrollier, N., Kourkoumelis, D., Micallef, R. and Stadler, F. (2006) 'Does Europe have Something to Offer the World?', *Fletcher Forum for World Affairs*, 30 (2): 179–90.

Alesina, A. and Giavazzi, F. (2006) *The Future of Europe: Reform or Decline*. Cambridge, Mass. and London: MIT Press.

Allen, D. and Smith, M. (2006) 'Relations with the Rest of the World', *Journal of Common Market Studies*, 44 (5): 155–70.

Baldwin, R. (2005) 'The Real Budget Battle: Une crise peut en cacher une autre', *CEPS Policy Brief*, June.

Bartolini, S. (2005) *Restructuring Europe: Centre Formation, System Building and Political Structuring between the Nation State and the European Union*. Oxford: Oxford University Press.

Bartolini, S. (2006) 'Should the Union be Politicized? Prospects and Risks', in *Politics: The Right or the Wrong Sort of Medicine for the EU?* Policy Paper No. 19. Paris: Notre Europe, Etudes et Recherche.

Blankart, C. B. and Kirchner, C. (2003) 'The Deadlock of the EU Budget: An Economic Analysis of Ways In and Ways Out', *CESifo Working Paper*, 989, July.

Boeri, T. (2005) *Reforming Labor and Product Markets: Some Lessons from Two Decades of Experiments in Europe*. IMF Working Paper WP/05/97, May.

Cameron, F. and Moravcsik, A. (2003) 'Debate: Should the European Union be Able to do Everything that NATO Can?', *NATO Review*, autumn.

Castles, F. G. (2004) *The Future of the Welfare State: Crisis Myths and Crisis Realities*. Oxford: Oxford University Press.

CEC (2005) *Communication from the Commission on the Social Agenda*. Brussels: CEC.

Citi, M. and Rhodes, M. (2007) 'New Forms of Governance in the EU', in M. Pollack, B. Rosamond and K. E. Jorgensen (eds), *The Handbook of European Union Politics*. London: Sage.

Coeuré, B. and Pisani-Ferry, J. (2005) *Fiscal Policy in EMU: Towards a Sustainability and Growth Pact*. Bruegel Working Paper 2005/01, December.

Creel, J., Laurent, L. and Le Cacheux, J. (2005) 'Delegation in Inconsistency: The "Lisbon Strategy" Record as an Institutional failure'. Paper presented to CONNEX workshop on 'Delegation and Multi-Level Governance', Paris, 11 May.

Crombez, C. (2003) 'The Democratic Deficit of the European Union? Much Ado about Nothing?', *European Union Politics*, 4 (1): 101–20.

Crum, B. (2005) 'Tailoring Representative Democracy to the European Union: Does the European Constitution Reduce the Democratic Deficit?', *European Law Journal*, 11 (4): 452–67.

Daly, M. (2006) 'EU Social Policy after Lisbon', *Journal of Common Market Studies*, 44 (3): 461–81.

Daveri, F. (2004) *Why is There a Productivity Problem in the EU?* CEPS Working Paper No. 205.

Dearden, S. (2003) 'Is EU Development Policy a Candidate for the Open Method of Coordination?', *Journal of European Affairs*, 2 (2): 17–26.

Dixon, M. and Pearce, N. (2005) 'Social Justice in a Changing World: The Emerging Anglo-Social Model', in N. Pearce and W. Paxton (eds), *Social Justice: Building a Fairer Britain*. London: ippr/Politico's.

Dodini, M. and Fantini, M. (2006) 'The EU Neighbourhood Policy: Implications for Economic Growth and Stability', *Journal of Common Market Studies*, 44 (3): 507–32.

Easterly, W. (2006) *The White Man's Burden: Why the West's Efforts to Aid the Rest have Done So Much Ill and So Little Good*. New York: Penguin Press.

Ederer, P. (2006) *Innovation at Work: The European Human Capital Index*. Brussels: Lisbon Council.

Ederveen, S., Van der Horst, A. and Tang, P. (2005) *Is the European Economy a Patient and the Union its Doctor? On Jobs and Growth in Europe*. ENEPRI Working Paper No. 35, April.

Emerson, M. and Noutcheva, G. (2005) *From Barcelona Process to Neighbourhood Policy: Assessment and Open Issues*. CEPS Working Document No. 220, March.

Epstein, R. (2005) 'NATO Enlargement and the Spread of Democracy: Evidence and Expectations', *Security Studies*, 14 (1): 59–98.

Epstein, R. (2006) 'Divided Continent: Globalization and Europe's Fragmented Security Response', in J. Kirshner (ed.), *Globalization and National Security*. London and New York: Routledge, pp. 231–57.

Esping-Andersen, G. (2002) 'A Child-Centred Social Investment Strategy', in G. Esping-Andersen, D. Gallie, A. Hemerijck and J. Myles, *Why We Need a New Welfare State*. Oxford: Oxford University Press, pp. 26–67.

Ferrera, M., Hemerijck, A. and Rhodes, M. (2001) 'The Future of the European Social Model in the Global Economy', *Journal of Comparative Policy Analysis*, 3 (2): 163–90.

Gavin, B. (2005) 'The Euro-Mediterranean Partnership: An Experiment in North–South–South Integration', *Intereconomics*, November/December: 353–60.

Gourlay, C. (2004) *Feasibility Study on the European Civil Peace Corps*. Brussels: International Security Information Service (ISIS) Europe.

Gros, D. (2006) 'Employment and Competitiveness: The Key Role of Education', *CEPS Policy Brief*, 93, February.

Gros, D. and Miscossi, S. (2005) 'A Better Budget for the European Union: More Value for Money, More Money for Value', *CEPS Policy Brief*, 66, February.

Hartley, K. (2006) 'Defence Industrial Policy in a Military Alliance', *Journal of Peace Research*, 43 (4): 473–89.

Hemerijck, A., Keune, M. and Rhodes, M. (2006) 'European Welfare States: Diversity, Challenges and Reforms', in P. Heywood, E. Jones, M. Rhodes and E. Sedelmeier (eds), *Developments in European Politics*. Basingstoke: Palgrave Macmillan, pp. 259–79.

Hix, S. (2006) 'Why the EU Needs (Left–Right) Politics? Policy Reform and Accountability are Impossible Without It', in *Politics: The Right or the Wrong Sort of Medicine for the EU?* Policy Paper No. 19. Paris: Notre Europe, Etudes et Recherche.

Howarth, J. (2004) 'The European Draft Constitutional Treaty and the Future of the European Defence Initiative', *European Foreign Affairs Review*, 9 (4): 483–508.

Hughes, H. A., Hougaard Jensen, S. E. and Richter, C. (2004) 'The European Economy at the Crossroads: Structural Reforms, Fiscal Constraints and the Lisbon Agenda', mimeo.

Jacobs, B. and Van der Ploeg, F. (2006) 'Getting European Universities into Shape', *European Political Science*, 5 (3): 288–303.

Keller, W. (2004) 'International Technology Diffusion', *Journal of Economic Literature*, 42 (3): 752–82.

Kelley, J. (2006) 'New Wine in old Wineskins: Promoting Political Reforms through the New European Neighbourhood Policy', *Journal of Common Market Studies*, 44 (1): 29–55.

Konings, J. and Murphy, J. P. (2004) 'Do Multinational Enterprises Relocate Employment to Low Wage Regions? Evidence from European Multinationals'. Available at <www.ecb.int/events/pdf/conferences/lmw/Konings.pdf>.

Lambert, R. and Butler, N. (2006) *The Future of European Universities: Renaissance or Decay?* London: Centre for European Reform.

Leonard, M. (2005) *Why Europe will Run the 21st Century*. New York: Public Affairs.

Levy, H., Lietz, C. and Sutherland, H. (2006) *A Basic Income for Europe's Children?* EUROMOD Working Paper EM4/06.

Majone, G. (2005) *Dilemmas of European Integration: The Ambiguities and Pitfalls of Integration by Stealth*. Oxford: Oxford University Press.

Majone, G. (2006) 'The Common Sense of European Integration', *Journal of European Public Policy*, 13 (5): 607–26.

Manners, I. (2006) 'Normative Power Europe Reconsidered: Beyond the Crossroads', *Journal of European Public Policy*, 13 (2): 182–99.

Moore, P. W. and Schrank, A. (2003) 'Commerce and Conflict: U.S. Efforts to Counter Terrorism with Trade May Backfire', *Middle East Policy*, 10 (3): 112–20.

Moravcsik, A. (2002) 'In Defence of the "Democratic Deficit": Reassessing Legitimacy in the European Union', *Journal of Common Market Studies*, 40 (4): 603–24.

Pelkmans, J. and Casey, J. P. (2004) 'Can Europe Deliver Growth? The Sapir Report and Beyond', *CEPS Policy Brief*, 45, January.

Pontusson, J. (2005) *Inequality and Prosperity: Social Europe vs. Liberal America*. Ithaca and London: Cornell University Press.

Raik, K. (2006) 'Promoting Democracy through Civil Society: How to Step up the EU's Policy towards the Eastern Neighbourhood', *CEPS Working Document*, 237, February.

Rhodes, M. (2005) 'Employment Policy', in H. Wallace, W. Wallace and M. Pollack (eds), *Policy-Making in the European Union*. Oxford: Oxford University Press, pp. 279–304.

Robert, P., Vilby, K. Aiolfi, L. and Otto, R. (2005) *Feasibility Study on the Establishment of a European Civil Peace Corps Channel Research*. Final Report, 29 November. Belgium, Ohai: Channel Research.

Sangiovanni, M. E. (2003) 'Why a Common Security and Defence Policy is Bad for Europe', *Survival*, 45 (3): 193–206.

Sapir, A., Aghion, P., Bertola, G., Hellwig, M., Pisani-Ferry, J., Rosati, D., Viñals, J. and Wallace, H., with Buti, M., Nava, M. and Smith, P. M. (2004) *The Sapir Report: An Agenda for a Growing Europe*. Oxford: Oxford University Press.

Sapir, A. (2006) 'Globalization and the Reform of European Social Models', *Journal of Common Market Studies*, 44 (2): 369–90.

Scharpf, F. (2000a) 'The Viability of Advanced Welfare States in the International Economy: Vulnerabilities and Options', *European Review*, 8 (3).

Scharpf, F. (2000b) 'Economic Changes, Vulnerabilities and Institutional Capabilities', in F. Scharpf and V. Schmidt (eds), *Welfare and Work in the Open Economy*, Vol. 1. Oxford: Oxford University Press.

Schleicher, A. (2006) *The Economics of Knowledge: Why Education is Key for Europe's Success*. Brussels: Lisbon Council.

Schmitt, B. (2003) 'The European Union and Armaments: Getting a Bigger Bang for the Euro', *Chaillot Paper*, 63. Paris: WEU Institute for Security Studies.

Smith, J. (2004) *Reinvigorating European Elections: The Implications of Electing the European Commission*. London: Royal Institute of International Affairs.

Soskice, D. (2007) 'Macroeconomics and Varieties of Capitalism', in B. Hancké, M. Rhodes and M. Thatcher (eds), *Beyond Varieties of Capitalism: Conflict, Contradiction and Complementarities in the European Economy*. Oxford: Oxford University Press.

Tsoukalis, L. (2005) *What Kind of Europe?* Oxford: Oxford University Press.

Vachudova, M. (2005) *Europe Undivided: Democracy, Leverage, and Integration after Communism*. Oxford: Oxford University Press.

Van der Horst, A., Lejour, A. and Straathof, B. (2006) 'Innovation Policy: Europe or the Member States?', *CPB Netherlands Bureau for Economic Policy Analysis Document*, 132, November.

Index

Compiled by Sue Carlton

Iraq *continued*
  and UK policy 85, 379–81
  war in 4, 54, 55, 85, 285, 371, 375,
    385
Iraq Study Group 380
Islam, deterritorialization 375
Islamic extremism 55, 99, 215, 375–6
Israeli-Palestinian conflict, two-state
  solution 375

Jay, Michael 375
jihadism 375
Jobseeker's Allowance (JSA) 193, 194
Joseph Rowntree Foundation/MORI
  survey 140–1

Kelley, J. 405
Khameini, Ali 378
Kilroy Silk, Robert 290
Kyoto Protocol 102

labour market 11, 59, 73–5, 97, 101–2,
    103
  accessing new opportunities 202–6
  adult learning 200–2, 208
  Anglo-Social model 192, 196, 198
  career ladders 206, 207–8
  changing 86–7, 105–8, 196–8
  employment support 192, 203
  flexibility 10, 168, 197, 198, 207,
    249–50
  and geographical inequalities
    197–8, 199
  individual's attitudes to
    advancement 198–200
  nature of work 206–8
  pre-employment support 198–200
  productivity 74, 103–4, 105, 196
  and regional inequalities 109, 113–14
  retention and progression 191–208
    extent of 194–6
    promoting career trajectories
      192–3, 203
    and skills 107, 156, 192, 197,
      198, 200–2, 208
    and social mobility 193–4
  and social justice 105, 108, 192,
    194, 200
  and technological change 196–7

land mines 379
Latin America, and protectionism 98
Le Grand, Julian 162
Leitch Review 108, 120, 201
Leventhal, G.S. 306
life expectancy 109, 110–11, 151,
    177, 47
The Limits to Growth 342
Lisbon programme 391, 392–3, 394,
    395, 396, 398
local government
  and empowerment 37
  and public participation 293
  and shared local identities 231, 232
London
  immigrants 84, 218
  July 2005 bombings 54–55, 365,
    373
London Citizens 298
lone parents 67–8, 155, 158–9, 238,
    247, 250
  and labour market 191–2, 193, 194,
    202, 203
  lone mothers 149–50, 157
Lovelock, James 342
Lukes, S. 299
Luxembourg Income Study (LIS) 149
Lyons, Sir Michael 231

MacTaggart, F. 291
Make Poverty History 39, 82, 285,
    353, 366
Malaysia 361
manufacturing sector 11, 74, 75, 98,
    102, 105–6, 192, 196
marriage 237–40, 323
  marital homogamy 149, 155, 167
Married Couples Allowance 323
maternity leave 153, 249
Maxwell, S. 355
media
  and accuracy 294
  and children 325–7
  and crime coverage 78–9, 262
  and immigration 54
  online interactivity 293–4
  regulation 294, 299–300
  simplification of issues 287–8, 293,
    294